yt11
17. 7. 07

In th...   ...ciful

He who does not thank people does not thank Allah.

People are the dependents of Allah: the closest to Him are the
most useful to His dependents.

He Who created Death and Life, that He may try which of you is best in deed, and He is the Exalted in Might, oft-Forgiving. (67:2)

أَلَّذِى خَلَقَ ٱلْمَوْتَ وَٱلْحَيَوٰةَ لِيَبْلُوَكُمْ أَيُّكُمْ أَحْسَنُ عَمَلًا وَهُوَ ٱلْعَزِيزُ ٱلْغَفُورُ (الملك)

O you who believe! Remain conscious of Allah, and {always} say words that are true to the mark {truthful, relevant and to the point}. (33:70)

يَٰٓأَيُّهَا ٱلَّذِينَ ءَامَنُوا۟ ٱتَّقُوا۟ ٱللَّهَ وَقُولُوا۟ قَوْلًا سَدِيدًا (الأحزاب)

Not a word does he utter but there is a sentinel by him, ready (to note it). (50:18)

مَّا يَلْفِظُ مِن قَوْلٍ إِلَّا لَدَيْهِ رَقِيبٌ عَتِيدٌ (ق)

《إِنَّما النَّاسُ كَإِبِلٍ مَائَةٍ، لَا يُوجَدُ فِيها رَاحِلَةٌ》

People are like camels; you may not find a suitable mount from even a hundred of them. (Sahih al Bukhari and Sahih Muslim)

《مَنْ اسْتَوى يَوْمَاهُ فَهْوَ مَغْبُونٌ》

He whose two days are equal [in accomplishment] is a sure loser.
(Sunan al Daylami)

《مَنْ لَمْ يَشْكُرِ النَّاسَ لَمْ يَشْكُرِ الله》

He who does not thank people does not thank Allah
(Sunan Abu Dawud, AlTirmidhi and Ahmad Ibn Hanbal)

《الـخَلْقُ عِيالُ الله، أَحَبُّهُمْ إِليه أَنْفَعُهُمْ لِعِيالِهِ》

People are the dependents of Allah; the closest to Him are the most useful to His dependents.
(Sahih Muslim)

Training Guide for
Islamic Workers

Acknowledgement

Many scholars and Muslim leaders have contributed to the evolution of this *Guide*. Two of them, Eltigani AbuGideiri and Isma'il al Faruqi, have passed away; may Allah bless their souls. We ask Allah to qualify them for His reward among those who leave behind useful knowledge for generations to benefit from after their demise.

We list other names in alphabetical order, realizing that this work would not have been possible without their contribution to its form and essence:

> *AbdulHamid AbuSulayman, Ilham Altalib, Anis Ahmad, Taha al 'Alwani, Jamal Barzinji, Anwar Ibrahim, Omar Kasule, Yaqub Mirza, Mustafa Othman, Mahmoud Rashdan, Ahmadullah Siddiqui, Dilnawaz Siddiqui, Sayyid Syeed, Mustafa Tahan, and Ahmad Totonji.*

We also acknowledge the invaluable assistance of those who edited, proof-read and reviewed this work. Among them were:

> *Ali Abuzaakouk, Zaynab Alawiye, Anas Ali, Muhyiddin Atiyyah, Suhaib Barzinji, Yusuf Delorenzo, Michele Messaoudi, Muhammad Totonji, and Jay Willoughby.*

This work would not have been completed without the efforts of Iqbal Unus, who contributed original material to it, designed its layout, and transformed the manuscript into a book.

All praise be to Allah! May He accept our work for His sake alone!

TRAINING GUIDE

FOR

ISLAMIC WORKERS

Hisham Altalib

The International Institute of
Islamic Thought

Herndon, Virginia, USA
1421/2001

Human Developments Series No.1

First Edition 1991
Second Edition 1992
Third Edition 1993
Fourth Edition 2001

Copyright©1411 AH / 1991 AC by:
    The International Institute of Islamic Thought
    P.O. Box 669
    Herndon, Virginia 20172-0669, U.S.A.

Library of Congress Cataloging-in-Publication Data

Altalib, Hisham, 1940-
    Training Guide for Islamic Workers/Hisham Altalib

    p.   cm.   —(Human Development; 1)
    Includes bibliographical refrences.
    ISBN 0-912463-89-9
    1. Leadership–Management–Organization–Youth Camps–Islam–Handbooks, manuals, etc.
    I. Title. II. Series: Human Development (Herndon, VA.); 1
BP190.5.L4A48 1991
297' .61'07–dc20   91-12896
                                                                      CIP

Printed in the United States of America
by International Graphics
10710 Tucker Street
Beltsville, MD 20705 U.S.A.
Tel: (301) 595-5999 • Fax: (301) 595-5888

OUR GOAL

To produce dynamic Islamic leaders who will pioneer social change by acquiring knowledge and wisdom, and practicing *da'wah* with perceptiveness and communication that is convincing and effective.

OUR MEANS

To achieve this goal, the training program offers a valuable opportunity that enhances commitment of the trainees, imparts knowledge to them and builds up their skills in communication, administration, and planning. Moreover, it aspires to enhance their physical and technical abilities, and develop healthy group attitudes, promote spiritual upliftment and nurture a positive problem solving mentality. The program seeks to transfer the experiences of elder brothers and sisters to the younger ones in a condensed format. We hope that the trainees will start from where the elders left off, avoid their mistakes and pioneer new strategies rather than duplicate old ones. In essence, the training program attempts to help raise a generation which knows its priorities, and which becomes a part of the solution rather than a part of the problem.

A Note about the Use of Islamic Terms

Many Islamic terms have become part of the vocabulary of Muslims, irrespective of the languages they speak or read. This is as it should be.

Like other languages, English is being gradually enriched when Muslims who speak and read English use these Islamic terms. While this is commendable, it is equally important that they pronounce the Islamic words, names and terms correctly. To help the readers do that, when necessary, we have italicised Islamic terms (except those that are found in standard English dictionaries) and have included their Arabic equivalents in the Index and Glossary of Islamic Terms at the end of this book. We urge you to refer to the Arabic equivalents whenever you are unsure of the correct pronunciation.

CONTENTS

PART FOUR: TRAINING FOR TRAINERS

PART FIVE: THE YOUTH CAMP
IN THEORY AND PRACTICE

A Step in the Right Direction

Although the Islamic movement conducts many camps and training activities, the area of human development and leadership training has not been given the attention it deserves; indeed, it needs to be studied more systematically and formalized in the form of textbooks and curricula. We are not aware of a single book or manual published to date that caters satisfactorily to such a dire need.

The fact that this is the first time a book of this kind has been published bespeaks the decline of our ummah in its present phase. If the ummah today is to be a witness unto other nations, as the Qur'an intended it to be, there should be hundreds of such books in the marketplace.

The *Training Guide for Islamic Workers* is a modest step in the right direction. If Allah wills, there will be many more to come. In the meantime, however, it is hoped that this one will serve as a foundation upon which improvements in format and content may be built; it is an encouragement for others to produce.

The contents of the *Guide* cannot satisfy everyone. We have targeted an international audience, and what applies to a country with a certain political system may not be valid for one under a different system. Each region of the world is unique and has its own peculiarities and specialities. Undoubtedly, there will be some material which may not correspond to or may even contradict some experiences of certain localities or individuals. Similar guide books and manuals have to be produced in each locality to answer their particular needs.

Although our experience covers a wide range of backgrounds, we do not claim to have addressed all situations. This is why we have intended our book to serve only as a guide and, as such, it should be used with wisdom. Indeed, the effectiveness of the *Guide* will depend to a great extent on the tactful supervision of the organizers who conduct the training programs. The only perfect book is the Qur'an. We offer this work as a first attempt and call upon its users to advise us of any improvements which can be made in future editions, *in sha'a Allah*.

We realize that human development and training is a rapidly developing field. We pray that several institutions will be established to cater to the development of human resources, particularly among our youth.

The task of producing training materials cannot be adequately undertaken by amateurs and part-time devotees. Rather, there must be a specialized and concerted effort of thoughtful scholarship and professionalism to bear the urgently needed fruit. The Islamic movement would do well to dedicate an important part of its resources to this highly specialized area, for it can no longer be served by well-wishing generalists of *da'wah*. Even though non-Muslims have expended tremendous effort in this area, their work has to be carefully sorted out, sifted, and thoroughly Islamized before we can utilize it. This is a challenge that demands top priority.

The *Guide* should be used in conjunction with the book *Tawhid: Its Implications for Thought and Life* published by the International Institute of Islamic Thought (IIIT), and later by the International Islamic Federation of Student Organizations (IIFSO), under the authorship of the late Professor Isma'il Raji al Faruqi, may Allah bless his soul. While the *Guide* basically focuses on the science and art of propagating the message and preparing the trainee, *Tawhid* deals with properly understanding the contents of the message itself: Islam.

To keep the *Guide*'s size manageable, we have been selective in the topics covered. We hope that the resources of the Department of Human Development in IIIT, including its library, can complement the *Guide* by offering material in other areas and by responding to inquiries from field workers.

Many items in these pages have been mentioned only as eye-openers or reminders. Interested readers must not limit themselves to this material, but should seek additional references and sources for a deeper understanding. This is a fast-growing field, one which is expected to be updated and expanded due to new research. We believe that keeping in touch with publications and conferences on these themes will be very rewarding for all trainers and trainees using this work.

All praise be to Allah, who made this humble work possible. O Allah! Guide us to the straight path, *al sirat al mustaqim!*

Dhu al Hijjah 1411 AH
June 1991 AC

Hisham Altalib
Department of Human Development
The International Institute of Islamic Thought

Historical Development

I. Our Story of Training

It all started in November 1973 in Gary, Indiana. We asked ourselves during an executive committee meeting of the Muslim Students Association of the US and Canada (MSA): "What is the purpose of it all? What do WE get out of these long and tedious organizational meetings month after month and year after year?"

We came to realize that in addition to administering the organization, committee members should also acquire education, skills, and spiritual upliftment during their terms of office. So we decided to dedicate the first day of each following executive committee meeting to leadership training. The impact of this decision was tremendous! One cannot forget that "three minute self-introduction session" when each member presented his or her background. What a discovery it was to know about one another!

The MSA leadership then realized that it was time to discard the policy of "doing what we can do" in favor of one of "doing what needs to be done!" To this effect, the MSA established the Planning and Organization Committee.

One can hardly remember anything more valuable to our Islamic work than the impact of this committee's efforts. Upon analyzing the movement's growth, they assessed the needs of *da'wah* and set in motion an action plan for the future. It must be noted that the term "movement" is used here in a very general sense, as it includes every group which professes the totality of Islam, practices it, and calls for its establishment in our lives and societies. With the expansion of the movement's work, more skilled and experienced field workers were needed. Hence, intensive crash training programs were a must. The establishment of a Department of Training, which would have a full-time director, became essential. The committee also recommended that a full-time secretariat, which would include a Department of Education and Information, a Department of Administration, and a Department of Finance be established. The Islamic concept of a full-time *da'iyah* was refined and practiced in a wonderful way; it continues to bear a bountiful harvest.

The dream of the Planning and Organization Committee materialized in 1395/1975 with the establishment of a permanent secretariat in Indianapolis, Indiana. One year later, the secretariat moved to the premises of the Islamic Center of North America in Plainfield, an Indianapolis suburb.

II. The Department of Training at the MSA Headquarters

Upon its establishment in 1395/1975, the first crucial issue this department faced was: "To train people in what?"

The general answer "to train them in Islam" does not help much, because Islam is so vast that such an answer is useless. While it is relevant to any given situation regardless of time and place, it does not impose the specifics required by many particular programs. Our great literary heritage was not an answer either, because suitable literature was in short supply. As a result, the department chose to write to eighty-six outstanding Muslim scholars all over the world. These scholars were requested to write articles in their area of specialization which would be less than ten pages long, relevant, practical, and concise.

The outcome was disappointing in two ways. First, only 10 percent of the scholars responded. Second, many of the responses received were deficient both in format and content, and the material was not readily usable in the American context of field work. So, the department set out to tap the rich resources of American literature, particularly in the areas of communication, administration, management, and skills suitable for *da'wah*. Two tasks were attempted simultaneously: to Islamize the American experience and to mold the Islamic materials into the contemporary context. The first was easier, because virtually anything that made sense was already advocated by an *ayah* or a hadith.

The early period between 1975 and 1977 was a pioneering experience in organized Islamic work. It has been documented in the *Report and Review* of Safar 1396/ January 1976. The report, which covers the first MSA training course, is available at the Islamic Society of North America (ISNA) headquarters. The benefit of this program was not confined to North America, but extended to Africa, Asia, and Europe.

Four basic themes for training the *da'iyah* were identified:
1. Spiritual uplifting
2. Knowledge and proper understanding of Islam
3. A working knowledge of contemporary ideologies and religions
4. *Da'wah* skills and tools

The first MSA training course spanned 103 contact hours and was conducted simultaneously at four training camps. Presentations included sixty-eight articles in the areas of Islamics, contemporary ideologies, and field skills. The course trained 120 participants, among them twenty-seven sisters. By the close of the 1970s, the idea of leadership training was adopted by many domestic and foreign Muslim organizations. In particular, IIFSO and the World Assembly of Muslim Youth (WAMY) contributed a great deal to training camps and the publication of relevant literature. The Muslim World League (MWL) sponsored several camps. May Allah reward all the brothers in these organizations who have assimilated, promoted, and developed the concept of Islamic leadership training since its inception.

By the dawn of fifteenth hijri century when the IIIT was established in 1401/1981, it had become apparent that the new mode of *da'wah* was to be found in "leadership training." The experience of a large number of national and international camps organized by WAMY and IIFSO added great insight, sophistication, and depth to the initial realization. As a result, during the IIFSO General Secretariat meeting in Ramadan 1409/April 1989, it was decided jointly with the IIIT board of directors to commission Dr. Hisham Altalib to produce the *Training Guide for Islamic Workers*. Hence, this *Guide* is the culmination of many contributions from ISNA, IIFSO, WAMY, MWL and IIIT. May Allah Guide them rightly.

We pray to Allah to make this *Guide* a source of benefit to the new Islamic civilization that will emerge during the fifteenth hijri century .

III. Milestones: Organizations and People

In the course of developments mentioned above, a number of organizations and people have played prominent roles. We will review them briefly below.

A. The Muslim Students Association of the US & Canada (MSA)

The Muslim Students' Association of the United States and Canada was established on 1 January 1963. A dozen concerned and committed Muslims, all students at various American universities and colleges, had gathered for just this purpose in Champaign-Urbana, Illinois. For two decades, the MSA continued to tap into the Islamic conscience of Muslims in America, both on and off campus, mobilize Muslim students and Muslim communities, and play the role of a catalyst for the realization of the Islamic presence in North America.

Led by volunteer elected leaders and assisted by a permanent general secretariat (established in 1395/1975), the MSA organized annual conventions and regional conferences, published a monthly newsletter and a quarterly magazine, conducted training programs, arranged seminars, and provided Islamic information to Muslims and non-Muslims. Through its specialized institutions like the North American Islamic Trust (NAIT) and the Islamic Teaching Center (ITC), the MSA forged ahead in the service of Islamic *da'wah*. For example, it published and distributed Islamic literature, preserved the integrity of Islamic centers and *masajid* by holding them in trust, and presented the teachings of Islam to both non-Muslims and new Muslims. On the international level, ISNA is a member of the International Islamic Federation of Student Organizations.

After twenty years of concerted action, the MSA leadership led the search for a new organizational structure to cater to the changing needs in the Muslim community. This resulted in MSA focusing its work on North American college and university campuses. On this front, its challenges and opportunities are matched only by its resolve to best serve the cause of Islam in this land. It became a part of the newly-founded Islamic Society of North America in 1403/1983.

1. The Planning and Organization Committee of the MSA

This committee was set up with the late Eltigani AbuGideiri as its first chairman. The committee conducted surveys, reviewed organizational structures, and generally evaluated all aspects of the organization to produce far-reaching reports including those that shaped the formation of the general secretariat and of the Islamic Teaching Center (ITC). It is fair to claim that the contribution of this committee was one of the most important factors in the achievements of the MSA and the Islamic renaissance in North America.

2. The Training Department

The MSA realized in its growing years that its future was linked to the availability of well-trained human resources. Therefore, when the permanent general secretariat was established in 1395/1975 , it transformed the Training Committee into a department with Dr. Hisham Altalib as its full-time director. The Training Department commissioned and gathered training literature and conducted a series of training programs for the MSA executive committee members, presidents of local chapters, and field representatives. The department has detailed the programs and analyzed the training approaches for Islamic work in North America in an exhaustive report available at the general secretariat.

Dr. Hisham Altalib was followed in 1398/1978 by Dr. Anis Ahmad and then by Dr. Abdul Hadi Omer as directors of training with brief periods of time when the position was combined with the Department of Education. The Department of Training was then advised by a committee.

B. The Islamic Society of North America (ISNA)

As the MSA reached its mid-teens, it began preparing for an expanded role in the service of Islam. It called an historic meeting of a cross-section of Islamic workers in Plainfield, Indiana, in early 1397/1977. This meeting set up a task force to recommend a new organizational structure to respond to the increasing challenges and responsibilities emerging in the growing North American Muslim communities. The task force concluded that the new environment would be best served by establishing a broader umbrella organization called the Islamic Society of North America (ISNA). This was accomplished during Rabi' al Awwal 1403/January 1983. The

MSA, the new Muslim Community Association of the US and Canada (MCA), and the three professional associations, namely, the Islamic Medical Association (IMA), the Association of Muslim Scientists and Engineers (AMSE), and the Association of Muslim Social Scientists (AMSS), became its founding constituents. The MCA is no longer functional, and ISNA has now become a federation of affiliated community organizations in addition to being a membership organization open to all Muslims. Three of its service institutions are the North American Islamic Trust (NAIT), the Islamic Teaching Center (ITC), and the Canadian Islamic Trust Foundation (CITF).

The strength of ISNA derives from its supraethnic character and its broad geographical base. Its priorities are the unity of Muslims, the education of Muslim children, and *da'wah* to non-Muslims. The *majlis al shura* (the consultative council) is the supreme policy-making body, the executive council is the governing body, and the general secretariat is the operational arm of ISNA. In the execution of its action plan, they are aided by service institutions — like NAIT and ITC — and a number of functional committees.

The major continental and community oriented functions of the MSA were assumed by ISNA. Thus the work of ISNA represents a continuity of the Islamic work in North America. The *Islamic Horizons* magazine, the annual convention, and other community-centered programs have expanded under ISNA, while the MSA concentrates on university and college campuses.

ISNA is one of the largest national Muslim organizations in North America. Over three hundred local organizations, mosques, and Islamic centers are affiliated with it. Among its constituent organizations are the Muslim Arab Youth Association (MAYA), the Malaysian Islamic Study Group (MISG), and the Muslim Youth of North America (MYNA). MYNA represents the future hope of Islam in North America because it encompasses a unique generation of youth born in North America and raised with a commitment to Islam. Its members combine both the heritage of immigrant Muslims and the indigenous opportunities for *da'wah*.

C. The International Islamic Federation of Student Organizations (IIFSO)

The International Islamic Federation of Student Organizations is comprised of Muslim student organizations located all over the world. Founded in 1389/1969, the organization has been the leading publisher of Islamic literature in those languages spoken by Muslims. It holds its general assemblies and training conferences in different countries to assist the development of Islamic work. IIFSO has published original works and translations in five hundred titles and eighty languages involving more than ten million copies. Dr. Ahmad Totonji was its first secretary general. **He was followed by Dr. Hisham Altalib, Dr. Sayyid Syeed, Br. Mustafa Tahan, Dr. Mustafa 'Othman, Dr. Syed Abdullah Tahir, and Br. Omar Farouq.**

D. The World Assembly of Muslim Youth (WAMY)

The World Assembly of Muslim Youth was founded in 1392/1972 in Riyadh, Saudi Arabia, at an international meeting of Islamic workers involved in youth activities and representatives of youth organizations. It has been active in holding international and local youth camps in many different countries. It helps youth and student organizations around the world execute their own planned projects. It holds its international meetings about every three years and publishes their proceedings.

The headquarters of WAMY is located in Riyadh. Its first secretary general, elected in 1383/1973, was Dr. Abdulhamid Abusulayman. He was followed by Dr. Ahmad Bahafzallah, Dr. Tawfiq al Kusayyer, and the current secretary general Dr. Maneh al Johani.

E. The Muslim World League (MWL)

The Muslim World League is a worldwide organization based in Makkah with offices and full-time *du'at* in many countries. The MWL espouses causes relating to the welfare of Muslims, especially in countries where Muslims are a minority. It holds international conferences and helps establish *masajid* all over the world. The current secretary general is Dr. Abdullah Naseef.

F. The International Institute of Islamic Thought (IIIT)

The International Institute of Islamic Thought, located in America, is an educational institute dedicated to Islamic research. It was founded in 1401/1981 by Dr. Isma'il al Faruqi, Dr. Abdulhamid Abusulayman, Dr. Taha al 'Alwani, Dr. Jamal Barzinji, and Br. Anwar Ibrahim to revive and promote Islamic thought and the Islamization of knowledge in the contemporary social science disciplines. It also explores the potential to package knowledge in specifically Islamic disciplines derived from *tawhid* and the Shari'ah.

The objective of IIIT's work is to address human problems pertinent to Muslims through the principles, concepts, and values of the Islamic paradigm. To accomplish its goals, IIIT holds specialized seminars and conferences, sponsors research projects at universities, supports the writing of Islamically-oriented textbooks, and publishes scholarly works in Arabic, English, and other languages from scholars around the world. In addition, IIIT is committed to developing material for youth programs.

Who Is This Guide for and How Should It Be Used?

I. Definition of Training, Development, and Education

Among human development professionals, training and development are sometimes used, interchangeably to primarily denote the betterment of one's ability to meet or exceed expectations of performance. More specifically, the three terms, may be defined as follows:

- **Training** is a set of programs (and their implementation) concerned with learning and improving a skill or ability so that one can perform as expected.
- **Development** is a set of programs which deals with the growth or sharpening of analytical and leadership skills and acquiring an understanding of supervisory and management functions.
- **Education,** on the other hand, is the acquisition of knowledge which can be applied to improve human faculties, behavior, and skills through training and development.

Among Islamic leadership trainers, the term "training" is used comprehensively to denote a set of activities which educate and motivate the trainees, enrich and uplift them spiritually, and improve their skills in leadership and *da'wah* delivery.

Islamic training programs assume a basic level of Islamic commitment, understanding, and consciousness, and then seek to build on it. Their methodology is based on relating the identified goals and their attainment to the core of humanity's relationship with its Creator, Allah. The educational material used in these training programs to date focuses on enhancing Islamic understanding and increasing the trainees' commitment to it.

II. Who Is This *Guide* for?

This *Guide* does not seek to make new Muslims. It assumes that its audience has some commitment to Islam and the willingness to establish its practice. The principal target audience of this *Guide* is university students, both undergraduate and graduate. In terms of age, it aims at young people in their twenties, although with some adaptations it can be useful for other ages. This *Guide* aims at training potential leaders and workers in Islamic *da'wah* at the local, national, and international levels. It can be used for self-training by individuals as well as for training others in groups.

Together with its recommended reading material, the *Guide* is intended to benefit mainly those experienced Islamic workers charged with the training of the next generation of Islamic leaders. Two main categories of potential trainees are described below.

A. **Young men**: Young Muslim men occupy positions of responsibility and authority in many Islamic organizations whose membership is generally open to both men and women. Such young men may be leaders of youth organizations, of youth programs, or of the general community-based organizations. In any case, they are mostly in the early stages of their leadership experience and conscious of the need to acquire those skills which will help them perform more effectively.

B. **Young women**: Young Muslim women are beginning to assume positions of responsibility in Islamic *da'wah* by taking charge of projects and activities in youth organizations and programs as well as in community organizations. Young women exercise positions of leadership in women's organizations, and their effectiveness in leading Islamic endeavors is critical to the overall growth of the Muslim community.

We realize that no single program is suitable for all organizations, countries, and backgrounds. Thus while some material may be less suited to certain locations, it may be decidedly relevant to others. Such situations can be resolved during the actual application and execution of the programs at various training events. We must also emphasize that while the language of the *Guide* mostly uses the masculine gender, the material is meant for both men and women.

III. How is the *Guide* to be Used?

This *Guide* is organized into five parts in addition to the opening section. Its underlying structure may be described in terms of the "why, what, and how" of training:

- WHY: An overview of the Islamic movement and the need for training is covered in part one.
- WHAT: The major elements of leadership and the essential individual and group skills are dealt with in parts two and three.
- HOW: How trainers train others effectively is discussed in part four, while part five focuses on organizing and running a youth camp as a major mode of training.

Some activities and aids to learning have been included in various chapters. Most chapters begin with "Learning Objectives" and end with "Questions for Discussion" and "Comprehension Exercises" in order to reinforce both group training and self-learning experiences. Relationships among subtopics are pointed out when doing so will extend the learning material. Action points, special exercises, reminders, and anecdotes are included with the lessons to highlight and reinforce the practical use of the basic material.

A. The most effective way to use the *Guide*?

The *Guide* is designed for easy reading and on-going self-evaluation. The most effective way to use it is to go over it chapter by chapter. Following that, read each chapter alone as the need arises. Use the material extensively in your presentations and preparation for various occasions.

For a group of people or an organization, it is highly beneficial to cover the whole *Guide* from cover to cover in a one-week-long training camp. A senior experienced person should be in charge of conducting such a program.

B. When to use it?

After the first reading, review the *Guide* every time you are faced with a situation covered by the *Guide*. For example, use it when asked to deliver a speech, organize an activity, make a decision, chair a meeting, or just participate in a training camp.

If you are in charge of an Islamic activity or a group of Islamic workers, you may want to make copies of specific pages and distribute them to those who need them. This will not only refresh the skills of those involved, but also help attain uniformity in how they approach their leadership tasks .

As you use the *Guide* in specific situations, try to add to it by recording specific case studies, trainee reactions, instructor evaluations, and the like. Using this material, try to "customize" your learning or presentation for the purpose at hand.

C. How to supplement it?

The *Guide* is intended to cover essential topics related to training youth for Islamic leadership. However, no such *Guide* can be a conclusive document. To reinforce what you learn from it, and to add to it, a collection of training material has been established to provide you with articles on a range of topics not covered by this *Guide*. Articles from the collection will be sent to listed users of the *Guide* on a regular basis for reading and feedback.

Part One

Perspectives on Training

When we speak of "training," it is essential to set the frame of reference in the right perspective. The following must be made clear to avoid speaking in a vacuum:

1. The role of humanity and its relationship with the environment;
2. The status of the Islamic movement during the fourteenth hijri century. (If everything is good, there is no incentive to train people to change the status quo.)

Only after we have formed a consensus on these two issues can we form realistic aims and objectives for a training program. If we are unable to pass this first stage, we shall be hindered by the questions: Why? What for? and How? To settle these critical issues, we turn to the Qur'an.

We have indeed created man in the best of molds, then do We abase him [to be] the lowest of the low, except those who believe and do righteous deeds: for they shall have a reward unfailing (95:4-6).

٤ لَقَدۡ خَلَقۡنَا ٱلۡإِنسَٰنَ فِىٓ أَحۡسَنِ تَقۡوِيمٖ
٥ ثُمَّ رَدَدۡنَٰهُ أَسۡفَلَ سَٰفِلِينَ ٦ إِلَّا ٱلَّذِينَ ءَامَنُوا۟
وَعَمِلُوا۟ ٱلصَّٰلِحَٰتِ فَلَهُمۡ أَجۡرٌ غَيۡرُ مَمۡنُونٖ (سورة التين)

The Prophet (SAW) reminds us that:

«إِنَّ اللهَ كَتَبَ الإِحْسَانَ على كُلِّ شَيءٍ، فإذا قَتَلْتُمْ فَأَحْسِنوا القِتْلَةَ، وإذا ذَبَحْتُمْ فَأَحْسِنوا الذِّبْحَةَ،

وَلْيُحِدَّ أَحَدُكُمْ شَفْرَتَهُ، وَلْيُرِحْ ذَبِيحَتَهُ».

Allah has decreed that for everything there is a better way. Then, when you kill in battle, do it in the best way; and when you slaughter [an animal] in sacrifice, do it in the best way. So every one of you should sharpen his knife, and let the slaughtered animal die comfortably (Sahih Muslim, Sunan Abu Dawud, Sunan al Tirmidhi, Sunan al Darimi, Sunan Ibn Majah, and Sunan al Nasa'i).

In light of these directives, the Islamic worker and the Islamic movement are obliged to carry out their tasks both efficiently and correctly. This is what Islamic training is all about.

In this part of the *Guide*, we offer an overview of the Islamic movement and its general condition today. Within that context, we seek guidance from the Qur'an to define the objectives of training.

Chapter

1

The *Da'iyah*, the Environment, and the Population

I. Aims and Means

A Muslim is not one who fights Satan with his sword and gets catapulted into *jannah*, but rather one who interacts actively with his environment in order to make a difference:

> That man can have nothing but what he strives for; that [the fruit of] his striving will soon come in sight; then will he be rewarded with a reward complete (53:39-41).

﴿ وَأَن لَّيْسَ لِلْإِنسَٰنِ إِلَّا مَا سَعَىٰ ۝ وَأَنَّ سَعْيَهُۥ سَوْفَ يُرَىٰ ۝ ثُمَّ يُجْزَىٰهُ الْجَزَآءَ الْأَوْفَىٰ ﴾ (سورة النجم)

Our actions are witnessed not only by Allah and His messenger but by others as well. Hence, the Muslim is not living in a vacuum; he is continuously acting and interacting with his surroundings. What makes him or her a better Muslim? According to the following hadith:

«الْخَلْقُ عِيالُ اللّهِ، أَحَبُّهُمْ إِلَيْهِ أَنْفَعُهُمْ لِعِيالِهِ»

People are the dependents of Allah; the closest to Him are the most useful to His dependents.[1]

Thus, the criterion for being a better Muslim is not simply salah, fasting, *dhikr*, and *tasbih;* it's one's utility to others! In this context, the following principle should alarm us: "He who does not concern himself with the affairs of the Muslims is not one of them."

The task of a *jama'ah* (group) of Muslims is not to serve itself; it is to serve others! The group is not the objective, for in reality it is only an organizational means to accomplish the objective. The interest of such an organization must be subservient to the interest of the ummah and of the outside world.

The Messenger of Allah directs us:

«ارْحَمُوا مَنْ في الأرضِ يَرْحَمْكُمْ مَنْ في السَّمَاءِ»

Have mercy on those in the land, so that the One in Heaven will have mercy on you.[2]

Muslim groups which confine themselves to their membership are losing sight of their objectives and becoming self-serving. In fact, all the preparation and training of the organization's members should be directed towards serving their nation. To establish an organization for the sake of the organization is like building a house for the sake of the house.

The environment and the population of which the *da'iyah* is a part are the only mediums through which he can perform. They are the only fields of operation in which Allah is testing him during his life.

II. Concept of Traveling and Exploration in the Qur'an

Nor did We send before you [as Messengers] any but men, whom We did inspire — [men] living in human habitations. Do they not travel through the earth, and see what was the end of those before them? But the home of the Hereafter is best, for those who do right. Will you not then understand? (12:109).

﴿وَمَآ أَرْسَلْنَا مِن قَبْلِكَ إِلَّا رِجَالًا نُّوحِىٓ إِلَيْهِم مِّنْ أَهْلِ ٱلْقُرَىٰٓ أَفَلَمْ يَسِيرُوا۟ فِى ٱلْأَرْضِ فَيَنظُرُوا۟ كَيْفَ كَانَ عَٰقِبَةُ ٱلَّذِينَ مِن قَبْلِهِمْ وَلَدَارُ ٱلْأَخِرَةِ خَيْرٌ لِّلَّذِينَ ٱتَّقَوْا۟ أَفَلَا تَعْقِلُونَ﴾ (سورة يوسف)

The *da'iyah* trainee must have four distinct and concurrent levels of enlightened awareness. The first one is known as *'alam al ghayb,* the world of the unseen; the other

---

1   Sahih Muslim.
2   Sunan al Tirmidhi.

three are *'alam al shahadah*, the witnessed world, as shown below:

A. The Unseen B. The Universal C. The International	Knowledge of these is common to all Muslims; they can be termed "constants" for all in any given generation.
D. The Local	Knowledge of this is specific and variable for each country and its individuals.

A. The Unseen

The Unseen is defined in the Qur'an and the *Sunnah* as belief in Allah, His angels, His books, His messengers, the Day of Judgment, and the divine decree. Belief in the Unseen saves our minds from vain wandering into areas beyond our limits of comprehension. This belief does not vary with the time and place of the Muslim; it is a constant for all times and places.

B. The Universal

The *da'iyah* must realize that time and space are Allah's creation and that the universe is for humans to use and derive benefit from:

Do you not see that Allah has subjected to your [use] all things in the heavens and on earth, and has made His bounties flow to you in exceeding measure, [both] seen and unseen? Yet there are among men those who dispute about Allah, without knowledge and without guidance, and without a book, to enlighten them (31:20).

أَلَمْ تَرَوْاْ أَنَّ ٱللَّهَ سَخَّرَ لَكُم مَّا فِى ٱلسَّمَٰوَٰتِ وَمَا فِى ٱلْأَرْضِ وَأَسْبَغَ عَلَيْكُمْ نِعَمَهُۥ ظَٰهِرَةً وَبَاطِنَةً وَمِنَ ٱلنَّاسِ مَن يُجَٰدِلُ فِى ٱللَّهِ بِغَيْرِ عِلْمٍ وَلَا هُدًى وَلَا كِتَٰبٍ مُّنِيرٍ (سورة لقمان)

Again, this is common knowledge for all Muslims and does not change with one's particular location.

C. The International

Every *da'iyah* must attain a minimum level of knowledge about other peoples and nations. He should view the Islamic movement as one global entity unbounded by geographical borders. He has brothers and sisters all over the world. The ummah of which he is a part includes Muslims not only in lands where they form the majority but also where they are a minority. He is obligated to defend the truth and stand against falsehood everywhere. His duty is to explain the message of Islam to all people. In fact, the whole world is considered a place of action and worship for the trainee, as Allah's Messenger explains:

«جُعِلَتْ لِيَ الأَرْضُ مَسْجِدًا وَطَهُورًا»

The Earth has been made for me a masjid and a means of purification.[1]

D. The Local

The local environment is where the trainee's primary obligation lies, and it is there that he must discharge the following responsibilities.

First: He must know and understand as best he can the prevailing reality of the country in which he lives and its population. He should learn about its geography, history, demography, and all other relevant aspects which will help him in his mission. Some of these are: What are its natural resources? What is the population breakdown in terms of its religions, *madhahib*, ethnic backgrounds, male-female ratio, etc.? What is the nature of its economy, imports, exports, industry, agricultural products, and the like?

He needs to have a good grasp of the country's political system: its political parties, publications, supporters, the process of decision making, and the "who," "what," and "how" of the political process. What are the major newspapers and magazines? Who are the opinion leaders and top scholars, authors, scientists, and *ulama*? The *da'iyah* cannot understand a country's people unless he has some basic knowledge of their history and their relations with people in other countries, particularly the neighboring ones. In short, the *da'iyah* must have a fair knowledge of the social, economic, educational, political, and religious conditions of the country in which he lives and works.

Second: The *da'iyah* should concern himself with the problems of his society. He should not take the negative attitude that he is not responsible for their solution because Islam did not create these problems. His behavior should be like that of a physician who takes it as his challenge and duty to cure the ills of his patients even though he did not contribute to their appearance. Even when he has no real remedy, he can at least lessen the pain and relieve the patient's agony. We do not hear of a successful doctor ridiculing and attacking his patients. He always tries to improve their situation, in the spirit of *ihsan* (improvement). Indeed, the trainee must put himself in the shoes of the political leader of his country and apply his mental powers to find ways to solve the problems. He must identify and analyze them and then provide viable Islamic alternatives. It is easy to be in the opposition and criticize the ruling party in an irresponsible way. The constructive-minded Muslim must provide honest, responsible, and enlightened opposition so that if one day he is asked to take charge, his plans

---

1   Sahih Muslim, Sunan Abu Dawood, Sunan al Tirmidhi, Sunan al Nasa'i, Sunan ibn Majah, Sunan al Darimi, and Musnad Ahmad ibn Hanbal.

and ideas will work and show results in real life situations. Imaginary, theoretical, and utopian claims are only wishful thinking. If he is unable to translate these claims into real and concrete accomplishments, the public will soon learn not to take him and his group seriously.

Some think of Islam as a bed of flowers which can be planted anywhere. That is not so in real life. Islam is more like a unique assortment of bouquets of flowers which can be offered to each people in a different arrangement. For each soil and climate there is a unique set of flowers. It has its specific and local flavors which suit that country. This beautiful mosaic of nations is what makes the ummah so colorful, resourceful, and attractive. While the *da'iyah* exhibits some major common traits acquired from the unseen, universal, and international aspects of Islam, he should also demonstrate the specificity related to local customs, tastes, dress, arts, and culture of the country in which he is living. At present, we have a serious imbalance in our Islamic education. We are more concerned with the general and common theoretical aspects of people's lives, and have thus become deficient in understanding their local and specific needs.

Obviously, the *da'iyah* has to achieve the right union of these factors within the framework of Islamic directives. But his contribution should not be simply a copy of past events across the spectrum of history or geography; that will not work. His contribution should be like the variety of delicious dishes in Muslim countries; they may all be different, but they are all *halal*.

III. Leadership through Service

One of the main principles which the Prophet (SAW) taught us is the principle of leadership through service:

«سَيِّدُ القَوْمِ خادِمُهُمْ»

The leader of the nation is their servant.[1]

This is how the *da'iyah* should proceed: provide service and help to the community. When the Islamists position themselves in their society as service-oriented agents offering viable alternatives and solutions to local problems, people will trust them and make them their leaders. They will not only give the Islamists their hearts but also their votes in the polls.

---

1   Sunan al Daylami and Sunan al Tabarani.

IV. A Recipe for Action

We prescribe action on three levels: individual, local, and national.

A. The Individual Level

On the individual level, the Islamist must try to educate himself about local and international issues by reading newspapers and magazines and listening to broadcast news on a daily basis. He should make it a habit to discuss events in the news with those he meets and try to benefit from their views. Every *da'iyah* should personally acquire an adequate general knowledge of the events around him.

B. The Local Level

At the local level, the *da'iyah* should participate in a local periodic meeting of about ten members or less. Such meetings, often called *halaqah* or *usrah*, normally focus on education and spiritual uplifting. This is not enough. The structure of these meetings needs to be further developed so that about half of the time is utilized to discuss plans for local community affairs and practical *da'wah* projects. In this area, the situation of the movement today is appalling! Its adherents concentrate on academic and theoretical issues alone. Only about 5 percent of the membership performs and gets overloaded with work, while 95 percent remain spectators; they only watch and criticize negatively!

The entire structure of the movement looks like an inverted pyramid where 5 percent of the members are assets and 95 percent are liabilities. With such a structure, an organization readily becomes entangled with itself instead of dealing with issues related to its aims and objectives. Hindrances are abundant and helping hands are scarce. Realistically speaking, the output of such an organization may be five times greater if the inactive 95 percent of its members were outside supporters rather than internal members. This way they would not have to be cared for by the group, which feels the burden of responsibility for their welfare.

To solve this problem of inactivity, each member must be assigned a specific responsibility. He may be a member of a small committee or he can become in effect a "one man committee" accountable to the leader to whom he must report periodically on his activities.

The group must assign well-defined tasks to individuals (or committees) and should follow up on them. These tasks are quite numerous, for there is a lot to be done in the society over and above memorizing an *ayah* or a hadith.

The movement is not healthy if it does not become like a beehive or an ant kingdom full of energy and vitality, performing purposeful tasks in its society.

C. The National Level

While at the individual level we demand at least an adequate level of knowledge and awareness, we should expect professional, high level, specialized committees working on the national level. There must be a highly qualified functional committee for every major issue facing the country. These advisory or action committees form the organization's think tank. Their objective is to research the issues and supply the leadership with realistic and practical alternatives and solutions in their areas of specialty. While the general followers may be satisfied with generalities and superficial treatment, these committees must delve deeply into the issues. They master the state of the art in their areas so that they can provide concepts, resource allocations, and action plans within their fields of expertise. They have to be able to demonstrate in a convincing manner that Islamic solutions are superior to any other in the marketplace of ideologies. If these committees do their job well, the nation voluntarily hands over leadership to them, due to their superb mastery of scholarship and command over the issues. The movement then rightly becomes the natural trustee of the nation.

The Lighter Side of Da'wah!

FROM THEORY TO PRACTICE

There was an able *shaykh* who trained students for *da'wah* — six months in theory and three months in the field for practice. A confident student graduating from the theoretical part felt that he could do the practical part by himself. The *shaykh* warned him against this view, but the student did not listen. He went off to a remote village to practice *da'wah*. On the first Friday, a phoney imam delivered a *khutbah* full of lies about Allah and the Prophet. The student stood up and shouted: "The imam is a liar. Neither Allah nor the Prophet (SAW) made any of these statements." The imam responded: "This young man is a *kafir* and deserves to be punished." The audience in the mosque beat the student badly. The student went back to his *shaykh* with bandages and broken bones! The *shaykh* said to him: "Let me show you a good example of practical *da'wah*." Next Friday, they went to the same mosque where the same imam delivered a similar *khutbah*. Having listened to the *khutbah*, the *shaykh* stood up and declared: "Your imam is a man of *jannah*. Anyone who takes even a single hair from his beard will earn *jannah*." At once, the people attacked the imam's beard and pulled one hair after another until he was left beardless and bleeding on the floor. Then the *shaykh* whispered in the ear of the imam: "Are you going to stop lying about Allah and the Prophet (SAW) and behave yourself, or do you want more punishment?" The imam admitted his mischief and repented. The student realized his mistake and pleaded to the *shaykh* to give him his three months of practical *da'wah* field training! There is a world of difference between theory and application.

STOP!

> **Read!** in the name of your Lord and Cherisher, who created – created man, out of a leach like stage: Read! And your Lord is Most Bountiful, – Who taught with the Pen, – taught man that which he knew not (96:1-5)

ﭐﭑﭒﭓﭔﭕﭖﭗﭘﭙﭚ ﭛﭜﭝﭞﭟﭠﭡﭢﭣ ﭤﭥﭦﭧ ﭨﭩﭪﭫﭬﭭ ﭮﭯﭰﭱﭲﭳﭴﭵ
(سورة العلق)

- If the Muslim ummah reads the most, it will lead human civilization.
- If the *du'at* read more, they will lead the Muslim ummah.
- Today: Westerners read the most, Muslims read the least! Moreover, we learn to read, but they read to learn.
- **Directed Action:** Islamists must pioneer campaigns to wipe out illiteracy among Muslims.

   Bonus: Muslim masses will look up to *du'at* as their hope, aspiration, and saviors. The rule is that those who solve the problems of the people get to rule them!

GO!

> Against them make ready your strength to the utmost of your power, including steeds of war, to strike terror into [the hearts of] the enemies, of Allah and your enemies, and others besides, whom you may not know, but whom Allah does know ... (8:60).

ﮱﯓﯔﯕﯖﯗﯘﯙ ﯚﯛﯜﯝﯞﯟ ﯠﯡﯢﯣﯤﯥﯦ ﯧﯨﯩﯪﯫﯬﯭﯮ ﯯﯰﯱ ... (سورة الأنفال)

Chapter

2

The Movement during the Fourteenth Hijri Century

I. General Background

We use the term "movement" in a very general sense. It includes every group which professes, practices, and calls for the establishment of Islam. Moreover, we are taking a "snap shot" look and analyzing the outcome as a whole at the present time. For the sake of fairness and objectivity, we must keep in mind the major factors mentioned below as we do our analysis. This is not an evaluation or an assessment of achievements, for we are only focusing on some aspects from which we seek to draw useful lessons.

A. Looking from Within

In speaking about the movement, we are talking about ourselves from within. We are not criticizing from the outside. As such, we are offering constructive self-criticism with the objective of identifying shortcomings to improve our in-house situation. Unless we are truly honest with ourselves, our training and subsequent efforts will be useless.

B. Achievements vs. Shortcomings

Although we need to identify our weaknesses, we do not intend to paint a negative and gloomy picture of the movement. There are dark spots as well as bright ones. Indeed, the preservation of Islamic *da'wah* and the global awakening of the movement are a testimony to the movement's great success. The fact that we are enumerating our deficiencies stems from our deep-rooted commitment to strive ahead in the right direction. We are ourselves the product of this movement.

C. Political Action and Reaction

The assault of the West on the Muslim world included political and military occupation. Naturally, the Islamic and national reaction was similar in kind. This explains why the liberation movements are largely political and confrontational in dealing with the oppressing colonialists and their successors. As a result, the social, economic, and educational aspects were given secondary importance by these movements. When these nations achieved independence from foreign rule, it was only superficial. Their leaders did not know what to do with their political freedom. This explains why the economic, social, cultural, and educational imperialism of the colonial period lingered on for a long time with the same, if not greater, intensity.

D. Backwardness

We must also realize that the Muslim world has been in a state pervasive decadence for several centuries. This negative state permeates the concepts, activities, and actions not only of the general masses but also of the reform movements. Our ability to analyze, diagnose, and prescribe remedies is sharply reduced by our weaknesses. The fact that we are believers hardly affects the way we conduct the affairs of our movement. This phenomenon of backwardness takes its toll in a similar fashion on religious, nationalistic, and leftist parties alike. It affects the total cross-section of the nation — leaders, educators, doctors, engineers, civil servants, army officers, soldiers, farmers, men, women, the poor, and the rich. Decadence is an epidemic that attacks everyone.

E. Could We Have Done Better?

We may claim that the movement did its best, but success can only come from Allah. Certainly we were not perfect in our methods and concepts, and there was a lot of room for improvement. Allah's reward for those who strive in His cause will be generous. But as far as real social change in the conditions of our ummah is concerned, we notice little headway being made. In order to move ahead, we have to admit our mistakes so that we can do something constructive about them. The fact that someone is criticizing the movement does not necessarily put him on a higher level than the movement itself. Nor does it classify him with the enemies of the movement. No one is superior to others; Allah alone will assign one's rewards. Our superiority rests in the message and the ideology, not in the persons involved.

F. Battle for Survival

The movement, stifled by restrictions on its freedom, was primarily fighting the battle of life and death on a daily basis. Hence, it did not have the opportunity to pause, reflect on, and reconsider its course of action. To do so was a luxury virtually unavailable to it. Such a condition may breed extremist, secretive, underground, ambiguous, unrealistic, and inexperienced members, which in turn impede any improvement. Therefore, the major responsibility for correcting our situation lies with those who live in countries where people enjoy the gift of freedom. The demand on them is very great. They should not compare themselves with those living in countries oppressed by dictatorial regimes, as the former command opportunities which the latter can only wish for.

This being the background of the ummah during this century, we can appreciate the nature of the movement's struggle and begin to realize areas of possible improvement.

Al hamdu li Allah, the movement has survived all oppression and hostility from within the Muslim world and from without. This in itself is a great blessing. A lot has been gained from this struggle, but better results can be achieved. What is needed now is for the movement to improve in the areas discussed below.

II. Identifying Areas of Improvement

We draw the attention of our youth to the following areas in the hope that they will do better than we did, *in sha'a Allah*!

A. Participatory *Shura* (Mutual Consultation)

The movement was not able to practice *shura* in its entirety. It focused, more or less, on another system of convenience called *"al sam' wa ta'a"* — listen and obey. The leadership preached *shura* in theory, but neither formalized nor institutionalized its practice. A lot of academic debate went on whether *shura* is *mu'limah* (informative) or *mulzimah* (binding) on the *amir*. Each side quoted from Islamic sources to support its position. Since this is an area of ijtihad (research), it cannot be resolved simply through a *fatwa* (ruling of law). Today we need a binding, systematized, institutionalized, and well structured system of *shura*. A reasonable number of members should actively participate in the decision-making process as well as in the execution of the resulting decisions. The advantages of this Qur'anic *shura* system can never be overemphasized, particularly in modern times.

B. Team Spirit

The movement was able to produce excellent individuals through its *tarbiyah* (training) programs. The problem arose when these individuals were asked to work together. The movement was run mainly by a few individuals, rather than by teams of many members, not realizing that working together yields a much higher level of performance than working alone. This approach reflected the backward environment where we see a "one man management" system dominant in many spheres of life. In the family, the father dominates overwhelmingly. The case is similar in schools, the government, the army, and all political parties. This system, a symptom of decadence, pervades most of our institutions. If we analyze the world scene, we find that Europe pioneered the call of freedom and established the national states. America surpassed Europe by practicing the theory of the melting pot of all nationalities coupled with hard work. Japan, on the other hand, beat America by adding team spirit and loyalty to their own traditions and beliefs. Think of Islamic work as a football team. If you assemble all the best players on one team but they do not practice team spirit, they will lose to a much less qualified group with good team spirit.

C. Women and Children

A lack of success is noted in the areas of women and children. While we were partially successful with men, we failed with the others. We have not been able to educate, mobilize, and establish an effective women's movement. With some exceptions, Muslim women are still unable to organize themselves and motivate others. The great majority of them cannot communicate well or debate social issues. While nationalistic and leftist parties were exploiting women as much as possible for political gains, we could not benefit from the enormous potentials of our own sisters. Except in limited cases, they are inert, ineffective, and unable to contribute to the movement. While we wish and claim that they bring up the leaders of the ummah, we take no positive steps to involve, train, or support them. This remains a paradox in the movement. Realistically, we cannot win the battle if 50 percent of our forces are secluded and excluded from participation.

Similarly, little effort was expended in developing children. For example, not even 5 percent of the Islamic literature is addressed to them. We expect them to read the literature for adults and be convinced of its truths. Child and youth education are specialties in themselves and require distinct types of publications. The movement is losing a great deal by neglecting this area.

D. The *Shaykh* Type Leader

In some cases, the movement has followed the *shaykh* model of a leader. It looks for an angelic, heroic person who knows all and does all. He is to head the organization as long as he lives. Once in power, he cannot be unseated, and the movement is stuck with him regardless of what he does. Even when he is out of the country for long periods of time, he continues supervising the organization by remote control. When he is present in a meeting, he dominates the entire agenda; he speaks when he wants and for the period he desires. The subject matter is irrelevant to him because he does not prepare, write, or even make short notes for the meeting. He can speak off the top of his head on any subject. He is to be respected and given the number one position in everything, regardless of the specialization needed for that position.

The standard puzzle of the second-line leadership is who can replace him? Every member around him thinks of himself as a dwarf because all his life he has been brought up to think that way. It is presumed to be a necessary condition for his Islamic humbleness. He has never been trained in leadership through collective, participative *shura*. His enormous respect for the *shaykh* prevents him from challenging or holding the *shaykh* accountable, or even questioning him. He typifies the Sufi motto: "The follower before his *shaykh* is like the deceased in the hands of his bather." In some cases, a very much needed decision from the *shaykh* transforms itself into a *du'a'* format instead! Considering the above, recent worldwide experiences show that the most suitable term of office for a leader should be 4-6 years, renewable only once. This gives a maximum of 12 years for a leader. When his term expires, he can best serve in one of the specialized committees and as a valuable consultant to the new leadership. We do not accuse all leaders of following this typical model, but we invariably find at least some of these characteristics in many leaders.

E. Absence of Institutions

The movement has relied on individuals to carry out various tasks. Functions have depended on persons, which resulted in instability and many operational changes. There was little if any institutionalization. Even in the few institutions formed, there was lack of planning, team spirit, and proper organization. The movement could not realize its principles and objectives through these institutions. Some of them became a burden rather than a help. Although many members had succeeded in their personal projects, they failed when it came to group work. The movement has not yet tackled the need for the new "fiqh of institutions" coded in today's terminology and concepts. *Da'wah* work remains only talk until one can point to several successful public Muslim institutions in the country. There have to be at least ten such sizable ones in each country before we can begin to claim that we have started a successful process of institutionalization.

F. Regionalism and Nationalism

In theory, the movement is convinced of the ummah's unity and universality. In practice, however, these qualities are not fully applied. We demonstrate regionalistic and nationalistic attitudes and habits in our behavior. A clear sign of that shortcoming is seen in our social gatherings where brothers and sisters cling to their own ethnic friends. They rarely socialize with others. At the leadership level, we still have no periodic regional or international forums for movement leaders of various countries. While such meetings of the mind are not binding, they are crucial for information exchange, consultations, strategy formulation, and coordination.

Though we admit that our enemies act against us according to a unified plan, we fail to respond through a similarly unified plan. We have been victims of a misconception well expressed by the proverb: "The people of Makkah know its valleys best." Today, a foreign specialist may know our country much better than we do. In the same way, some brothers may give valuable advice to their counterparts in other countries which may benefit them in their local struggle. The world is getting smaller every day, and the concept of the global village is becoming a reality. Islam has advocated this concept of universality since its inception, but the movement is still dealing with its affairs locally and treating each locality in isolation from others.

G. Absence of Planning

Often the movement is living one day at a time, fighting only the immediate battle for survival. Hardly any thought is given to a five-year or a ten-year plan. Its work is managed by crisis, where routine maintenance situations become emergency operations. Lack of planning in advance has resulted in fuzzy aims, misallocation of resources, wrong priorities, and the loss of a sense of direction. At any given time, we do not know where we stand, how far we are from our goals, or how are we to evaluate our activities. Thus we continue to do what we are doing without knowing its benefits and costs. It is high time we resorted to proper planning and moved from the phase of doing what we can to that of doing what we must!

H. The Islamic Alternative

Up until the fifties, the movement was busy in proving that Islam is good. Then it went on to asserting that Islam is better than all the "isms." However, it stayed within these generalities and did not mature beyond them. We have yet to provide the Islamic alternative in the form of a university level textbook, for example. This is needed in every social science discipline.

This is not a voluntary part-time job for the general, sincere, and zealous member; it is the duty of full-time specialized scholars. The movement has to establish several high level academic institutions to tackle these areas of ijtihad. This work can no longer be assigned to the "know-it-all" type of individual *'ulama'*. It must be a collective effort. It is tedious, time-consuming, expensive, nonpartisan, and continuous hard work. But it is a necessary prerequisite if the ummah is to experience a renaissance. Without it, the superiority of Islamic systems remains an emotional conviction. An enlightened living example is needed to attract the East and the West towards Islamic civilization. This explains why more engineers, doctors, and natural scientists are attracted to the movement and its leadership than social scientists. The nice pure generalities convince them of the rationality and the beauty of Islam. However, the specialist social scientists must be particularly convinced of the details. The generalities are not adequate enough to lure them to the Islamic fold. This current state of affairs is an abnormal phenomenon. When we begin to witness that the majority of the movement's leaders are social scientists, we can signal the true rebirth of Islamic civilization.

I. Objectives and Means

There exists among some members a confusion between objectives and means. In many cases, the interest of the group is held up as the criterion for action, even though in fact the group is only a means to serve the objective of Islamizing the society. This has made the movement busier with itself than with the society which it seeks to change. A rough statistical analysis of how the time, money, and efforts of members are spent shows that approximately 70 percent of it is dedicated to the movement's internal affairs and maybe only 30 percent to the external society. The healthy set up must be the exact opposite.

The concept of the party has become sacred in itself, as if the party has been established for its own sake. It is considered almost as a sports club or a cooperative society servicing its own members exclusively. The image of the party has been that of a special group concerned only with its members and having no real stake in the society at large. This is why when political persecution falls on this group, the general public does not respond with concern. This handicap is also clearly manifested when credits earned by Islamists are lost to secularists due to lack of cooperation among Muslim groups and subgroups. Their organizational structures stand in the way of realizing their objectives. It cannot be emphasized enough that the movement must adopt the problems of the ummah as its challenge and undertake the task of solving them. Most of the movement's effort must be expended on these issues so that the ummah recognizes the movement as the true guardian of its affairs. The ummah should be able to sleep comfortably knowing that a reliable trustee, the Islamic group, is taking good care of it.

J. Crisis of Thought

In general, the movement did not achieve uniformity or unity of thought among its members because it clung to generalities. The main thrust of the movement was on activities rather than thought and education. In addition, when the group did not take a formal stand on some important issues, the membership espoused various opinions, adding to the problem of nonunified thought. Indeed, the vacuum was sometimes filled with the viewpoints and positions of secular parties or hostile ideologies.

K. Nondialogue

The movement appears to stifle ideological dialogue on three levels — internally among its members, with other Islamic organizations, and with non-Islamic groups — religious or secular. This resulted in nurturing utopian and idealistic concepts among some members. Theoretical puritan ideas remained untested for their practicality. The lack of dialogue produced a static intellectual atmosphere which did not provide the enrichment needed for maturity within the movement. Concurrently, this stagnant atmosphere generated a lack of understanding among some groups which bred mistrust and enmity among various factions in the society.

L. Neglect of the Media

To some extent, the movement neglected the area of communication with the outside world. It did not direct its members to fill this gap early enough. Thus its impact on the society was much less than what it could have been. Meanwhile, its competitors controlled the media and painted a distorted image of the movement. The movement needs to direct members to specialize in the media. This was particularly noticeable when the movement contested elections in several countries. The level of its public campaign was mediocre in some areas. Islamic publications are often unattractive and sometimes repulsive. Only committed members have the patience to go through the agony of reading them. Nonmembers avoid the movement's literature. The low circulation of our periodicals is a true index of this fact.

The movement has also ignored the importance of directing its high school graduates to the most needed areas of specialization like social sciences, media and communications, education, civil service, and the police and law enforcement agencies. The absence of this kind of planning has taken its toll on the movement.

M. Followers' and Leaders' Accountability

The norm in the movement has been that members are accountable to the leadership. The latter demands absolute obedience of the former at times of pleasure and hardship alike. However, the need for the leaders' accountability has not been satisfactorily addressed, and it is far from being systematized, formalized, and practiced. Whenever the leaders report to the membership, it is in generalities like "the situation is under control," "the *da'wah* is progressing," "the future is bright for Islam," "Allah's victory is near," "you must increase your *iman*," "give more sacrifices," "have patience," and so on.

Mainly, there are no statistics, no facts and figures, no quantitative or qualitative analysis of membership data, publications, finances, public opinion polls, institutional assessment, or proper evaluations of performance. Thus there is no foundation upon which to base accountability.

Sometimes leaders may refuse to answer questions under the pretext of confidentiality. A movement is unhealthy unless it periodically holds its leaders accountable. Leaders should be confronted with true challenges and asked to improve their performance. Of legal importance is the financial accountability. The movement must have its financial reports and statements audited on a regular basis.

N. Ordering of Priorities

"Efficiency" leads to doing things right while "priority" leads to doing the right things. There is a lot of difference between the two, but both are necessary. We can be very efficient while doing the wrong task. Hence, priority takes precedence, even if only because there are more tasks and demands than resources. Thus, prioritizing becomes essential, and this results in giving the right issues your very valuable and scarce human and material resources. As history moves on, things happen faster and the need to prioritize becomes increasingly more crucial. It is not enough to do the important things; we must do the most important things first.

O. Organizational Freeze

It has been noticed that once the movement's organizational structure is set up, it stays unchanged for a long time in spite of the organization's growth, the change of issues, and the reordering of priorities. To serve its purpose, however, the formal structure of an organization must reflect its real functioning. It should be modified to accommodate any development of the group. The administrative configuration which it represents is only a means to serve the objective and cannot be considered sacred and unchangeable. As a general rule, revisions are recommended every five years .

P. Underground vs. Open

Too much time has been wasted in discussing whether the movement should work openly or underground. In some instances, taking a position on this issue was portrayed as part of one's faith. Each side sought examples from the Prophet (SAW) and the legacy to support its point of view. This is a purely organizational issue and both ways are Islamic. What needs to be done is a realistic assessment of existing social realities in order to determine which option is more beneficial to the movement in the long run. In some cases there is no choice; the country's conditions dictate which way to go. Whenever the environment allows it, the movement should be open to the public. There is no virtue in working underground if we are allowed to work openly.

Q. The Qur'an and the *Sultan* (Ruler)

Due to the historical background of twentieth-century imperialism, the movement has been in a state of continuous confrontation with the governing regimes. This attitude may be justified in several cases, but should not be accepted as the normal state of affairs. It must be reversed. The movement must strive to change this condition by seeking new realities. On the other hand, the country's regime must be convinced that the movement means well and wishes good for the country and its rulers. The nation stands only to lose in an atmosphere of mistrust. The movement exists to construct, sacrifice, educate, serve, and guide to what is better. It should not be perceived as power-hungry and therefore "out to get" the rulers. To rule is not the objective of the movement; it is only a means. If this objective cannot be fully achieved through the authority of a government, it can at least be partially implemented through the actions of the masses in a free and democratic manner. The movement should seek to change the image of confrontation into one of cooperation. There is no virtue in confrontation: virtue lies in easy, simplified, and relaxed dealings, as the Prophet (SAW) taught us. While external powers may be pushing for hostilities between the Muslim masses and their governments, enlightened Islamists should watch for such alarming trends and try to avert them whenever possible. The movement should learn the wisdom of the maxim: "Do not fight a losing battle." We have to avoid being drawn into a confrontation before we are ready.

R. Absence of Adequate Feedback

Our management functions as an open loop system where corrective feedback information is neither solicited nor used. Some members aim at just delivering the message without monitoring its desired effect. The idea that a Muslim gets his reward from Allah in the hereafter if not in this life has been confused with abandoning efforts to seek successful results. The prevailing concept is that the work is our responsibility and the results are in Allah's hands. This concept has been misused and has caused a lack of emphasis on performance and success. Our motto has been to work but not to seek success.

This is like the case of a ship captain who delivers his passengers to shore — dead. He establishes no communication with them. The time has come when the movement must engage the best of its specialists in the fields of psychology, sociology, communication, mass movement, political science, and public relations in order to analyze our work and its impact on people. How do they respond to it? This feedback must then be utilized to modify and correct our approach and interaction with people. We should realize that our "expression" is not necessarily the "impression" people get from us. There exists a gap between what we mean and what people understand. This gap must be reduced to a minimum; the smaller it is, the more successful we are delivering our message, as expressed by the equation:

(Expression - Impression) = Error

OR (Expression - Error) = Impression

S. The Partisan Issue

More often than not, the upbringing of members in the movement is based on partisan considerations and not on the merits of the issues. The member is more biased towards the party than towards the truth. He tends to become emotional and judges truth by people instead of judging people by truth. In a manner of speaking, he is not taught to think freely; rather, he is shackled by biased opinions and viewpoints. This makes it difficult for him to deal openly with others, particularly those outside the movement. He has undue difficulty in speaking with scholars because he is not trained to examine issues objectively. He has similar trouble with non-Islamic minded persons. Normally, the movement does not encourage self-criticism and has not established a formal system to channel the opinions of members to the leaders. On the contrary, criticism is unwelcome; those who venture to stick their necks out are sometimes accused of hostile intentions and ulterior motives. The response to criticism is to attack personalities instead of addressing the contents of the argument. The focus is not on what is being said but on who is saying it, and objectivity is lost in the process. This approach has stifled efforts to introduce much-needed productive reform.

T. *Adab al Ikhtilaf* — The Etiquette of Differing

We are not always following the Prophetic guidance in our manners when we disagree with one another. We have lost tolerance. Instead of differences becoming blessings and sources of enrichment, they bring about disunity and fragmentation. Differences of the mind are transformed into differences of the heart. Brotherly love is turned into hatred. The group loses its bonds and degenerates into a collection of hostile individuals. This turns any new opinion into a threat to unity, a development which causes an alarm to be sounded immediately and loudly to protect the integrity of the group. The creation of such an emergency situation gives an excuse to the leaders to suspend Islamic manners and indulge in extraordinary un-Islamic behavior so that the atmosphere becomes saturated with backbiting, slander, rumors, accusations, lying, and character assassination. Indeed, some disputes among Islamists have led to bloodshed within the ranks of believers, as happened in Afghanistan. We often do not follow the Qur'anic guidance of observing Islamic manners in all our disputes. If we do, it will guarantee us success against our opponents in the long run.

U. Long Agenda

Occasionally, the movement fell into the trap of demanding everything from its opponents all at once. We did not crystallize or prioritize our demands. We did not submit a program that spelled out material and human resources with a time schedule. Some think that an immediate, totally perfect and pure version of Islam is achievable on demand. They want everything done at once, and are unable to understand that this process takes time.

They confuse the mental belief in the totality of the message with the gradual application of its teachings in real-life situations. They fail to reconcile the statement "accept Islam totally or leave it" with the hadith:

«إِنَّ هَذا الدِّينَ مَتينٌ فَأَوْغِلْ فيه بِرِفْقٍ»

This religion is strong, so deal with it delicately and nicely.[1]

A nice and gradual step-by-step application is what the Prophet (SAW) taught us. The lesson to learn is to keep our agenda short, precise, and clear. Once we achieve it, we put together another short and well-timed agenda, and so on. This was done effectively by the communists and nationalists in Muslim countries. Their slogans were highly attractive and viable because they were precise and clear, like:

- "We want bread"
- "We demand fewer working hours"
- "Higher wages"
- "Free health service," etc.

III. Looking Back

Looking back at the Islamic movement, there is no doubt it did a lot of hard work. However, sometimes the harvest of its efforts was hijacked by its adversaries. This is particularly obvious in the liberation movements like those in Algeria, Egypt, Libya and Pakistan.

The library of Islamic literature today produces a static Muslim. Normally, he is legalistic and literal in his approach to life. We failed to produce the dynamic, convincing *da'iyah*. The Prophet (SAW) prayed to win the leaders of Quraysh to Islam:

«اللّهمَّ أعِزَّ الإِسْلامَ بِأَحَبِّ هٰذينِ الرَّجُلَيْنِ إِلَيْكَ، بِأَبِي جَهْلٍ (عمرو بن الحكم) أوْ بِعُمَرَ بْنِ الخَطَّاب»

Oh Allah! strengthen Islam by the more lovable one to You of the two men: Abu Jahl (meaning 'Amr Ibn al Hakam) or 'Umar ibn al Khattab.[2]

In his prayer, the Prophet (SAW) was identifying the potential leaders of the society in order to Islamize them, thus gaining power for *da'wah*. The opposite is happening today, for the dynamic and intelligent members often end up leaving the Muslim group. The *jama'ah* becomes unable to absorb or deal with them. They become like the ripe fruit which falls because the mother tree cannot bear them anymore. There is hardly any sorting and sifting; the bright ones graduate and leave the movement while the mediocre stay behind, forever becoming a burden and a liability. We end up with a top-heavy organization which does not respond promptly and effectively to urgent needs. Our movement is not alone in the field; the arena is full of competitors and challengers. Hence, the movement has to develop a policy on how to deal with other Islamic and non-Islamic organizations; it has to give up placing everything under one name, one

---

1   Musnad Ahmad ibn Hanbal.
2   Musnad Ahmad ibn Hanbal and Sunan al Tirmidhi.

roof, one center, and one entity; and it should try to influence and control rather than possess and own. Whenever a task can be adequately performed by others, it should be entrusted to them. Islam belongs to all, and no single organization can claim exclusive title to it. The fact that some dedicated volunteers are willing to make sacrifices does not give them an open mandate to dominate the work, regardless of their effectiveness. If their performance is superior, they will take the lead and keep it; otherwise, they will be displaced.

> ... If you turn back [from the path], He will substitute in your stead another people; then they would not be like you (47:38).

$$\text{... وَإِن تَتَوَلَّوْا يَسْتَبْدِلْ قَوْمًا غَيْرَكُمْ}$$
$$\text{ثُمَّ لَا يَكُونُوا أَمْثَالَكُم (سورة محمد)}$$

Although it is important to gain a favorable public opinion, the movement should not be led by public opinion. Rather, it should have its own plans and strategies to form, modify, change, and lead public opinion.

When it comes to dealing with the West, some Muslim thinkers have portrayed the West as one of two extremes: either like a *jannah* (paradise) or a *jahannam* (hell). The truth is that the West is like neither one of them; it has both positive and negative features. As Muslims, we must always be fair, as Allah teaches us:

> ... Give just measure and weight, and do not withhold from the people the things that are their due ... (7:85).

$$\text{... فَأَوْفُوا الْكَيْلَ وَالْمِيزَانَ}$$
$$\text{وَلَا تَبْخَسُوا النَّاسَ أَشْيَاءَهُمْ ... (سورة الأعراف)}$$

The West is making the *haram* attractive, inviting, and abundant. We are making the *halal* difficult, repulsive, and scarce. The movement has to give up the easy route of issuing *fatawa* and adopt the much-needed approach of offering viable solutions. While we prevent people from the *haram*, we must provide them with *halal* alternatives. For example, we have not yet developed *halal* radio and television programs. The entertainment arena is wide open for Islamization, but very little work has been done in this field.

To sum up, the West has an inferior product with superior salesmen, while we have a superior product with inferior salesmen. And although their man-made system is fallible, the secularists are relentlessly working to rectify and correct it. Their likeness is that of driving an old car that keeps breaking down, but the passengers are engineers and mechanics who can always fix it. We are driving a new imported car with no knowledge of how it works. Once it breaks down, we are stuck forever. The challenge of the movement is to prove the excellence of *iman*, to establish the superiority of Islamic thought in various disciplines, and to demonstrate a practical model for the Islamic alternative. A small but successful pilot project will suffice! This is the real challenge facing the ummah in the fifteenth *hijri* century!

IV. Questions to Ask!

A. Tug of War!

It is claimed that most people in the Muslim world do not work hard. But how about those good Muslims who do work very hard? Why are they unproductive? Their problem is one of attitude, orientation, and lack of team spirit. As a result, individuals in a group may work very hard but in opposing directions. The total effect of their forces can be zero, or even negative.

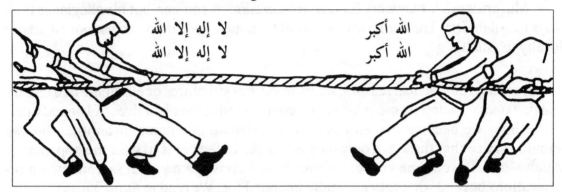

Islamic work has a magnitude and a direction like a mathematical vector quantity. Unless individuals work in unison with one another with a clear plan and a sense of direction, they will not produce results in spite of the tremendous energy they expend. If we continue picking on one another's mistakes, neglecting positive contributions, and belittling others' achievements, we shall not get anywhere. We have to abandon the feeling that we are always right and others are always wrong. We must recognize all the workers in the Islamic field and try to coordinate our efforts.

B. Existing Conditions: Worst or Best?

It is often claimed that "our situation today is the worst it can get, and it is not possible to work under such circumstances. We must wait for a better and more conducive environment." The fact of the matter is that over the last several decades conditions have continuously deteriorated in a number of Muslim countries. The healthy attitude of the *da'iyah* should be that the current conditions are the best available and that he must get the most out of them. We do not know what may happen tomorrow, nor can we be sure how long the status of things today will last. The light-hearted story of the man falling from a twenty-story building applies here. As he was falling down past the seventh floor a man asked him from the window: "How are you doing?" He replied: "So far, so good!"

Our overly-guarded optimism regarding *da'wah* can be viewed through the Qur'anic account of the prophets Musa (AS) (Moses) and Harun (AS) (Aaron), and Pharaoh.

Go, both of you, to Pharaoh, for he has indeed transgressed all bounds; but speak to him mildly; perchance he may take warning or fear [Allah] (20:43-44).

وَأَذْهَبَا إِلَىٰ فِرْعَوْنَ إِنَّهُ طَغَىٰ ﴿٤٣﴾ فَقُولَا لَهُ قَوْلًا لَّيِّنًا لَّعَلَّهُ يَتَذَكَّرُ أَوْ يَخْشَىٰ ﴿٤٤﴾ (سورة طه)

We are not better than Musa (AS), nor are the people any worse than Pharaoh. Hence we must keep up the hope and not despair from our present situation.

C. Is Loyalty to Allah or to Acronyms?

A Muslim worker may work for one organization or another, but his allegiance is always to Allah first. The acronyms we invent to name organizations must not cloud our loyalty to Allah.

For strategic or tactical reasons, we form various structures or eliminate and change existing ones. Their purpose must not be confused with the objectives of Islamic work. Sometimes we become overenthusiastic and defend one name or another, but we should realize that these are only means, for the objective is to gain the approval of Allah alone. It would be very dangerous if we imposed a mystical sacredness on organizations beyond what they are really intended for. We read in *Surat* Yusuf:

If not Him, you worship nothing but names which you have named — you and your fathers — for which Allah has sent down no authority: the Command is for none but Allah: He has commanded that you worship none but Him: that is the right religion, but most men understand not (12:40).

مَا تَعْبُدُونَ مِن دُونِهِ إِلَّا أَسْمَاءً سَمَّيْتُمُوهَا أَنتُمْ وَءَابَاؤُكُم مَّا أَنزَلَ اللَّهُ بِهَا مِن سُلْطَانٍ إِنِ الْحُكْمُ إِلَّا لِلَّهِ أَمَرَ أَلَّا تَعْبُدُوا إِلَّا إِيَّاهُ ذَٰلِكَ الدِّينُ الْقَيِّمُ وَلَٰكِنَّ أَكْثَرَ النَّاسِ لَا يَعْلَمُونَ ﴿٤٠﴾ (سورة يوسف)

This is the phenomenon that has been plaguing our movement, and it is clearly due to our lack of comprehension of the highest objective.

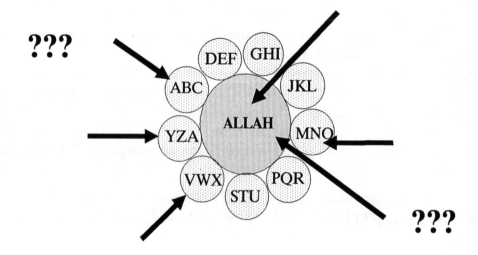

V. The Balance ...

By nature, we often take things for granted and forget the great blessings delivered by the Islamic movement during this century. In fact, to say the least, the movement acted as the guardian of Islam and Muslims. It kept the banner of the Islamic call high despite extreme hardship.

Undoubtedly, the movement stood as a formidable fortress against the vicious attacks from the right and the left. While the nationalists were hollow and bankrupt ideologically and morally, the movement continuously enriched the ummah with the immunity and enlightened spirituality needed to guide it towards righteousness. It worked hard to preserve the identity of the ummah. Without such struggle, the masses would have dissolved in the various "isms" of socialism, capitalism, materialism, racism, and nationalism. We can claim with some certainty that when compared to non-Islamic parties, the Islamic movement, on balance, surpassed them all. The movement pioneered the jihad against dictators and oppressors. It carried the torch in the fight against corruption and evil. For these it paid the heavy price of martyrdom, imprisonment and persecution. It stood up to the transgressors and tyrants to tell them: "You are *zalim*s; you must step down; you must give freedom to the people." As a result, victimization and torture fell heavily on the Islamists.

It was the movement's selfless members who put up the strongest resistance against the colonialist occupiers in Palestine, Algeria, Afghanistan, and Kashmir. Clearly this was due to sincerity, sacrifice, and dedication among the God-fearing followers of the movement.

The manifest awakening in the Muslim world today can only be credited to the movement's relentless jihad. This revival was not confined or localized, but rather was pervasive in nature. It swept many countries, like Malaysia, Bangladesh, Pakistan, Afghanistan, Iran, Turkey, Egypt, Sudan, Tunisia, and Algeria. Hardly any Muslim country escaped the winds of Islamization of some sort. It suffices to say that our existence today as Islamists is owed to the global Islamic movement.

While we may assign a failing grade to groups championing Westernization, secularism, and communism in the twenieth century AC, we feel confident that the Islamic movement has earned a passing grade during the fourteenth *hijri* century. All praise be to Allah, to Whom we pray to guide us to the Right Path in this fifteenth *hijri* century.

The Timeline of Events in Training

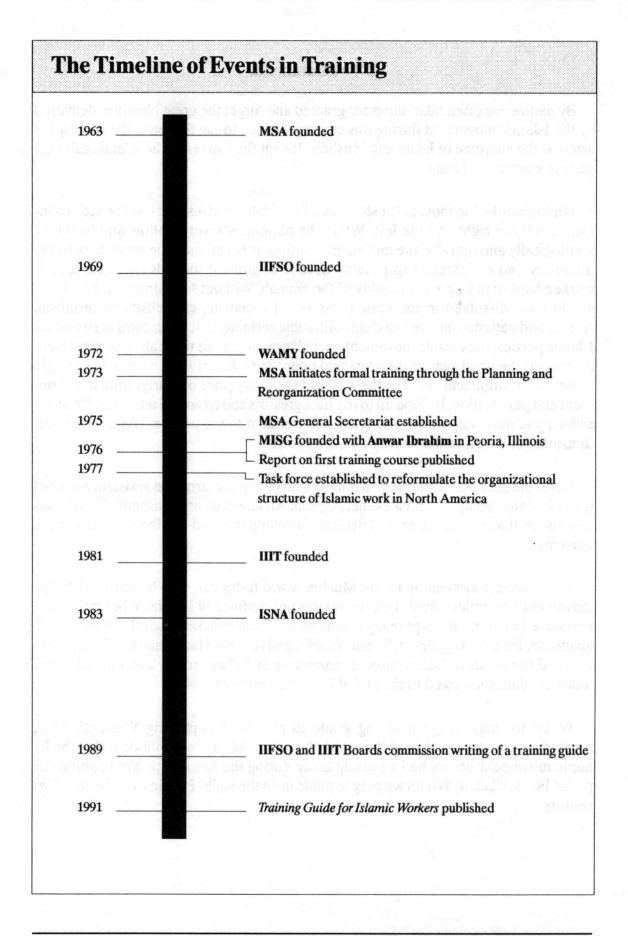

1963	**MSA** founded
1969	**IIFSO** founded
1972	**WAMY** founded
1973	**MSA** initiates formal training through the Planning and Reorganization Committee
1975	**MSA** General Secretariat established
1976	**MISG** founded with **Anwar Ibrahim** in Peoria, Illinois
1977	Report on first training course published
	Task force established to reformulate the organizational structure of Islamic work in North America
1981	**IIIT** founded
1983	**ISNA** founded
1989	**IIFSO** and **IIIT** Boards commission writing of a training guide
1991	*Training Guide for Islamic Workers* published

Chapter

3

Our Objectives

I. The Historical Steps

The objective of training is not to make Muslims, for we assume that the trainees are already committed and practicing Muslims who aspire to do something more to promote the cause of truth.

The historical steps of our existence on earth, as related in the Qur'an, throw light on our objectives.

A. The Will of Allah to Make a *Khalifah* (Vicegerent) on Earth

When Allah willed our creation, He spoke to the angels:

Behold, your Lord said to the angels: "I will create a vicegerent on earth." They said: "Will You place therein one who will make mischief therein and shed blood? — While we do celebrate Your praises and glorify Your holy [name]?" He said: "I know what you know not" (2:30).

۞ وَإِذْ قَالَ رَبُّكَ لِلْمَلَٰٓئِكَةِ إِنِّي جَاعِلٌ فِى ٱلْأَرْضِ خَلِيفَةًۖ قَالُوٓا۟ أَتَجْعَلُ فِيهَا مَن يُفْسِدُ فِيهَا وَيَسْفِكُ ٱلدِّمَآءَ وَنَحْنُ نُسَبِّحُ بِحَمْدِكَ وَنُقَدِّسُ لَكَۖ قَالَ إِنِّىٓ أَعْلَمُ مَا لَا تَعْلَمُونَ (سورة البقرة)

Of significance is the angels' focus on the anti-objective — to make mischief, spread evil, and shed blood. This is the opposite of reform (*islah*): to civilize and build the planet.

B. Knowledge

After the creation of Adam, the first thing Allah did was:

And He taught Adam the names of all things; then He placed them before the angels, and said: "Tell Me the names of these if you are right." They said: "Glory to You: of knowledge we have none save what you have taught us: in truth it is You who are perfect in knowledge and wisdom" (2:31-2).

وَعَلَّمَ ءَادَمَ ٱلْأَسْمَآءَ كُلَّهَا ثُمَّ عَرَضَهُمْ عَلَى ٱلْمَلَٰٓئِكَةِ فَقَالَ أَنۢبِـُٔونِى بِأَسْمَآءِ هَٰٓؤُلَآءِ إِن كُنتُمْ صَٰدِقِينَ ۝ قَالُوا۟ سُبْحَٰنَكَ لَا عِلْمَ لَنَآ إِلَّا مَا عَلَّمْتَنَآ إِنَّكَ أَنتَ ٱلْعَلِيمُ ٱلْحَكِيمُ (سورة البقرة)

He taught Adam "the names of all things," which is the prerequisite for attaining the power of reasoning, without which neither Adam nor the angels would know anything.

C. The Test

Adam and Eve failed their first test. Allah told them and Satan:

We said: "Get you down all from here: And if, as is sure, there comes to you guidance from Me, whosoever follows my guidance, on them shall be no fear, nor shall they grieve" (2:38).

قُلْنَا ٱهْبِطُوا۟ مِنْهَا جَمِيعًا فَإِمَّا يَأْتِيَنَّكُم مِّنِّى هُدًى فَمَن تَبِعَ هُدَايَ فَلَا خَوْفٌ عَلَيْهِمْ وَلَا هُمْ يَحْزَنُونَ (سورة البقرة)

Whether human beings would follow guidance or falsehood was a test for them. This theme of testing is stressed in the Qur'an.

He who created Death and Life that He may try which of you is best in deed; and He is the Exalted in Might, Oft-Forgiving (67:2).

ٱلَّذِى خَلَقَ ٱلْمَوْتَ وَٱلْحَيَوٰةَ لِيَبْلُوَكُمْ أَيُّكُمْ أَحْسَنُ عَمَلًا وَهُوَ ٱلْعَزِيزُ ٱلْغَفُورُ (سورة الملك)

Do men think that they will be left alone on saying, "We believe," and that they will not be tested (29:2).

أَحَسِبَ ٱلنَّاسُ أَن يُتْرَكُوٓا۟ أَن يَقُولُوٓا۟ ءَامَنَّا وَهُمْ لَا يُفْتَنُونَ (سورة العنكبوت)

And We shall try you until We test those among you who strive their utmost and persevere in patience; and We shall try your reported [character] (47:31).

وَلَنَبْلُوَنَّكُمْ حَتَّىٰ نَعْلَمَ ٱلْمُجَٰهِدِينَ مِنكُمْ وَٱلصَّٰبِرِينَ وَنَبْلُوَا۟ أَخْبَارَكُمْ (سورة محمد)

D. The Prophets as Our Models

How do we prepare for and pass this test of life? Knowledge alone is not enough; otherwise, the scriptures would have sufficed for guidance. A model which we can follow is needed. The prophets, peace be upon them, are such models. They show us the light and take us from the "what and why" of life into the "how." Beyond knowledge, the prophets are granted *hikmah* (wisdom), which is the proper application of knowledge.

> When Yusuf attained his full manhood, We gave him power and knowledge: thus do We reward those who do right (12:22).

Surveying the Qur'an, we see the mission of the prophets as that of proclaiming the message clearly:

> And our duty is only to proclaim the clear Message (36:17).

> Therefore, do you give admonition, for you are one to admonish. You are not one to manage [men's] affairs (88:21-2).

> Therefore, give admonition in case the admonition profits [the hearer] (87:9).

> Invite [all] to the Way of your Lord with wisdom and beautiful preaching; and argue with them in ways that are best and most gracious; For your Lord knows best, Who have strayed from His Path, and who receive guidance (16:125).

The prophets perform one major task which consists of clear warning, explaining with wisdom, good preaching, and irrefutable aurgument — they remind others of the truth. They do not use force in fulfilling their mission and cannot grant guidance to individuals, for these come from Allah alone.

> Let there be no compulsion in religion; Truth stands out clear from Error: Whoever rejects Evil and believes in Allah has grasped the most trustworthy handhold, that never breaks. And Allah hears and knows all things (2:256).

It is true that you will not be able to guide those whom you love; but Allah Guides those whom He will and He knows best those who receive guidance (28:56).

إِنَّكَ لَا تَهْدِى مَنْ أَحْبَبْتَ وَلَكِنَّ اللَّهَ يَهْدِى مَن يَشَاءُ وَهُوَ أَعْلَمُ بِالْمُهْتَدِينَ (سورة القصص)

II. The Course of Action

A. Our Task

Our task and our role are derived directly from this verse in *Surat* Yusuf:

Say you: "This is my Way: I do invite unto Allah — on evidence clear as the seeing with one's eyes — I and whoever follows me. Glory to Allah! and never will I join gods with Allah!" (12:108).

قُلْ هَذِهِ سَبِيلِى أَدْعُوا إِلَى اللَّهِ عَلَى بَصِيرَةٍ أَنَا وَمَنِ اتَّبَعَنِى وَسُبْحَنَ اللَّهِ وَمَا أَنَا مِنَ الْمُشْرِكِينَ (سورة يوسف)

This is my way, the Prophet (SAW) asserts, to call for the sake of Allah with vividness and clarity (*basirah*) for himself and for those who follow him. Our training strategy has to prepare the trainees to attain this state of *basirah*. Their goal in life should be expressed the way the prophets verbalized it — the Straight Path. Since the Prophet Muhammad (SAW) is the last of the prophets, the task and role designated in the verse above is now solely for us, the followers of his way, to fulfill. While the Qur'anic verse above is addressed to the Prophet Muhammad (SAW) and his followers in general, the following one applies directly to the trainees in their role as *du'at* :

Who is better in speech than one who calls [men] to Allah, works righteousness, and says, "I am of the Muslims?" (41:33).

وَمَنْ أَحْسَنُ قَوْلًا مِّمَّن دَعَا إِلَى اللَّهِ وَعَمِلَ صَلِحًا وَقَالَ إِنَّنِى مِنَ الْمُسْلِمِينَ (سورة فصلت)

Hence the mission of a trainee is to:
● Call for the sake of Allah,
● Act in the best way, and
● Declare that he is a Muslim.

The last point eliminates the possibility of the trainee becoming just an isolated super individual. On the contrary, he must get involved and aim at effecting social change. All the personal preparations are to enable him to become an agent of social transformation. This role of the trainee is further clarified by the verse:

For each [such persons] there are angels in succession, before and behind him: they guard him by command of Allah. Verily never will Allah change the condition of a people until they change within their own souls ... (13:11).

لَهُ مُعَقِّبَتٌ مِّنْ بَيْنِ يَدَيْهِ وَمِنْ خَلْفِهِ يَحْفَظُونَهُ مِنْ أَمْرِ اللَّهِ إِنَّ اللَّهَ لَا يُغَيِّرُ مَا بِقَوْمٍ حَتَّى يُغَيِّرُوا مَا بِأَنفُسِهِمْ ... (سورة الرعد)

The beauty is in the word "themselves" — in the plural form, not the singular. Excellent individuals — even supermen — alone are not enough; they must work effectively with team spirit in groups to qualify for the title "excellent."

B. *Islah*, *Ihsan*, and *Itqan*: Reform, Improvement, and Perfection

The training program trains the trainee to advance through the stages of Islam — *iman*, *ihsan*, and *itqan* — ever striving to qualify for successively higher levels. Having attained *iman* he reaches for *ihsan*. *Ihsan* means to continue improving performance without giving up. It is a continuous process that involves *islah*, the opposite of *ifsad* (undermining), of performance. Alluding to the improvement he sought in his people, the Prophet Shu'ayb (AS) said to them: "I seek nothing but reform."

He said: "O my people! See you whether I have a Clear [Sign] from your Lord. And He has given me sustenance [pure and] good as from Himself? I wish not, in opposition to you, to do that which I forbid you to do. I only desire [your] betterment to the best of my ability; And my success [in my task] can only come from Allah. In Him I trust, and unto Him I look" (11:88).

قَالَ يَقَوْمِ أَرَءَيْتُمْ إِن كُنتُ ﴿٨٨﴾
عَلَىٰ بَيِّنَةٍ مِّن رَّبِّى وَرَزَقَنِى مِنْهُ رِزْقًا حَسَنًا
وَمَا أُرِيدُ أَنْ أُخَالِفَكُمْ إِلَىٰ مَا أَنْهَىٰكُمْ عَنْهُ
إِنْ أُرِيدُ إِلَّا ٱلْإِصْلَٰحَ مَا ٱسْتَطَعْتُ وَمَا تَوْفِيقِى
إِلَّا بِٱللَّهِ عَلَيْهِ تَوَكَّلْتُ وَإِلَيْهِ أُنِيبُ (سورة هود)

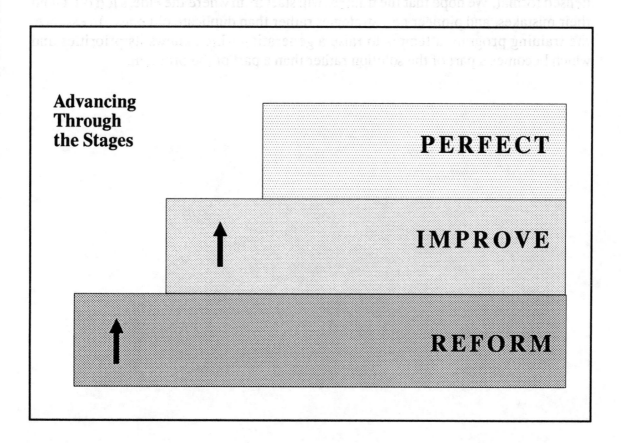

Advancing Through the Stages

PERFECT

IMPROVE

REFORM

Whenever one is confronted with a difficult situation, one should make the best of it, improve upon it, and reform it, just as Allah tells the Prophet (SAW):

Nor can Goodness or Evil be equal. Repel [Evil] with what is better: Then will he between whom and you was hatred become as it were your friend and intimate (41:34).

وَلَا تَسْتَوِى ٱلْحَسَنَةُ وَلَا ٱلسَّيِّئَةُ ٱدْفَعْ بِٱلَّتِى هِىَ أَحْسَنُ فَإِذَا ٱلَّذِى بَيْنَكَ وَبَيْنَهُ عَدَاوَةٌ كَأَنَّهُ وَلِىٌّ حَمِيمٌ

(سورة فصلت)

C. The Goal

The above verses of the Qur'an direct us to our goal: to produce dynamic Islamic leaders who will pioneer social change by acquiring knowledge and wisdom and practicing *da'wah* that is convincing and effective with perceptiveness and communication.

D. The Means

To achieve this goal, the training program offers a valuable opportunity that enhances the trainees' commitment, imparts knowledge to them, and builds up their skills in communication, administration, and planning. Moreover, it aspires to enhance their physical and technical abilities, develop healthy group attitudes, promote spiritual upliftment, and nurture a positive problem-solving mentality. The program seeks to transfer the experiences of senior brothers and sisters to the younger ones in a condensed format. We hope that the trainees will start from where the elders left off, avoid their mistakes, and pioneer new strategies rather than duplicate old ones. In essence, the training program attempts to raise a generation which knows its priorities and which becomes a part of the solution rather than a part of the problem.

Part Two

Functions of Leadership

The training of the *da'iyah* — the Islamic worker — is centered on learning "how" to exercise leadership among one's peers as well as in the public at large. In fact, leadership is part of the Islamic personality. The Prophet (SAW) told us that:

«كُلُّكُمْ رَاعٍ وَكُلُّ رَاعٍ مَسْئُولٌ عَنْ رَعِيَّتِهِ»

Every one of you is a shepherd and every one is responsible for what he is shepherd of (Sunan al Tirmidhi, Sunan Abu Dawud, Sahih al Bukhari and Sahih Muslim).

This part of the *Guide* deals with some selected elements of leadership. It begins with a discussion of its Islamic basis. This is followed by discussions on problem solving, decision making, implementation of decisions, planning, evaluation, and teamwork. This covers the fundamentals of leadership and should prepare the user of the *Guide* for action and further training in this area.

Chapter

4

Leadership in Islam

LEARNING OBJECTIVES

On completing this chapter, you should be able to:
- define the responsibilities and limitations of leadership
- identify the characteristics and behavior of leaders
- understand the Islamic model of leadership
- function as a more effective Islamic leader

I. Definition of Leadership

Leadership refers to the process of moving people in a planned direction by motivating them to action through noncompulsive means. Good leadership moves people in a direction that is truly in their long-term best interest. The direction could be as general as reaching out to the world with Islam or as specific as holding an issue-oriented conference. In any case, the means and the ends should serve the best interests of the people involved in a real and long-term sense.

Leadership is both a role and a process of influencing others. The leader is a member of a group who is given a certain rank and is expected to perform in a manner consistent with that rank. Also, a leader is the person who is expected to exercise influence in forming and accomplishing the group's goals. An honest leader is the one who leads and not the one who manipulates to lead.

The phenomenon of leadership may be explained in terms of the following fundamental concepts:

1. It is a force which in some unknown manner flows between leaders and followers and impels the followers to release their energies in concert towards collectively formulated objectives. Working towards an objective and its attainment is satisfying to leaders as well as followers.
2. It gives character to and takes character from the media, the environment, and the atmosphere in which it functions. It does not operate in a vacuum, but in an atmosphere created by many elements.
3. It is constantly active. It may fluctuate in degree, intensity, or extent, but it does not turn on and off. It is either dynamic or nonexistent.
4. It employs, in a purposeful way, principles, tools, and methods of some definiteness and consistency.

II. Effective Leadership

A. What Is Effective Leadership?

Effective leadership is the process of creating a vision, developing a strategy, enlisting cooperation, and motivating action. The effective leader:
- creates a vision of the future that takes into account the legitimate long-term interests of the parties involved;
- develops a rational strategy for moving toward that vision;
- enlists the support of the key power centers whose cooperation, compliance, or teamwork is necessary to produce that movement; and

- highly motivates that core group of people whose actions are central to implementing the strategy.

A combination of complex biological, social, and psychological processes determine the leadership potential in an individual. This potential must be practiced successfully to be effective. It is possible to possess qualities of leadership and not exercise them. In different people's lives, these qualities may express themselves in a variety of situations and may emerge at different stages. The exercise of leadership is influenced by the environment and its opportunities and limitations.

B. Leaders, Supervisors, and Followers

Leaders direct their subordinates toward their goals through motivation and personal example. Supervisors obtain the desired behavior by exercising their higher official authority in the organizational structure.

Good leaders recognize that they must also be good followers. Usually, leaders report to someone or some group. Thus, they must be able to follow as well. A good follower must avoid competition with the leader, act as a loyal "devil's advocate," and constructively confront the leader's ideas, values, and behavior.

The followers and leaders are tied into a purposeful relationship. The leader must always be concerned with the welfare of the followers.

III. Characteristics of an Islamic Leader

The Prophet (SAW) said that the leader of a *jama'ah* is its servant. Thus, a leader should be in the business of serving and helping others get ahead. Some important factors that characterize Islamic leadership are as follows:

A. Allegiance

The leader and the led are bound in allegiance to Allah.

B. Global Islamic Goals

The leader perceives the goals of the organization not only in terms of the interests of the group but also in terms of wider Islamic objectives.

C. Adherence to the Shari'ah and Islamic Manners

The leader is not above observing Islamic injunctions, and can only continue in office as long as he adheres to what the Shari'ah has enjoined. In the conduct of his affairs, he must adhere to Islamic manners, particularly in dealing with the opposition or dissidents.

D. Delegated Trust

The leader accepts his authority as a divine trust of great responsibility. The Qur'an commands the leader to do his duty for Allah and to show kindness to those under his authority:

> Those, who, if we give them power in the land, establish worship and pay zakah and enjoin right and forbid wrong... (22:41).
>
> ﴿٤١﴾ الَّذِينَ إِن مَّكَّنَّاهُمْ فِي الْأَرْضِ أَقَامُوا الصَّلَاةَ وَآتَوُا الزَّكَاةَ وَأَمَرُوا بِالْمَعْرُوفِ وَنَهَوْا عَنِ الْمُنكَرِ... (سورة الحج)

IV. Basic Operational Principles of Islamic Leadership

There are three basic principles that govern Islamic leadership: *shura*, justice, and freedom of thought.

A. *Shura* (Mutual Consultation)

Shura is the first principle of Islamic leadership. The Qur'an has made it clear that Muslim leaders are obligated to consult those who have knowledge or those who can provide sound advice:

> And those who answer the call of their Lord and establish prayer, and who conduct their affairs by consultation and spend out of what We bestow on them for sustenance (42:38).
>
> ﴿٣٨﴾ وَالَّذِينَ اسْتَجَابُوا لِرَبِّهِمْ وَأَقَامُوا الصَّلَاةَ وَأَمْرُهُمْ شُورَىٰ بَيْنَهُمْ وَمِمَّا رَزَقْنَاهُمْ يُنفِقُونَ (سورة الشورى)

The Prophet himself was directed by the Qur'an to consult his companions:

> It is part of the Mercy of Allah that you do deal gently with them. Were you severe or harsh-hearted, they would have broken away from about you: So pass over [their faults], and ask for [Allah's] forgiveness for them; and consult them in affairs [of moment]. Then, when you have taken a decision, put your trust in Allah. For Allah loves those who put their trust [in Him] (3:159).
>
> ﴿١٥٩﴾ فَبِمَا رَحْمَةٍ مِّنَ اللَّهِ لِنتَ لَهُمْ وَلَوْ كُنتَ فَظًّا غَلِيظَ الْقَلْبِ لَانفَضُّوا مِنْ حَوْلِكَ فَاعْفُ عَنْهُمْ وَاسْتَغْفِرْ لَهُمْ وَشَاوِرْهُمْ فِي الْأَمْرِ فَإِذَا عَزَمْتَ فَتَوَكَّلْ عَلَى اللَّهِ إِنَّ اللَّهَ يُحِبُّ الْمُتَوَكِّلِينَ (سورة آل عمران)

The practice of *shura* enables members of the Islamic organization to participate in the decision-making process. At the same time, *shura* serves to check the conduct of the leader in case he deviates from the collective goals of the group.

Obviously, the leader is not obligated to engage in *shura* in all matters. Routine matters should be dealt with differently from policy-making ones. What is routine and what is not should be worked out and defined by each group according to the prevailing size, needs, human resources, and circumstances. The leader must abide by and implement a decision made within the realm of *shura* so established. He should avoid manipulating and playing on words to serve his own opinions or defeat decisions reached by *shura*.

Generally speaking, the following guidelines help define the scope of *shura*:
- **First:** Administrative and executive affairs should be left to the leader.
- **Second:** Affairs needing prompt, urgent decisions should be handled by the leader and presented to the group for review at the next meeting or through a telephone conference call.
- **Third:** Group members or their representatives should be able to verify and question the leader's conduct freely and without any feeling of embarrassment.
- **Fourth:** Policies should be adopted, long-term objectives set, and major decisions taken by elected representatives in a consultative manner. These should not be left to the leader alone.

B. Justice

The leader should deal with people justly and fairly regardless of their race, color, national origin, or religion. The Qur'an commands Muslims to be fair even when dealing with those opposed to them.

Allah does command you to render back your trusts to those to whom they are due, and when you judge between man and man, that you judge with justice ... (4:58).

﷽ إِنَّ ٱللَّهَ يَأْمُرُكُمْ أَن تُؤَدُّواْ ٱلْأَمَٰنَٰتِ إِلَىٰٓ أَهْلِهَا وَإِذَا حَكَمْتُم بَيْنَ ٱلنَّاسِ أَن تَحْكُمُواْ بِٱلْعَدْلِ ... (سورة النساء)

... And let not the hatred of others to you make you swerve to wrong and depart from justice. Be just, that is next to piety ... (5:8).

... وَلَا يَجْرِمَنَّكُمْ شَنَآنُ قَوْمٍ عَلَىٰٓ أَلَّا تَعْدِلُواْ ٱعْدِلُواْ هُوَ أَقْرَبُ لِلتَّقْوَىٰ ... (سورة المائدة)

O you who believe! Stand out firmly for justice, as witnesses to Allah, even as against yourselves, or your parents or your kin, and whether it be against rich or poor, for Allah can protect both ... (4:135).

﷽ يَٰٓأَيُّهَا ٱلَّذِينَ ءَامَنُواْ كُونُواْ قَوَّٰمِينَ بِٱلْقِسْطِ شُهَدَآءَ لِلَّهِ وَلَوْ عَلَىٰٓ أَنفُسِكُمْ أَوِ ٱلْوَٰلِدَيْنِ وَٱلْأَقْرَبِينَ إِن يَكُنْ غَنِيًّا أَوْ فَقِيرًا فَٱللَّهُ أَوْلَىٰ بِهِمَا ... (سورة النساء)

In addition to observing the comprehensive principle of justice, which is the basis of an Islamic society, the leader of an Islamic organization must establish an internal judiciary or arbitration committee to settle any dispute or grievance within the group. The members of such a committee must be selected from among knowledgeable, pious, and wise people.

C. Freedom of Thought

The Islamic leader should provide for and even invite constructive criticism. Members of the group should be able to freely voice their views or objections and have their questions answered. *Al khulafa' al rashidun* considered this to be an essential element of their leadership. When an old woman interrupted 'Umar Ibn al Khattab (RA) to correct him during his address in the mosque, he readily acknowledged his error and thanked Allah (SWT) that there were those who would correct him if he were wrong. 'Umar (RA) once asked an audience what they would do if he violated an Islamic principle. When a man responded that they would correct him with their swords, 'Umar (RA) thanked Allah (SWT) that there were people in the ummah who would correct him if he went astray.

The leader should strive to create an atmosphere of free thinking, healthy exchange of ideas, criticism, and mutual advice so that the followers feel very comfortable in discussing matters of interest to the group.

Muslims are advised to provide sincere advice whenever necessary. Tamim ibn Aws narrated that the Prophet Muhammad (SAW) said:

«الدِّينُ النَّصِيحَةُ» قُلْنا لِمَنْ؟ قَالَ «لله، وَلِرَسُولِهِ، وَلِكِتَابِهِ، وَلِأَئِمَّةِ المُسْلِمِينَ وَعَامَّتِهم»

"Religion is sincere advice." We said: "To whom?" He said: "To Allah, His Book, His Messenger, the leaders of Muslims, and to their common folk."[1]

In short, Islamic leadership is neither tyrannical nor uncoordinated. The Islamic leader, after basing himself on Islamic principles and consulting respectfully and objectively with his associates, makes decisions as fairly and impartially as possible. He is accountable not only to his followers but also, and much more importantly, to Allah (SWT).

This type of participative leadership is optimal. It fosters unity among the members and enhances the quality of their performance.

---

1   Sahih Muslim.

V. Leadership in Practice

A. The Continuum of Leadership

In practice, leadership styles vary from autocracy to laissez-faire:

Autocrat:
- has little trust in group members
- believes only material rewards motivate people
- issues orders to be fulfilled with no questions

Benevolent Autocrat:
- listens carefully to followers
- gives impression of being democratic
- always makes his/her own personal decisions

Democrat:
- shares decision making with group members
- explains to group reasons for personal decisions
- objectively communicates criticism and praise

Laissez-faire:
- has little confidence in his leadership ability
- sets no goals for the group
- minimizes communication and group interaction

The democratic leadership style is the most effective and productive. It is also the one in keeping with the Shari'ah. It leads to new ideas, positive changes, and a sense of group responsibility.

B. Leadership Habits

There are five habits that Muslim leaders should cultivate:

1. **Know** where your *time* goes. Control it, rather than letting it control you, by making every second work for Islam.
2. **Focus** on concrete *results*. Concentrate on results rather than just the work itself. Look up from your work and look outward towards goals.
3. **Build** on *strengths*, not weaknesses. This includes not only your own, but those of other brothers/sisters. Acknowledge and accept your strengths and weaknesses and be able to accept the best in others without feeling that your position is threatened.
4. **Concentrate** on a few major *areas* where consistent hard work will produce outstanding results. Do this by setting and sticking to priorities.

5. **Put** your complete *trust* in Allah and aim high instead of limiting your goals to only the safe and easy things. As long as you are working for Him, be afraid of nothing.

CAN YOU TELL ME? *Who is the Nonleader?*	The nonleader is the one who comes to the assembly unprepared and says: "I am just one of you; you tell me what to do. Whatever you agree upon, I'll try to go along!" The leader's job is to do his homework before he comes in front of the members, and to prepare alternatives for them to discuss and decide upon. There was a brother who used to say: "Don't inform me about the topic of my speech in advance. Just whisper it in my ear as I go up to the podium." What an insult to the intelligence of the audience!

The Lighter Side of Leadership!

THE PLEASING TYPE OF LEADER!

A person was visiting a supervisor in a factory. The foreman came and complained about an employee. The supervisor said: "You are right!" Then after the foreman left, the employee came and complained about the foreman, to which the supervisor responded: "You are right!" The visitor was puzzled and asked: "They complained about each other and you told both of them they were right! How can that be?" The supervisor said to the visitor: "You know, you are right, too!"

This type of management gets you nowhere! It wrecks the organization. You will soon be discovered and lose trust among your people.

THE LEADER AND THE PEOPLE

DeGaulle: "If the people do not like me, I will leave the country."

Dictator: "If the people do not like me, they are free to leave the country."

THE SACRED BALLOT BOX

In the fifties during elections between Zahidi and Musaddiq in Iran, a bedouin came to the ballot box and started kissing and worshipping it. The soldiers guarding the box asked him: "What are you doing; this is only a box." The bedouin replied: "Oh, no! You don't know this box. It is sacred and worthy of worship. You put in Musaddiq but out comes Zahidi, *subhana Allah!*"

C. The Peter Principle

The Peter Principle states that every person in a hierarchy tends to rise to the level of his or her incompetence. That is, a person starts off competent, then rises through promotion to a position where he or she is not competent to perform the prescribed work. Everyone eventually faces this situation.

The Peter Principle results from a condition called demand overload. The person is performing to his or her maximum capacity yet cannot meet the job demands. The skills, the role, and the knowledge needed for the job are beyond his capacity.

The classic example of the Peter Principle in an Islamic organization is when the best local organization president gets elected as regional representative and so on up the ladder. Eventually the person may end up as vice president and may still do a good job. But when he is elected president of the national organization, he may fail. He may have functioned well so far, but may not have the ability to make independent decisions as president.

Discussion Point

Some people claim that the major weakness in the application of the Peter Principle is that the person's ability to grow is ignored. Many people do grow as they move upward.

However, others say that the ability to grow is already taken into account. The person rises till he can no longer grow.

*What
Do You
Think?*

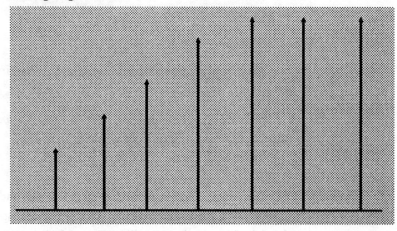

Leaders lead. Followers follow. Or do they?

Sometimes some leaders follow the followers. They abandon the functions of leadership when their actions become mere reflections of the followers' desires or practice. They no longer determine the direction in which to move, and their followers mistakenly judge the leaders' actions to be popular decisions. Sooner or later, the followers discover that they can do without such leaders.

Islam promises rewards and punishments to leaders for the actions of their followers.

John F. Kennedy once remarked: "We don't want to be like the leader of the French Revolution who said: 'There go my people. I must find out where they are going so I can lead them.'"

Quoted in the Indiana Daily Student, February 6, 1958, Rex Allen Redifer painted a striking picture of such a leader in the following piece:

ACTION POINT

Is the leadership following the followers?

> *"Follow the Leader — A Modern Fable."*
>
> *A parade was passing in the street, and from the crowd that watched a voice was heard to cry:*
>
> *"Beware you fools, you march the wrong way. That street leads nowhere— it is a dead end!"*
>
> *The paraders paused....alarmed.... "But how can this be?" they thought, and looked, as if they were one, toward the front where, tall and proud, their handsome leader made his way.*
>
> *"He must be going the right way," they thought, "for look how well he marches! And look how tall he stands. Oh yes, he is most certainly going the right way!"*
>
> *.... and they marched on.*
>
> *The handsome leader paused....alarmed.... "But how can this be?" he thought, and stole a glance behind.*
>
> *"I must be going the right way," he thought, "for look how many follow me. Oh yes, I am most certainly going the right way."*
>
> *.... and he marched on.*

The lesson? Although we may elect a leader and follow him, we must always watch, think, and evaluate. Our personal responsibility for doing the right thing continues until the Day of Judgment when we face Allah all by ourselves.

An Exercise in Leadership

Criteria of Leadership

On the occasion of his installation as the first *khalifah*, Abu Bakr (RA) stated his policy in a *khutbah*, as follows:

«أيُّها الناسُ: قد وليُّتُ أمرَكم ولستُ بخيرِكم وإنَّ أقواكم عندي الضعيفُ حتى آخذ بحقِّه، وإنَّ أضعفَكم عندي القويُّ حتى آخذ منه الحقَّ، أيها الناسُ: إنَّما أنا متبعٌ ولستُ بمبتدع، فإن أحسَنْتُ فأعينوني وإن زغْتُ فقوّموني. وحاسبوا أنفسَكم قبلَ أن تُحاسبوا، ولا يدعُ قومٌ الجهادَ في سبيل الله إلاَّ ضَرَبَهُم الله بالذُّلِّ، ولا ظهرت الفاحِشةُ في قوم إلاَّ عمَّهُم الله بالبَلاء. فأطيعوني ما أطَعْتُ الله، فإذا عَصَيْتُ الله وَرَسَولَه فَلا طَاعةَ لي عليكم. وَلَوَدَدْتُ أنَّهُ كفاني هذا الأمرَ أحَدُكُم، وإنْ أنتم أردتموني على ما كانَ الله يقيمُ نبيَّهُ مِنَ الوحي ما ذلكَ عِندي، إنَّما أنا بشرٌ فَراعوني...» (كنز العمال، جزء ٣، صفحة ١٣٠–١٣٥)

O People! Even though I am not the best of you, I have been given the responsibility of ruling you. I will consider the weakest among you strong until I claim for them whatever is their due. And the strongest among you I will consider weak until I have taken from them whatever is due from them. O People! I am a follower (of the Prophet), not an innovator. So, if I do well, assist me! And if I deviate, straighten me out! And reckon with yourselves before you are taken to reckoning! No people ever abandoned jihad in the way of Allah except that Allah afflicted them with disgrace! And never did an obscenity appear among people except that Allah caused disaster to spread among them! Then obey me for as long as I obey Allah! But if I disobey Allah or His Prophet, you owe me no obedience! I really prefer that another one of you should have been given (and thus spared me) this responsibility! And if you expect me to assume the same role as the Prophet in relation to *wahy* (revelation), I cannot do that. I am only human, so make allowance for me (*Kanz al 'Ummal* III 130-135).

If you were elected *khalifah* today what would you add to or subtract from, Abu Bakr's speech. (Note: To repeat Abu Bakr exactly will not be acceptable because the world has changed a lot since then! Be concise.)

A DIVINE REMINDER!

...And We raise some of them above others in ranks so that some may command work from others. But the Mercy of your Lord is better than the [wealth] which they amass (43:32).

وَرَفَعْنَا بَعْضَهُمْ فَوْقَ بَعْضٍ دَرَجَٰتٍ
لِيَتَّخِذَ بَعْضُهُم بَعْضًا سُخْرِيًّا
وَرَحْمَتُ رَبِّكَ خَيْرٌ مِّمَّا يَجْمَعُونَ
(سورة الزخرف)

QUESTIONS FOR DISCUSSION

1. What is the role of vision in leadership?
2. How are followers different from leaders?
3. What are the three basic principles that govern the operation of Islamic leadership?
4. What is the role of *shura* in Islamic leadership?

COMPREHENSION EXERCISE

THE GENERAL ASSEMBLY OF YOUR ISLAMIC ORGANIZATION HAS JUST ELECTED YOU ITS PRESIDENT. YOU HAVE COME A LONG WAY SINCE YOU WERE ELECTED PICNIC COORDINATOR TEN YEARS AGO. MUCH IS EXPECTED OF YOU. MANY MEMBERS ARE ENTHUSIASTIC ABOUT YOUR LEADERSHIP QUALITIES, BUT SOME ARE SKEPTICAL. THIS IS YOUR FIRST VISIBLE ROLE IN THE COMMUNITY AT LARGE EVEN THOUGH YOU WERE FINANCE SECRETARY LAST YEAR.

1. *Make an outline for your first speech as president. Include remarks to win over the skeptics.*

2. *Write a memo to your executive committee members explaining how you will function as president within the Islamic model.*

3. *Outline a contingency plan to resolve conflicts when they arise.*

Chapter

5

How to Identify Potential Leaders

LEARNING OBJECTIVES

On completing this chapter, you should be able to:
- identify the qualities of leadership
- recognize persons who possess such qualities
- test and evaluate specific individuals for leadership potential

I. Who Are Potential Leaders?

Since the community of Muslims is based on the Islamic ideology, the more a Muslim fears Allah and avoids evil and performs good actions, the greater respect he or she commands in a Muslim society. One's wealth, sex, color, or race are of no avail in raising one's position in the eyes of Allah and among practicing Muslims. The Qur'an states:

... Verily, the most honored among you is the one most conscious of Allah ... (49:13).

... إِنَّ أَكْرَمَكُمْ عِندَ اللَّهِ أَتْقَنكُمْ ... (سورة الحجرات)

An ideal Muslim, however, is not one who renounces life but one who actually involves himself in the struggle of establishing the socioeconomic and political system of Islam. Men and women differ in their capacity to organize others so as to lead them to a specific goal. It was in recognition of this fact that the Prophet Muhammad (SAW) used to pray to Allah that men like 'Umar should join the Muslims. Since 'Umar possessed certain rare qualities, the Muslim community and the Islamic cause greatly benefitted from him.

In every group of human beings we find persons with certain qualities. We must locate these gifted persons and prepare them to move ahead. If they are practicing Muslims, we must provide them opportunities to serve the community. They should be selected or elected to suitable positions where their special qualities will become good assets.

Persons with exceptional qualities may decline to be in positions of authority and responsibility. It is our duty to promote their qualities of leadership for the benefit of the community at large. If we identify potential leaders among nonpracticing Muslims, we should try in a systematic way to interact with them and them engage them in a positive dialogue. If we find these uncommon qualities in some non-Muslims, we should use all legitimate means to explain Islam to them. The Prophet of Islam has categorically said:

«النَّاسُ مَعَادِنُ خِيَارُهُمْ في الجَاهِلِيَّة خِيَارُهُمْ في الإِسْلامِ، إِذَا فَقُهُوا»

People are like mines [in terms of their nature]. Thus the best of them in *Jahiliyah* [period of ignorance] will be the best of them in Islam; so long as they attain a proper understanding of Islam.[1]

II. What Qualities Should We Look for?

Even though we may differ on the semantics of leadership, we can observe that some people are effective in influencing others while others are not. Factors which represent what it takes to be a leader can be grouped into:
   a: those established by scientific research,
   b: those extracted from executive experience, and
   c: those expressed by followers.

Naturally, we find some overlapping in these three approaches because they all pertain to leadership.

---

1   Sahih al Bukhari, Sahih Muslim, Sunan al Darimi, Musnad Ahmad ibn Hanbal.

A. Factors Established by Scientific Research

These factors are common in the published findings of research projects conducted on successful leaders, business organizers, and entrepreneurs. (Although stated below in masculine terminology, essentially the same factors are applicable to women.)

1. **Mental Ability**: Not necessarily a super-intelligent prodigy.
2. **Broad Interest and Abilities**: He is not a narrow specialist. He possesses a wide general understanding, and has many and varied abilities. He is sensitive to and broadly interested in the work with which he is most directly connected, plus many other important activities and aspects of his environment. As such, he is a broad and broadly endowed individual.
3. **Communication Skills**: One of the titles of the Prophet of Islam is "The most eloquent speaker of Arabic." According to the Cambridge History of American Literature: "Not his policies, nor his action had won for Lincoln his commanding position in his party in 1860, but his way of saying things. In every revolution, the men who can phrase it can lead it."
4. **Maturity**: A successful leader is free from leftover childishness; his attitude and behavior patterns are those of a responsible, mature adult. He is psychologically secure within himself and represents psychological security to his followers.
5. **Motivational Strength**: Drive, energy, initiative, courage, ability to "self-start," and consistency have long been recognized as clear marks of a strong leader. The successful leader likes the work of planning, organizing, and directing the efforts of others. He has a strong desire to accomplish.
6. **Social Skill**: Leadership fundamentally means accomplishing through others, which makes it entirely obvious that the successful leader must rely heavily on social skills. He must be sensitive to human feelings and attitudes, whether spoken or not, and he must be empathetic in order to be effective in influencing others.
7. **Administrative Ability**: Envisioning, originating, planning, organizing, directing, completing, evaluating people, selecting, teaching, inspiring, reviewing, analyzing, observing, improving, applying insight, summarizing, deciding, getting things done: these, more than the technological ones, are the skills on which the leader particularly relies.

B. Factors Extracted from Executive Experience

These factors have been collected from the experiences of executives, leaders, and business organizers:

i) Qualities: The leader is expected to be:

1. Morally sound	14. Enthusiastic
2. Imaginative	15. Energetic
3. Management-minded	16. Coaching minded
4. Fair to all concerned	17. Expressive (speech and writing)
5. Varied in interests	18. Logical
6. Instruction minded	19. Mentally keen, alert
7. Emotionally mature	20. Responsible
8. Planning minded	21. Improvement minded (practicing *ihsan*)
9. Respectful toward self and others	
10. Studious	22. Resourceful
11. Decisive	23. Initiating, hard working
12. Organized	24. Loyal to all concerned
13. Dependable	25. Humane

ii) Knowledge: The leader should have the knowledge of:

1. Aims, principles, and objectives of the organization
2. Organization structure and orientation
3. Duties and responsibilities
4. Organization policies, practices, and procedures
5. Basic economics
6. Scientific management principles and methods
7. Products, processes, and markets of the organization
8. Planning, scheduling, and control
9. Cost requirements and control
10. Job, trade, technical, and professional knowledge
11. Quality requirements and control
12. Basic mathematics, language, and science
13. Pertinent legislation
14. Professional standards (in his field)
15. Personal strength and development needs
16. The art and science of creative thinking
17. Human relations principles and methods
18. Selection and placement principles, tools, and methods
19. Training principles, tools, and methods
20. Compensation systems in the organization
21. Care of machines, material, and equipment
22. Functions of line and staff units
23. Communications
24. Safety at work, home, and during leisure time
25. People, machines, materials, and methods
26. Getting high production, good quality, and low cost

iii) Skills: The leader should have skills in the areas of:

1. Creative thinking
2. Planning, organizing, executing, and following up
3. Teaching, training, and coaching
4. Assigning work
5. Providing materials, equipment, and supplies
6. Selecting and placing people
7. Keeping people informed
8. Controlling quality
9. Reducing or eliminating waste
10. Controlling costs
11. Quality requirements and control
12. Carrying out policies, contracts, and procedures
13. Looking after employee conduct and welfare
14. Cooperating with others
15. Keeping adequate records
16. Enforcing rules and regulations
17. Handling employee problems
18. Correcting unsafe working conditions
19. Handling emergencies
20. Maintaining good housekeeping
21. Studying for continued improvement
22. Giving and getting a fair day's work for fair pay
23. Keeping informed and keeping in shape
24. Setting a good personal example
25. Leading for high production, good quality, and low cost

C. Factors Expressed by Followers

These factors have been expressed by followers about their leaders in different situations:

1. Thoughtfulness
2. Impartiality
3. Honesty
4. Proficiency
5. People knowledge
6. Control
7. Courage
8. Directness
9. Decisiveness
10. Dignity
11. People interest
12. Helpfulness

To this list we can add those factors that may pertain only to a particular situation, such as specific type of education or physical condition.

III. Who Has These Qualities?

To find out who does or does not possess what it takes to be a leader, it is necessary to evaluate the candidates in some way. The following are three common techniques.

A. Test

Whether objective or subjective, tests can measure:
   a. Tendencies (not absolute characteristics)
   b. Potential abilities (not necessarily developed)
   c. Possible disabilities (possible until proven otherwise) in three basic areas:
      i. Capacity for work (aptitude, knowledge, skills, and abilities)
      ii. Desire to do the work (interest, drive, and initiative)
      iii. Ability to get along (with self and others)

B. Probation

It may be possible to place each candidate in a specially designed, multiple and diverse problem-ridden trial leadership position for a limited period, during which time he would be kept under constant critical observation by qualified judges who would then make detailed analyses and appraisals of him in action.

C. Observation

Of the total knowledge that we seek to gain about a candidate using tests and probation, our methods and instruments will yield some significant information. But, they will also leave out some equally significant pieces of information. To complement tests and probation, we have to observe the candidate in general life situations.

REMEMBER
- That person has what it takes to be a leader who neither falls short of nor exceeds the standards you have established for leadership in your organization.
- That person has what it takes to be a leader who is not disqualified by a shortcoming so serious as to outweigh his positive qualifications.
- That person has what it takes to be a leader who is capable of mastering the work under conditions of intensive, accelerated learning.
- That person has what it takes to be a leader who evokes an automatic, emphatic "yes" to the question: "Will we be safe in his hands?"

IV. Leadership Proficiency Measurement

To evaluate a certain potential leader, we can fill in the questionnaire below to measure his leadership proficiency. The questionnaire may be filled out by one or several experienced persons who know him well, and the points can be averaged to provide a more objective result.

INSTRUCTIONS:
    Respondent: Please check one blank in each item.
    Evaluator: Count points stated against each item checked. Average the score for each item if you have several respondents filling the form. Then add all item scores to obtain the total score for each candidate.

QUESTIONS (with explanation):

1. **Pioneering:** Some persons have a distinct talent for leadership. They are looked up to by their fellows, are put in positions of honor, and are expected to take the lead in any new enterprise. At the other end are persons who are content to be followers, who are never asked to head up any sort of undertaking. In between lie persons of varying degrees of leadership ability. Based on your observation of his past performance, how would you estimate this individual in comparison with his fellows?
    (5 pts.)_____ Outstanding as a leader
    (4 pts.)_____ Very often a leader
    (3 pts.)_____ Average
    (2 pts.)_____ Inclined to follow rather than lead
    (1 pt.) _____ Distinctly a follower

2. **Original:** Some people are independent and creative in their thinking. They have "ideas of their own." They analyze and interpret, invent, write, and propose ways of doing things. Others are not original in this fashion, but seek to know how things are done by others before trying anything themselves. Your estimate of the individual should be based on what he actually does.
    (5 pts.)_____ Unusually original in thinking
    (4 pts.)_____ Distinctly more creative than the average person
    (3 pts.)_____ As original as most people
    (2 pts.)_____ Inclined to depend on others for ideas
    (1 pt.)_____ Shows no inclination to do original thinking

3. **Charismatic:** Some persons are quite generally pleasing to their fellows. Others make an unfortunate impression on most of the people with whom they meet. The distinctly agreeable personality is welcome in all circles, is invited out, and has a large number of acquaintances. The unpopular personality is not sought after by others and

is frequently neglected, if not positively shunned. Consider the individual you are estimating in terms of his attitude and in terms of the attitudes actually shown by others towards him:

(5 pts.)_____ One of the best-liked persons in the community
(4 pts.)_____ Quite popular
(3 pts.)_____ Average, welcome, but not distinguished
(2 pts.)_____ Not so fortunate as most in social standing
(1 pt.)_____ Impresses most people unfavorably

4. **Communicating:** Some persons are able to speak in such a way as to hold people's attention and communicate ideas clearly and readily. At the other extreme are persons whose speech is slow, hesitant, and very ineffectual. In between are varying degrees of ability. Consider the person you are estimating in comparison with others. Do people understand him quickly and readily? Do people listen to him with ease and pleasure? Or is the opposite true? Try to recall concrete experiences.

(5 pts.)_____ Outstanding as a speaker
(4 pts.)_____ Above average in ability to convey ideas
(3 pts.)_____ Does as well as most people
(2 pts.)_____ Not a very good talker
(1 pt.) _____ Distinctly inferior in his speech

5. **Trustworthy/Reliable:** Some people arouse the greatest confidence in others. They are regarded as trustworthy in any situation, and people generally have the greatest respect for their integrity. The opposite extreme is the wholly unworthy person who is known not to be reliable and is never depended on. Consider this person as you know him yourself and as he is known to be viewed by others, and indicate where he stands, in the matter of reliability, in comparison with his fellows.

(5 pts.)_____ Most highly respected and trusted
(4 pts.)_____ Has a good reputation for dependability
(3 pts.)_____ As reliable as most people
(2 pts.)_____ Frequently found to be dependable
(1 pt.)_____ Does not have a good reputation for reliability

SCORING CHART:

	Item 1	Item 2	Item 3	Item 4	Item 5	
Response						
Response						
Response						
Response						
Response						
Item Avg.						
Total Score						

CHECK LIST: HOW TO TELL A WINNER FROM A LOSER

A WINNER	A LOSER
- makes commitments.	- makes promises.
- goes through a problem.	- goes around a problem and never gets to it.
- respects other winners and tries to learn from them.	- resents winners and tries to find chinks in their armor.
- knows what to fight for and what to compromise on.	- compromises on what he shouldn't and fights for what isn't worth fighting about.
- feels responsible for more than his job.	- says: "I only work here."
- isn't nearly as afraid of losing as a loser.	- is secretly afraid of winning.
- says: "I'm good, but not as good as I ought to be."	- says: "I'm not as bad as a lot of other persons."
- would rather be admired than liked, although he would prefer both.	- would rather be liked than admired and is even willing to pay the price of mild contempt for it.
- when he makes a mistake, says: "I was wrong."	- when he makes a mistake, says: "It wasn't my fault."
- shows he is sorry by making up for it.	- says: "I am sorry" but does the same thing the next time.
- works harder than a loser, yet has more time.	- works less than a winner, yet has less time.
- paces himself.	- has only two speeds: hysterical and lethargic.
- feels strong enough to be gentle.	- is never gentle — he is either weak or pettily tyrannical by turns.
- explains.	- explains away.
- listens.	- just waits until it's his turn to talk.
- says: "There ought to be a better way to do it."	- says: "That's the way it's always done here."
- says: "Let's find out."	- says: "Nobody knows."

EXERCISE

Things Leaders Do

Explain in a few words what you understand from these two leadership mottos:

QUITTERS NEVER WIN;
WINNERS NEVER QUIT.

FOLLOW, LEAD, OR
GET OUT OF THE WAY!

Can you relate a specific experience of your own to each of the two mottos? Share your findings with your group in a workshop.

REFLECTION EXERCISE

Having absorbed the material in this chapter, do you think you can find a leader satisfying ALL the qualities discussed here? If not, what does this suggest to you?

How about:
— group or collective leadership?
— frequent effective consultation?
— complementing one another?
— team spirit?
— other ideas?

Discuss these thoughts in a workshop.

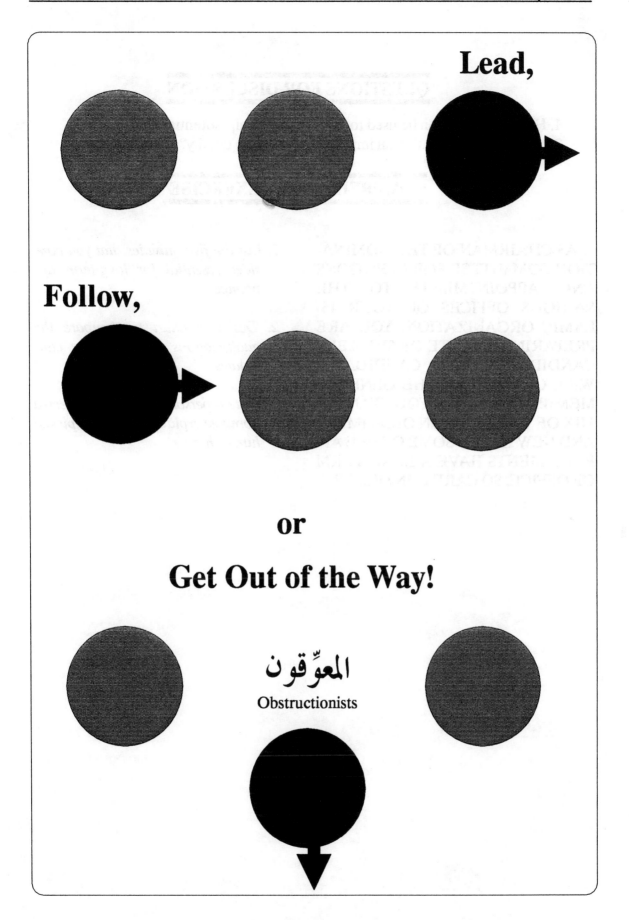

Lead,

Follow,

or

Get Out of the Way!

المعوِّقون

Obstructionists

QUESTIONS FOR DISCUSSION

1. How can probation be used to test for leadership potential?
2. Why is communication an important leadership quality?

COMPREHENSION EXERCISE

AS CHAIRMAN OF THE NOMINA-TION COMMITTEE FOR ELECTIONS AND APPOINTMENTS TO THE VARIOUS OFFICES OF YOUR IS-LAMIC ORGANIZATION, YOU ARE PREPARING A SLATE OF SUITABLE CANDIDATES. THE CANDIDATES WILL COME FROM THE GENERAL MEMBERSHIP, BUT YOU WANT A MIX OF WELL-KNOWN OLD-TIMERS AND NEW FACES. SOME OF THE AP-POINTMENTS HAVE A LONG TERM OF OFFICE, SO CARE IS IN ORDER.

1. List the five qualities that you con-sider essential for long-term ap-pointees.

2. Design a chart to compare the qualifications of prospective can-didates.

3. Write a personal letter to a selected nominee explaining why you picked him or her.

Chapter

6

Essentials of Problem Solving

I. Problem Identification
    A. Defining the Problem
    B. Classifying the Problem
II. Solution Alternatives
III. Solution of Choice

LEARNING OBJECTIVES

On completing this chapter, you should be able to:
- define present problems and recognize potential problems
- identify and analyze problems
- use specific methods to find acceptable solutions
- minimize future problems through preventive analysis

I. Problem Identification

A. Defining the Problem

The cause of a problem is always a change that has taken place through some distinctive feature, mechanism, or condition to produce a new unwanted effect. To define a problem, we must first ask what specific activity or behavior is out of the ordinary. What activity or behavior is violating the norm of the situation? In what way is the norm being violated? Is the result of such activity or behavior unacceptable? Must it be changed? What is the desirable result that is sought by solving the problem at hand?

It is imperative that we first understand a problem before trying to solve it. The process of identifying the problem consists of defining it and then classifying it on the basis of relevant experience. The awareness that a problem exists is a very important step in the problem-solving process.

To recognize and define a problem, we may use primary sources of information, such as:

1. Historical data that includes information about past activities, results, problems, and solutions. For events of a cyclical nature, we should analyze performance data in the previous cycles of a day, a month, a year, or longer, as the case may be.
2. Planning data that compares results with objectives that were expected to be achieved.
3. Criticism by outsiders from all affected categories, including elected leaders, appointed officers, committee members, and the general membership.
4. Comparisons with others in similar circumstances when such criticism is unfavorable. This comparison could be impromptu or carefully designed to yield results.

 Action Point

SORTING AND CLASSIFICATION OF ISSUES!

In the morning the guard told the king: "I dreamt that you will be killed at noon." The king took necessary precautions, and saved his life. In the afternoon the king told the guard that he would reward and punish him.

Why?

The reward, because he saved his life. The punishment, because he was not supposed to sleep and dream during the night watch. The lesson of this story is to identify, isolate, and deal with issues separately. Nowadays, we put emphasis on global and universal concepts but neglect the microaspects. We must take care of both.

We have to deal on an item-by-item basis. Reward the good action and punish the bad, but explain your action clearly. Don't mix and confuse issues, or misuse the law of averages. This will be like putting your right hand in boiling water and your left hand in freezing water and saying that the average temperature is fine.

It is important that the problem be defined accurately. Otherwise, the proposed solution may not bring about the desired results. If you follow the systematic way of defining a problem, you will be amazed to discover how many problems disappear when you try to define them, and how many new problems emerge that were not felt to be problems.

B. Classifying the Problem

Problems may be classified by their degree of risk. After determining each problem's rank, we can then concentrate on those problems which are the most threatening to the endeavor's success. Smaller risk problems may have to be overlooked if the resources or opportunities to solve them do not exist.

II. Solution Alternatives

Identifying alternative solutions is the next step in solving problems. This task can be accomplished in one of several ways. We can approach it in a routine way if there are standard operating procedures or a knowledgeable supervisor to tell us what to do. We can also adopt a systematic scientific approach, a decisional approach, a quantitative approach, or a creative approach. Most situations in Islamic organizations call for a creative approach, to problem solving.

Creativity can be helpful only when the reason or the need for ideas is recognized and aided by a positive attitude towards the freedom of ideas. Creative ideas develop from a broad base of knowledge and experience based on personal observations, discussions with informed people, and informed interaction with the Qur'an and the *Sirah* of the Prophet (SAW). A large number of ideas must be generated, but none should be evaluated until the process of idea generation can proceed no further. At this stage, we must then allow the unconscious mind to draw upon the myriad of facts and experiences it holds by stepping back from active engagement with the problem. Depending on the individual circumstances, one or more ideas will begin to emerge with brilliance, bringing into focus how the problem will be solved. This stage may come quicker for a mind which is alert and receptive than for one which is not.

III. Solution of Choice

The solution of choice emerges from a careful process of grading possible alternatives in order of acceptability within relevant constraints. No solution may be perfect in that it eliminates all of the damage caused by the deviation from the standard that was the cause of the problem. We must focus on the ones that:
    a. limit the damage;
    b. do not cause deviations that damage other parts of the planned activity;
    c. are feasible within the constraint of available or accessible resources.

Each alternative identified above may serve as a solution. Each may offer a way to reach the desired results within the constraints of the situation. Which of the alternatives may be the most suitable depends on which characteristics of the outcome may be most applicable to the situation. On the other hand, an alternative may require the expense of material resources in short supply. A generalized list of characteristics of ac-

ceptable solutions may be needed. An acceptable solution must:
  (a) produce at least the minimum outcome that is desired, but
  (b) not require an expenditure of more resources than are available

We should use formal procedures whenever possible to solve problems. Not only is this efficient and effective, but this method of working also documents our experience and creates records that can be referred to when a similar situation arises in the future, thus eliminating the wasteful duplication of work.

At times, it is not possible to carry out formal procedures. This may be due to the short time needed to respond, or to other circumstances or unusual constraints, like sensitivity or security considerations. Informal procedures in such circumstances call for consultations with those aware of the problem and able to assess it. Whenever possible, proper records should be created when it becomes practical to do so.

"PREVENT A PROBLEM" CHECKLIST

The preventive approach to problem solving calls for actions to minimize or possibly prevent the effects of potential problems. To do so, list all major potential problems. Then, for each problem (on an enlarged version of this checklist):
  1. Identify the problem: _____
  2. Describe it accurately: _____
  3. Classify it by degree of risk: _____
  4. Identify its possible causes: _____
  5. Assess its probability of occurrence: _____
  6. Decide how to handle it: _____

A Question of Attitudes!

— Are you a part of the problem or a part of the solution?
— How can you improve the "problem-solution" attitude in your group?

A Case Study

AN INTERACTIVE APPROACH TO PROBLEM SOLVING

1. What is the situation?
   Many members complain that they get the newsletter late.

2. What should the situation be?
   Members should get the newsletter on time.

3. What prevents the situation from changing?
   a. Material comes in late from departments and field units.
   b. There are many last-minute changes.
   c. Laying out the pages takes more time than anticipated.
   d. The mailroom has a backlog of mailings.

4. What is the highest priority obstacle?
   Material comes in late from departments and field units.

5. What can I do?

   ACTION NEEDED
   a. Survey departments and field units to determine causes for delay.
   b. Establish firm deadlines and follow up.
   c. Give recognition to early respondents.

   RESOURCES NEEDED
   a. Ask someone to develop and conduct the survey.
   b. Communicate and consult with those who cause delay.
   c. Ask the head of the organization to write appropriate letters.

QUESTIONS FOR DISCUSSION

1. Which of the four sources of information recommended for problem identification is the most accurate? Which is the least accurate? Why?
2. What is the role of resources in choosing a solution?
3. What is the role of record keeping in identifying potential problems?
4. How does the "degree of risk" affect problem solving?

COMPREHENSION EXERCISE

AS CHAIRMAN OF THE CONVENTION COMMITTEE OF THE UNITED CENTRAL SOCIETY, YOU HAVE JUST BEEN INFORMED THAT THE COST OF RENTING MEETING FACILITIES AND DECORATIONS WILL BE 50% MORE THAN YOU HAD BUDGETED. YOU HAVE ALREADY SENT THE REGISTRATION FORM TO THE PRINTER WITH SITE INFORMATION AND REGISTRATION FEES BASED ON EARLIER ESTIMATES. MEMBERS OF THE SOCIETY EXPECT A HIGH STANDARD OF MEETING FACILITIES, WHICH YOU ARE DETERMINED TO GIVE THEM.

1. *State what the problem is.*

2. *List all sources of information which you may need to solve this problem.*

3. *Make a table to help you compare various alternatives and their merits.*

4. *Name specific steps you could have taken to prevent this problem from happening.*

On Decision Making

LEARNING OBJECTIVES

On completing this chapter, you should be able to:
- relate decision making to choosing between alternatives
- identify steps and actions leading to decisions
- determine who should make decisions and how
- make effective, implementable decisions

I. Introduction

Although many techniques may be acquired through learning, decision making is not that easy to learn. Some leaders are better decision makers than others. When complete information is not available, decision making becomes much harder. The decision maker must frequently deal with uncertainty. Leaders must make decisions and move on even though mistakes may be made. Not making decisions is the worst mistake we can make. Islamically, we must strive hard to come up with the right decision. If none of the alternatives is good, we should select the least unsatisfactory among them. Having done all we can under the circumstances, if our decision is wrong Allah rewards us once, and if we are right He rewards us doubly. Leaders should not consider all decision making a fiqh issue. More often than not, it is simply a matter of political, organizational, or public policy. Even when it is purely a matter of jurisprudence, the leader should examine various schools of fiqh before selecting the ruling which is the most advantageous for the organization and the ummah.

Being open-minded is essential in decision making, for decision making is a dynamic, not a static, process. One must monitor the outcome of a decision and modify it as and when needed. When we make a decision, we choose between alternatives. The choice may not always be between right and wrong or black and white. Sometimes we must choose between "almost right" and "probably wrong." A decision can be a choice between various courses of action, none of which can be proved to be more nearly right than the others.

The desired end result of a decision is action and behavior on the part of people.

Before making a decision, we must ask the question: "Is a decision really necessary?" One standard alternative is the alternative of doing nothing. A decision is required when the existing condition is likely to degenerate if nothing is done, or if an important opportunity is likely to be lost unless we act promptly.

The important elements in decision making are to define the question, to decide whether there is need for a decision, and what the decision is about. If we focus on fully understanding the situation, we are most likely to consider all possible alternatives. In other words, we should direct the whole process to finding out what the decision is really about before deciding what it should be.

The effective decision maker does not start with a closed mind and assume that only one proposed course of action is right and that all others are wrong. We must be concerned first with understanding the question and then using the conflict of opinions as a tool to make sure all major aspects of an important matter are looked at carefully.

The prerequisites for effective decision making are to:
  a. focus on deciding what the decision is all about, i.e., focus on defining the question, not giving an answer,
  b. bring out and discuss dissenting opinions until a common understanding emerges; consider a wide variety of opinions and approaches,
  c. seek alternatives first rather than the "right solution."

This approach to arriving at a decision defines at what level and by whom a certain decision should be made. It builds effective execution into the decision-making process.

II. The Decision-Making Process

Decision making is both an art and a science.

The acquisition, analysis, and manipulation of information in a scientific manner activates the process of making decisions. This leads to the identification of possible alternatives. To select an alternative usually requires us to consider human sensitivities when examining the utility or desirability of all possible consequences of opposing alternatives. Good decision making relies as much on sound judgment as on dependable information.

The process of decision making can also be viewed as a black box. Parameters of the situation at hand are fed into it as the input. Decisions are extracted from it as the output. The box performs the task of searching for alternatives and, after adequate evaluation, selects the best alternative. The black box may be split into several smaller black boxes. The process within the box then becomes the sequential making of a series of minor decisions which are components of the major decision.

A. Steps in Decision Making

Faced with a diagnosed and well defined need or an opportunity, we must do the following to arrive at a decision:
  1. Identify alternative courses of action that may be taken and consider all possible consequences of these actions. This step is relatively straightforward. It involves drawing up a list of alternatives to deal with a particular situation, assuming the situation has already been diagnosed and defined. However, sometimes the situation is too complex for simple alternatives. In that case, a deeply intellectual and inventive function may need to be called upon.
  2. Gather relevant information that will help determine whether a particular action will lead to a particular consequence. This step is the collection of all relevant information. We must then try to assess how such information will

modify the relationship between an action and the different possibilities that may result from that action. In some cases, the information may be such as to decisively exclude some possibilities. In other cases, several pieces of information may be needed, since each piece may be suggestive and not conclusive. A common problem is being flooded with irrelevant or unwanted information, while not receiving the needed relevant information.

3. Evaluate the utility or desirability of each of the consequences resulting from each alternative. This step can usually be best accomplished by discussion among those most familiar with the situation and by opinion formation through *shura*, which is a Qur'anic injunction. The Qur'an encourages openness and honesty in the expression of one's opinions and discourages secrecy in consultation. Examine the possible actions and consequences for their acceptability from an Islamic point of view. A step-by-step review process employing standard techniques should be used to determine acceptability.

4. Make a decision by selecting one of the alternatives that will lead to the desired consequence. This final step of decision making must be viewed within the framework of the organization's objectives and selected by considering the goals to which the organization is committed. Consequently, we may judge how much better or worse one decision is than another by relating each to the goals of our organization.

To recapitulate, decision makers should:
  a. **assemble** all possible action **alternatives** A1, A2, etc.,
  b. **determine** their likely **consequences** C1, C2, etc.,
  c. **estimate** the probability that each consequence may **occur** P1, P2, etc., and
  d. **assess** the usefulness of **each** consequence U1, U2, etc.

From there, it is a procedural job of combining probabilities (P) with usefulness (U) to determine the most desirable course of action (D). Mathematically, we get this functional relationship:

$$U = U (C) \qquad D = (U, P)$$

B. Decision Analysis

The character of a decision may be affected by one or more of these four factors: futurity, impact, qualitative considerations, and recurrence.

⇒ **Futurity** refers to how long into the future the decision is going to commit the organization. Is the decision a short-term one or a long-term one?

⇒ **Impact** refers to the influence the decision will have on other areas of the organization or on the organization as a whole. Will its effect be confined or global? Will it optimize performance in one area at the expense of other areas?

⇒ **Qualitative considerations** refer to the ethical bias or the worldview of the organization. Will the decision subvert or strengthen the Islamic character of the organization?

⇒ **Recurrence** refers to the frequency with which the same decisions may need to be made. Can the decision, once made, be transformed into a permanent, standardized policy?

The above analysis helps to determine the level of authority at which a decision may be made. Generally, decisions should be made at the lowest level of competence where detailed knowledge and experience exist. However, they should also be made at a level at which the objectives of all parts of the organization and of the whole are well served. Together, these considerations determine the hierarchy of activities in an organization. For example, if the answers to all four questions in a particular case are high on the scale, the top executive must make the decision. The relationship between the character of decisions and the level of authority at which the decision is made is shown below.

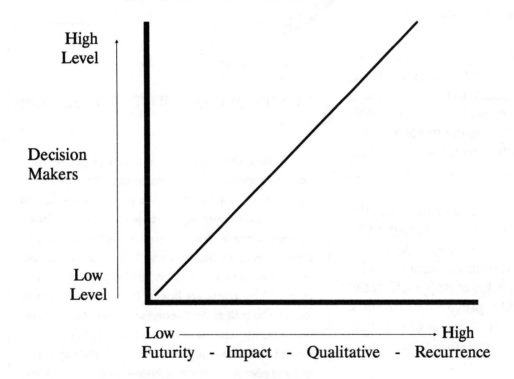

C. Systems Approach

Decision making can benefit from the systems approach. In a nutshell, a system is anything that does a job in an organized way. The essence of a systems approach is to find out what the problem is before trying to solve it and to determine some basis for making choices, and probable constraints, before choosing a solution.

D. The Creative Process

The rational decision-making process, as discussed above, is often supplemented by the creative decision-making process, which may include essentially five steps.
- ⇒ The *first* step, **saturation**, involves becoming thoroughly familiar with a situation and its activities and ideas.
- ⇒ In the *second* step of **deliberation**, the decision maker analyzes and challenges these ideas from different angles.
- ⇒ **Incubation** is the *third* step, during which the decision maker abandons conscious effort and lets the subconscious mind work. A bright idea then strikes the decision maker in the *fourth* step that can be defined as **illumination**.
- ⇒ Next comes the *fifth* step of **accommodation**: refining and adapting the idea to fit the requirements of the situation.

E. Strategic Decisions

Decisions may be characterized as either administrative or strategic. Generally, administrative decisions are concerned with short-term goals and deal with routine matters. They are basically repetitive. Strategic decisions are more complex and concern long-term goals. Consequently, we are often faced with the task of assessing unpredictable factors bearing on strategic decisions. At the same time we must consider factors which, for example, affect the quality of life, prevailing economic conditions, etc. Such decisions may relate to the very survival of the organization.

Action Point

DON'T DECIDE JUST TO PLEASE OTHERS!

Suppose that someone submits a project to you, and you approve it just to please him. You have committed a big mistake. When the projects fails, he will blame you for approving it. He will not blame himself for submitting it. Why did you not voice your objections? It is much better to say "no" in the beginning and displease him than to say "no" at the end and disappoint him. If you are honest from the start, he will love you later when he discovers you were the only one who gave him true *nasihah*, while everybody else was smiling and showering him with praise. Be very objective and give your honest opinion based on merits and not emotions or self-interest. Remember that people can change their opinions; if you want to please them, you will be trailing them every time they change.

III. Information Gathering

A. Main Factors in Information Gathering

The gathering of "good" information is critical to good decision making. A number of formal and informal methods can be used to gather information, including interviews, questionnaires, data bases, reports, and documented records. Four factors play an important part in information gathering: relevance, timeliness, legitimacy, and accuracy.

RELEVANCE

Information can be used only when it is relevant. Technically, when it is irrelevant to the subject at hand, it is not information but "noise." What may be information in one instance may be noise in another. For example, if we were going to decide on a theme for the annual convention, the fact that a popular convention site is located next to a highway is not information but noise. However, when we want to decide where to hold the convention, this same "noise" becomes vital information.

TIMELINESS

Information is not useful if it is not available in time or not up-to-date in its contents. For example, the knowledge that another group has selected the theme that we were going to select is useful only if available to us before we make our decision. The knowledge of the participants' distribution with respect to their states of residence is not information if it is dated so long ago that patterns of distribution have completely changed since then.

LEGITIMACY

Information must be legitimate in order to be used for decision making; i.e., it must be acceptable within the value system of the decision maker. Specifically, it must not violate injunctions of the Qur'an or the Sunnah or be otherwise Islamically unacceptable. For example, data to help make decisions should not be gathered by cheating or through immoral dealings.

ACCURACY

Information must be accurate. Inaccurate information can cause irreparable damage if it is used as the basis of making a decision. Ideally, the process of decision making must assume that all information fed into the process is accurate. From a practical point of view, however, we must verify its accuracy through cross-checking with related information or by directly questioning the source about its accuracy. For example, if we want to pick a site for the annual convention based on distance from major highways, an accurate road map showing the latest exits and any highway construction detours will be essential to making the right decision.

B. Methods of Information Gathering

INTERVIEWS

Informal interviews may be no more than social chit chats with someone who has the information we are looking for. Formal interviews should be well-structured in order to be the most beneficial. When possible, give the interviewee an opportunity to prepare by telling him the goal and the context of the interview. Set an appropriate time and location to minimize interruptions and distractions.

QUESTIONNAIRES

Questionnaires can be administered in person or by mail. In either case, they should be well designed, unambiguous in content, and precise about the answers they seek.

DATA BASES

Data bases containing needed information may be available in print in libraries, university departments, or government agencies. Alternatively, the data base may be available on an electronic data base system accessible through an office or home computer.

REPORTS

Reports published by research groups or consumer agencies as well as academic or government institutions may be a source of required information. However, we must always make sure that the report is objective and up-to-date.

DOCUMENTS

Documents including books, encyclopedias, and magazines can be obtained through libraries. They can be helpful for background and underlying information, but will not usually contain current statistical information.

IV. Brainstorming

Brainstorming is a technique for stimulating the generation of new and relevant ideas and facilitating their expression, or for gathering needed information during a meeting. This technique is used when ideas are not available on a certain subject and need to be created. It is an unfettered process as opposed to a structured discussion.

A brainstorming session must have a theme around which to generate ideas. The session generally has three stages. In the **first** stage, members of the group suggest ideas and a recorder writes down all ideas so that all members can see them. It may help if the group leader has a couple of ideas to get started. No criticism of any idea is permitted at this stage. In the **second** stage, participants are invited to speak out on their ideas. It is advisable to ask them to state the pros and cons of their ideas to minimize any unnecessary pride of ownership. In the **third** stage, each idea is discussed from the point of view of merit, feasibility, priority, etc. Ideas may then be rated according to an agreed-upon set of criteria.

A. Suitability

The brainstorming technique is suitable for decisions that may spring from a wide variety of alternatives. The technique can be used as long as the group is knowledgeable or concerned about the situation and the leader is familiar with the procedure. One example of the effective use of brainstorming would be when an organization wants to select a theme for its convention. A mixed group of officials, staff, and committee members could stimulate a spectrum of creative ideas rooted in the vision and culture of the organization. The final theme could be selected from this rich pool of ideas.

B. Techniques for Productivity

The contribution of the participants to the brainstorming process can be made most productive by employing the techniques below:
  a. Hold the session when the group is fresh and not tired;
  b. Have as varied a group as possible, keeping in mind that they should be somewhat equal in status, so that all will feel free to contribute, and that they should also have a similar level of familiarity with the situation;
  c. Keep the group small enough to be manageable, yet large enough to provide many potential sources of ideas — five to seven is a good size;
  d. Seat the group around a round table facing each other so that free discussion can take place;
  e. Set a time limit long enough for everyone to get a chance to contribute, but short enough for the session not to become tiring;
  f. Write down all ideas so that everyone can see them, regardless of how strange they might be, as long as they are positive and build on another's ideas;
  g. Do not evaluate suggestions and allow no comments or criticism at the beginning of the ideas being presented;
  h. When necessary, rephrase the problem clearly.

C. Drawing Conclusions

The purpose of brainstorming is to derive conclusions from the gathered data. In order for that to happen, the session should be planned in the following way:
  a. Let each person state the pros and cons of his suggestions;
  b. Assign priority and feasibility ratings to suggestions;
  c. Ask for possible ways to implement the best suggestion;
  d. Decide on suggestions most likely to succeed;
  e. Convey selected suggestions to the appointing body.

V. *Shura* (Mutual Consultation)

A. The Nature of *Shura*

Shura is the Islamic process of consultation among those with knowledge of the issues involved, and is best accomplished by discussion among those most aware of the situation. *Shura* is one of the most important organizational and constitutional principles in Islam.

The Qur'an instructs Muslim leaders to administer the affairs of the people through consultation with them. It encourages openness and honesty in the expression of opinions.

It is part of the mercy of Allah that you deal gently with them. Were you severe or harsh hearted, they would have broken away from about you: so pass over [their faults], and ask for [Allah's] forgiveness for them; and consult them in their affairs [of moment]. Then, when you have taken a decision, put your trust in Allah. For Allah loves those who put their trust [in Him] (3:159).

فَبِمَا رَحْمَةٍ مِّنَ ٱللَّهِ لِنتَ لَهُمْ وَلَوْ كُنتَ فَظًّا غَلِيظَ ٱلْقَلْبِ لَٱنفَضُّوا مِنْ حَوْلِكَ فَٱعْفُ عَنْهُمْ وَٱسْتَغْفِرْ لَهُمْ وَشَاوِرْهُمْ فِى ٱلْأَمْرِ فَإِذَا عَزَمْتَ فَتَوَكَّلْ عَلَى ٱللَّهِ إِنَّ ٱللَّهَ يُحِبُّ ٱلْمُتَوَكِّلِينَ (سورة آل عمران)

The Sunnah of the Prophet is full of examples of his consultation with his companions. Abu Hurayrah confirmed this by saying: "I have never seen anyone who seeks consultation with his companions more than the Prophet (SAW)." The Prophet (SAW) sought the opinions of the community in deciding about worldly affairs, and departed from it only in the case of a direct revelation to the contrary. One example was the Prophet's decision to consult Muslims about the treatment of captives from the Battle of Badr. Abu Bakr (RA) and 'Umar (RA) presented opposing points of view, and Muslims were generally divided among themselves. The Prophet (SAW) gave full consideration to their opinions before deciding that Muslims could accept ransom for the captives before releasing them. Another example was when some Muslims proposed to fight Quraysh outside Madinah in the Battle of Uhud. Other Muslims wanted to fight from within fortifications in Madinah. The Prophet (SAW) preferred the latter option but, in consideration of the general view in the community, chose to go to battle outside the city.

B. The Practice of *Shura*

The most important consideration in the practice of *shura* is the presence of opposing points of view. One often does not need to make a decision unless there is disagreement and dissent. To profit fully from the practice of *shura*, an effective decision maker

organizes his dissent. The principal benefits of doing so are:
- ⇒ Disagreement safeguards the decision maker against being unduly influenced by the majority's view;
- ⇒ Disagreement can provide viable alternatives to choose from;
- ⇒ Disagreement is needed to stimulate the imagination; well-reasoned, thought through, and documented disagreement is the most effective stimulus to imagination.

To prepare for a decision by consultation, there must be an open and organization-wide debate debate on the proposal so that everybody is familiar with the facts and the options. The result of this debate should be a meeting of the minds as to whether there is (or is not) a need for change.

To arrive at a consensus on the facts, we must first find the facts. To determine what is a fact pertaining to the situation at hand, first seek an agreement on the criteria of relevance, especially on the appropriate measurement.

The understanding that underlies the right decision grows out of the clash and conflict of divergent opinions and out of the serious consideration of competing alternatives. This is a lesson clearly embedded in the Prophet's decisions at Badr and ʿUhud noted above.

Present technology has greatly improved our capability to fulfill the demands of *shura*. On one hand, it has become possible to quickly disseminate information that may be the basis of a decision. On the other, the exchange of views itself can be helped by modern means of communication. Some of the many possibilities are briefly described in the chapter on communication in this *Guide*.

VI. Tips on Negotiating and Compromising

Often we are faced with coming to an agreement with others having interests, perspectives, or constraints different from our own. Solving problems in such cases calls for a process of give and take, usually referred to as negotiating.

Negotiating is an art that demands an understanding of human psychology. Specifically, the more we know about the needs and motivational drives of the other party, the greater are our chances of making a good decision and solving the problem at hand effectively. However, negotiating is not a game we win or lose, nor is it an attempt to overwhelm the other party such that it must say "yes" to all our demands. In fact, good negotiations are focused on reaching a wise outcome based on principles, reason, and objective criteria.

In negotiating, being "soft" is as much a problem as being "hard." In such cases, whoever applies greater pressure gets what he wants, regardless of what is in the best interest of both sides. The solution to this problem is to concentrate on the merits of the case as the basis of negotiation. Negotiating is a very wide subject. Some hints on the negotiating process described as follows by Roger Fisher and William Ury in their *Getting to Yes — Negotiation* are very helpful in getting results.

PROBLEM Positional Bargaining - Which Game Should You Play?		SOLUTION Change The Game - Negotiate On Merits.
SOFT	HARD	PRINCIPLED
Participants are friends.	Participants are adversaries.	Participants are problem-solvers.
The goal is agreement.	The goal is victory.	The goal is a wise outcome reached efficiently and amicably.
Make concessions to cultivate the relationship.	Demand concessions as a condition of the relationship.	Separate the problem from the people.
Be soft on the people and the problem.	Be hard on the problem and the people.	Be soft on the people, hard on the problem.
Trust others.	Distrust others.	Proceed independent of trust.
Change your position easily.	Dig in to your position.	Focus on interests, not positions.
Make offers.	Make threats.	Explore interests.
Accept one-sided losses to reach agreement.	Demand one-sided gains as the price of agreement.	Invent options for mutual gain.
Disclose your bottom line.	Mislead as to your bottom line.	Avoid having a bottom line.
Search for the single answer: the one they will accept.	Search for the single answer: the one you will accept.	Develop multiple options to choose from: decide later.
Insist on agreement.	Insist on your position.	Insist on objective criteria.
Try to avoid a contest of will.	Try to win a contest of will.	Try to reach a result based on standards independent of will.
Yield to pressure.	Apply pressure.	Reason and be open to reasons; yield to principle, not pressure.

Limits on Compromise

Compromise is often the byword in the negotiating process. Islamic guidelines on compromising between what is right and what is wrong have been explained by, among others, Ibn Taymiyah in *Hisba fi al Islam*. In his view, the limits of compromise are as follows:

a. It is not permissible to command or forbid a course of action between right and wrong without thorough investigation.

b. If the right is preponderant it should be commanded, even if it entails a lesser wrong.

c. If the wrong is predominant it should be forbidden, even if it entails the loss of a greater right.

d. A wrong should not be forbidden if doing so entails the loss of a greater right.

e. If the right and wrong are equally balanced and inseparable, neither is to be commanded or forbidden.

Some people think that since we have the perfect code of life in the Qur'an we can just go ahead and apply it to our life without **thinking**. Allah gave us a brain to use in the understanding and application of our faith. This is what makes us different from animals. We are not the fastest, the biggest, the strongest, or the tallest of creatures. But we are the "brainiest" of them all!

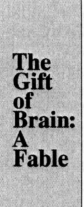

The Gift of Brain: A Fable

There was a lion in the forest who told his young cub: "You have nothing to fear from any animal, but beware of that two-legged creature called man; he has a brain." One day the cub met a man, overpowered him, and was about to kill him. He remembered his father's advice and asked the man: "My father warned me about you. Can you show me your brain?" The man said: "Oh yes, but I left it at home. If you release me, I will go and get it for you." The cub agreed. The man then said: "But you may go away and I won't be able to find you. Let me tie you to the tree so that you cannot leave." The cub agreed. After the man tied the cub, he got a stick and beat the cub to death. In his last moments, the cub remembered his father's advice: "Beware of man; he has a brain."

Unfortunately, we do not make full use of the brains we have. In some cases we leave them brand new, never used! Seriously, scientific research has shown that the average man seldom taps into more than 5-10% of his potential brain power.

QUESTIONS FOR DISCUSSION

1. When should one NOT make a decision? Why?
2. What should one NOT do to make an executable decision?
3. What are the four steps in the decision-making process? List them in the right sequence.
4. What are the five steps in the creative approach to decision making in the right sequence?
5. So that information is useful, which of its characteristics is the most critical; the least critical?
6. So that a brainstorming session is successful, which step is most critical; the least critical?
7. What is the Qur'anic command about shura?
8. If the Prophet (SAW) was engaging in shura with the Muslims about the Battle of Uhud in our times, which means of shura would be the most effective; the least effective? Why?
9. How does the discussion of shura here relate to that on leadership?

COMPREHENSION EXERCISE

AS VICE PRESIDENT FOR ISLAMIC OUTREACH FOR THE UNITED CENTRAL SOCIETY, YOU HAVE BEEN ABLE TO ATTRACT A FEW MUSLIM STUDENTS FROM THE LOCAL CAMPUS TO VOLUNTEER IN YOUR NEW LITERATURE DISTBUTION PROGRAM. THIS PROGRAM HAS BEEN SUCCESSFUL BY YOUR STANDARDS. NOW THE LEADERS OF A SMALL NEIGHBORING COMMUNITY HAVE ASKED YOUR HELP TO RUN A SIMILAR PROGRAM THERE WITH THE SAME VOLUNTEERS. YOU WANT TO HELP BUT YOU BELIEVE SUCCESS IN YOUR OWN COMMUNITY IS MORE CRUCIAL TO OVERALL MUSLIM INTERESTS.

1. List some of the acceptable alternatives you may consider.

2. Prepare a chart to gather information you will need to make your decisions.

3. Will you make an individual decision or will you involve others? Why? How?

4. Examine your possible decision in terms of futurity, impact, qualitative considerations, and recurrence. Which of the factors, in this case, is the most important; the least important?

Decision vs. Implementation

LEARNING OBJECTIVES

On completing this chapter, you should be able to:
- relate the implementation of a decision to its making
- plan the implementation of a decision
- build implementation into the decision-making process

I. What Is Implementation?

A decision is only as good as its implementation. An effective decision calls for an action or a certain behavior on the part of the persons affected by it. It may also call

---

for no action. When it calls for an action to be performed, the decision must be properly implemented in order to make its impact felt.

Implementation is the act of carrying out a decision. A designated person or group of persons must perform an action or a set of actions at or within a certain time using a given set of material resources. This is the implementation of the decision.

II. The Implementation Factor in Decision Making

A decision is only a good intention until it has been carried out in work and action and has become an accomplishment. Deciding and doing are complementary. The Qur'an admonishes us not to say what we do not do, and to be firm in doing what we have decided to do.

O You who believe! Why say you that which you do not? (61:2)

يَٰٓأَيُّهَا ٱلَّذِينَ ءَامَنُوا لِمَ تَقُولُونَ مَا لَا تَفْعَلُونَ ۝
(سورة الصف)

... Then, when you have taken a decision, put your trust in Allah. For Allah loves those who put their trust [in Him]. (3:159)

... فَإِذَا عَزَمْتَ فَتَوَكَّلْ عَلَى ٱللَّهِ إِنَّ ٱللَّهَ يُحِبُّ ٱلْمُتَوَكِّلِينَ
(سورة آل عمران)

Making a decision means that the specifications of the situation have been thought through, various alternatives explored, risks and gains weighed, and who will have to do what understood. At this point it is reasonably clear what course of action should be taken.

An effective decision is a commitment to action and results. First rule: make sure that everyone who will have to do something to make the decision effective, or who could sabotage it, has participated responsibly in making the decision. It is equally important to build, from the start, a commitment to action into the decision itself. For all practical purposes, no decision has been made unless carrying it out in specific steps has become someone's work assignment and responsibility.

An effective decision has its implementation built into the decision itself. This is accomplished through the extensive involvement of those affected by the decision in its making, and by a thorough discussion during the process leading up to the final decision. In this way, the necessary input and commitment is secured from all involved parties.

Further, a decision is based on certain underlying expectations which must be continuously tested against the real world. This is accomplished by building a feedback loop into the decision-making process around direct exposure to reality to ensure that the decision is implementable in the real world.

III. Elements of Implementation

Converting a decision into action requires answering several distinct questions on which its successful implementation is based. These are:

- Who should be informed?
- What should be done?
- Who should do it?
- When should it be done?
- Who will cover the cost?

These questions are answered through the following steps:

A. Communicate Decision

"Who should be informed?" Everyone who is affected by the decision should be informed about it. Some of them may have contributed to making it; others may not have contributed. Some may become involved in implementing it; others may only be touched by its results.

B. Outline Action

"What should be done or what action has to be taken?" This is the core of the decision. The answer must be specific and applicable to the situation at hand because it states the action commitments a decision requires. For this reason, it is necessary to understand the situation thoroughly before taking the decision that is called for. The action or the series of actions must be outlined in a manner so that the people who have to do it can do it. Specific work assignments must follow from it and should be clearly stated.

C. Assign Responsibility

"Who should do it?" Responsibility should be assigned to someone for accomplishing what the decision seeks to accomplish. This could be a person or a unit of the organization qualified to do it. In either case, the assignment of responsibility should be specific by name or title of the doer to remove any ambiguity and to prevent shifting of accountability to others. If EVERYBODY is

> *THE KING AND THE HONEY TANK*
>
> A king, who loved expensive honey, wanted to test how much people loved him. He put an empty barrel in the city square and announced that anyone loving him should pour one cup of pure honey into the barrel. One person thought that since everyone else was pouring in honey, he could pour in a cup of water instead. After all, one cup of water will not be noticed in a barrel of honey. When the king opened the barrel later, it was full of water. It seems everyone had the same idea.

responsible for one task, it will not get done, because EVERYBODY thinks somebody else will do it. Remember the story of "The King and the Honey Tank"; the tank ended up being full of water, because everybody thought somebody else would put in the honey.

D. Schedule Activities

"When should it be done?" A time schedule of activities must be established. A decision may be very time-sensitive and may lose its effect if executed too early or too late, or if component decisions and actions are not carried out in the right sequence. For example, what a poor image we give when we send out a letter that reaches its destination after the deadline of the response required by the letter!

E. Budget Resources

"How much does it cost?" If the answer is not accurately known, an approximate but realistic and enlightened estimate should be made. An effective decision is one that can be carried out within the constraints of an approved budget.

ACTION POINT Think and Research Before You React!	In 1959, I was a student at Norwood Technical College in London. One morning a brother told me: "You are always joyful and smiling. I wish I could be like you." That same afternoon another brother exclaimed: "Why do you always look serious? What is wrong with you?" In 1979, I was in charge of a training camp organized by WAMY and IIFSO in Cyprus. On the third day, two brothers told me: "This is a very strict camp. We feel as if we were in a military environment." On the fourth day, two other participants told me: "This is an extremely loose program. We must change it to train ourselves like soldiers." It would be disastrous if we instantly reacted to people's opinions and change our plans to please them. People have different backgrounds and perceptions, and we should analyze, investigate, confirm, and consult before we change our plans. Management by reaction leads us astray. We must listen to everyone but act according to a well-thought-out plan. Although we represent our members, we also have a responsibility towards Allah to lead wisely. The movement should position itself to lead people and NOT to be led by them.

IV. The Nuts and Bolts of Getting Things Done

Now that we have gained some familiarity with the process of implementation, we can benefit from some practical pointers for getting things done on an everyday basis. Through the few short anecdotes and reminders that follow, we will examine what makes the difference between succeeding and failing to get the job done: for example, carrying a notebook to record "things to do," acting on plans more than talking about them, carrying each job to a hundred percent completion, and keeping an eye on performance when comparing people.

A. Note That Pocket Notebook

Man is forgetful. To remedy this, always carry a small notebook, a card, or just a piece of paper in your pocket. List all the important things you want to remember, preferably in their order of priority. Look at it at least twice a day, preferably once in the morning and once in the afternoon. Keep adding more things to the list and strike out the items you have completed. This gives you a sense of accomplishment. No matter how sharp your memory is, try this system; it is very rewarding. You will be astonished by its impact on your performance.

B. Action Deficiency Disease!

It is a fact that good action is based on a sound theoretical foundation. However, conceptualization and theorization are mainly done by leaders and scholars. What about the followers? They have been victims of "action deficiency disease." Just watch what happens during meetings and measure the ratio of talk to action.

We have to concentrate on doing rather than talking. Allah, the Prophet, and the believers will see our deeds, not our words. A major problem with talking is that talk becomes a substitute for action. When we talk a lot about a project, after some time we tend to believe that it has been taken care of. An example of this is the curricula and syllabi of full-time Islamic schools. So much talking has been done about it , but it is still waiting to be accomplished.

It is human nature to sometimes substitute words for action. The less action, the more words needed to justify the inner feeling of guilt. To put this concept into operation, we can think of words and actions as debit and credit. Each word is debit cost, as in a telegram, and each action is a credit. Looking at it this way could transform us from a talking person to an action-oriented one.

C. Do 100%, Not 99.99%

We estimate that roughly 90% of the people do only one-half of their jobs; 9% do jobs 95% complete. Only 1% can complete 100% of the task. This means that if you are a manager, you cannot fully entrust tasks except to 1% of the work force. This puts a heavy burden on top management, which has to carry out the actual final completion of the job. This is often crippling. You often hear people saying the job is complete, and that we need only to do "this and that." It means it is not complete. Why do they not do "this and that" before coming to you?

The majority of people come to you with excuses for not being able to complete a job. The world is full of excuses. What is needed is a reliable performer who, in spite of all valid excuses, can solve problems and complete the job 100%. These types are self-motivated and self-supervised. If your manager does not rely on you, ask yourself: Am I reliable? Do I complete the task 100% or 99.99%. The Prophetic wisdom puts it this way:

«إنَّما النَّاسُ كَإِبِلِ مائَةٍ، لاَ يُوجَدُ فيها رَاحِلَةٌ»

People are like camels; you may not find one suitable mount from even a hundred of them. [1]

Try to be that 1% reliable performer who completes 100% of the assignment.

D. The Father and Three Sons!

People came angrily to the father. "Why do you prefer your youngest son to his two brothers?" they asked. He replied, "Wait here and discover for yourselves." Then he called his three sons and told them to go to the seaport and come back after one hour with their reports. They came back with their reports:

The Eldest: We received a shipment of machinery.

The Middle One: We got three machines from Japan yesterday.

The Youngest: We got three machines, spare parts are missing, one unit is damaged, and I have filed a claim with the insurance company. We must complete the documents next week to meet the deadline and avoid demurrage.

Do a complete job first and admit your own shortcomings before you compare yourself with others.

---

1   Musnad Ahmad ibn Hanbal, Sahih al Bukhari, Sahih Muslim, Sunan al Tirmidhi, and Sunan ibn Majah.

Exercise

THE SIX PHASES OF A PROJECT

Can you remember a project where the following six phases took place according to this sequence?

1. Enthusiasm
2. Disillusionment
3. Panic
4. Search for the guilty
5. Punishment for the innocent
6. Praise and honors for the nonparticipant

Try to imagine if the same project were to be done again, what would you do differently? Share your experiences with the group in a workshop.

A PARADE OF IMPLEMENTORS!
Do you know how to work with them?

 K  D 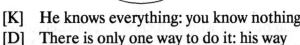 B

The Know-It-All	[K]	He knows everything: you know nothing
The Dictator	[D]	There is only one way to do it: his way
The Backstabber	[B]	Every time you turn your back, there's another knife sticking in it
The Constant Complainer	[CC]	He finds fault with everything: except himself
The Competitor	[C]	Every day is a battle: he has to win and you must lose
The Exploder	[E]	A psychological powder keg: on a very short fuse

 CC  C 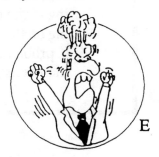 E

Action point

ORGANIZATIONAL PENTAGON OF SUCCESS

When we become aware of a problem, it does not mean that we have solved it. We need to identify it and make the right diagnosis first.

Then a solution has to be proposed and a remedial medicine prescribed. We then ask ourselves: "Is the solution applicable to this situation? How? In what dose? With what timetable?" All these decisions must be made. They constitute a plan of action. Finally, we come to the stage of following up on these decisions and following through with their implementation. The first four stages are theoretical and help us reach the right decisions, but until we implement them we have not moved ahead. In the course of execution, we need feedback and continuous monitoring of the progress of the situation. Experience shows that in the majority of cases, the organization gets through most of the stages but stops short of execution. The reason is lack of follow up and follow through. The answer to this is to assign one member of the governing body to the job of following up. He is like the "whip" member in a parliament. He should keep in mind the following four points:

1. It should be clear who is to carry out the decisions that are made. What is the deadline? What is the budget? What are the terms of reference and authority required to carry out the job?
2. Minutes of the meeting should be recorded and distributed to the members.
3. Regular contact should be maintained with those assigned to the tasks, not only as a reminder but also to receive progress reports. Such contact can be daily, weekly, or monthly, according to the urgency. The reports may be written or oral, depending on the circumstances.
4. If problems arise while carrying out his duties, the "follow up" member should consult with the president.

PENTAGON OF SUCCESS (FALAH)

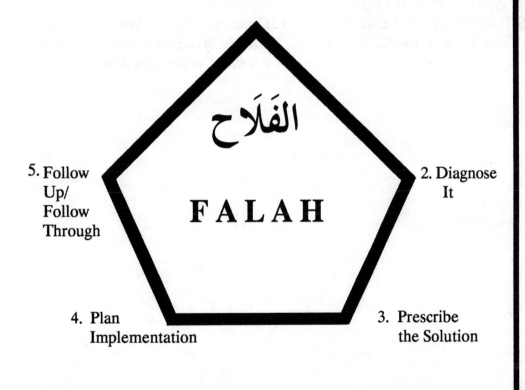

1. Feel the Problem

5. Follow
Up/
Follow
Through

الفَلَاح

FALAH

2. Diagnose
It

4. Plan
Implementation

3. Prescribe
the Solution

QUESTIONS FOR DISCUSSION

1. How can you build implementation into a decision?
2. What role does feedback play in carrying out decisions?
3. What are the five steps in implementing decisions?
4. What should be the primary concern in assigning responsibility for carrying out a decision?

COMPREHENSION EXERCISE

THE UNITED CENTRAL SOCIETY HAS DECIDED TO BUILD AN IS-LAMIC CENTER IN A MAJOR TOWN WITHIN THE NEXT TWO YEARS. THE DECISION HAS BEEN TAKEN CAREFULLY AND IS TURNED OVER TO YOU, AS THE SOCIETY'S EXECU-TIVE SECRETARY, FOR IMPLEMEN-TATION.

1. *Outline the steps you will take to carry out the decision.*

2. *State specific pitfalls you will seek to avoid.*

3. *Create a project plan to monitor progress of implementation; include schedules, milestones, costs, etc.*

Chapter

9

Basics of Planning

LEARNING OBJECTIVES

On completing this chapter, you should be able to:
- define planning and its role in managing work
- distinguish between various levels and formats of planning
- identify interrelationships between planning levels
- develop plans including annual action plans

I. What Is Planning?

Planning is a way of making our mistakes on paper. It is a way of charting our course to get from here to there. On the way to there, we tend to get off the highway and into sidestreets and bylanes. When this tendency is not checked so that we can remain on course, we fail to get there at all. We may get to somewhere, but that will not be where we wanted to go. Planning, and then controlling, keeps us on course.

In getting to a destination or accomplishing a great objective, the maxim remains true: If we fail to plan, we plan to fail.

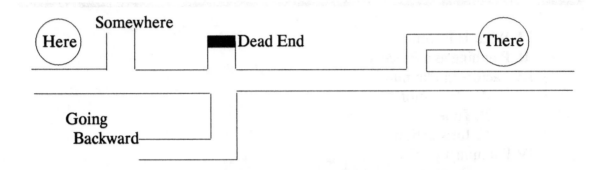

II. Planning as a Process

In one sense, planning is a sequential and loop-around process. It ceases to be meaningful if the loop-around path is interrupted or the direction is reversed. In the triangular diagram below, one can start anywhere in the loop:

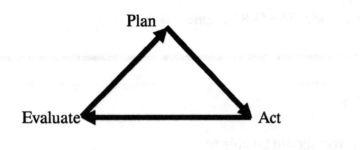

Planning is the process of gathering information and making assumptions about the future to formulate those activities necessary to achieve organizational objectives.

Planning ensures purposeful and orderly activities by directing all efforts towards results. It points out the need for changes in the future. Planning provides a basis for controlling so that the results of planned activities do not deviate from the expected ranges. It encourages achievement and enables us to conceptualize and visualize the whole enterprise. Finally, planning optimizes the utilization of resources and facilities.

From a behavioral point of view, it is expected that our commitment to Islamic work will be strengthened when we engage in the process of planning through the exercise of *shura* (mutual consultation).

III. Factors in Planning

A. Motivation

Planning is a function of the leadership's motivation, whether it is focused on what happens in the immediate future or on what may happen in the distant but certain future. Long-range planning aimed at moving the organization towards where it should be is called strategic planning. On the other hand, short-range planning aimed at the consequences of specific actions yielding comparatively quick results is called tactical or action planning.

"Strategic" plans lay down the organization's primary directions and priorities. They are the result of the process of making decisions systematically and with the greatest knowledge of their future impact, systematically organizing the efforts needed to carry out those decisions, and measuring the results of those decisions against expectations through systematic feedback. They also take into account the organization's external environment shaped by social, political, and economic factors. On the other hand, "action" plans chart specific activities and projects. While "tactical" generally covers a period of one year, "strategic" covers a longer time span of five, ten, or more years.

B. Time

Planning is a function of time because plans are concerned with decisions for action, and action always focuses on results in a dimension of time—the future. We can plan for a month, a year, or a decade. The longer the duration of the planning period, the more demanding the process becomes. A plan represents the sequence of activities which must be carried out for a goal to be accomplished. Plans can be classified according to the time span built into them as:
    a. Short-term plans,
    b. Medium-term plans and
    c. Long-term plans.

Short-term plans must be integrated into long-term plans. Conversely, long-term plans must be divided into short-term plans. Continuity and compatibility within these plans are essential to the optimal utilization of the human and material resources which have been committed to carrying out the plans.

a) Organizational Goals

Long-term plans, also called strategic plans, may cover a period of five to ten years. A vital element in long-term planning is the establishment of goals. Let us briefly consider what organizational goals are.

An organizational goal is a desired state of affairs which the organization attempts to realize as a group. This organizational goal is in part affected by the goals of the elected leadership, those of the rank and file membership, and those of the Muslim community in general. The goals of an Islamic organization are based on the injunctions of the Qur'an, the teachings of the Prophet (SAW), and the practice of *shura* within the membership of the organization.

b) Long-Term or Strategic Plans

In developing strategic plans, the executive committee must consider two sets of assumptions:
   - a: assumptions about uncontrollable factors, i.e., population trends, political issues, etc.
   - b: assumptions about controllable factors, i.e., budget allowances, *da'wah* priorities, etc.

The format for formulating strategic plans is to gather and analyze background information, assess environmental dimensions relating to the objectives, conduct a resource audit of the organization, establish strategic alternatives, and make the principal strategic choice and alternate choices that will accomplish the stated objectives.

Once strategic plans are formulated, an organization may establish medium-range plans spread over one to two years. It is important that medium-range plans flow logically from long-term plans. An Islamic organization whose long-term plan is to build an Islamic center may establish a medium-range plan to raise funds for construction. This plan would be a logical step toward the attainment of its long-term plan.

c) Short–Range or Tactical Plans

Short range or tactical plans provide the guidelines for the year-to-year operations of the organization and delineate the step-by-step methodology by which they are to be carried out. Tactical planning done to support strategic planning provides a charter, as it relates to the future. The Islamic organization with a long-range plan to establish an Islamic center and a medium-range plan to raise funds may set up a short-range plan to have an architect design and prepare fund raising materials.

Short-range plans themselves can be broken down into very specific targets or immediate action plans lasting usually from one to thirty days. Thus, continuing the above example, immediate action would be required to find an architect, contact him, and agree on a budget for design work. Someone must be commissioned to prepare a brochure for fund raising.

C. Jurisdiction

Planning is also a function of jurisdiction. We must plan for each unit of the organization and also for the entire organization. The two must be compatible. For mission-inspired, membership-based organizations, the planning process works in two ways:

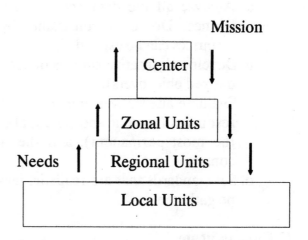

1. **Top to bottom:** A good understanding of the mission determines the planning framework or priorities. This information is communicated to the units to serve as guidelines.

2. **Bottom to top**: A clear understanding of the membership's needs and roles determines relevant activity at the grass roots level. This information is woven into a unit plan and communicated to the center. Unit plans are then synthesized into a central plan.

The jurisdictional levels of the planning process are illustrated above.

IV. Planning by MBO

We will now introduce a method of planning known as Management by Objectives. Put simply, such planning determines WHO is going to do WHAT, HOW, and WHEN. There are four steps to MBO planning: preparing, deciding, communicating, and controlling.

A. Prepare

In the preparation stage of the planning process, the organization should do the following:
   a. State the objectives as clearly and as specifically as possible.
   b. Collect facts, data, opinions, and experiences of others which bear on these objectives.
   c. Consult with those involved with the plan or its execution either directly or indirectly. Also consult with other knowledgeable and original thinkers who may not be involved.

B. Decide

In the decision-making stage of the planning process, the organization should perform the following steps:
   a. Analyze all the data and construct scenarios with every possible consequence. Do not be constrained by scarcity of resources at this stage, since resources can be expanded.
   b. Develop alternative courses of action; each course of action must lead to the desired objective(s).
   c. Evaluate alternatives and choose the best one. Consider the availability of resources (present and potential), community benefits (the maximum and the most permanent), and the time framework (set by environmental constraints).
   d. Set standards that are realistic, feasible, and for which measurable data can be gathered.

C. Communicate

The communication stage of the planning process takes place after a concrete plan has been decided upon:
   a. Decide upon precisely who will be directly or remotely involved with the plan by using information gathered about the "targeted" audience.
   b. Select and implement the best methods of communicating the plan to them.
   c. Check to be sure that everyone involved understands and accepts the plan and allow them some flexibility in the way they carry out the plan's assignments.

D. Control

The control stage of the planning process includes the following steps:
   a. Set up check points to evaluate the program. Are we on target or not?

b. Compare actual results with anticipated ones; be sure to distinguish between deviations caused by natural and uncontrollable factors and those caused by inadequate plan implementation.

c. Take remedial action when necessary; namely, revise current targets in the plan if they are no longer feasible, or change the whole plan if necessary. Corrections on the way are better than disasters at the end.

V. Effectiveness in Planning

A. Preplanning Considerations

An action plan, when formulated with foresight and commitment, should direct the course of work during the year. It should serve as a constraint on "crisis planning" which wastes manpower, money, time, and goodwill. To yield desirable results, such a plan should be monitored for compliance and reviewed every three months.

The preplanning discussion should be guided by the following considerations which may seem contradictory at first:

1. We cannot plan to do more than our projected resources for the year would allow.
2. We must be bold in breaking new ground and in conceiving new programs for the coming year. Our ability to attract new resources depends on such initiatives.

B. Centralized and Decentralized Planning

Planning may be either centralized or decentralized. In centralized planning, the process is in the form of a pyramid. The president sets goals for members of the governing body, states the standards and the results expected, provides the information and training that the members need, explains the procedures for action, develops and improves the current methodology, and applies discipline to ensure that everybody implements his or her part of the overall plan.

On the other end, in decentralized planning the president and the governing body consult with membership at various stages of planning and implementation. Information is freely accessible, and training is more of a supervised on-the-job learning type. Members are not forced out of the organization if they make mistakes, but are strongly encouraged to learn from them.

Characteristics of Effective Plans

1. Plans need to be **specific** if they are to motivate our members towards concrete actions.
2. Plans must be **action oriented** — neither too easy nor too difficult. They must be cast in language easily understandable by those who are to carry them out.
3. Plans must be **flexible**. The greater the number of uncontrollable factors, the more flexible the plan should be.
4. Plans must be **consistent with the goals** of the Muslim community at large.

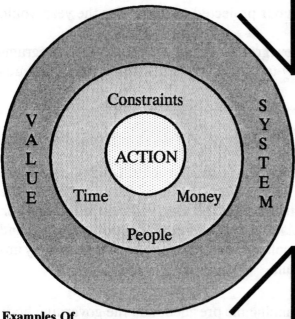

Examples Of
(interrelated) Time And Money Constraints:
a: Mailing scheduled by third class bulk rate; delay causes TIME to run out and mailing has to be sent first class at over three times the COST.
b: More EXPENSIVE airline tickets have to be purchased because of DELAY in sending invitations to a planned activity.

Tips for Effective Planning

1. The plans that are carried out are the ones made by people who will be **responsible** for their execution.
2. All participants in planning must see their world in more or less the same way, both now and in the future; they must share a common **worldview.**
3. Planners work best if they first concentrate on **issues** rather than on machinery, on *what* rather than on *how*. The *how* should come later.
4. Most people dislike planning because a plan represents a **commitment** that they may not be able to honor. The planning coordinator should withhold addressing the *how*s of achieving future goals until the planning group has become excited about the evident needs and opportunities the future holds.
5. Since only a limited number of strategies can be implemented at any given time, it is important to identify the truly fundamental **goals** and to design a few basic strategies to achieve them.
6. Planning gets neglected because it is a **difficult** task. It demands deep original thinking, like research. However, the results of planning are very rewarding.
7. To benefit most from planning, remember to PLAN; DO; CHECK.
8. Plans must be designed to yield **results** within the constraints of time, people, money, and value system.

VI. The Annual Action Plan

An action plan is a document that charts the course of an organization during a specified period. In an Islamic organization with an elected governing body and a full-time general secretariat, the task of preparing this document rests with the head of the secretariat who works in consultation with the head of the organization's executive committee. The latter official, usually called the president or the chairman, has the final responsibility to present a viable plan to the executive council for approval and to ensure that it is implemented as approved.

A fairly accurate projection of the scheduled dates for the beginning and the ending of each activity is the most crucial element of the action plan.

We can establish this schedule by first determining the expected duration of the activity. Then, we establish the activity's role in the unit plan's fulfillment so as to establish the beginning date. Scheduling should also take into account the availability of persons and equipment that may be needed. We have to identify major milestones in the progress of each activity.

The final draft of the annual action plan must be prepared through a process of integrating the unit plans. Each regional representative should prepare a regional plan based on plans from units in his region. Each zonal representative should make a zonal plan based on his regional plans. Similarly, each department head in the secretariat should prepare a department plan based on plans from the field. A planning coordinator in the headquarters should then integrate all plans to prepare the final draft.

The final draft becomes the official annual action plan of the organization after its review and approval by the organization's highest policy-making body.

VII. The Envelope of Planning: The Q-8 Scheme

The concepts and techniques of planning are applicable to a variety of situations. We will examine two cases as different in time and circumstances as possible to illustrate this point. Further, the narrative or commission paragraph at the end of each case shows how, using the Q-8 scheme, the organization's leadership may define the planning function to the planning group.

To review how an action plan may be prepared, we resort to the "envelope of planning." The envelope is determined by what we have called the Q-8 Scheme, a set of eight questions the planner(s) must answer.

Q
8

Q-1: **What** is the objective of this planning effort?
Q-2: **Why** is this objective meaningful?
Q-3: **Who** will be the implementor and the "audience" of the plan?
Q-4: **How** will they achieve the objective and evaluate results?
Q-5: **When** will the implementation be most effective?
Q-6: **Where** will the activity/event be most effective?
Q-7: **At what cost**, in people, time, and money will the plan work?
Q-8: **To what benefit**, overall, is the plan directed?

Finally, we must ensure that the unit plans, including their projected activities, are fully integrated into the central plan.

Action Point

Are You Task Oriented or People Oriented?

In general, people exhibit two types of behavior. One type includes those who focus on accomplishing objectives regardless of people; the other comprises those who concentrate on pleasing people regardless of objectives. The ideal method of operation is to try to accomplish objectives and please people. But this is easier said than done and it can rarely be accomplished, particularly in the short run. We need the group wisdom provided through consultation on how to proceed in moderation, to accomplish our objectives, and to preserve good relations with individuals at the same time. Certainly complete dedication and loyalty to Allah is a prerequisite, but in the accomplishment of tasks we also need the collective wisdom of those with greater experience.

THE CASE OF MUSLIM STUDENTS LEADERSHIP TRAINING

1. Q-1: **What?**
   What is the objective of this planning effort?
   Example: To train Muslim student leaders to do a better job.
2. Q-2: **Why?**
   Why is this objective meaningful?
   Example: So that the organizations they lead may become more effective.
3. Q-3: **Who?**
   Who will be the implementors and the "audience" of the planned activity/event?
   Example: ISNA HQ staff and office holders of MSA, MAYA, and MISG chapters.
4. Q-4: **How?**
   How will they accomplish the objective of this effort?
   Example: Through some type of training camps and reading materials.
5. Q-5: **When?**
   When will the activity/event be most effective?
   Example: During the winter of 1992.
6. Q-6: **Where?**
   Where will the activity/event be most effective?
   Example: At the Islamic Center of North America in Indiana.
7. Q-7: **At What Cost?**
   What will the activity/event/action cost in people, time, and money?
   Example: About five people working in a committee for about five hours a week for five weeks at a total cost of $500.
8. Q-8: **To What Benefit?**
   What will be the overall benefit of this effort?
   Example: Muslims and non-Muslims in the jurisdiction of the involved organizations will receive improved services and more effective *da'wah, in sha'a Allah.*
9. Narrative or Commission:

> To train Muslim student leaders to do a better job so that the organizations they lead may become more effective, office holders of MSA, MAYA, and MISG chapters will be offered some type of training program during the winter of 1992 at the Islamic Center of North America.
>
> About five people working in a committee for about five hours a week for five weeks at a cost of $500 may be needed to achieve this. As a result, Muslims and non-Muslims in the jurisdiction of the involved organizations will receive improved services and more effective *da'wah, in sha'a Allah.*

THE CASE OF NUH'S ARK

1. Q-1: **What?**
   What is the objective of this planning effort?
   Example: To transport selected living beings to safety.
2. Q-2: **Why?**
   Why is this objective meaningful?
   Example: So that life may continue after the flood.
3. Q-3: **Who?**
   Who will be the implementors and the "audience" of the planned activity/event?
   Example: Nuh (AS) (Noah) and pairs of animals and believers.
4. Q-4: **How?**
   How will they accomplish the objective of this effort?
   Example: Through some type of sea transportation system.
5. Q-5: **When?**
   When will the activity/event be most effective?
   Example: Immediately after the beginning of the flood.
6. Q-6: **Where?**
   Where will the activity/event be most effective?
   Example: To the east of town.
7. Q-7: **At what cost?**
   What will the activity/event/action cost in people, time, and money?
   Example: Nuh (AS), working together with believers volunteering their labor for many days, had to pay for required material only.
8. Q-8: **To what benefit?**
   What will be the overall benefit of this effort?
   Example: The earth will be once again populated by human and animal life submitting to Allah (SWT).
9. Narrative or Commission:

   To transport selected living beings to safety so that life may continue after the flood, Nuh (AS) and pairs of animals and believers should be moved through some type of sea transportation system immediately after the beginning of the flood from the town's east side.

   Nuh (AS), working together with believers for many days at the cost of required material, would be able to achieve this. As a result, the earth will be once again populated by believers and animals submitting to Allah (SWT).

VIII. Goals

Goals are the currency of action in planning. In other words, planning is directed towards the accomplishment of goals. If the goals are unclear or unwanted, no amount of planning will enable us to achieve them.

Writing a goal statement is, therefore, not just an academic exercise. A well written goal statement can make the difference between success and failure. To understand how a good goal statement is constructed, let's think of it as a "being."

The heart of a goal statement is the "action verb." The head of the statement is the "responsible person" who inspires and undertakes action. The body of the statement comprises the "specific time period or date" and "cost in dollars or time." The legs of the goal statement are the "specific measurable end results" that take the responsible person performing the action where he wants to go.

We show below the "anatomy" of a goal statement and the checklists necessary to analyze it.

ANATOMY OF A GOAL STATEMENT

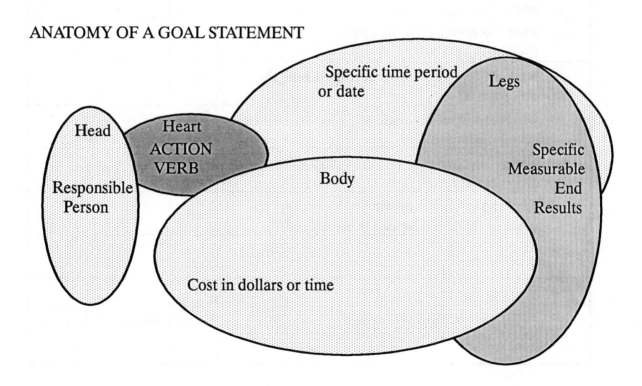

CHECKLIST
FOR ANALYZING YOUR WRITTEN GOAL

To analyze your written goals, think of the questions that follow. Answer YES or NO. To do it right, all your answers should be YES. Work on those with a NO answer.

Add your own questions in the blank cells.

QUESTION DOES THE GOAL STATEMENT STATE.....	YES/ NO?	If NO: What will you do?
⇒ what the objective, in explicit and concrete terms, is?		
⇒ whether the objective is quantifiable?		
⇒ what is to be done?		
⇒ what the objective hopes to achieve?		
⇒ who has responsibility for doing it?		
⇒ when it is to be completed?		
⇒ what the approach to be employed to achieve the objective is ?		
⇒ what the justification for accomplishing the objective is?		
⇒ what resources, in detail, are necessary for its accomplishment?		
⇒ who is to coordinate different parts of the over-all objective?		
⇒ what the criteria is by which the accomplishment of the objective can be measured?		
⇒		
⇒		
⇒		

CHECKLIST
OF COMMON DEFICIENCIES IN GOAL STATEMENTS

To analyze your written goals, think of the questions that follow. Answer YES or NO. To do it right, all your answers should be NO. Work on those with a YES answer.

Add your own questions in the blank cells.

OBJECTIVES ARE.....	YES/ NO	If YES: What will you do?
⇒ set too low to truly challenge capabilities.		
⇒ inappropriate or impossible to achieve because individuals or groups have overestimated their capabilities.		
⇒ not reflective of the responsibilities of the individual making them.		
⇒ concerned with how to do something rather than what is to be done.		
⇒ not assigned to someone with the responsibility to achieve them.		
⇒ not revised or deleted if proven unfeasible, irrelevant, or impossible.		
⇒		
⇒		

QUESTIONS FOR DISCUSSION

1. In what ways do strategic plans differ from tactical plans?
2 What role does control play in MBO planning?
3. What are the four major features of effective plans?
4. What are the five most important elements of a goal statement?

COMPREHENSION EXERCISE

IT IS TIME TO MAKE THE ANNUAL ACTION PLAN OF THE ISLAMIC OR-GANIZATION. YOU SERVE AS ITS SECRETARY. YOU EXPECT COOP-ERATION AND ASSISTANCE FROM THE EXECUTIVE COMMITTEE, FUNCTIONAL COMMITTEE MEM-BERS, AND FIELD OFFICERS. YOU HAVE AN ASSISTANT TO HELP YOU MAINTAIN RECORDS. THE ORGAN-IZATION WANTS TO NOT ONLY CON-TINUE SUCCESSFUL EXISTING PROJECTS BUT ALSO TO BREAK NEW GROUND IN SERVICES TO THE COMMUNITY. HOWEVER, THE FINANCIAL AND HUMAN RESOUR-CES AVAILABLE ARE ALREADY STRETCHED THIN.

1. *List the officials whose input you will need to make the annual action plan. Also identify the areas of input.*

2. *Make a project management schedule for this project from being assigned to the task to handing over the draft plan to the president.*

3. *Write a short introduction to the annual action plan to establish its adherence to the organization's mission.*

Fundamentals of Evaluation

LEARNING OBJECTIVES

On completing this chapter, you should be able to:
- identify how evaluation helps plan implementation
- choose appropriate types of evaluation for each case
- use different evaluation techniques
- gather data and information for controlling

I. Introduction / Concept

How often we quarrel among ourselves about whether the organization is doing well or not! We are not manipulating one another; we simply mean different things in our evaluation. This is a deficiency on which the movement has to start focusing. We have to evaluate our work systematically before we can begin meaningful improvement. More of the same is not a solution. Otherwise, we are like a manufacturer who is losing money but produces more units, thinking that he will thereby reduce his loss. He is actually increasing his loss because his cost per unit is larger than his sale price. He cannot know where he stands unless he calculates his cost. It is time we started an objective evaluation of the movement to really know where we are. Otherwise, we shall continue to be driven by whims and conjecture.

Evaluation is defined as the basic feedback mechanism that helps improve performance. We shall discuss three areas of evaluation: evaluation of organizational programs, evaluation of personnel, and evaluation of training activities.

II. Evaluation and Control of Programs

In the context of managing programs, evaluation is the key component of a broader process called controlling. Controlling is the twin aspect of planning. While planning identifies commitments to action intended for future accomplishments, controlling ensures the effective implementation of the plans. Whether it relates to a specific activity or to a whole year of programs, a plan is viable only if it identifies and specifies the necessary controls.

We can view controlling as a mechanism for detecting and correcting significant variations in the results obtained from planned activities. Its purpose is positive — to improve, not negative — to blame. It is to make things happen, not to hinder the achievement of stated objectives. Effective controlling regulates actual performance, making it proceed as expected.

Controlling consists of the following steps:
1. Finding out where we stand in our performance — that is, evaluating performance, then
2. Comparing results with expectations, which leads to
3. Approving the results, or
4. Not approving the results, and in that case
5. Applying corrective measures so that performance takes place according to what we want.

Why should we evaluate performance? There are at least three reasons:
1. To maintain what is good and to improve or remove what is not.
2. Workers need assurance that they are moving in the right direction and that we care enough to check on what they are doing.
3. Sponsors and donors want to know that their contributions are producing the desired results.

A. The Controlling Process

Establishing a standard or a yardstick is the key in controlling. Since it will be the basis for evaluation, the standard should use some form of measurement — quantitative if possible. Controlling diminishes in effectiveness as standards become inexact or confused.

The process of control, including evaluation, may be divided into three stages:

1. **Establish standards and monitor actual performance.** Effective control requires some type of measurement comparable to the terms specified in the statement of objectives. For example, if the organization's goals are stated in terms of service to the Muslim community, some index of measurement of the service received by the community is required. This may be the number of conference attendants, the number of requests for publications, the number of people who have accepted Islam, the number of successful projects, etc.

2. **Evaluate "actual" performance data** against "projected" performance. For example, did we register the projected number of attendants at our conference? Did we receive the projected number of requests for publications, or did the projected number of people accept Islam?

3. **Correct those deviations from the objectives** and targets which are outside acceptable limits by taking "corrective" action. If we answered "no" to any of the questions in the second stage, we should give feedback to the planners to either "fine tune" the human and material resources committed to the task or adjust the plan. We should ask if we fell short of implementing some part of the plan or whether our goals are unrealistic within the constraint of our resources. Should the objectives be reevaluated and restated?

Certain deviations from the standard may be within acceptable limits. Others may not be critical to the success of the operation. Therefore, to expedite controlling we should concentrate on those outstanding variations which exceed acceptable limits.

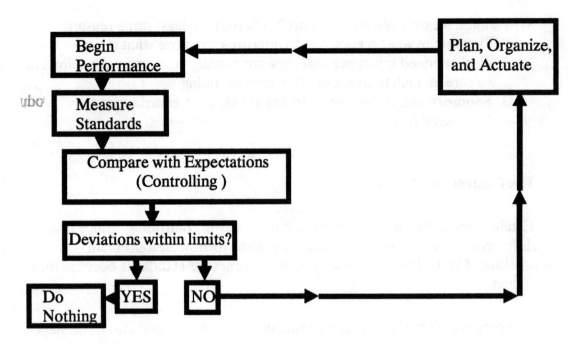

B. Types of Control

The designing of control processes and activities should be part of any good planning method.

Any activity can be controlled with respect to any or all of the following factors:
1. Quantity
2. Quality
3. Time use
4. Cost

Anything likely to go wrong and require controlling will fall under one of these categories. The most common causes of things going wrong are:
1. Human error and inadequate training
2. Unexpected circumstances
3. Equipment failure
4. Uncertainties in decisions and projections

A matrix like the one below, when used as a concluding part of the planning process, can help prepare us for effective controlling.

CONTROL FACTOR	WHAT CAN GO WRONG?	WHEN AND HOW WILL WE KNOW?	WHAT ACTION – BY WHOM?
Quantity			
Quality			
Time Use			
Cost			

We can separate the controlling process into its three phases: preventive, concurrent, and evaluative.

1. Preventive Control

Preventive controlling aims at preventing deviations from taking place in the conduct of the organization's programs. Also called preliminary or anticipatory controlling, it takes place before operations begin and includes the development of policies, procedures, and rules designed to ensure that planned activities will be carried out properly. Since people are critical to the success of Islamic work, we can exercise preventive control by optimizing their ability to perform through their selection, training, and development. The following factors come into play:

a) Recruiting and Training

First, we should attempt to recruit and train Islamic workers whose education and experience reflect their talents and commitment to perform to the best of their ability. Following selective recruitment, training programs should be arranged, taking into account the expected diverse levels of preparedness. A variety of techniques may be used to recognize the extent of leadership potential in them before assigning responsibilities. The following points must be considered in order to achieve preventive control through recruitment and training:

1. **Informal interviews** in person or on the phone dealing with subjects considered important to the organizational work at hand;
2. **Structured** pre-job or on-the-job **training** with limited responsibilities for potential volunteer workers. This will enable them to test their understanding and ability and allow others to gauge the strength of their commitment to Islamic work;
3. Following several training sessions, a **follow-up interview** to determine whether the volunteer is still as committed as before and capable of handling the expected assignments;
4. Adherence to the **Islamic code of behavior** by all workers on the premise that one must live Islam to be effective in Islamic *da'wah* .

b) Renewal of One's Consciousness of Allah

Key staff workers and volunteers should periodically engage in collective activity to renew their consciousness of Allah (SWT) through educational and spiritual experiences. The purpose is to equip them with a sense of constant purification and self-evaluation encouraged by Allah's promise of judgment and reward.

2. Concurrent Control

Concurrent controlling takes place during the "action" phase of carrying out the plans and includes the direction, monitoring, and fine tuning of activities as they occur.

3. Evaluative Control

Evaluative, or feedback, controlling analyzes data from actual performance and aims at improving performance to eliminate deviation from the organization's projections. Evaluative control focuses on the use of information about previous results to correct future deviations.

Evaluative control methods provide information "after the fact" and use such information to identify the need for corrective measures. Every program must be reviewed within the framework of the organizational objectives and evaluated for its effectiveness in attaining these objectives. Such objectives in Islamic work should be measurable and verifiable, in either quantitative or qualitative terms, to serve as yardsticks against which to measure performance.

The number of volunteers involved, the length of time they stay on, the number of Muslims they reach — all are factors that can be used to assess a program. Surveys, interviews, or informal contacts with the community served by the program can pinpoint areas where corrective action needs to be taken.

III. Evaluation of People

In programs, especially those involving volunteers, evaluation should be focused not only on the program itself but also on the people involved, including staff, volunteers, and the audience or target population.

Only Islamically acceptable considerations should influence the evaluation of an individual's performance. At the same time, without discouraging anyone from active participation in Islamic work, we should assign responsibilities according to the abilities of those involved. Commitment to Islam, the most vital ingredient of an Islamic personality, should be coupled with the ability to perform in order to be effective.

'Amr ibn Ma'di Karab and Tulayhah ibn Khalid were outstanding warriors who had no gift for statesmanship or administration. When 'Umar (RA) sent them to the conquest of Iraq under Al Nu'man ibn Muqrin, he instructed Al Nu'man not to give them any administrative position, as they were not qualified for such appointments. Ammar ibn Yasir was a companion who commanded high esteem and respect for his piety, but he had no administrative capacity or political insight. 'Umar nevertheless appointed him to the governorship of Kufah. However, 'Umar soon dismissed him because 'Ammar could not work efficiently.

Here are some broad questions which help evaluate people:
1. Are the groups for whom the program has been designed satisfied with it? Do they consider it to be of any help?
2. Does the program have adequate support from responsible persons in the organization's leadership and the community?
3. Can the volunteers involved work together on this program effectively? Does each know what is expected of him?
4. Are those committed to the program giving enough time to it both individually and as a group?

Who Evaluates Whom?

Just as almost everyone affected by a project should have an input in its planning, all those concerned should also be involved, to some degree, in its evaluation. This could include the program committee, the key workers, and the communities involved.

The head of the organization's planning committee should generally be the one to oversee the evaluations. Occasionally, an outside observer may be more effective in assessing the workers' performance, especially when a program has run into problems, the staff and volunteers are at odds, or when the community expresses dissatisfaction. Resorting for program and people evaluation to someone who is not directly involved with them, or even with the organization itself, may provide valuable and impartial expert feedback in some cases.

The key to effective control (evaluation being its most critical phase) is the development of a satisfactory psychological contract between the implementor and his or her supervisor. This contract must be rooted in a commitment to the excellence that Islam requires of all Muslims, and its fulfillment should be sought by using all Islamically acceptable methods of motivation.

Adequate authority for the person doing the evaluating and controlling is also important. Taking the proper corrective action with respect to people and programs necessitates sufficient authority to do the task.

IV. Evaluation of Training

A. Purpose

The objective of training in an Islamic organization is to enhance the commitment of individuals to *da'wah*, to develop their Islamic personality, and to equip them with the skills necessary to accomplish, with excellence, the organization's goals. The effectiveness of training itself must be evaluated to ensure that the objective is achieved with the optimum utilization of human and material resources. Towards this end, we can use evaluation to:

   a. determine whether the training achieves its objectives; if yes, to what extent
   b. assess the value of courses, seminars, and workshops
   c. identify program areas that need improvement
   d. help us decide to continue or eliminate a program
   e. identify the right audience for programs of this type and, similarly, the right program for the given audience
   f. review and reinforce key program points
   g. convince leaders and participants about the program
   h. help manage the training activity better

B. Criteria and Tools

The tools that we design and adopt to evaluate the efficacy of our training program can be based on one or more criteria relating to the target audience of the training effort. The objective is to determine certain parameters that indicate progress. Some of these criteria are:

⇒ REACTION: Determine participants' reaction to the program. Were they satisfied with it?

⇒ LEARNING: Determine what participants learned. What new knowledge or skills did they acquire and demonstrate?

⇒ ATTITUDES: Determine whether the program affected participants' attitude. How has the training changed their opinions, values, and beliefs?

⇒ BEHAVIOR: Determine the changes in behavior. How has the training affected the way participants perform on the job?

⇒ RESULTS: Determine the impact of training on the organization. How has it contributed to accomplishing organizational goals and objectives?

C. Test Methods

Comparing scores of trainees on tests given before and after a training program is one effective way of evaluating the training. Higher scores on the same test question after the training indicate an increase in skill or knowledge, or desirable changes in behavior, on the part of the trainee. Test methods can be of three types:

⇒ NORM-REFERENCED: These tests compare the trainee's scores to those of the average performance in the group, i.e., the group norm. The group must be large enough to have statistically significant averages. Test results can rank each person as being better or worse than the norm.

⇒ CRITERIA-REFERENCED: These tests measure performance according to well-defined training objectives. They focus on determining what the participants have learned based on performance standards related to those objectives. Individuals successfully meeting the standard will have mastered the skills as specified in the training program. For example, the objective for a speaker-in-training could be to speak extemporaneously for five minutes with no more than one grammatical mistake, one case of unconnected ideas, etc. These then becomes the criteria for determining if the speaker has or has not been successfully trained.

⇒ PERFORMANCE: These tests require a physical demonstration of skills or knowledge. They may be used for demonstrating skills in specific job related training (like computer use or artwork) or for performance testing in the form of role play and skill practice exercises (like problem solving or communication).

D. Test Questions

Tests for training program evaluation may contain one of several types of questions. A partial list of types includes:

⇒ MULTIPLE CHOICE: Participants are asked to choose the most accurate response from a list of possible responses.

⇒ OPEN-ENDED: No specific response is suggested, and participants are permitted to write at length to answer the question or solve the stated problem.

⇒ CHECKLIST: Participants are presented with a list of items that may or may not apply to the given situation or match corresponding items on another list. They must choose the ones that are applicable.

⇒ TWO-WAY: Also called true/false, these questions are provided with both the correct and alternative answers.

⇒ RATING SCALE: A list of items is presented to the participants, who are then asked to rank the items according to a given criteria and scale.

E. Evaluation Methods

Methods to evaluate the training acquired by the trainees include:

⇒ PAPER AND PENCIL TESTS are given in class to measure the participants' progress in learning the program content.

⇒ ATTITUDE SURVEYS are used to gather information about the participants' attitude in relation to work habits, values, relationships, etc. Surveys conducted before and after training assess any improvement in attitudes.

⇒ SIMULATION AND ON-SITE OBSERVATIONS help determine whether the participants have improved the skills they are demonstrating.

⇒ PRODUCTIVITY REPORTS measure actual improvement in performance based on job-related hard data and statistical reports.

⇒ POST-TRAINING SURVEYS, conducted periodically, measure continuing progress and performance improvement on the job.

⇒ NEEDS/OBJECTIVES/CONTENT COMPARISON is done by trainers and organizational leaders as well as trainees to determine whether program objectives were related to analyzed training needs, and if the program was relevant to the participants.

⇒ EVALUATION FORMS, when completed by the participants at the end of the program, indicate what they liked or disliked about the training. Their recommendation may be valuable.

⇒ PROFESSIONAL OPINIONS given by those with expertise in the design of instructional material assesses the program.

⇒ INSTRUCTOR EVALUATION by professional trainers helps determine the instructor's competence, skills, and effectiveness.

⇒ COST ANALYSIS is done by calculating the cost of materials, facilities, compensations, travels, etc. and assessing the value of the training to the organization per trainee.

⇒ COST-EFFECTIVENESS ANALYSIS is a comparative analysis of alternative methods/formats of training.

V. Evaluation: Obtaining Data on Performance

Data about performance may be obtained by several means, some of which are:

⇒ PERSONAL OBSERVATIONS: The personal observations approach means going to the area of activities and taking notice of what is being done.

⇒ ORAL REPORTS: Oral reports maintain certain elements of the personal observation method in that the information is transmitted orally and personal contact is included.

⇒ WRITTEN REPORTS: Written reports lend themselves to comprehensive data and are adaptable for statistics that are somewhat involved and detailed. Written reports also supply a permanent record for comparison or study at a future date. Frequently, written reports are supplemented by oral reports and direct observation.

⇒ SURVEYS: Surveys can be effective when data must be gathered from a large number of people. An evaluation form seeking feedback on specific questions regarding an activity of the organization is one way of conducting such an evaluation survey.

How to Use and Improve Evaluation

Needless to say, evaluation is a waste of time and money if the results are not used. However, it is not uncommon to see extensive evaluation being done and then stacked away without engaging in any follow up. To prevent this from happening, we should:

    a. NOT KEEP the results to ourselves, but inform all key people involved with the program;

    b. DISCUSS the evaluation through a process of *shura* using group discussion techniques, brainstorming sessions, etc;

    c. DRAW UP a plan of action to reinforce good performance and to correct deficiencies, and then ACT on that plan;

    d. NOT SHELVE the evaluation report.

To improve evaluation, we should assess our own use of the techniques and the instruments of evaluation. Did we receive the right information? Was it too little, too much, or too late? Did we use Islamically acceptable means to gather information? Asking questions such as these can help us select the right form of evaluation and identify any weakness in the way we use it.

It is advisable to evaluate our programs and projects on a regular basis instead of conducting an annual ceremonial evaluation. This will help us benefit from evaluation as we go along. Do not evaluate "bad" programs only. Evaluate the "good" ones also to determine why they are working and then act to make them even more effective.

We must also conduct follow-up evaluation to measure lasting results of the training imparted and to identify areas where learners show the greatest and the least improvement. The comparison of end-of-program evaluation responses with the follow-up responses at projected milestones yields valuable information about the degree of training retention by the trainees.

A Word of Caution about Evaluation

It may be claimed that statistics are biased, misleading, and misused. The fact of the matter is that statistical data are neutral, but politicians and others may misuse them and misquote them out of context. Hence it is crucial to be extremely careful in reaching conclusions from evaluation data. For example, if the audience is very pleased with the entertainment session and is only marginally satisfied with the Islamization of sociology session, it does not mean that we expand the first session and eliminate the second one. Our objective is not just to please our audience, which may be the aim of a secular system, or just to get people's approval and votes. We should lead public opinion in the right direction and not simply follow and become led by it.

On the other hand, we must not ignore evaluation data. These data are extremely valuable to the task of improving our performance. But we should not lose our perspective and become trapped, framed, or misled by the data of evaluation to such an extent that we treat them as sacred.

An Exercise in Evaluation

Assume you are a visitor who has just arrived at a meeting. Evaluate the meeting. Be specific about what you observe.

Positive Points:

_____
_____
_____
_____
_____

Negative Points:

_____
_____
_____
_____
_____

Other Comments:

_____
_____
_____
_____
_____

QUESTIONS FOR DISCUSSION

1. What is the role of standards in evaluation?
2. How can preventive controls improve performance?
3. What are the differences between preventive and evaluative control?
4. What factors stand out in evaluating how people perform?
5. Why is an "outsider" sometimes useful for conducting an evaluation?
6. What is the main difference between the norm-referenced methods and the criteria-referenced methods of testing?
7. How do "reaction" and "result" differ as criteria when evaluating training?
8. What are the advantages of sharing the results of an evaluation with others who are involved?
9. What kind of information does a "follow-up" evaluation yield?

COMPREHENSION EXERCISE

THE EXECUTIVE COMMITTEE HAS ASKED YOU TO EVALUATE THE PERFORMANCE OF YOUR ISLAMIC ORGANIZATION'S NEXT ANNUAL MEETING. YOU DECIDE TO PLAN AHEAD AND PUT CONTROL AND EVALUATION MECHANISMS INTO PLACE. YOU WANT TO EVALUATE MAJOR STEPS AS THEY ARE COMPLETED AND THEN GIVE CORRECTIVE FEEDBACK TO THE MEETING PLANNERS. THEN YOU WILL EVALUATE THE ON-SITE PERFORMANCE.

1. Design "standards" you would use to "control" major steps in planning the meeting.

2. Define quantifiable and measurable parameters that will enable you to reduce evaluation data to ratios which can be easily tracked.

3. Develop a chart to monitor performance and track deviations from standards.

Chapter

11

Team Building and Group Achievement

LEARNING OBJECTIVES

On completing this chapter, you should be able to:
- identify qualities that distinguish effective teams
- design working teams for specific work
- design task forces to accomplish specific goals
- recognize where committees may be most effective

«يَدُ اللّهِ مَعَ الجَمَاعَةِ، وَمَنْ شَذَّ شَذَّ إلى النَّارِ»

The Hand of Allah is with the *jama'ah*. Then, whoever singles himself out (from the *jama'ah*), will be singled out for the Hell-Fire.[1]

I. Team Building

A. What Is a Team?

Team building is a way of getting people to work with one another as a harmonious unit. Organizing such units, or teams, is one of the functions of good leadership. Working together is an Islamic directive. There are blessings and operational efficiency in individuals working together as a team.

A team is not a random collection of individuals with separate agendas, but a group of people who work together on a continuing mission with common goals and objectives. This mission is accomplished through specific and defined tasks that may be simultaneous or sequential and that may change from time to time. Members of the team may represent the whole organization or may be drawn from various areas in order to represent a variety of backgrounds, skills, and knowledge pertaining to the mission. At times, a large team may be divided into subteams. Everyone on the team is expected to take responsibility for the success of the team as a whole — the fulfillment of a specific task or the accomplishment of the mission.

The work and performance of each member and of the whole team must relate to a clearly defined objective. Both the team's composition and the leadership may change from one specific task to another. While each team member contributes particular skills and knowledge, the team as a whole, as well as each member, is responsible for the task on which it is focused. The operational responsibility to make decisions and issue commands rests with the member having the knowledge and skills for the specific task. The responsibility of the leader is to determine who that member is, not to personally assume command and then hand down a decision on every issue.

To be effective, members of the team must be trained in communicating within the team, their roles in it, and consensus formation. They must also understand the sources of power that supplement established authority. For example, a member with information, or expertise, or one likely to be referred to, attracts power to motivate action. Team members must also be trained in the theory of how organizations change and how to deal with conflict and collaboration.

---

1   Sunan al Tirmidhi.

B. How Do Teams Function Effectively?

Teams function at all levels, but are most useful at the highest levels of leadership and management. Effectiveness at this level rests on a clear understanding of and commitment to the task and who has responsibility. Adhering to certain basic rules helps teams succeed. For example:

1. The team member with primary responsibility in a given area both determines and is expected to make the final decision.
2. Conversely, a member does not make decisions with regard to matters for which he does not have primary responsibility.
3. Team members do not undermine one another publicly, even if they do not like one another, or disagree on issues and opinions.
4. A team is different from a committee which makes decisions by voting, for the team leader leads rather than chairs the effort.
5. A team has systematic and intensive communications links among its members, be they formal or informal.

C. Performance: Individual vs. Team

The success of the team is dependent on the characteristics of the individual members—the team players. Some very talented individuals are not team players by nature or due to a lack of training. Besides the necessary skills and knowledge, effective team players must be willing to sacrifice for the benefit of the team. While they contribute their best as members, they must be willing to let the leader lead. They must have the ability to see things clearly and to solve problems easily. They must be willing to try something new and exhibit a spirit of compromise in dealing with other members. In short, they have to be task oriented, not people oriented.

II. The Task Force Approach

A. A Tool for Group Accomplishment

The task force is one vehicle of effective group action. We form a task force when the problem at hand needs the input and consultation of people from a variety of interests and backgrounds. Task forces work best when challenged with a well-defined goal and invested with authority to seek a potentially acceptable solution.

To form a task force, we should:
  a. define the task: set the goal that the task force is expected to work for
  b. establish a time frame, including a deadline and milestones along the way
  c. issue an appointment document containing the above and a list of members
  d. specify a budget

To optimize the task force's performance, we should ensure that the task at hand is communicated clearly and is understood by all members in the same way. The work of the task force should be supported by giving it easy access to information in the files or with individuals. We should encourage the task force to issue periodic reports, especially if the task is long and will have a large impact, for individual task force members are likely to benefit from the feedback they receive.

Not all work destined to be done by a group instead of an individual is appropriate for a task force to handle. The task force is an effective tool for group accomplishment when the group has a common understanding and a unified sense of direction. The focus of the task force is not to weigh alternatives at that level but, given the support, to chart a course of action for moving in that direction.

B. A Case Study

One example of a task force is the Islamic Society of North America Task Force on the Structure of Islamic Work. Appointed in 1977, it laid the groundwork for the establishment of ISNA. A profile of the task force is as follows:

a) Task
To formulate a vision of a new organizational structure for Islamic work in North America

b) Members
1. Prominent Islamic workers active with MSA
2. Prominent Islamic workers with a known commitment to Islamic work but not necessarily active with MSA at the time
3. Ex-officio members, like past presidents of MSA

c) Meetings
General meeting of the task force followed by meetings of three committees focusing on specific subjects

d) Reports
1. Questionnaire in the monthly newsletter to solicit public opinion
2. Minutes of each task force committee
3. Final report on the findings

e) Recommendations
A continental organization should be formed to integrate the following organizations: MSA, MCA (a new organization of Muslim communities), and the three existing professional associations of Muslim doctors, scientists and engineers, and social scientists.

III. Functional Committees

Functional committees are the most popular way of benefitting from a group's achievement potential. By definition, such committees have assigned functions. The nature, composition, and management of committees have been discussed elsewhere in this *Guide*. Some do's and don't's of committee operation from the perspective of effective group achievement are:

DO:
1. Forge a mission statement for the committee;
2. Designate a "product" and a time frame for the committee;
3. Specify the committee's place in the organizational structure.

DON'T:
4. Use the committee to legitimize individuals' actions;
5. Bypass the committee in taking actions that lie within its jurisdiction;
6. Subject committee achievement to another committee's review unless there is a specific reason and purpose for doing so.

IV. One-man Committees

A one-man committee is one way to get the job done within an institutional framework, especially in those cases in which a larger group may not be practical. This committee should have a specific job description and a reporting responsibility. It must also engage, when necessary, in *shura* with those having relevant knowledge and experience. We must hold it accountable for its actions and for achieving the planned results.

V. Individual Roles in Group Performance

Most groups consist of individuals with varying competencies, characteristics, and interests. Each of them plays a role determined either by inherent personality or assigned function. An awareness of such roles helps one understand why the group performs as it does. Some of these roles are listed below.

GROUP TASK ROLES

Initiator-contributor	Proposes new ideas or approaches to problem solving; a person who plays this role may suggest a different approach, procedure, or methodology for the problem-solving task.
Information seeker	Asks for clarification of suggestions; an information seeker also asks for facts or other information that may help the group deal with the issues at hand.
Opinion seeker	Asks for a clarification of the values and opinions expressed by other group members.
Information giver	Provides facts, examples, statistics, and other data that pertain to the problem the group is attempting to solve.
Opinion giver	Offers beliefs or opinions about the ideas under discussion.
Elaborator	Provides examples based upon experience, personal or otherwise, that help to show how an idea or suggestion would work if the group accepted a particular course of action.
Coordinator	Tries to clarify and note relationships among the ideas and suggestions provided by others.
Orienter	Attempts to summarize what has occurred and tries to keep the group focused on the task at hand.
Evaluator critic	Makes an effort to judge the evidence and conclusions that the group suggests.
Energizer	Tries to spur the group to action and attempts to motivate and stimulate the group to greater production.
Procedural technician	Helps the group achieve its goal by performing tasks such as distributing papers, rearranging the seating, or running errands.
Recorder	Writes down all suggestions and ideas; makes a record of the group's progress.

GROUP BUILDING AND MAINTENANCE ROLES

Encourager	Offers praise, understanding, and acceptance of others.
Harmonizer	Mediates disagreements among group members.
Compromiser	Attempts to resolve conflicts by trying to find an acceptable solution to disagreements among group members.
Standard setter	Helps to set group standards and goals.
Group observer	Keeps records of the group's process and uses the information later.
Gatekeeper and expediter	Encourages less talkative group members to participate.
Follower	Basically goes along with the suggestions and ideas of other group members; serves as an audience in group discussions and decision making.

INDIVIDUAL ROLES

Aggressor	Destroys or deflates the status of other group members; may try to take credit for someone else's contribution.
Blocker	Is generally negative, stubborn, and disagreeable without apparent reason.
Recognition seeker	Seeks the spotlight by boasting and reporting on his or her personal achievements.
Self-confessor	Uses the group as an audience to report personal feelings and observations.
Loner	Lacks involvement in the group's process; lack of interest may result in cynicism, nonchalance, or other behavior that indicates a lack of enthusiasm for the group's activities.

Dominator	Makes an effort to assert authority by manipulating group members or attempting to take over the entire group; may use flattery or assertive behavior to dominate the discussion.
Help-seeker	Tries to evoke a sympathetic response from others; often expresses insecurity or feelings of low self-worth.
Special interest pleader	Speaks for a special group or organization that best fits his or her own biases to serve an individual need.

VI. The Nuts and Bolts of Teamwork

Teamwork does not just happen. It has to be organized and nourished through effective leadership and management. In the preceding sections we have discussed a number of approaches to building teams. In this section we will focus on some practical pointers that help achieve results through working in groups on a daily basis. First we need to know about the group itself.

A. Who Are We and What Do We Want?

It may be an easy question to answer in the singular form, i.e., Who am I and What do I want? But in the group form, it is a challenging question. Try it out in a group session. It is not enough to say we are Muslims; there are more than one billion of us. What is our justification for forming a distinct organization? How are we different from other Muslims? We must have a good reason. The second part of the question — What do we want? — is more involved than the first part. You will be amazed at the extent to which the objectives of our organization are unclear, how fuzzy they are, how much we differ in our understanding of them, and most importantly, how far apart we are in our priorities and perceptions of a plan of action. This will provide you with a yardstick to measure the degree of disunity in our thought. The major cause of members leaving the organization is differences in thought and opinion.

Thinking together leads to finding common goals and a sense of direction. Next comes the task of moving forward. Who should lead the march?

B. Who Can Make It to the Top?

People respond to this question in different ways. They may say: the smartest, the strongest, the best communicator, the manipulator, the most pious, the most knowledgeable, and so on. When a number of people at the top were polled, it was found that the most important common trait among them was the ability to work well with others. This implies being a team player, possessing a team spirit, and having the ability to get along with superiors, colleagues, and subordinates. Such a person tolerates differences, listens, and tries to understand others. He both modifies his position if he is convinced of the need and readily admits his mistakes. He has an open mind and does not behave stereotypically. He seeks wisdom and grasps it even if it comes from his opponent. One person working in harmony with another does not add up to two only; they become eleven.

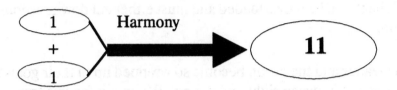

Moreover, three persons become:

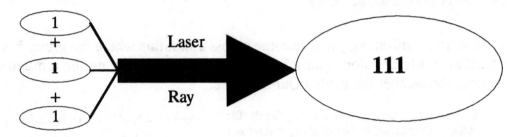

This is what marks the difference between a band of light rays that disperses in all directions and a coherent laser beam. A laser is no more than harmonious rays of light operating at similar frequencies to create intense energy. Such a laser ray can penetrate thick concrete and iron walls.

Making it to the top does not mean making it alone. Delegation, trust, and feedback are keys to involving the group. However brilliant, the leader always needs help to perform at his or her best.

C. The Overload Disease

"Overload" has become a chronic disease in our organizations. Either the leader is selfishly doing everything himself or others around him are lazy. Whenever symptoms of overload appear in a leader, the group must pause, rethink the situation, and solve the overload problem. The most efficient and organized person can be rendered unproductive and disorganized through heavy overload.

The remedy to overload is not to have more muscles but to distribute the load appropriately, train the second-line leadership, and do better planning and prioritizing. Overloaded leaders must be relieved and given some vacation time to replenish their energy and vitality. Otherwise they may become dull, sick, and eventually collapse. If the leaders lose their energy and luster, the movement will suffer tremendously.

How do we detect an overload? We should look for signs that the leader is not fully aware of the major aspects of all the projects under him and starts losing control. He is not expected to follow up on daily details, but he should be in control of all the significant factors. If he is not, he is overloaded and must either cut down responsibility or get additional help.

Sometimes the leader and the group become so wrapped up in their goals that they gloss over the distinction between right and wrong. Watch out for this trap.

D. Always Do the Right Thing!

In your organization, you may come across a situation where the group has to make an unfavorable decision against someone. He may or may not be a member of the group. Remember the golden Qur'anic rule:

O you who believe! Stand out firmly for Allah, as witnesses to fair dealing, and let not the hatred of others make you swerve to wrong and depart from justice. Be just: that is next to piety: and fear Allah. For Allah is well acquainted with all that you do (5:8).

يَٰٓأَيُّهَا ٱلَّذِينَ ءَامَنُواْ كُونُواْ قَوَّٰمِينَ لِلَّهِ شُهَدَآءَ بِٱلۡقِسۡطِ وَلَا يَجۡرِمَنَّكُمۡ شَنَـَٔانُ قَوۡمٍ عَلَىٰٓ أَلَّا تَعۡدِلُواْ ٱعۡدِلُواْ هُوَ أَقۡرَبُ لِلتَّقۡوَىٰ وَٱتَّقُواْ ٱللَّهَ إِنَّ ٱللَّهَ خَبِيرُۢ بِمَا تَعۡمَلُونَ (سورة المائدة)

Always seek justice and fairness in your verdict against someone.

A good practice is to put yourself in his place and pass your judgment carefully. This is empathy. Do not be misled by emotions or group euphoria to form a hasty opinion. You will regret it later. At some point in the future, Allah may put you in the same position, and any injustice you cause will come back to you in kind. Make sure in all such cases that you follow Islamic manners and etiquette. Never deviate from them. You will find that Allah will always be on your side if you have enough patience (*sabr*).

Have you noticed how dictators, cheaters, criminals, thieves, and gangs get rid of one member unjustly, then another and another until they eat themselves up? Unjust practices used by the group against outsiders usually end up being used against insiders as well. Avoid using double standards; they will end up being used on you!

In order to appreciate the merit of someone else's opinion, imagine yourself to be on his or her side of the table.

As the group moves forward, knowing itself and its leadership and acting rightly, it must attend to details with careful planning.

E. Everybody's Responsibility Is Nobody's Responsibility

This happens when we leave the responsibility of doing something to everybody. It is very common in our meetings that tasks do not get assigned to specific individuals. They then remain undone because every one thinks that someone else is responsible for doing them. Remember the story of the king who loved expensive honey and wanted to test how much people loved him. He put an empty barrel in the city square and announced that any one loving him should pour one cup of pure honey into the barrel. One person thought that since every one else was pouring honey he could pour in a cup of water instead. After all, one cup of water would not be noticed in a barrel of honey. When the king opened the barrel later, it was full of water. It seems everyone had the same idea.

This story teaches us that responsibility is personal. You cannot excuse yourself from it by thinking that others will perform. The Prophet (SAW) expressed it this way:

«كُلُّكُمْ رَاعٍ وَكُلُّ رَاعٍ مَسْئولٌ عَنْ رَعِيَّتِهِ»

Every one of you is a shepherd and every one is responsible for what he is shepherd of.[1]

---

1   Sunan al Tirmidhi, Sunan Abu Dawud, Sahih al Bukhari, and Sahih Muslim.

Action Point

GETTING

THE

BEST

OUT

OF

PEOPLE!

A major obstacle in our teamwork is the pervasive feeling that unless we agree with a person 100%, we cannot work with him or her. Since this does not exist in reality, we find that very few groups among us are working harmoniously. In the majority of cases, one person dominates and dictates his way of thinking and approach on the group. Our institutions are victims of one-man management styles. No nation can progress with this kind of mentality. We have to realize that each person is different. We have about 90% areas of common agreement among ourselves. We should make these agreements the foundation of our cooperation. Today we make the 10% of difference a strong foundation for our disunity.

Moreover, nobody is perfect. Everyone has strengths and weaknesses. The movement should focus on points of strength and put aside points of weakness. This way the dynamic equation of the total group effort becomes the sum of all individual strengths—a very powerful resultant force indeed.

Remember that we shall not find the excellent worker or leader who is devoid of all shortcomings. If we think that someone has it all, it means that we have not yet discovered the negative sides of his personality!

We have to generate a new attitude within ourselves, one which focuses on the strengths of our brothers, and then work with them and complement them to minimize their weaknesses. Such an attitude is a necessary condition for team spirit and group work.

REMEMBER!

IF TWO PEOPLE ALWAYS AGREE WITH ONE ANOTHER, YOU NEED ONLY ONE OF THEM!

A FORMIDABLE CHALLENGE IN THE FIFTEENTH *HIJRI* CENTURY

The single most important deficient aspect of Islamic work in the fourteenth *hijri* century was TEAM SPIRIT!

Team spirit requires much more than knowledge, sincerity, dedication, and sacrifice. It is nourished by a much higher level of understanding, appreciation, and *hikmah* (wisdom). It functions among individuals who are able to sacrifice their own personal differences and learn how to work with others effectively. When Islamists attain team spirit, we can herald the onset of a true modern Islamic civilization. Nothing can stop it then! It will only be a matter of time, because the blessings and mercy of Allah are with the team-spirited brothers and sisters!

Question: What theme do you see developing here?

Answer: _____
          (12 words or less)

QUESTIONS FOR DISCUSSION

1. Who makes decisions in a team? Why?
2. What qualities can help a team member be effective?
3. What are the differences between a team, a task force, and a committee?
4. When is a one-man committee suitable for group work?

COMPREHENSION EXERCISE

IT HAS BEEN OBVIOUS FOR SOME TIME THAT MEMBERS OF YOUR ISLAMIC ORGANIZATION ARE NOT SATISFIED WITH THE DELIVERY OF MEMBERSHIP SERVICES LIKE SPEAKERS, PUBLICATIONS, LITERATURE, ANNOUNCEMENTS, ETC. YOU ARE DETERMINED TO FIND OUT WHAT IS WRONG, WHY, AND WHAT CAN BE DONE TO GAIN THE MEMBERS' SATISFACTION. YOU WANT TO SET UP A GROUP TO ACCOMPLISH THIS GOAL. THERE ARE NO CONSTITUTIONAL RESTRICTIONS.

1. Decide which type of group you should set up to get the best results.

2. Write a model letter of appointment containing all that is required for effective group achievement.

3. Prepare a chart of members and of similarly qualified nonmembers who are relevant to the type of group you have selected.

Part Three

Skill Enhancement and Self-Development

To be effective in accomplishing their objectives, leaders as well as followers must acquire certain skills. Some skills are individual, like public speaking, writing, giving advice, listening, and managing time. Others are group skills, like forming and chairing committees, arranging and chairing meetings, using audiovisuals, talking to the media, and establishing local organizations. All of these are discussed in this part of the *Guide*.

By no means is this a complete inventory of skills that set an effective *da'iyah* apart from others. One must always be in a learning frame of mind to identify and acquire whatever it takes to get the job done.

The last chapter of this part deals with additional aspects of self-development. Through a lively string of practical pointers, it reminds the user of the many facets of the Islamic character. The conscientious trainee should use it to develop his own action plan for growth and self-development.

PART THREE: SKILL ENHANCEMENT AND SELF-DEVELOPMENT

Chapter 12

On Public Speaking

I. Planning and Preparation of Content
  A. Step-by-Step Approach
  B. Increasing Effectiveness
II. Delivery Techniques: Highlights
  A. Practice
  B. Body Language, Voice, and Visual Contact
  C. Stopping to Talk
  D. The Speaker's Self
III. Questions and Answers: Challenge and Opportunity
IV. Models of Effective Public Speaking
V. Public Speaking Checklist

LEARNING OBJECTIVES

On completing this chapter, you should be able to:
- identify the elements of a good speech
- know how to strengthen weaknesses in your presentation
- deliver an effective public speech
- critically review speeches delivered by others

Speaking in public to a friendly or a hostile audience is one of the most important tasks of leadership. The purpose of speaking may vary from communicating information to changing opinions to motivating action. Basic principles of preparing and delivering a speech are common to all situations. These will be discussed below.

I. Planning and Preparation of Content

A. Step-by-Step Approach

1. Preliminary Considerations

a) *Know the audience*

The first step in planning a speech is to know our audience. For example, we should know the group or causes represented in the audience, who has already spoken to it, and what their various positions on the subject at hand are. We should seek information on whether there are "troublemakers" in the audience as well as "friends" sympathetic to the speaker's views.

To gain rapport with the audience and thus improve communication, arrive early and stay late. This permits us to meet early arrivals and perhaps discover allies in the audience. We can also talk with those strongly opposed, enabling us to mention their names and concerns in the presentation, thus showing respect for their opinions. We can also use this opportunity to reinforce points made in the speech.

b) *Establish credibility*

Our audience will respond to us if we are credible in their eyes. To establish credibility, the speaker must have expertise in the subject he is addressing, be believable in his presentation, and act in a manner that makes the audience like him. When the Prophet (SAW) was ready to tell the people of Makkah that he had been chosen to deliver Allah's Message to them, he called them to gather around a high place in Makkah and said: "Tell me, if I give you the news that an army is about to come from the foot of this mountain, will you believe me?" All said: "Yes," for so far they had not experienced any kind of lie from him. Having thus established credibility, he said: "I warn you of a severe punishment which is before you, if you disbelieve."[1]

2. How to Structure the Speech

What follows is a general model outline of a speech. However, it may not always be suitable, as a specific occasion or topic may dictate a different structure. In each case,

---

1   Sahih al Bukhari.

the aim should be to prepare a well-rounded and integrated speech which conveys the message clearly.

a) State the subject

State the subject, describe its elements, and explain the topic. Explain why the issue is significant for the ummah and why the audience should be concerned. State what we expect to achieve in the speech.

b) Analyze the subject

Explain the historical background and state the lessons from the past. It is more effective to arrange the material in a topical order than a chronological order. The audience must clearly understand why the problem came to be a problem today.

c) Report previous solutions

Review specific cases, if possible, in the Muslim as well as non-Muslim past and discuss solutions then suggested in terms of their successes and failures. If the problem is entirely new, discuss similarities with past problems.

d) Diagnose and suggest solutions

Begin to creatively diagnose the problem by invoking the Qur'anic principles under which the search for a solution may be conducted. Search the Sunnah for clarification or elaboration of those principles. Examine their applicability to the present and to the Muslim ummah or Muslim individuals. Consider the reinterpretation (ijtihad) of the Qur'anic legacy as an attempt at a solution. If needed, suggest creative new elements in the search for one.

e) Conclude

Normally end the presentation on three notes: **First**: the Islamic expression of humbleness, the crown of the critical attitude of mind, which is the acknowledgement that human knowledge is but little. **Second**: the optimism that Allah (SWT) has established a cause for everything and, with His help and guidance, the ummah will discover that cause and change the world affected by it for better. **Third**: salaam and thanks to the organizers and the audience who lent us their ears.

A well-planned talk begins with a satisfactory introduction, covers the main points, draws a proper conclusion or summary, and ends within the allotted time period. We should plan our time to present all our speech, cutting down when necessary on ideas and data within each part of the speech.

B. Increasing Effectiveness

1. Continuity

Before we deliver our speech, we must decide how we are going to move from one idea to the next. Our speech should have continuity and should flow smoothly from beginning to end. However, the need for transitions is not just an artistic one. Although we know in our own mind how and what we are saying relates logically to our last point, that relationship may not be so clear to our audience. Our listeners are more likely to grasp what we are saying if they can see how our information falls into place instead of having to stop and figure it out for themselves.

There are two kinds of transitions we can employ: rhetorical, which is a sentence or phrase that links what was said before with that which is to come, and vocal, which is effected chiefly through a change in volume and pitch. An example of the first kind will be the transition from the first paragraph to the second in the example below:

> "... This leads to the conclusion that hunger is a primary concern of much of the world's population."

> "Hunger, though, is not a result of the shortage of food alone ..."

2. Diction

Always use the best diction possible. Nothing will mark us more quickly as immature than the use of immature language—words such as "swell," "guy," and "stuff." The use of contemporary vernacular can sometimes be an effective means of establishing rapport with an audience that is in tune with it, but it should be used selectively.

There are a few "shortcuts to eloquence" that work well when used judiciously:
⇒ repetition of key points (preferably repetitions of three);
⇒ use of rhythmic tempo in choice of words;
⇒ alliteration to give a beat to the speech;
⇒ clever lines that express a point—people remember them;
⇒ similes, metaphors, and analogies to convey complex ideas;
⇒ statistics that can lend authenticity to the position;
⇒ active voice and action verbs that appeal to the emotions as well as to the intellect;
⇒ dynamic attention-getting opening statements and memorable conclusions that drive home the central message.

On the other hand, some sayings must be avoided. For example, we should not use the following phrases unless we really mean them:

"I am not sure but I think ..."   "Always"
"So far as I know ..."   "Never "
"I believe that ..."   "Everybody"
"We should know ..."   "Nobody "

3. Notes

If we prepare notes to help deliver the speech, it is best not to stray from them even if we feel that the presentation is going well. It is more than likely that we shall suddenly find ourselves floundering, either because of unconfirmed information or because of overelaborate figures of speech, i.e., mixed metaphors.

We should not read continuously from our notes, but we do not need to attempt to hide them either. Our attitude should be that we have taken the trouble to prepare our talk and we are covering all of the points that we wish to make. Furthermore, if we have any trouble knowing what to do with our hands, we could solve the problem by holding our lecture notes.

II. Delivery Techniques: Highlights

The best speeches can be ruined by an inadequate delivery. The Prophet Musa (AS), preparing to address the Pharaoh's court, prayed to Allah (SWT):

O My Lord! Expand my breast, and ease my task for me; and remove the knot from my tongue that they may understand my saying (20:25-28).

قَالَ رَبِّ ٱشْرَحْ لِى صَدْرِى ۞ وَيَسِّرْ لِىٓ أَمْرِى ۞ وَٱحْلُلْ عُقْدَةً مِّن لِّسَانِى ۞ يَفْقَهُواْ قَوْلِى (سورة طه)

Delivering a speech involves the whole person of the speaker. We need to pay attention to our body, our voice, and our eyes, and direct our whole being to the task of communicating with the audience. This requires observing a few rules and a great deal of practice. Some considerations are discussed below.

A. Practice

We may spend many hours researching the material and preparing our outline, and then produce only a mediocre speech due to our failure to take the easiest step of all — practicing our delivery. Perhaps we feel that rehearsing a speech will change our presentation from honest communication into a "performance" or an "acting situation." A good speech should be natural and an honest reflection of our personality.

However, remember that public speaking is structured, and the goal of structured communication is to effectively convey the greatest amount of information in the shortest possible time. We do not do our audience any favor by taking up their time with dull, long-winded discourses; they probably will not listen to us if we do so. For that matter, practice in structured speaking will stand us in good stead in unstructured, informal discourse as well. The more clearly and succinctly we can say what we have to say, without a lot of irrelevant sidetracking, the more people in any situation are going to listen to us with interest.

Sometimes, tape record the entire presentation in order to review and learn from it. You will be pleasantly surprised at how much you learn from listening to your own speech. Try it! Tape recording has another advantage—you can give the tape to others for evaluation.

B. Body Language, Voice, and Visual Contact

1. Body Position

a) Gesturing

Just as we need not feel glued to one spot, we should not feel that our elbows are glued to our ribs. If we can, we should rehearse our speech in front of a mirror. Experiment with different kinds of gestures to see how they look. Do not plan them for specific points in the speech. If we bring them in on cue, that is exactly how they look: acting unnaturally! The important thing is to overcome the reluctance we may have to use any gestures at all.

b) Standing

We must appear confident, especially during that all-important moment of approaching the lectern. During the speech, body language should be consistent with the words being spoken. Above all, we had better learn how to stand — on both feet. Standing with our weight on one foot is not forbidden. However, when we do that, we tend to shift to the other one and are likely to end up rocking back and forth without being aware of it. Our audience will be aware of it. With a firm foundation, we are less likely to distract either ourselves or our audience with awkward poses.

There will certainly be occasions when we can speak to a group while we are seated or even perched on the edge of a desk or table. Generally speaking, though, avoid the temptation to lean on things. Tables, chairs, and lecterns are not crutches. To speak effectively, we should display a certain amount of physical vitality; leaning on the furniture gives the impression that we just cannot summon up the necessary energy. Once behind the lectern or the desk, do not feel that you have taken root there. Feel free to move around as long as the movement has some purpose. Do not pace the floor just to dissipate energy, but do move when there is a reason to do so. We may want to walk to the chalkboard to write something down or turn once in a while to face a part of the audience that cannot see the speaker too well.

One particular reason to step out from behind the lectern and move toward the audience is to close the distance between the speaker and the audience in order to emphasize an important point. It has long been known that the effectiveness of communication varies with the distance between the speaker and the audience. As the distance between the speaker and audience decreases, a greater impression of intimacy and a special effect is created.

2. Visual Contact

We hear all kinds of advice about how to maintain good eye contact, but the only way it can really be done is to look people in the eye. This should be done within the guidelines of Islamic modesty that require us not to fix our gaze when facing persons of the opposite sex. When facing our audience, we look directly at each person; as soon as the person we are looking at returns our glance, move on to the next one. Do not focus over the tops of people's heads or stare off into space. Our faraway gaze will make them feel that we are not really in touch with them. Above all, we should not fix our eyes on our notes or on the lectern. Remember, we are talking to people, not just projecting our voice into the room. One of the things we must get used to is that public speaking requires more volume than we normally use. We may be mumbling because we are not really sure of our material and are afraid someone might hear us. If so, we might do well to review our material.

Keep in visual contact with the audience. Try to speak to each person or at least each area of the audience, like a speaker on TV who seems to speak through the screen to each individual in his audience. It helps to write "VC" (visual contact) on the top of two or three lines of our trigger cards or lecture notes to remind us of this most important element of communication.

Under certain circumstances, it may help to maintain eye contact with those in the audience believed to be supportive or neutral and to avoid those known to be most adamantly opposed.

3. Voice

a) Volume

Speeches are made to be heard. Whether a microphone is being used or not, we should make a deliberate assessment of the volume level to which we must raise our voice in order to be heard clearly. A reminding mark on our lecture notes can prompt us to address our opening sentences to the persons sitting at the back left- and right-hand corners of the hall, as they are the farthest from the speaker.

b) Pitch

Pitch problems can be difficult to overcome, but the first step is to identify them. There are two basic kinds: the monotone and the patterned pitch. The former is tiring to listen to, like the same key sounded over and over on a piano. As a result, it becomes difficult to concentrate on what is being said even when the speaker's material is good. A speaker with a patterned pitch has what is known as a "sing-song" voice. It goes up or down at regular intervals, and the audience tends to concentrate on the pattern rather than on the words being spoken. This problem is often a result of having memorized the speech. A tape recorder is helpful for identifying the pattern and practicing to overcome it. Vocal emphasis may be important for the sake of oratory, but it is often essential for clarifying our meaning. Vocal emphasis entails some kind of vocal change to set off what we are emphasizing from the surrounding material.

c) Rate

People can listen faster than we can talk (on the average, 800 words per minute vs. 250), and if they are left for long without something to listen to their attention will wander. We shall probably have to speak faster than we usually do in casual conversation. There is no one rate of delivery that is best for all speakers, but we should talk as fast as we can without stumbling over words or slurring syllables. In this, clarity is important; every word and every syllable must be understood.

Enunciation is at the heart of good delivery. We must pronounce each word clearly and avoid distracting habitual filler words like "I mean," "you know," "uh," "hmm," and "em."

d) Pause

Most people are used to absorbing detail and new information from the printed page. Therefore, it is important that we allow our talk to breathe. If we make a particularly important point, pause slightly longer than usual at the end of the sentence to permit the audience to absorb the information. Pausing at critical points can add punch and drama.

C. Stopping to Talk

For some reason, many people who are reluctant to undertake a speech are equally reluctant to stop talking as their lecture nears its end. They wish to make sure that the audience has fully understood and appreciated the various points they have made and start a repeat performance with the words "What I have been trying to say is..." While a brief recapitulation of the main points, preferably by means of a chart of diagrams, can be most useful, an impromptu rambling summary with many repetitions of "Finally, brothers and sisters...." can ruin an otherwise successful talk. We should, therefore, stick to our planned delivery and refrain from saying "Finally ..." or "In conclusion..." more than once. To safeguard against this, plan a definite beginning and ending to the speech, making sure that both of them contain a strong element of dramatization.

D. The Speaker's Self

Now that we have some ideas about how to put our speech across, let us give some thought to the factors involved in putting ourselves across. The message our audience receives and its willingness to accept it is going to be determined in large measure by its perception of the speaker as a person. To be an effective speaker, we must not only possess the qualities that will win the audience's respect, but also project them. The characteristics of ethos are elusive, but there are some fundamental points on which the audience will base its judgment, such as sincerity, affability, and energy.

Communication is whole-body interaction. It is essential that the whole self — body, voice, expressions — communicates a feeling of excitement, interest, and enthusiasm. If we are not excited, interested, and enthusiastic about the subject, we have chosen the wrong subject or are the wrong persons to speak on it. The audience is quick to recognize this deficiency and soon loses rapport with the speaker and, in a sense, turns itself off to the speech.

Our purpose is not just to speak, but to communicate. If we are not communicating with our audience, we have a problem. As a speaker, we are part of every speech we give, and it is up to us to develop the individual style that will make us as effective as our words.

III. Questions and Answers: Challenge and Opportunity

The time for taking questions from the audience after a speech can be a challenging opportunity to accomplish any remaining goals of the presentation. If we do a good job gathering "intelligence" on the audience, we can often anticipate certain questions.

To neutralize hostility, restate the question without the questioner's emotionally loaded words. Though answers should normally be short, if a question presents the opportunity to offer new information, do so. To gain a broader perspective on this subject, see the chapter entitled "How to Chair a Meeting."

IV. Models of Effective Public Speaking

The Prophet (SAW) set up models to emulate. His public speaking abilities were of no small consequence in the deliverance of the message he carried. Among the many outstanding examples to learn from are his Last Sermon and his speech to the Ansar after the campaigns of Hunayn and Ta'if. His companions also spoke brilliantly. One of the many good examples to study is the speech of the leader of the Muslim immigrants in the court of the Abyssinian emperor. These and other such discourses are available in published Islamic literature. One easy reference is the *Life of Muhammad* by M. Haykal. Read these speeches and analyze them in the light of this chapter.

Action Point

PURE DISHONESTY

In 1973 at the Annual Conference of FOSIS (Federation of Student Islamic Societies) in Manchester, England, a brother was translating into English for a speaker. The translator said several times: "The speaker is wrong and the right thing is what I am saying." He did not convey a true and faithful translation of the speech. He was stabbing the speech before even transmitting it to the audience. This is gross dishonesty and a misuse of trust. A translator's job is to translate the contents accurately regardless of his own opinions. If he must express his own opinions, he must indicate that clearly and give ample chance to the speaker to respond.

Speech organization:
A GENERAL RULE OF THUMB IS:
- *Tell them what you are going to tell them;*
- *Tell them;*
- *Tell them that you've told them!*

V. Public Speaking Checklist

How to Use: You can use the checklist during your practice or after the speech, from memory or while watching a videotape of the speech. You can also have someone else listen to your speech and complete the checklist for you. This might be more effective and objective, since you may not be able to accurately assess your own behavior and style.

How to Score: Mark 1 for YES or 0 for NO in the boxes below. A total score of 17 or above indicates good speech preparation and delivery skills. A score of 11 or less calls for serious planned effort for improvement.

1. PLANNING

Is my talk well-planned in terms of:
[ ] A satisfactory introduction?
[ ] Coverage of the main points?
[ ] A proper conclusion or summary?
[ ] The allotted time?

2. DELIVERY

a. Poise

Do I convey poise in terms of:
[ ] Looking relaxed and in control?
[ ] Standing straight, not rigidly, with weight distributed evenly and feet comfortably apart?
[ ] Dressing comfortably and appropriately for the occasion and the audience?
[ ] Approaching the speaker's podium calmly and pausing before starting?

b. Movement

Do I convey self-confidence in terms of:
[ ] Using deliberate full-body movements to change mood, draw attention to visual aids, reinforce ideas, and avoiding random, nervous movements?
[ ] Gesturing naturally to reinforce comments and refraining from nervous and frozen gestures?
[ ] Having an animated facial expression?

3. VOICE AND VISUAL CONTACT

Do I employ my voice and eyes to communicate in terms of:
[ ] Speaking in an audible voice?
[ ] Speaking in a warm, pleasant tone?
[ ] Varying the rate and tone at an effective pitch?
[ ] Avoiding speaking too slowly or too quickly?
[ ] Maintaining visual contact with the audience?
[ ] Looking at the whole audience?

4. SELF-PROJECTION

Do I come across effectively in terms of:
[ ] Speaking with expressiveness and enthusiasm?
[ ] Using notes effectively?
[ ] Using visual aids when warranted?
[ ] Noting any good or bad mannerisms?
[ ] Making a positive delivery?

EVALUATION OF SPEAKERS — A SHORT FORM

Answer each question by grading the indicated behavior on a scale from 1 to 5 with 5 being the most desirable standard in the indicated behavior. Circle the grade.

1. Voice level	1	2	3	4	5
2. Eye contact	1	2	3	4	5
3. Physical projection	1	2	3	4	5
4. Body motion	1	2	3	4	5
5. Subject matter	1	2	3	4	5
6. Time control	1	2	3	4	5
7. Starting and concluding	1	2	3	4	5
8. Tidiness of podium	1	2	3	4	5
9. Dress	1	2	3	4	5
10. Inducement of audience	1	2	3	4	5
11. General performance	1	2	3	4	5

Action Point

DON'T SHOOT YOURSELF IN THE FOOT!

In 1973 I was invited to a church at Logansport, Indiana, to talk about Islam. Seven priests spoke about their denominations first, then a Hindu professor of electrical engineering spoke about Hinduism. He started by saying: "Although I am a Hindu, I know nothing about Hinduism. So, I will read to you a few chapters from a book written by a Christian American lady who spent a few years in India." Towards the end he said: "Finally, I shall read you this chapter...Finally, I will read another chapter...Finally, I will read you one more page." When he said: "Finally, I will read you this paragraph," no one believed him because his "finally" actually meant "not finally." The audience was extremely bored with his speech.

The point in all this is that, no matter what the circumstances are, do not pass judgment on, or make confessions about your presentation like: I am sorry I had no time to prepare; my speech is not going to be good; the organizers only told me to speak now; I do not know much about the subject; you the audience can make a better speech, etc. Avoid all of the above, enter into the subject directly, and do your best. Do not grade yourself before people; they will give you the grade. You may deliver the best presentation without your knowing it.

It is reported that the third khalifah, 'Uthman ibn 'Affan, once could not deliver the Friday *khutbah* from the *minbar*. As he was stepping down, he said: "Allah accomplishes things at the hands of the ruler which cannot be accomplished through the Qur'an alone." Hearing this, the audience exclaimed: "Had he said this on the *minbar*, it would have been one of the best *khutab* ever delivered."

Action Point

TRAIN PEOPLE ON HOW NOT TO SPEAK

We normally emphasize to the trainees how to speak. Sometimes it is more important to teach ourselves how to stop speaking. For example, if you are delivering a speech and some people are under the rain, or exposed to the hot sun, you must be very brief and cut your talk to a minimum. Similarly, if the air conditioner has stopped and the atmosphere is suffocating the audience, you must stop speaking. Or if you are late and the program chairman instructs you to stop, you must heed and abide. Unfortunately, some of us become stubborn and insist on delivering the speech in full without regard to the changes in the situation. This is where dynamic thinking and continuous updating of the program is essential. We often miss the objective. What matters is not to deliver the message, but for the audience to receive it. If we have a package to deliver and we do not find the right addressee, we don't just throw it away; we keep it and deliver it at another convenient time to ensure it gets to the recipient.

Action Point

"I Can Only Speak of Rat Poison."

A rat poison specialist went to a social party with his wife. After a while he was standing alone. His wife approached him saying: "Why don't you socialize with other people? Go and talk to them." He replied: "Whenever I speak with them about rat poison, they turn away and leave me."

Unfortunately, he could only speak about his speciality and nothing else. The *da'iyah* has to be highly diversified and well-read. He should be able to initiate and maintain a good conversation on a variety of subjects beyond his major and minor areas of speciality. This will give him the right image of a concerned and caring member of society. He must have a deep interest in what goes on around him. He should have some hobbies, sports involvement, and membership in several organizations.

EXERCISE

Ask someone to deliver a speech full of mistakes, both in content and delivery, and let the audience compete to count the maximum number of mistakes.

Use the following outline to identify mistakes and remedies. Count one point for each mistake and one point for each remedy identified.

CONTENT:

Mistake #1 _____

Remedy _____

Mistake #2 _____

Remedy _____

Mistake #3 _____

Remedy _____

DELIVERY:

Mistake #1 _____

Remedy _____

Mistake #2 _____

Remedy _____

Mistake #3 _____

Remedy _____

QUESTIONS FOR DISCUSSION

1. What is the role of credibility in speech making?
2. What is an effective way to end a speech? Give an example.
3. What is rhetorical transition? Give an example.
4. What are the possible disadvantages of practicing a speech? How can you minimize them?
5. Why is visual contact important in speech making?
6. How does pitch affect delivery? Give examples.

COMPREHENSION EXERCISE

AS THE NEW PRESIDENT OF YOUR ISLAMIC ORGANIZATION, YOU ARE SCHEDULED TO ADDRESS THE FIRST MEETING OF MEMBERS. THE GROUP IS GENERALLY FRIENDLY BUT NOT MANY KNOW YOU WELL. YOU MUST COVER NOT ONLY ORGANIZATIONAL BUSINESS BUT ALSO THE GENERAL WELFARE OF THE COMMUNITY. IT IS YOUR OPPORTUNITY TO ESTABLISH CONFIDENCE IN YOUR LEADERSHIP AND SOLICIT FUNDING SUPPORT. YOU HAVE ONLY A SHORT TIME TO PREPARE AND SPEAK.

1. Make a checklist of specific actions you must take to prepare your speech.

2. List specific steps you would take to get to know your audience before the speech and establish your credibility during it.

3. List three major points you would make. For each point, state how you put the needed emphasis on it through a specific delivery technique.

4. Write a concise ending to your speech.

Chapter

13

Towards Better Writing

LEARNING OBJECTIVES

On completing this chapter, you should be able to:
- identify the elements of good writing
- write more effectively
- critically review writing by others

I. Purpose

Writing is a many-faceted tool. We write to inform, persuade, inspire, or even threaten others. It is important to write well because writing can:

⇒ make ideas and information permanent in a form easily accessible for reference and duplication;

⇒ move others to act according to its message;

⇒ free up the writer's time by enabling his ideas to be duplicated and distributed among wider audiences;

⇒ guide and direct learners by communicating new or different ideas in a precise manner;

⇒ establish credibility and authority by introducing the writer to the reader;

⇒ increase chances for success by precisely and permanently spelling out choices or courses of action;

⇒ be a very effective means of *da'wah*.

As a tool for communication with others, writing must be sharpened through practice. Our choice of words and subject matter are very important in making our writing not only clear and precise but also understandable and interesting.

II. Problems

Among the most common mistakes that writers make are:
⇒ researching and collecting too little or too much data
⇒ organizing the subject matter poorly
⇒ failing to revise the first draft
⇒ using words or sentences that are too long
⇒ expressing a writer-centered point of view
⇒ directing the writing to the wrong audience

In addition to the above, there are mistakes of grammar and style that include:
⇒ redundancy
⇒ run-on sentences
⇒ cliches and overused expressions
⇒ lack of structure
⇒ archaic language
⇒ inadequate introduction and conclusion
⇒ weak transitions

We will discuss only how writing should be accomplished, leaving the discussion of grammar and style to standard works in the field. Writing is a powerful and effective tool and a very important means of *da'wah*. As such, we should pay personal attention to developing our ability to write well.

III. The Writing Process

Writing is a process that seems to be complicated but actually demands merely the accomplishment of a few basic skills. It can be made easier if we understand our subject, our purpose, and our audience. Given that, we can minimize the frustrations associated with writing by breaking up the process into manageable steps. These steps are described below:

A. Planning

Writing begins with planning. This means thinking about what can and may be written about the subject at hand. It can also mean taking notes, making lists, or creating a rough outline of the ideas being presented. We jot down the ideas and supporting details so that we will not miss a point or present the ideas in an unorganized manner. The thinking, verbalizing, and imagining that precede putting the first word down are just as important as the mechanics of writing the entire piece.

B. Drafting

To begin writing, we prepare the first draft in concise form, using no more words than necessary and avoiding vague words that will confuse the ideas being conveyed. While doing so, we must keep the readers and their ability to comprehend the main ideas in mind. Our use of descriptive examples can often clarify difficult ideas.

The time devoted to drafting is well spent, because the draft is the foundation of the written piece. Once it is ready, we review it to recognize usable elements — ideas, examples, and style — so that we may develop them in the revision stage. We should be prepared to throw out part or all of the draft if it does not work.

C. Revising

Revision can significantly improve our draft. We go over it to weed out unimportant details and clarify any vague ideas. However, revision is not to be considered merely a mechanism for fixing the first draft; it should be treated as a means to create the final product. In this phase of writing, it is not unusual to change a major portion of our work, its tone, or the point of view from which it is written. This is also the time to eliminate any confusion.

D. Proofreading

When the final draft is ready after one or more revisions of the rough or first draft, we then proofread the final manuscript to check for grammar, spelling, and punctuation errors. For quick reference, it helps to have a dictionary and a handbook of grammar rules handy. We should make it a rule that if we do not have time to proofread, we do not have time to write.

IV. Writer's Block

Writer's block is the commonly used term for the condition when we seem to be stuck and can't think of another word to write about our subject. Several strategies might help to overcome this condition. For example, we could:

⇒ Force ourselves to keep writing, such that one idea leads to another and we find we are slowly getting back to the subject;

⇒ Talk to someone about our dilemma and, in the process, generate new leads or ways of approaching the subject;

⇒ Leave our writing aside for a while and come back to it later with a fresh outlook.

V. Tips

Some tips for good writing include:

⇒ Base your prose on facts; stay simple, brief, and exact.

⇒ Avoid business jargon, overused phrases and terms.

⇒ Edit for a leaner, crisper style; shorten sentences.

⇒ Strengthen the prose by using more verbs than nouns.

⇒ Eliminate unnecessary words by changing nouns to verbs.

⇒ Avoid use of nouns or adjectives as verbs.

⇒ Use the active voice by making subjects do the action.

⇒ Avoid repetition of words; use synonyms instead.

⇒ Start your first draft by jotting down all your relevant ideas and key words on a piece of paper. Do not worry about ordering and sequence at first; you can group subsections later.

⇒ Remember what the Prophet (SAW) said: "The best of words are those that are precise and concise."

Writing Creates and Conveys ...

There is a story that a former chairman of a scientific institution in Pakistan was once talking to the head of a very wealthy business family. As part of his energetic campaign for literacy and education, he was trying to convince the mother to encourage her son to go to school and college instead of becoming an apprentice in her family business at a young age. "What would college do for him," she wanted to know. "The college will teach him, for example, how to write well," said the chairman. "Why would he want to write?" shot back the old lady. "He will always have a secretary!"

Of course, there is more to writing than can be delegated to a secretary. Writing is a tool of leadership. It is a way of conveying part of yourself, your priorities, your focus, and your sense of direction to those you lead. Think of the many forms in which you can do that, for example:

⇒ internal memos to staff and volunteer workers

⇒ speeches to members or the public

⇒ appointment or orientation letters to committees

⇒ agreements with other individuals and organizations

⇒ briefs, working papers, or proposals for superiors

⇒ resolutions or minutes of meetings

Do not write to just fill paper. Use the CAR formula. Be:

Creative

Accurate

Result Oriented

QUESTIONS FOR DISCUSSION

1. How is writing different from speaking as a means of communication?
2. Into what four steps can the writing process be divided? What are the major mistakes you might make in taking each step?

COMPREHENSION EXERCISE

AS THE PUBLIC RELATIONS OFFICER IN YOUR ISLAMIC ORGANIZATION, YOU HAVE BEEN ASKED TO PREPARE A WHITE PAPER ON ITS FOUNDING AND GROWTH. THE PAPER WILL BE USED TO SUPPORT A FUNDING APPEAL TO A MAJOR DONOR AS WELL AS TO HELP NEW MEMBERS BECOME COMMITTED TO ITS PROGRESS. YOU WILL DETERMINE THE CONTENT, STYLE, AND LENGTH OF THE PAPER.

1. *Outline your plan for writing this white paper.*

2. *Write a memo to someone you have asked to edit and improve your initial draft. Point out what the editor should be looking for in improving your draft.*

3. *List five things you will NOT do in completing this specific writing project.*

Chapter

14

Nasihah (Advice)

I. The Nature of *Nasihah*
II. *Nasihah* as Feedback
III. *Nasihah* as an Obligation
IV. *Nasihah* in Action
      A. From Generalities to Specifics
      B. From Knowledge to Behavior

LEARNING OBJECTIVES

On completing this chapter, you should be able to:
- identify the elements of the advice-giving process
- give advice in an Islamically recommended way
- receive advice in an Islamically acceptable manner

I. The Nature of *Nasihah*

One of the most crucial attributes of a *da'iyah* is the practice of giving advice to his fellow Muslims, as expressed by the comprehensive Qur'anic term *nasihah*. *Nasihah* is an essential tool of true, faithful feedback in an Islamic society. Indeed, the Prophet (SAW) spoke of religion as the practice of giving advice to Muslims by saying:

«الدِّيْنُ النَّصِيْحَة»

Religion is sincere advice.[1]

---

1   **Sahih Muslim.**

The significance of this attribute is evident from the fact that the Prophet (SAW) took homage from Jarir ibn 'Abd Allah on three actions: establishing prayers, giving zakah, and offering advice to every Muslim. Every Muslim includes the ruler and the ruled.

If we claim to love our fellow Muslims, one measurement of that love is how much sincere advice we convey to them. To care about others means to accept the responsibility of pointing out their mistakes to them. If we do not, our love may only be a superficial, verbal claim and not a warm, heartfelt feeling.

Giving advice has always been the mission of Allah's messengers.

I [Hud] deliver to you the messages of my Lord and I am to you a sincere advisor (7:68).	۞ أُبَلِّغُكُمْ رِسَالَاتِ رَبِّي وَأَنَا۠ لَكُمْ نَاصِحٌ أَمِينٌ (سورة الأعراف)
... I [Shu'ayb] delivered to you [his people] the messages of my Lord and I gave you good advice ... (7:93).	... لَقَدْ أَبْلَغْتُكُم رِسَالَاتِ رَبِّي وَنَصَحْتُ لَكُمْ ... (سورة الأعراف)

II. *Nasihah* as Feedback

As human beings, we perform all our actions without the ability to observe ourselves during the act. This is undoubtedly a limitation of our capabilities, but Allah (SWT) has compensated for our limitation by making our brothers and sisters in Islam mirrors for each other. Through them, in a sense, we can watch our own actions while performing.

According to prophetic teachings, the believer is a mirror of his brother. Remember that a mirror gives us a true reflection, nothing more, nothing less. We must do the same when we transmit the picture to our fellow Muslims through advice.

A wise man benefits from the expressed criticism of adversaries to his actions by correcting the mistakes that others see but are unnoticed by him. Indeed, a faithful friend who conveys advice to us is an indispensable companion in this life. Once 'Umar (RA) exclaimed: "May Allah have mercy on him who sends me my faults for a gift!"

Advice is two-way communication; the one who is being advised must welcome it with an open heart and open mind, a smiling face and an appreciative expression of gratitude, followed by a determination to start improving himself. On the other hand, the one who is giving advice must be patient, tactful in using appropriate words, and should choose the proper emotional atmosphere. He should not be offended or discouraged if he does not detect an immediate change in the attitude or behavior of the advisee. Such changes often need a time lag between determination and implementation.

To be most effective, the advisor must demonstrate love, affection, and sincerity. The tone must not show any superiority, censure, ridicule, or indictment.

Islamic manners require us to communicate advice in private and not in public so as to prevent any sort of ill-feelings from developing. The purpose of advice is to correct the shortcomings of individuals rather than publicize their mistakes.

While we should be open to receiving advice, we should guard against being deceived.

He [Iblis] swore to them [Adam and his wife] both that he was their sincere advisor (7:21).	﴿٢١﴾ وَقَاسَمَهُمَآ إِنِّى لَكُمَا لَمِنَ ٱلنَّٰصِحِينَ (سورة الأعراف)
...We [Yusuf's brothers] are his sincere well-wishers (12:11).	... وَإِنَّا لَهُۥ لَنَٰصِحُونَ (سورة يوسف)

III. *Nasihah* as an Obligation

Giving advice is obligatory on us regardless of the way it is received. Societies, the Prophet (SAW) has reminded us, were destroyed due to the neglect of advice. Above all, advice must be offered for the sake of Allah alone and not for any worldly purpose. In this respect, every *da'iyah* must be a good example of the proper practice of this Islamic virtue, *nasihah*.

We should not be put off by those who do not seem receptive to our sincere advice. Experience has shown that even those who were upset by frank, corrective advice at times were very appreciative and grateful in their hearts months or years later.

Finally, a word of caution is in place here. The fact that we convey advice to someone does not necessarily mean that our opinion on the issue is correct. It might be that we are in error and that the advisee is correct. In such cases, the practice of advice must not turn into a vain argument; rather it should become a fraternal discussion. This is the shared responsibility of the advisor and the advisee.

Advice is sometimes not well-received.

> ... I [Salih] certainly delivered to you [his people] the message of my Lord and I gave you good advice; but you do not love those who give good advice (7:79).

... لَقَدْ أَبْلَغْتُكُمْ رِسَالَةَ رَبِّي وَنَصَحْتُ لَكُمْ وَلَكِن لَّا تُحِبُّونَ ٱلنَّاصِحِينَ (سورة الأعراف)

Let's recapitulate the Qur'anic principles:
1. Giving advice has been the mission of Allah's messengers.
2. Advice is sometimes not well-received.
3. We should guard against being deceived in advice.
4. Our responsibility is to offer advice, but it will be profitable only by the permission of Allah.

IV. *Nasihah* in Action

A. From Generalities to Specifics

Reminders benefit believers. Allah (SWT) says:

> And remind, surely reminding benefits the believers. (51:55)

(٥٥) وَذَكِّرْ فَإِنَّ ٱلذِّكْرَىٰ تَنفَعُ ٱلْمُؤْمِنِينَ (سورة الذاريات)

Reminding is not educating; it assumes that knowledge is already there. Knowledge is a must, but it is not enough! Sometimes we forget; at other times we are unaware of our behavior. When we perform an act, we do not see ourselves; others see us. If they do not tell us how we are "acting," we remain unaware of our strengths and weaknesses. This is a handicap in us, but Allah has prescribed the solution to it. It comes through our involvement with the "community of remembrance."

First, there is the continuous remembering of Allah (SWT). Islam has institutionalized this through the instrument of *dhikr*:

> Men who celebrate the praises of Allah, standing, sitting and lying down on their sides, and contemplate [the wonders of] creation in the heavens and the earth, [with the thought]: "Our Lord! not for naught have You created [all] this! Glory to You! Give us salvation from the Penalty of the Fire" (3:191).

(١٩١) ٱلَّذِينَ يَذْكُرُونَ ٱللَّهَ قِيَٰمًا وَقُعُودًا وَعَلَىٰ جُنُوبِهِمْ وَيَتَفَكَّرُونَ فِى خَلْقِ ٱلسَّمَٰوَٰتِ وَٱلْأَرْضِ رَبَّنَا مَا خَلَقْتَ هَٰذَا بَٰطِلًا سُبْحَٰنَكَ فَقِنَا عَذَابَ ٱلنَّارِ (سورة آل عمران)

Second is the behavioral level of believers. It comes through the "mirror believer" in the hadith:

«المُؤْمِنُ مِرآةُ المُؤْمِنِ»

The believer is the mirror of the believer.[1]

In the physical mirror, one sees himself and the mirror speaks to him visually. In the brotherly mirror, the believer has to speak out loud to his brother. This is where the breakdown occurs, and where we fail in our duties towards each other. Our brothers are usually willing to correct their mistakes if they know them. But if the mirror brothers do not identify to them their mistakes, the former continue to repeat them. Furthermore, it is not enough to tell a brother to be clean; he knows that he must be clean. You must go from generalities to specifics. You should point out to him that he stinks, his feet smell, he has bad breath, he has a ring around his shirt collar, his clothes are dirty, and so on.

B. From Knowledge to Behavior

In fieldwork, we should go from the level of generalities to specifics, as and when they occur. This way the one advised realizes where the problem lies and starts acting to correct it. Once we spot a mistake, it becomes our duty to point it out; otherwise on the Day of *Qiyamah* the brother will hold us accountable. 'Umar ibn al Khattab said: "May Allah have mercy on him who sends me my faults for a gift."

He perceives of his faults as gifts, and indeed it is not only valuable but also an indispensable gift. This is particularly so today, when we have lost this beautiful practice. This practice springs out from our love and care for others. If you love them, you should point out their mistakes to them, not to others. They should reciprocate. Otherwise *iman* is in question according to the hadith:

«لا يُؤْمِنُ أَحَدُكُمْ حَتَّى يُحِبَّ لأَخِيهِ مَا يُحِبُّ لِنَفْسِهِ»

You shall not attain *iman* until you love for others what you love for yourself.[2]

This is the opposite of the selfishness which we find in materialistic societies. There, people are only concerned with themselves. Their objective is the personal freedom to enjoy lusts and desires. Hence they do not have to tell others what they do not like to hear.

Our objective is to establish the truth in the society, even if we have to tell others things they may not like to hear.

---

1   Sunan abu Dawud and Sunan al Tirmidhi.
2   Sahih al Bukhari and Sahih Muslim.

So next time you see your brother with an unbuttoned shirt, skewed tie, open zipper, dirt on his face, untied shoe lace, or speaking loudly, make sure to remind him, alone, instantly. He should be very grateful to you for this great gift. If we practice this "on the spot," specific, *nasihah* reminder with love and concern in our training programs, our performance will go up by more than 50%. We will feel the blessings of getting closer to the "community of remembrance."

It works like this:

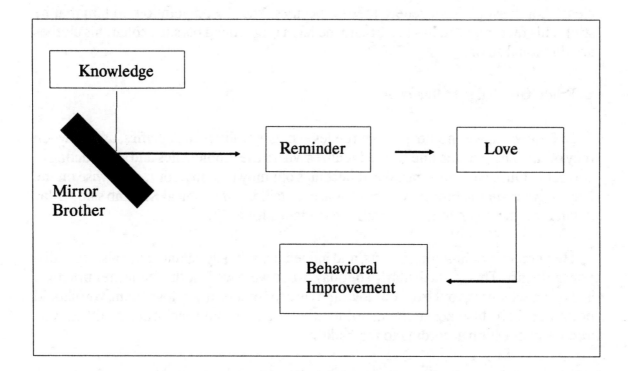

This is advice in action. It converts theoretical knowledge into better behavior through the catalysts of brotherly mirroring and caring love.

NASIHAH IN PRACTICE

Giving and receiving advice calls for strength of character. As with other traits of the Islamic personality, determination and practice will help us become better advisors and advisees. Perhaps we could set a target for ourselves. In the coming three months, we can offer advice to several brothers and sisters we care about at least once and then analyze our behavior during and after this process according to what has been discussed in this chapter.

AN EXERCISE IN *NASIHAH*

Divide your local small group (*usrah* or *halaqah*) into groups of two each. Let them offer *nasihah* to each other privately for five minutes. Then exchange the lessons of this experiment and discuss the mechanics and procedures of *nasihah* in a meeting.

QUESTIONS FOR DISCUSSION

1. What is the goal of reminding others about their faults?
2. How does a Muslim function as a mirror to a fellow Muslim?

COMPREHENSION EXERCISE

AS YOU GO THROUGH THE RECORDS OF YOUR ISLAMIC ORGANIZATION AS THE NEW CHAIRMAN OF THE EVALUATION COMMITTEE, YOU DISCOVER SEVERAL IMPROPRIETIES. ONE OF THEM IS REPEATED OVERSPENDING MERELY DUE TO FAILURE BY THE TREASURER TO SCHEDULE THE PURCHASES AHEAD OF TIME. YOU DO NOT WANT TO MAKE IT AN ADMINISTRATIVE ISSUE YET, BUT FEEL THAT THE MATTER SHOULD BE BROUGHT TO THE ATTENTION OF THE TREASURER. YOUR AIM IS TO STREAMLINE FINANCIAL PROCEDURES.

1. Outline a scenario which will be most suitable for giving advice in this case.

2. Draft the script for a possible dialogue between you and the treasurer.

3. List three possible reasons why you could be wrong in your assessment of the situation.

Chapter

15

On Communication

I. What Is Communication?
    A. Judgment and Interpretation
    B. The Prophetic Way
    C. "Please Make Me Feel Important"
II. Ways to Communicate
    A. Tips on Communicating
    B. "Do You Say What You Mean and Mean What You Say?"
III. Cross-Checking of Information
IV. Communication Checklists
    A. Communicating without Words:
       How We Use Non-Verbal Language
    B. Do's and Don't's of Communication

LEARNING OBJECTIVES

On completing this chapter, you should be able to:
- understand the need for communicating with others
- recognize the pitfalls in communication
- understand and be understood better

Allah (SWT) says:

[Allah] Most Gracious! It is He Who has taught the Qur'an. He has created man: He has taught him speech [and art of communication] (55:1-4).

ٱلرَّحْمَٰنُ ﴿١﴾ عَلَّمَ ٱلْقُرْءَانَ ﴿٢﴾

خَلَقَ ٱلْإِنسَٰنَ ﴿٣﴾ عَلَّمَهُ ٱلْبَيَانَ ﴿٤﴾

(سورة الرحمن)

Allah (SWT) taught us communication. Our role is simply to communicate the message with clarity and purity. There are many obstacles to effective communication. Today, many things are blamed on communication; be it divorcing a spouse, firing an employee, or dropping out of school. Communication involves people; it is sometimes claimed that everybody is in the "people" business. Thus, everyone is a manager, contrary to general thinking. Children manage their parents, students manage their teachers, and secretaries manage their managers.

Unfortunately, we are brought up to be less than honest from childhood. Hence, in our communication we hide behind a thousand masks. People live artificial lives and are afraid that others may discover them, ridicule them, and reject them. We should not be fooled by what others say, but "listen" carefully to what they do not say! It is better to be rejected for what we are than to be accepted for what we are not. A survey once asked a group of students what was the one thing they most regretted? The majority of them replied: "I do not know who my parents are." Although they lived under one roof, they did not know and understand each other well.

I. What Is Communication?

To communicate is to let people know you, and allow them to come to mutual understanding with you. If they do, they will respect you. This process, however, involves sharing your ideas and feelings with people honestly.

A. Judgment and Interpretation

A major obstacle in dealing with people is prejudgment and interpretation. If Allah (SWT) does not judge a person until his life is over, why should we? The Prophet (SAW) taught us that deeds are judged by their ends.

We should replace evaluation and judgment of people with factual description of behavior. For example, do not say someone is dirty; say he stinks, spits on the floor, or throws litter in the street. No one can dispute these statements of fact. A good criterion is to restrict oneself to describing behavioral data that can stand up in a court of law. It is not what happened that causes people to feel bad, but rather their interpretation of what happened. For example, if someone does not greet you at a party, you will feel bad if you think he purposely ignored you. But if you think he did not see you, you will feel all right. Thus the same event has two completely different interpretations and judgments.

B. The Prophetic Way

People put on a facade because they are afraid of being discovered and rejected. To counteract this, we should receive them with love and accept them as they are.

We have to be honest, genuine, and spontaneous. Treat people with care, gentleness, and encouragement. Be sensitive to their needs and show them sympathy and affection. We have to be understanding. Allah described the Prophet (SAW):

Now has come unto you a Messenger from among yourselves; it grieves him that you should perish: ardently anxious is he over you: to the Believers is he most kind and merciful (9:128).

(١٢٨) لَقَدْ جَآءَكُمْ رَسُولٌ مِّنْ أَنفُسِكُمْ عَزِيزٌ عَلَيْهِ مَا عَنِتُّمْ حَرِيصٌ عَلَيْكُم بِٱلْمُؤْمِنِينَ رَءُوفٌ رَّحِيمٌ
(سورة التوبة)

It is part of the Mercy of Allah, that you deal gently with them. Were you severe or harsh-hearted, they would have broken away from you... (3:159).

(١٥٩) فَبِمَا رَحْمَةٍ مِّنَ ٱللَّهِ لِنتَ لَهُمْ وَلَوْ كُنتَ فَظًّا غَلِيظَ ٱلْقَلْبِ لَٱنفَضُّوا۟ مِنْ حَوْلِكَ ... (سورة آل عمران)

This explains how the kindness of the Prophet (SAW) attracted others. On the other hand, it asserts that if the Prophet (SAW) were severe and hard-hearted, people would have distanced themselves from him.

C. "Please Make Me Feel Important"

It is said figuratively that everyone is born with a sign on his forehead saying: "Please make me feel important!" This was the Prophet's way. He used to address everyone, fully turning his body towards the addressee, and making even children feel important and responsible like adults.

People hate being neglected or ignored. Every time they communicate they convey an unspoken message: "Please validate me!" "Please approve of my presence." "Do not pass me by unnoticed." Any time they do not get responses to their letters or telephone messages, you are in effect discounting them and telling them: "You do not exist!"

TRUST OR MISTRUST?

Are we going to trust everyone? Certainly not! We have to be very careful, since people do act and pretend. 'Ali ibn Abi Talib (RA) says: "I am not a cheat, but the cheat cannot deceive me."

We have to listen to others but also verify and check. Especially at times of decision and action, we need to cross-check the information.

Must we always agree with people? Of course not. We just have to be honest and straightforward. True, similarity brings familiarity, but differences make us grow and develop. Either way, we have to be truthful and say what is right.

II. Ways to Communicate

There are as many ways to communicate as there are reasons to do so. However, for the critical purposes of making decisions, some words and phrases have become common and standardized. We will discuss them after offering some general tips for effective communication.

A. Tips on Communicating

1. Powerful communication comes from inner strength. Do not try to seek power over people.
2. Interact with everyone in your work, camp, or *jama'ah*. Lack of time is not an excuse.
3. Spend each break period in a meeting with someone different. Plan to share meals with others. You will establish meaningful relationships with everybody in a short time.
4. Don't wait for latecomers in a meeting. If you do, you are teaching them that being late is okay and also punishing those who are punctual.
5. Paraphrase the message you hear to ensure proper transmission and reception.
6. Remember that the more we understand, the more we manage. The less we understand, the more we manipulate!
7. When it comes to interpretation, the Prophet (SAW) teaches us to find over seventy excuses for the bad behavior of others and, if none of them is correct, to say that there must be another interpretation of which we are unaware.

B. "Do You Say What You Mean and Mean What You Say?"

The 500 most commonly used words in the English language have collectively 14,000 dictionary definitions. This yields an average of twenty-eight meanings per word. When you utter a word, which one of the twenty-eight meanings do you intend?

Remember that:
⇒ Words don't have meanings, people do!
⇒ Words are just symbols, not realities.
⇒ Words are not absolute; they are taught or learned in a certain context.
⇒ Meanings can be hidden and buried.
⇒ Words reflect cultural and personal dimensions. They are laden with influences of race, religion, and male/female connotations.

Below are words to avoid and words to use:

WORDS TO FORGET	WORDS TO REMEMBER
I should, I have to	I want to, I choose to
I shall try to do it	I will do it, *in sha'a Allah*
Someday	Today, now
But (negates previous statement)	And
Risk	Opportunity
Problem	Challenge, Opportunity
Too difficult	Challenging
Worried	Interested
I am sorry	Excuse me, I regret
Why (stopper, attack)	Help me understand
I feel helpless	I would like your help
That is just the way I am	My potential for change is
I need you to	I want you to
You (it is blameful, accusative)	I (honest, responsible)

There are words of categorization that decrease our perception. They limit our options to only two. For example:

> either/or; male/female; black/white; old/young; American/foreign;
> right/wrong; boss/subordinate; smart/dumb

Whenever you hear or read these, do not ignore other possibilities. We often encounter these words which are pregnant with ideological connotations:

> East/West; capitalism/communism; center/outside; Muslim/non-Muslim;
> *Dar al Islam/Dar al Harb*; democracy/dictatorship; centralization/decentralization.

Words of this nature tend to obscure our vision and decrease our understanding. Watch your words carefully; angels are always recording accurately:

Not a word does he utter but there is a sentinel by him, ready [to note it] (50:18).

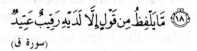

III. Cross-Checking of Information

How many times do we hear: "It is a problem of communication, lack of communication, miscommunication, or misunderstanding." Often it is true. The response should be: "Fix it!" One effective way of doing just that is to cross-check the information on which the communication is based. As a message travels, we add to or subtract from it; in either case, the message gets distorted. The engineering term "noise" is used to measure this distortion. Consider these two examples:

1. A man was driving with his son and got killed in an accident. The son needed an operation but the surgeon said: "I cannot operate. The patient is my son." Who is the surgeon?
2. A man left his house and put the keys in his pocket. A thief came and robbed the house. How did he enter?

In both these cases, our minds jump to conclusions and we give the wrong answer. The surgeon was the mother of the patient but we assumed erroneously that the surgeon must be a man. The thief entered through the door because it was not locked. We assume wrongly that the man locked the door before putting the key in his pocket. It is amazing how often we fall into this trap of assumptions, become presumptuous, inaccurate and approximate. In our work today, this tendency is affecting our performance considerably.

Try this interesting exercise in your group. First, write a very short story. Then make a circle of ten brothers. Whisper the very short story to the person on your right and tell him to whisper it to the one on his right and so on until it comes back to you from the last one on the left. You will be astonished that you may not even recognize the story, because it changes so radically in the inaccurate transmission and communication.

Although we trust our brothers and sisters, we should put news in the "hold" mode until we confirm it. Particularly when we need to act upon such information, we must verify it first.

It is useful to repeat instructions loudly to assure correct transmission and reception. Repeat the appointment time and place again to make sure. When someone dictates a telephone number or spells a name to you, do not say "umm," "OK" or "yes." Repeat after him the numbers and letters to eliminate the possibility of error. Of course, we should not overdo the cross-checking. The guiding rule must be the pure good intention of getting to the truth, not to trap or accuse others of purposely misleading us. If we follow the route of continuous suspicion, the results of cross-checking will be counter-productive.

IV. Communication Checklists

A. Communicating without Words: How We Use Non-Verbal Language

Use this checklist to make your notes about how various elements of your "self" add to or detract from effectively communicating your message to your audience. Remember, different audiences may be affected differently by the same element. For example, a larger audience needs a louder voice than a smaller one; a pep talk may be all right in informal dress but a project presentation may need formal dress.

Part of my SELF	How I shall use it to communicate
BODY	
Head position	_____
Face, especially mouth	_____
Eyes	_____
Shoulders	_____
Posture	_____
Movement	_____
Actions and Gestures	_____
Dress	_____
VOICE	
Tone	_____
Softness	_____
Speed	_____
SPACE	
Distance	_____
Marking, changing	_____
TOUCH[1]	
Shaking hands	_____
Hands on shoulder	_____
Holding hands	_____
Hug	_____
Kiss	_____

[1] TOUCH is permitted only among persons of the same gender.

B. Do's and Don't's of Communication

Use this checklist to rate yourself on your use of communication skills. First, add your own point (#8) in the DON'T column. Then, for each DO and DON'T, give yourself 5 points for "Often" and 1 point for "Never" and 2, 3, and 4 points for use in between.

DO points >4 x DON'T points   Good communicator
DO points >2 x DON'T points   Acceptable communicator
DO points = or <2 x DON'T points   Must improve communication skills

DO	RATING	DON'T	RATING
1. Make eye contact (same gender only) when listening	[ ]	1. Interrupt when having a point to make	[ ]
2. Check for understanding and use of paraphrase	[ ]	2. Ridicule what others say, even if it seems silly	[ ]
3. Affirm with nods and gestures	[ ]	3. Gossip	[ ]
4. Share laughter with people	[ ]	4. Give personal opinion on issues	[ ]
5. Share feelings of sadness	[ ]	5. Ask "why" all the time	[ ]
6. Get others involved in the conversation	[ ]	6. Carry the conversation single-handed	[ ]
7. Graciously accept opinions that are different	[ ]	7. Criticize the ideas of others without being asked to do so	[ ]
8. Compliment other people	[ ]	8. _____	[ ]

WORDS OF IMPORTANCE

The **6** most important words	*"I appreciate you and your efforts."*
The **5** most important words	"I am proud of you."
The **4** most important words	**"What is your opinion?"**
The **3** most important words	**"Would you please?"**
The **2** most important words	**"Thank you."**
The **1** MOST important word	**"We"**
The LEAST important word	"I"

S   E
   M   L
      I

It helps communicate ...

Bonus: You will be rewarded for it, according to the hadith:

﴿تَبَسُّمُكَ في وَجْهِ أَخِيكَ صَدَقَةٌ﴾

Your smile in the face of your brother is an act of charity (*sadaqah*).
(Sunan al Tirmidhi)

"The Whole

world

is Wrong

Except

I."

Or is it? Think about it!

QUESTIONS FOR DISCUSSION

1. What are two of the elements of the Prophet's communication with the believers? How did they help communication?
2. What approach should we adopt if we disagree with someone?
3. In what way are the words you must avoid different from the ones you should use?
4. What are the three common techniques for cross-checking information?
5. What should be our assumptions in cross-checking?

COMPREHENSION EXERCISE

YOU ARE STAFF ADMINISTRATOR OF A NATIONAL ISLAMIC ORGANIZATION. DUE TO HIGH TURNOVER, YOU HAVE SEVERAL SUBORDINATES WHO ARE NOT YET FAMILIAR WITH YOU PERSONALLY OR WITH THE ORGANIZATION'S CULTURE. YOUR OWN SUPERIOR IS ALSO NEW TO THE ORGANIZATION. THE ANNUAL GENERAL ASSEMBLY MEETING IS VERY NEAR AND ALMOST EVERYBODY IS UNDER PRESSURE TO PERFORM AT HIS PEAK. A GROUP OF MEMBERS HAS SERVED NOTICE THAT IT WILL CHALLENGE THE ANNUAL REPORT ON THE FLOOR.

1. *List two common elements and two differences in the way you will communicate with the three groups in this case: subordinates, superiors, and members.*

2. *Write a memo to the subordinates explaining your strategy for handling the floor challenge. Keep it simple and focus on it being unambiguously understood and implemented.*

3. *Write a memo to your superior advising him on how to cross-check information from the dissenting members.*

Chapter

16

How to Manage Your Time

LEARNING OBJECTIVES

On completing this chapter, you should be able to:
- identify and minimize major time-wasting habits
- identify and cultivate time-saving habits
- do more in the time available
- lead a more productive work and personal life

I. The Nature of Time

Perhaps you are aware of the saying: "What is the longest, yet the shortest; the swiftest, yet the slowest; all of us neglect it, and then we all regret it? Nothing can be done without it, it swallows up all that is small and it builds up all that is great?"

It is time.

It is the longest because it is the measured eternity; it is the shortest because none of us have time to finish life's work; it is the swiftest to those that are happy, slowest to those who suffer. Nothing can be done without it because it is the only theater in which we live. Time is what life is made of! It swallows up into oblivion all that is unworthy of posterity, and it builds and preserves all that is great and unselfish.

II. The Use of Time

Successful people spend their time doing things that people who fail are unwilling to do. The average person finds it easier to adjust to the hardships of failure than to spend the time adjusting to the sacrifices that lead to success. It means little to have goals and destinations in life unless there is a time schedule attached to each. Only then we can start moving towards these goals and arrive at the destination.

We fall into two categories: first we have the unfortunate, disenchanted group which is always going to start something tomorrow. Then we have that wonderful group which is ready to go right now. For them there is no tomorrow.

Killing time is not just a crime, it's murder! If you must kill it, why not work it to death? Whenever you say: "I don't have time," all you are saying is that there are other things more important to me.

A. One Day at a Time

Every morning when we wake up, our pocketbook is filled with twenty-four hours. The Prophet (SAW) tells us that:

«مَا مِنْ فَجْرِ يَوْمٍ يَنْشَقُّ إلاَّ وَيُنادي مَلَكانِ، يا ابْنَ آدَمَ أنا يَوْمٌ جديدٌ، وَعَلى عَمَلِكَ

شَهيدٌ، فَتَزَوَّدْ مِنِّي فَإنِّي لا أعُودُ إلى يَوْمِ القِيامَةِ».

Not a single dawn breaks out without two angels calling out: "Oh! Son of Adam, I am a new day and I witness your actions, so make the best out of me because I will never come back till the Day of Judgment."[1]

Each day must be filled with things to be proud of. Unless we are ready to start right now, regardless of our good intentions, this time tomorrow, this time next week, this time ten years from now we shall still be bogged down.

---

1   Al Ma'thur of the Prophet (SAW).

B. The Meaning of Time

The meaning of time to some is the moment when opportunity is at its highest. They put great emphasis upon good timing. The time when opportunity is most favorable has special significance to

WHAT IS A BAR OF IRON WORTH?	
As a plain bar of iron	$ 5
Cast into horseshoes	$ 11
Made into needles	$ 355
Transformed into knife blades	$ 2,285
Spun into ballistic springs for watches	$ 250,000

many. Advertising people tell us that there is nothing as powerful in industry as an idea whose time has come. If you can learn to recognize the right moment when it comes, and act before it goes away, the problems of life become vastly simplified.

Time to others is simply a measure or yardstick of seconds, minutes, hours, and years. When they think of time, they see either a clock or a calendar; it has only one dimension—duration. This is the shallowest concept of time. No great masterpieces were created by those who gave importance to this concept. The tragedy of this concept of time is that it destroys initiative, discourages creative impulses, and leaves nothing to fill the time allotted to it. If we have a full week to perform a task, it will take a week. If we are given ten days for its completion, it will consume ten days.

Finally, we have those individuals who give real meaning to life by giving the great quality of depth to time. To those people, time is no longer imprisoned by the clock or shackled by the calendar. Their accomplishments are governed by a spirit of dedication and enthusiasm, not by hours or weeks. They believe strongly in what they are doing, they are drawn towards their goal of success by a powerful, spiritual force which does not even recognize time. They have committed their hearts to a task they love and their work is a mission blazing with purpose.

This third approach to time should be a challenge to us all. The proper use of time determines the failure or success of the average employee today even more than his knowledge of his product or service. The proper organization of time is certainly one of the first items on any formula for success. The most difficult task ever found among groups is that of getting people to organize their time. This is why every individual must spend some time at the beginning of the week planning, in detail, the exact schedule for that week.

III. Spare Time

What do you do with your unused minutes; your so-called, lost time? Do you realize that books can be written, Qur'an and hadith can be fully memorized, and degrees may be obtained by a proper use of this spare time? Such spare time may be the few minutes while waiting for or traveling by train, plane or bus. Would you call this spare time or creative time? Fifteen minutes a day means eleven full days a year; thirty minutes a day means twenty-two full days a year, which is more than one month of working time. Some business persons start out with the premise that no one can be successful in business without adopting the equation that time equals money. We would never think of letting people steal our money, and yet we let people and things rob us of time. We believe that time is more than money; it is our life.

One salesman used to make $20 per hour. He wanted to paint his house himself. His friend asked him: "If you were to select a painter, would you employ an amateur at $20 an hour, or an expert at $5 an hour?" The answer is obvious, and yet many of us take valuable time from our own business or profession to do work which could be done far better by others at much less cost.

IV. How Time Passes

This chart shows what you might be doing with your time in a life of average length.

ACTIVITY	TIME
Tying one's shoes	8 days
Waiting for traffic lights to change	1 month
Time spent at the barber shop	1 month
Dialing the telephone	1 month
Riding elevators (in big cities)	3 months
Brushing one's teeth	3 months
Waiting for the bus (in cities)	5 months
Time spent in the shower or bath	6 months
Reading books	2 years
Eating	4 years
Earning a living	9 years
Watching television	10 years
Sleeping	20 years

So the way the whole thing adds up — if you are going to have the time to do some of the things you want to do, you are just going to have to plan it and program it into your busy schedule. If you wait for the right time to present itself, you might wait forever.

When you put a doctor's appointment, or business meeting, or special event on your calendar, as a rule you keep it. Do the same thing with the time you want to set aside for things you want to accomplish. Set aside a certain time each day and then stick with it as best you can.

For example, by setting aside an hour for every working day, you gain up to 260 hours a year, or the equivalent of thirty-two full working days. You can get a great deal accomplished in such a period of time. You could

⇒ memorize many parts of the Qur'an,
⇒ learn speed reading techniques,
⇒ acquire some specific skills,
⇒ have the best-looking yard in the neighborhood,
⇒ learn a foreign language,
⇒ write a book,
⇒ pick up a diploma, or
⇒ make yourself some extra money.

But with the way time flies by — taken up as it is by a thousand minor events, most of which do not contribute to our success or fulfillment as persons — you just have to schedule it and then stick with the schedule. And it is not easy. Regret for time wasted can become a power for good in the time that remains. And the time that remains is time enough — if we will only stop the waste and the idle, useless regretting.

V. Some Hints for Saving Time

Follow these suggestions for a few days and you will be astounded at the results:

1. Plan your day each morning by writing down the things to do and check them off as they are done.
2. Never visit a friend without informing or calling him by telephone.
3. Always have a pencil and paper or a small note book in your pocket so that you can jot down plans and ideas during spare time.
4. Plan rest times and try to match them with prayer times.
5. Utilize spare time by reading, memorizing, or doing something constructive.
6. When you make an appointment, be sure that both parties understand the exact time.
7. Adjust your traveling time to the distance involved, making reasonable allowance for the unexpected, so that you will arrive at the appointed time.
8. Have all items on hand before starting a job, whether it be cooking, writing an article, or preparing a speech.
9. Avoid people who are thoughtless and selfish enough to steal your time.
10. Do not make a trip in person if you can accomplish the same through a letter or a telephone call.
11. Fill your car with gas when you are passing your favorite filling station. Avoid a special trip and, by all means, never run out of gas; it will make you look stupid!
12. Keep proper change at all time for parking meters or telephone calls.

13. If you have errands or shopping to do, make a written note of all items and plan your activities so that you will not double your journey but cover the least amount of distance.

There are other time savers you can write down. Finish up this list and then try to use some of these suggestions. We should not be against rest and enjoyment, but against wastage of time. Recreation itself means to recreate. One of the greatest tragedies of modern living is that in our feverish existence we often let our bodies get so far ahead of our souls that it is doubtful if the two will ever get together again on this earth. How wonderful it would be if we would let our souls catch up with our bodies. Take time off periodically to pray, meditate, contemplate, and recharge the batteries of faith.

VI. Things to Remember about Time

A. Take time ...
Take time to think, for it is the source of power;
Take time to play, for it is the cistern of perpetual youth;
Take time to read, for it is the foundation of wisdom;
Take time to pray, for it is the greatest power on earth;
Take time to love and be loved, for *iman* is nothing but love and hate;
Take time to be friendly, for it is the road to happiness;
Take time to laugh, for it is the best lubricant;
Take time to give, for life is too short to be selfish;
Take time to work, for it is the price of success; but
Never take time to waste;
Remember that the Prophet (SAW) says:

$$\text{«مَنِ اسْتَوَى يَوْمَاهُ فَهُوَ مَغْبُونٌ»}$$

He whose two days are equal [in accomplishments] is a sure loser![1]

B. Time Well Spent

A good portion of our lives is spent with our friends. What kind of conversation do we indulge in during that time? Remember the following wisdom:
Great minds discuss ideas,
Average minds discuss events,
Small minds discuss people,
Very small minds discuss themselves.

---

1 Sunan al Daylami.

VII. A Case Study: What Does a Minute Cost?

The Central Issue: The Value of Time

We often speak of the value of time, its importance, and cost. Yet we seldom calculate the cost of time in a meeting or a camp or a conference. If we come up with a dollar figure per minute, we will realize that for every minute we waste we lose that much money. This places a heavy burden of responsibility on the organizers to plan every minute of the activity in an optimal way. Let us take a practical case "The Seminar on Islamization of Attitudes and Practices in Science and Technology" which was held at IIIT headquarters in Washington, D.C., in 1987.

The Situation: The Cost of the Seminar

a. Calculation of direct costs for thirty outside scholars attending:

Airline Tickets (30 x $200/scholar)	$ 6,000
Lodging (30 x $40/room x 2 nights)	2,400
Food (30 x $8/meal x 5 meals)	1,200
(15 local attendees x $8 x 3)	360
Local transportation (2 cars x $60/day x 2 days)	240
Secretarial help	1,000
Telephone	400
Stationary & Duplication	1,200
Overheads	1,000
Honorarium for 6 x $200	1,200
	$ 15,000

b. Calculation of presentation time:
10 sessions x 1 hour and 30 minutes   15 hrs.
(Friday 3 + Saturday 5 + Sunday 2)

c. Calculation of direct cost per session hour:

= ($ 15,000 / 15 hrs.) $ 1,000/hr.

d. Calculation of cost per minute
= ($1,000 / 60 min.) $ 17/min.

This is only direct cost which does not take into account salaries of the scholars and organizers for the 48 hours they spent plus their traveling time. If we do include their salaries at 45 persons x $100/day x 2 days = $9,000, the cost per session/hour becomes
= ($ 15,000 + $ 9,000) / 15 hrs. $ 1,600
Cost per minute = ($1,600 / 60 min.) $ 27

The Lesson: Cost Effectiveness in Meetings

If we learn to calculate the cost per minute for all our activities, we shall realize the tragic waste of the ummah's resources when we misuse the time spent during conferences, camps, seminars, and meetings. Gathering people is a very serious matter. Indeed, we are responsible before Allah for using it efficiently.

ALWAYS TRY HARDER!

DON'T POSTPONE TODAY'S WORK TILL TOMORROW

We can always increase our output by 10 to 15 % by exerting a little more effort. If you planned to read a certain number of pages, work until a certain hour, clean a certain area or make certain calls, you can always push yourself to do a bit more. This habit increases production and helps achieve more. Since duties are always more than the time available, this habit can make us more productive and beneficial.

If you procrastinate, the work keeps piling up. You do not know what tomorrow will bring. It is a great relief if you start the day with no work left over from yesterday. A good practice is to do any task on the spot if it takes five minutes or less. If it takes more than five minutes, schedule it according to its priority. This golden rule can make you a great achiever in life. Just imagine that you can do twelve jobs in one hour. By yourself, you can have an impact equal to that of a huge organization. If there are only ten individuals like you in the organization, your total impact will be astronomical. On top of that, Allah will bless your efforts for His sake infinitely!

ACTION POINTS!

Two Time Tamers!

The Pareto Principle (Also known as the 80/20 Rule)

> THEORY: The significant items in a given group constitute a relatively small portion of the total items in the group.

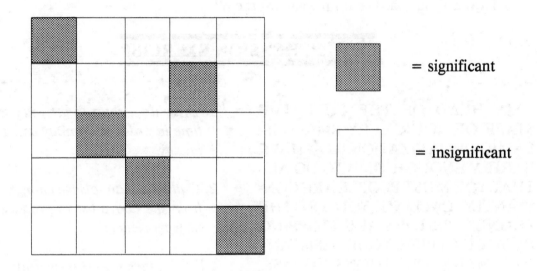

> APPLICATION: List all items you must act on. Recognize the 20% of the items that are likely to yield 80% of the desired results. Act on them first.

Parkinson's Law

> THEORY: Work expands to fill the time available for its completion.

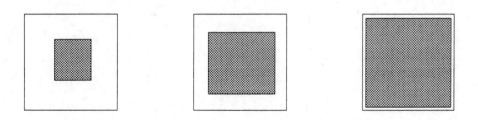

> APPLICATION: Set a deadline for each task and hold to that deadline.

QUESTIONS FOR DISCUSSION

1. Why is time today more valuable than time tomorrow?
2. How do people who succeed differ in their use of time from those who fail?
3. How do you calculate the monetary value of time? Give an example.
4. Why is making schedules necessary for good time management?
5. What are the three common major time-wasting actions?
6. How do you guard your time against them?

COMPREHENSION EXERCISE

AS HEAD OF THE FULL-TIME STAFF OF YOUR VERY SMALL ISLAMIC ORGANIZATION, YOU HAVE BARELY ENOUGH TIME TO DO ALL THAT YOU MUST. PEOPLE ARE CONSTANTLY CALLING YOU ON THE PHONE. VISITORS ARE STOPPING BY YOUR OFFICE. YOUR ASSISTANT HAS MANY QUESTIONS TO ASK. MAIL COMES IN LARGE QUANTITIES. NOW THE EXECUTIVE COMMITTEE WANTS YOU TO START ANOTHER NEWSLETTER.

1. *Draw up a chart to list your use of time in order of quantity as well as quality.*

2. *Outline a plan to save enough time from the above list to produce the new newsletter.*

3. *Write a memo to your assistant telling him how he can save you time.*

Chapter

17

The Art of Listening

I. What Is Listening?
II. Learning to Listen
III. Verifying the Message
IV. Listening and Physical Posture

LEARNING OBJECTIVES

On completing this chapter, you should be able to:
- identify the elements of good listening
- speak to others with their listening needs in mind
- listen to others with better results
- help others speak such that they are better understood

I. What Is Listening?

Listening takes place when a message that contains information is transmitted from a source to a receiver in an environment which suppresses noise and encourages feedback.

The **message** is whatever is communicated and **information** is whatever reduces the uncertainty in the message. One may ask: "How much information is contained in this message?" The source is the **sender** of the message and the **receiver** is the one who gets it. The **environment** is the set of conditions or circumstances within which listening takes place. Noise is whatever hinders the flow of information between a sender and a receiver. Feedback is the receiver's response to the sender's message as it has been interpreted. All these elements of the listening process are shown below.

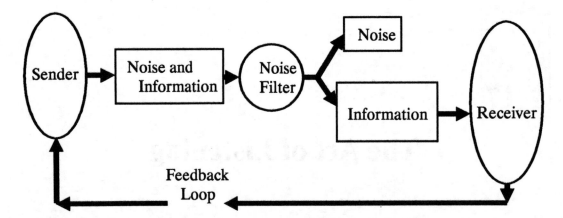

Listening is a two-way street. The speaker must follow basic rules of comprehension to help listeners understand. Listeners should also observe some guidelines to grasp the speaker's message. Remember, there can be more than one listener for one speaker at any time. The information received by each listener may or may not be the same unless all involved adhere to the principles of good communication.

To help listeners understand, as speakers we should consider how to organize the words and the details of what we are going to say. We should select the appropriate audience and the proper time and format (busy time or relaxed time), a formal meeting or an informal visit. Even the location—work area, conference room, social space— can help or hinder communication. Finally, we must decide whether or not a follow up, verbally or in writing, is required.

On the other hand, as listeners we must:
    a. keep an open mind about what the speaker is saying
    b. not let our attention be diverted by our own reaction to what is being said
    c. give consideration to the speaker's body language
    d. focus on the information being given
    e. be physically prepared to listen.

If we cannot understand the message, we may ask the speaker to repeat, specify, or explain the subject. A better time or another location may also help.

II. Learning to Listen

We are not all gifted with the same ability to listen, but we can all work at learning to listen if we make a conscious effort to listen well. To be successful listeners, we must practice:

a. listening intently
b. not letting our minds wander
c. concentrating on what is being said
d. resisting distractions
e. keeping our minds open
f. sitting in front and taking notes

We must repress our own egos and not think only of what we want to say when the speaker finishes. We must listen for ideas and judge the message on the merit of its contents, not its delivery. We must have the patience to hear the speaker out and hold our fire by not interrupting. We must find an area of interest in and be concerned and caring about what the other person is saying. We must consciously practice all of these aspects of listening.

III. Verifying the Message

It is often beneficial to respond to the speaker and give feedback on what we understand as listeners. We could ask questions to get more information from the speaker or help him tackle a difficult point. We could restate what he said to verify if it was what he meant. We could use body language and feelings to convey to the speaker our ease or difficulty in understanding him.

We could also ask open-ended questions (when, what, where, who, and so on) to get more information. We could ask other probing questions to get more details or to help the speaker deal with a difficult point.

IV. Listening and Physical Posture

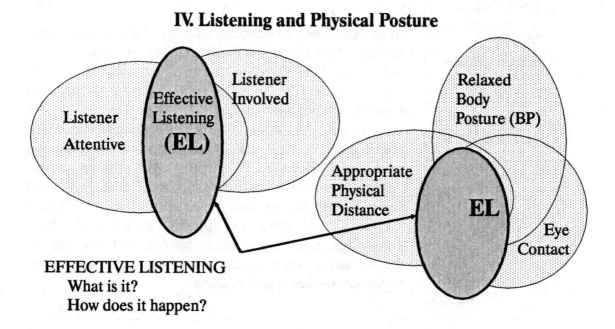

EFFECTIVE LISTENING
    What is it?
    How does it happen?

Listening is Dependent on .....
- Individual Factors AND
- Cultural Factors

THROUGH

- Eye contact
- Body language

When Eye Contact is .....

- **Present**
  ⇒ Speaker sends a stronger and more effective message
  ⇒ Listener is able to hear more accurately

- **Absent**
  ⇒ Speaker avoids a show of feelings
  ⇒ Speaker and listener follow Islamic guidelines for male/female interaction

ARE YOU MISSING THE POINT?

There was a man named Mr. John Donkey. His wife pleaded with him for years to change his name, but he refused. One day, he announced that he was changing his name. She was thrilled with joy and celebrated all night. In the morning she happily asked: "What is your new name, John?" He replied: "David Donkey!"

You will be amazed how many of us miss the essential point in our activities. We need to do a lot of explaining to our associates to prevent this from happening! One day a brother came to me and said: "You say the money of the organization must be protected because it is *amwal al Muslimin* (the property of the Muslims)? Since I am Muslim, give it to me." He certainly missed the point!

ADJUSTMENT FACTORS ARE A NECESSITY

A student in our community tells me: "I do not know why many people think I have very high grades. I am only an average student." The reason is that his parents tell others that he is a top student! Are they lying? No, it turns out that this is their perception of their son as a top-notch student.

When you listen to people, you must apply an adjustment factor. This could be more than 1.0 or less then 1.0. When you hear someone for the first time saying: my child is smart, the house is very clean, he is very rich, meeting attendance was very poor, the project is very big, the airport is very close, etc., remember these statements could mean to you exactly the opposite of what you perceive. Beware of forming an opinion before determining the adjustment factor of that individual. Every person has his own factor relative to you. This is the result of different cultural background, taste, knowledge, experience, family history, maturity, etc. Be doubly aware when making decisions or taking actions. **Verify, cross-check, and confirm!**

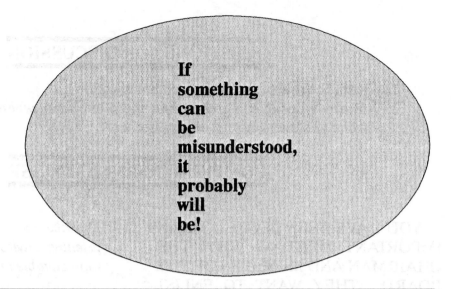

If
something
can
be
misunderstood,
it
probably
will
be!

A
Training
Exercise
for
Listening

One of the many exercises that can be used to improve listening skills is shown below.

REQUIREMENTS

- A tape or film, tape player or film projector, room for projection.

METHOD

- Divide the group into several roles, such as those who agree with the main theme, those who disagree with it, those who are required to implement action, or those who explain it to others; playing such roles will help members listen with a goal.

- Ask each member to listen according to his role.

- Play the tape or show the film.

- At the end, ask each member to report to the group what he heard.

- Comment on the discrepancy, if any, between what was said and what was heard; play or show poorly communicated parts of the tape or film again.

QUESTIONS FOR DISCUSSION

1. What is the role of feedback in communication?
2. Why are "rules of comprehension" more important when a speaker addresses many listeners instead of one listener?

COMPREHENSION EXERCISE

YOU HAVE BEEN INVITED TO AN IMPORTANT MEETING WITH THE CHAIRMAN AND MEMBERS OF THE BOARD. THEY WANT TO ENLIST YOUR SUPPORT IN PROMOTING THE NEW POLICIES OF YOUR ISLAMIC ORGANIZATION AND MOBILIZING THE MUSLIM PUBLIC IN FAVOR OF THOSE POLICIES. THEY, AND YOU, WANT TO COMMUNICATE WELL BECAUSE OF THE SENSITIVITY OF THE POLICIES.

1. *Describe the characteristics of the listening environment that will be most suitable in this case.*

2. *List possible communication pitfalls in this meeting and outline your plan for overcoming them.*

3. *List three questions you could ask the speakers to seek clarification when needed.*

Chapter

18

How to Form a Committee

LEARNING OBJECTIVES

On completing this chapter, you should be able to:
- identify when to form a committee and when not to
- write a charter or job specification for a committee
- select appropriate membership for a committee
- establish committees

I. What Is a Committee?

A committee may be defined as a group of people performing a certain task for the organization. Committees are indispensable. They seem to exist everywhere, even when they are not formally appointed, because of the fact that collective judgment and consultation are needed and valued more than individual and autocratic decisions.

For example, after he had collected all verses of the Glorious Qur'an from all over the empire, 'Umar (RA) appointed a committee to supervise the copying of the whole Qur'an in one volume. Sa'd ibn al 'As dictated and Zayd ibn Thabit wrote. Anticipating differences with regard to the pronunciation of some words, 'Umar (RA) laid down the guideline that the dialect of the Mudar tribe was to be accepted in such cases.

Generally speaking, committees may be used for:
   a) disseminating information and giving advice
   b) generating ideas and solving given problems
   c) facilitating coordination, communication, cooperation, and
   d) recommending actions and making decisions

A. Advantages and Disadvantages

Important **advantages** of committee action are:
   a) It makes possible integrated group judgment. People from different specializations, geographical regions, and hierarchical levels can be tapped for tackling a problem.
   b) It helps bridge demarcation lines in matters that involve more than one organizational unit.
   c) It helps bring about better teamwork through formal and informal interactions.

There are also some **disadvantages** of committee action:
   a) The monetary cost of committees in the form of such expenses as travel and lodging should prohibit their use for trivial and routine matters.
   b) Too much compromise and indecision may result.
   c) A new member or a minority may dominate the proceedings.
   d) It may be difficult to hold a group accountable for its actions.

B. Types of Committees

Committees are of different kinds, based on their functions, terms of reference, and sometimes size. Some committees are permanent; others have a relatively short life span.

Did You Hear This About Committees?

- *A committee—the unwilling appointed by the unfit to achieve the unattainable!*
- *Committees keep minutes and waste hours!*
- *A camel is a horse designed by a committee!*

Committees may be created for a special purpose and dissolved when their mission has been accomplished. Two kinds of committees are generally used in most organizations:

a) Standing committees, which exist for handling responsibilities that are of a generally continuing nature and call for collective rather than individual judgment, such as planning, membership, finance, etc.

b) Ad hoc committees, which exist for handling responsibilities that are specific, both in their nature and duration, and for generally noncontroversial, nonrecurrent tasks such as studying a situation or arranging an event.

II. Forming the Committee

A. Assignment

Some committees are created by provisions of the organization's constitution and bylaws. Their specific assignment is stated in those documents. Other committees are appointed by the organization's governing body. They must be given a commission or charter or terms of reference that clearly spells out what they are to do. This definitive document should also clarify the committee's reporting and other relationships within the organization. No committee should be appointed without a clear understanding of its purpose.

B. Membership

The question of who should be included in the committee is closely related to the nature of the committee's purpose. A committee that is primarily concerned with informational, advisory, or problem-solving functions should include individuals who have the required knowledge and skills. Functional proficiency may not be the primary consideration in selecting membership for a committee designed to promote better coordination or cooperation. A coordinating committee, for example, should include personnel from the organizational units concerned. Committee members should be appointed with a clear view of the goals the committee must achieve and of the skills brought by each committee member to assist in the achievement of these goals.

The ability of individuals to effectively participate in group activities also warrants attention in making up a committee roster.

The size of the committee will vary with its responsibilities. Larger committees may be needed for areas such as membership recruitment, but smaller committees are preferred for their efficiency in reaching a consensus and in accomplishing their tasks.

As a rule of thumb, a standing committee should have a minimum of five members and a maximum of nine, although there are of course justifiable exceptions. The reason for the minimum of five is that it implies a working majority of three, which represents about as narrow a spread of collective judgment as can suffice in a situation that calls for collective judgment. The maximum of nine is a less rigid limit, but since most standing committees must meet regularly without the stimulus of an emergency, the difficulty of scheduling meetings for a larger number of people suggests an upper limit in this neighborhood. This will be true unless the business of the committee is so overwhelmingly important that none of its members is likely to develop conflicting obligations. The membership of a standing committee should be as broadly representative as its size permits with regard to organizational seniority, personal characteristics, and factional affiliations.

Many ad hoc committees have three members; some have only two; five is about the practical maximum. It is important that the members of an ad hoc committee be compatible with one another and competent with respect to the committee's assignment. They do not need to be representative of the organization in any other way and usually it does not matter which of them is named as chairman.

C. Chairmanship

The key to an effective committee is an effective chairman, for he is the member who sets the tone, the pace, and the strategies for the whole committee. Even if a committee has capable members and clear objectives, the ability of its chairman to lead and direct the committee's work is essential for its success. To be effective, the chairman should himself accept responsibility while encouraging others to contribute. He must be thoroughly acquainted with the goals of the organization and the part that his committee plays in the achievement of these goals.

Especially in the case of a standing committee, the chairman ought to be able to solicit cooperation from members and to allocate work to them from time to time. He or she ought not to be a person of extreme opinions with respect to the standing committee's area of responsibility, or someone new to the organization who does not understand its informal norms and culture. The effective committee chairman maintains harmony with committee members and the governing board itself, and is clear in his communications with them.

WHOSE JOB IS IT?

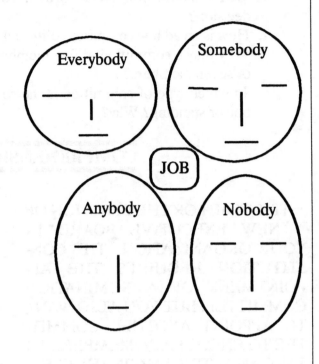

This is a story about four people named Everybody, Somebody, Anybody, and Nobody.

There was an important job to be done and Everybody was asked to do it.

Everybody was sure Somebody would do it.

Anybody could have done it, but Nobody did it.

Somebody got angry about that, because it was Everybody's job.

Everybody thought Anybody could do it but Nobody realized that Everybody would not do it.

It ended up that Everybody blamed Somebody when Nobody did what Anybody could have done.

WHOSE

JOB

WAS

IT

?

QUESTIONS FOR DISCUSSION

1. When should you NOT form a committee, even if you need a group decision?
2. How is an ad hoc committee different from a standing committee?
3. Why may a committee of five members be more effective than one of three or seven members?
4. In which type of committee is the role of the chairman more crucial — ad hoc or standing? Why?

COMPREHENSION EXERCISE

IT IS TIME FOR THE ELECTION OF A NEW EXECUTIVE BOARD IN YOUR ORGANIZATION. THE CONSTITUTION REQUIRES THE APPOINTMENT OF A NOMINATION COMMITTEE, BUT YOU ALSO WANT TO APPOINT ANOTHER COMMITTEE TO ENCOURAGE MEMBERS TO TAKE AN ACTIVE PART IN THE ELECTION PROCESS.

1. Write a job description for the two committees; indicate type, membership size, assignment, chairmanship, and term.

2. Draw up a plan for interaction between the two committees.

Chapter

19

How to Chair a Committee

LEARNING OBJECTIVES

On completing this chapter, you should be able to:
- identify elements of the committee chairman's role
- lead your committee in action and productivity
- help your committee achieve its goals

The task of chairing a committee is one of exercising leadership. The key to successful chairmanship of a committee is the chairman's ability to lead, motivate, delegate, and communicate with the members. The committee, as an organizational unit, is more than meetings, even though meetings are the most common and visible form of the committee conducting its business. The committee functions through many other formal and informal means of interaction, like writing reports, making observations, evaluating ongoing activities, monitoring performance, executing ceremonial functions, etc. Above all, the committee is a group whose continued existence as a group itself must be sustained through times of difficulties or differences. The chairman must lead the committee in more than its meetings.

I. The Chairman's Duties

Committee chairmen should take their assignment seriously, because their position is a mark of trust from the organization and its leadership. They should not do the committee's job all by themselves. That is self-defeating, since the purpose of the committee is to tap the varied resources of its members. A good chairman should lead and yet be a good listener.

The duties of the chairman may be classified as follows:
1. Planning the committee's work,
2. Conducting its meetings,
3. Maintaining records and information, (unless that task is assigned to a secretary-member of the committee),
4. Getting action from committee members, and
5. Evaluating results of committee action.

A. Planning the Committee's Work

The first responsibility of the chairman is to fully understand the committee's task. Based on this understanding, he should plan a tentative strategy of action that may include:
1. A preliminary schedule of meetings,
2. Assignments to individual members,
3. Background research work to staff,
4. Coordination with other committees,
5. Approvals for a budget, or
6. Other actions from authorizing bodies,
7. Time line and milestones for expected achievements, and
8. Other logistic and public relation concerns.

In a real sense, the committee is a miniorganization within a bigger one. The chairman should bring to bear all his leadership and management skills on moving the committee towards its commissioned objective.

B. Conducting Committee Meetings

A good committee meeting is the result of an action-oriented plan. It is based on a sound agenda, with all necessary conditions for decisions to be made met. The agenda and background material should be sent to members well in advance of the meeting date. Preferably, a meeting schedule for the entire year should be agreed upon before or during the first meeting. All members may not be able to attend all meetings, but the absence of a member from two or more meetings should be handled seriously within the scope of the chairman's authority and its limitation. (Discussion on chairing a meeting is covered in another chapter of this *Guide*.)

C. Maintaining Records and Information

Records of past actions, minutes of past meetings, reports of related committees, job description of the committee, and similar documents are needed for making informed decisions. In addition, the committee may need to set up data bases to store and manage information about members and the public who feel the impact of its work. Generally, the chairman should delegate record keeping to a committee member designated as the secretary. However, encouraging members to creatively apply all available information to furthering the committee's objectives rests with the chairman.

D. Getting Action from Committee Members

Committee members act as a group when they meet to decide upon plans and activities. At other times, each member must assume responsibility for specific actions. In either case, the chairman must help members procure resources and in general assist them in fulfilling their commitments. This calls for the ability to lead, motivate, delegate, and communicate with members. Also needed is the skill to recognize deficiencies in performance and taking corrective action. The chairman must set an example by attending to his assignment with promptness and seriousness.

E. Evaluating and Reporting Results of Committee Action

Committees must produce results, whether it is the successful staging of an event, producing a solution for a problem, or charting a course of action. In any case, the chairman must ensure that the results are evaluated for quality control purposes as well as for feedback. Time and resources should be set aside for evaluation as a part of the planning process discussed above. In fact, the performance of the chairman and members should also be evaluated to help improve future performance.

In most cases, the result of the committee's work must be reported to the appointing authority or the governing body of the organization. The chairman must direct the process of preparing the report and ensure that it truly reflects the views and accomplishments of all members. The report must serve its purpose of establishing clearly whether the objectives of the committee were achieved and make recommendations for further action if they were not. Presenting the report of the committee's work is a major responsibility of the chairman.

II. Limitations

A committee chairman must obtain full clarification of the mandate, scope, and limitations of his authority in operating the committee. Generally, a chairman cannot do any of the following:
  a. Appoint new members without appropriate approval,
  b. Remove any member without prior consultation with the governing body,
  c. Involve the organization in substantial, long-range commitments, financial or otherwise, or
  d. Alter organization policies, procedures, or bylaws.

III. Checklist for the Performance of Committee Chairman

Committee chairmen can use this checklist to make an assessment of their performance. Ask yourself:

DO YOU	YES	NO
1. Communicate effectively with committee members?	[ ]	[ ]
2. Listen to their views with an open mind?	[ ]	[ ]
3. Command their attention and inspire them?	[ ]	[ ]
4. Control the committee without dominating it?	[ ]	[ ]
5. Know and apply parliamentary procedures?	[ ]	[ ]
6. Take initiative in committee matters?	[ ]	[ ]
7. Understand interpersonal relationships?	[ ]	[ ]
8. Know the subject area of the committee?	[ ]	[ ]
9. Think and act in terms of committee goals ?	[ ]	[ ]
10. Create the right atmosphere for action and work?	[ ]	[ ]
11. Clearly understand the role of the support staff?	[ ]	[ ]

Give yourself 1 point for each YES and 0 for each NO. A score of 10-11 points is excellent, 8-9 points is good, 7-8 points is acceptable. A score of 6 and below is not acceptable for a committee chairman. Focus on improving in areas of deficiency and repeat the checklist test after three months to monitor your progress.

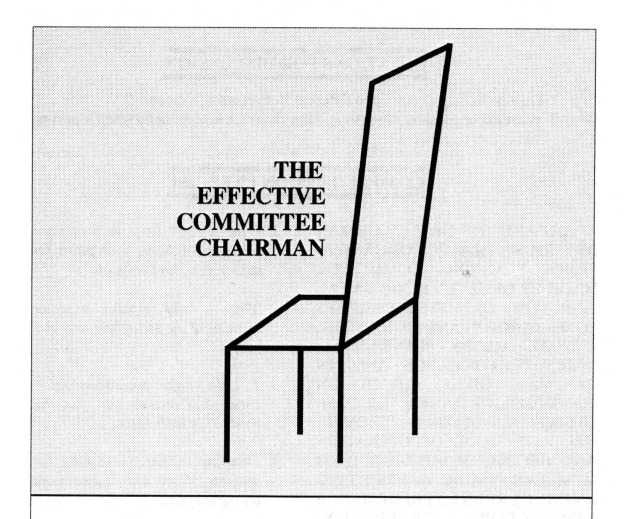

THE EFFECTIVE COMMITTEE CHAIRMAN

⇒ **C**ONSULTS before acting

⇒ **H**ESITATES before passing judgment

⇒ **A**CTS when it is time to do so

⇒ **I**NITIATES discussion without dominating it

⇒ **R**ECEIVES feedback willingly

⇒ **M**ODERATES his criticism

⇒ **A**CCEPTS new ideas without prejudice

⇒ **N**OTIFIES members about what he does in their name

QUESTIONS FOR DISCUSSION

1. How is chairing a committee different from chairing a meeting?
2. What major considerations should the chairman keep in mind when reporting the committee's work?

COMPREHENSION EXERCISE

YOU ARE THE NEW CHAIRMAN OF YOUR ISLAMIC ORGANIZATION'S PLANNING COMMITTEE. MADE UP OF SEVEN SENIOR MEMBERS, THIS COMMITTEE DISCUSSES LONG-RANGE PLANS, GUIDES THE ANNUAL ACTION PLANS, EVALUATES PERFORMANCE AND, IN GENERAL, GIVES ADVICE ON MAJOR POLICY ISSUES. THE COMMITTEE HAS DECIDED TO OVERHAUL ITS MODE OF OPERATION AND BECOME MORE VISIBLE TO MEMBERS. IT ALSO WANTS TO EXAMINE CURRENT PERFORMANCE AND LAY DOWN A STRATEGY FOR ORGANIZATIONAL GROWTH.

1. *Write a short letter to committee members outlining your plans for achieving committee goals.*

2. *Write a brief response a senior member of the committee may give you.*

3. *List the major documents, references, and records that you will need to use in this case.*

4. *Draw up a chart to monitor the progress of the committee's work during the year.*

How to Arrange a Meeting

LEARNING OBJECTIVES

On completing this chapter, you should be able to:
- identify various elements of a successful meeting
- prepare a plan for a meeting that has a given purpose
- arrange an effective meeting
- achieve above-average success in meeting arrangements

I. Purpose of a Meeting

Group meetings have grown to occupy a major role in organizational performance. Meetings give members a sense of belonging and importance, offer them an opportunity for participation, and provide a vehicle to distribute information. Against these advantages are the disadvantages of meetings. Only a few participants make any real contribution, many others come without any meaningful preparation, and discussion tends to get off the subject. Meetings take considerable time and give excessive advantage to the convincing speaker who may not necessarily offer the best idea or the best comment.

At heart, people attend meetings generally to satisfy their own self-interest. They may believe in the cause and receive satisfaction from working for it or they may perceive the organization as serving some special purpose for them.

An example of a special purpose would be that of people looking for companionship and a sense of belonging. Understanding the reasons for which people attend our meetings helps us plan better meetings and assign appropriate tasks to potentially productive participants. Some participants may withdraw if the tasks assigned to them do not meet their needs or are beyond their capabilities.

Meetings can be of any size: small, medium, or large. In any case, there are four basic purposes for having a meeting;
1. to make decisions,
2. to distribute information,
3. to develop relationships among people, and
4. to provide motivation.

The size and purpose of a meeting are often interrelated. For example, the bigger the meeting, the more difficult it is to make decisions. The physical presence of a large number of people is not always conducive to original thinking, but it does help to generate a sense of togetherness and motivate the participants.

II. Your Role as a Planner

Planning successful meetings requires following some fundamental planning guidelines and strategies that apply to any type of event. Good planning can make the difference between success and failure.

A. Leadership and Management

Arranging an effective meeting calls for leadership and management skills on our part. The first step is usually the appointment of a committee to plan the event. We must exercise effective leadership by getting committee members and co-workers to work as a team and do their share. However, when the committee does not have the resources or capabilities in certain areas, we must know how to draw upon resources of organizations that can perform in those areas.

The simplest way to start planning for an event is to use the time line planning method. One form of this method is to draw a time line between now and the date of the event. Then mark all that needs to be done, and when, at appropriate intervals on this time line.

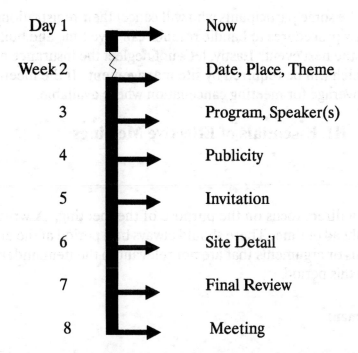

Day 1	Now
Week 2	Date, Place, Theme
3	Program, Speaker(s)
4	Publicity
5	Invitation
6	Site Detail
7	Final Review
8	Meeting

As meeting planners, we must have the ability to present plans and budgets to the appropriate authorizing bodies for their approval. These bodies must make necessary decisions at the right time. When meetings are being held out of town, we must establish procedures for inspecting the site and booking accommodations with help from local associates. Above all, we must anticipate and, when possible, avoid last minute problems.

B. Financial Control

We must always attempt to get the most for our meeting dollar, since the financial resources made available to us are a trust from Allah and our membership. Major areas of expense are travelling, lodging, meeting space, food on site, printing, and mailing. In each case, we should use competitive bargaining to negotiate the lowest prices consistent with the quality we want. We should find out about hidden costs on all items, especially when negotiating menu prices. We should understand what is negotiable in contracts and the penalty for any breach of agreement. Keeping track of invoices and other postmeeting paperwork is necessary for avoiding payment disputes with hotels and caterers.

By planning ahead, we can trim printing costs on brochures for publicity as well as on handouts and program material. We should develop cost-effective mailings that disseminate the information the attendants need by using the right mailing list, sharing the cost with any other mailing, allowing enough time for slower but cheaper mail delivery, and keeping the size small but attractive.

There will always be some participants who will cancel their registrations at the last minute. Safe and easy procedures to handle refunds can save time and build a reputation that will help in the next event. Lastly, let's not neglect the insurance needs of the meeting, some of which will be required by site management. If the meeting is large, also get insurance coverage for meeting cancellation where available.

III. Essentials of Effective Meetings

A. Purpose

There should be a direct focus on the purpose of the meeting. A written agenda must be passed out ahead of time. There should always be a period at the end for open discussion. Questions or arguments that are not relevant to the item under discussion can be postponed to this period.

B. Meeting Environment

Physical arrangement of the room is critical to the meeting's success. As for size, the room should comfortably accommodate the anticipated number of people. It should be neither too large nor too small, although it is prudent for motivational meetings to use a slightly smaller room since physical closeness will help generate a feeling of greater solidarity among the participants. The temperature should be comfortable and the room well lit, especially if decision making is expected. Seating arrangements are important. A speaker in front of rows of people tends to create a psychological barrier between himself and the audience. We should avoid this when possible since it inhibits participation. The room should be free of distractions such as excessive noise or inappropriate decorations.

Even if we don't know how many will come, our knowledge and experience should help us choose the size that may be the most proper. Select the best from the classic seating arrangements: Theater Style, Classroom Style, Conference Style, Banquet Style. Before the meeting, check the acoustics, lighting, and temperature control of the room so as to keep people comfortable. Plan on making more space in a crowded meeting room. Get things in writing from the facility manager.

C. Time

It is very important to start on time, to get to the point of the meeting, and to end it on time; this adds an organized appearance to a meeting, leaves a good impression on the participants, and helps get work done in an orderly and efficient manner. It is harmful to drag the meeting on by allowing discussion to go off on tangents. Socializing can occur after the meeting.

D. Chairman

The authority of the chairman must be well-established if he is to run the meeting effectively. When introducing him, we must stress the chairman's credentials and qualifications to chair the meeting. This promotes an acceptance of his authority. The chairman's appearance and manner of speaking must project him well. He should be neutral when controversial points are discussed. He should keep the thinking of the group focused on the agenda item. He should not ask: "Well, what do you think we should do?" Instead, he should summarize opportunities and alternatives as fairly as possible.

E. Participation

Participation is of the utmost importance. If one person does all the talking, others are turned off and the meeting becomes dull for them. We can plan participation ahead of time by asking different people to present various items on the agenda. Such involvement helps build and maintain an active and interested group. When we make the participants feel they are part of the focus of the meeting, we enhance their motivation to contribute and accept assignments for work.

To get shy participants to open up, we can use any number of "ice breakers" that will get the meeting off to a friendly start. To keep it that way, we should make attractive and legible name tags available, and encourage the participants to wear them.

F. Assignments

An effective meeting must not be concluded without assigning tasks to participants. These tasks can be as general as "Think about this on your way home" or as specific as "The three of you will research this topic and draft a document by the end of the week." A meeting in which nothing seems to have been accomplished, or which does not bring the participants closer to the solution of a problem, can be demoralizing in the long run. In assigning tasks, we should keep in mind the varied interests and abilities of those attending. Use a well-designed evaluation form at the end of the meeting to solicit feedback and comments. This will enhance a sense of participation and identify pitfalls to avoid in the future.

G. Decisions

Any decision-making sessions of a meeting should be well-structured. We should think through possible options and alternatives ahead of time and present them as such at the meeting. We should focus our discussion on definite choices and alternatives and avoid posing question like: "What do you think?" There are more effective ways of obtaining participants' thoughts on a subject without providing an invitation to digression or irrelevant discussion. For example, we might ask them to criticize a specific part of a given alternative or to state briefly their reasons for preferring one alternative over another. Advance preparation is the key if the meeting is to result in significant accomplishment.

H. Unity

Unity of the meeting helps propel it towards its purpose. The effective chairman should strive to maintain unity at all times by enforcing the procedural rules as well as by motivating those present. We should not let a meeting end with people divided, upset, or angry. Often we can assess the participants' inner feelings by carefully observing their facial expressions. Sometimes, a well-timed story, a joke, or wisdom from the hadith literature, can ease the tension and help reunite divided factions. Often times it is good to remind the group of the Islamic goals of the organization. If factions do develop, it often helps to designate a speaker for each faction and recognize only that person. Special effort should be made to keep everybody in the room until the end of the meeting, since entries and exits are distracting.

In general, either as chairman or as participant, we should never lose our temper and always display a positive attitude. A negative attitude tends to depress everyone. If the meeting is a long one, it is important that we provide time for strategic breaks. We should also try to instill in the participants a sense of being together on a mission.

After they have had time to reflect on the meeting and what followed from it, we could seek their opinions by mail or telephone, thus nurturing a group spirit among them.

I. The Unexpected

There will always be the unexpected, however well we plan. For example, the audio-visual equipment may not work or never arrive, the keynote speaker may cancel at the last minute, reservation errors may cause a shortage of meeting rooms, inclement weather may make outdoor activities impossible, or there may be insufficient parking at the site due to an emergency. We should anticipate as much as we can and develop alternative plans.

IV. Developing a Meeting Agenda

We should plan our meetings to maximize benefit from the participants' efforts. This requires a carefully drawn agenda which is neither too vague nor too restrictive. Agreement on the extent of the discussion on any item is vital to the success of any meeting.

The agenda should include items that really need group consultation, excluding those that only require an individual's decision. Place the most exciting items later in the agenda but allow enough time for them; discussion of such points will help the meeting pick up at the tail end when the participants begin to lose energy. Sequence agenda items so that they build up logically, keep their number limited, and allocate more time to items that are complex and controversial. One easy way to construct a schedule is to list times for the daily prayers and meals, and place ninety-minute sessions between and around them. Appoint a timekeeper to help you keep track of the time being spent on each agenda item. Allow enough time to discuss the topics in depth and leave some time free at the end for brainstorming, which helps anticipate potential problems.

With the notice of every meeting, participants should get a detailed agenda and minutes of the last meeting. Urge them to read and understand this material. Ask if they have any questions with regard to the minutes of the last meeting. Have them approve these minutes before proceeding with the new meeting.

> Example of an Agenda
>
> 1. Continuing Business
>   1.1 Approval of the Agenda
>   1.2 Minutes of the Last Meeting
>   1.3 Review of Decisions of the Last Meeting
>   1.4 Reports of Members
> 2. New Business
>   2.1 Mission Statement
>   2.2 Performance Standards
>   2.3 Action Plan and Budget
> 3. Other Business
> 4. Next Meeting, Date, and Agenda

V. Miscellaneous Tips

1. To book accommodation for an out-of-town meeting, first consult the city's hotel directory, often available at the local library.
2. A good way to judge a hotel's efficiency is to check the cleanliness of its rest rooms, the length of time registrants spend at the front desk, and the quality of food in its restaurant.
3. The most important consideration when choosing a room should be adequate size.
4. The best seating arrangement for audience involvement and participation is conference style.
5. All printed material must be completed early enough to allow for sufficient time for reprinting if an error is detected.
6. In meetings that have simultaneous (parallel) sessions, coffee breaks should be scheduled all at one time.

VI. Checklist for Arranging a Meeting

The following must be checked and tested before a meeting (also ask if the meeting site has its own checklist relating to special features of the site):

ITEM	Responsible	Deadline	Comments
Meeting Room Basics			
Chairs	_____	_____	_____
Tables	_____	_____	_____
Waste receptacles	_____	_____	_____
Pencils	_____	_____	_____
Note pads	_____	_____	_____
Name tags	_____	_____	_____
Refreshments	_____	_____	_____
Signs	_____	_____	_____
Presentation Items			
Stage and lectern	_____	_____	_____
Curtains and screens	_____	_____	_____
Lighting/projectors	_____	_____	_____
Spare bulbs	_____	_____	_____
Extension cords	_____	_____	_____
Easels and pointers	_____	_____	_____
Water at lectern	_____	_____	_____
Location Diagrams			
Equipment location	_____	_____	_____
Fire extinguishers	_____	_____	_____
Emergency exits	_____	_____	_____
Vending machines	_____	_____	_____
Location of signs	_____	_____	_____
Washrooms	_____	_____	_____
Audience Arrangement			
Acoustics	_____	_____	_____
Room temperature	_____	_____	_____
Adequate space	_____	_____	_____
Coat hangers	_____	_____	_____

Handouts for audience   _____ _____ _____
Seats for press/guests   _____ _____ _____
Prayers/baby-sitting   _____ _____ _____

The Speaker (s)
Invitation   _____ _____ _____
Exact time/place   _____ _____ _____
Purpose and topic   _____ _____ _____
Type of audience   _____ _____ _____
Detailed program   _____ _____ _____
Chairman or panelists   _____ _____ _____
Audiovisual capability   _____ _____ _____
Transportation   _____ _____ _____
Food and lodging   _____ _____ _____
Expense reimbursement   _____ _____ _____
Request for handout   _____ _____ _____

Whenever you see a successful meeting, you should automatically assume that a tremendous amount of preparation and effort has gone into it. Excellent meetings never happen accidentally!

For Organizers: Half a Dozen Ways to Wreck a Meeting

1. Do not let anyone know in advance what subjects will be discussed. (They might come with data, prepared to discuss the matter intelligently.)

2. Do send out notice of the meeting at least several months in advance. (Participants will put off preparation, figuring they have lots of time. They may even manage to forget it.) Or, give notice only a few hours ahead of time, through a member who does not know one thing about the meeting.

3. Do announce that the meeting will start "about" a certain time. (Assures interruptions when latecomers will take advantage of the vague timing and disrupt the meeting by their arrival—and by asking for a report on what's happened so far.)

4. Do see to it that the topics for discussion are not studied in advance and do be unprepared with leading questions to stimulate discussion.

5. Do encourage everyone to think they're going to be asked for advice and suggestions even if the purpose of the meeting is only to transmit information. (Participants will feel betrayed when their comments are ignored or overruled, and you can be assured of their resentment at future meetings.)

6. Do invite everyone you can, even if the meeting's purpose is to make a policy decision requiring a base of information about your organization. (Assures meeting will be doomed from the outset as uninformed participants exercise their influence and voting rights along with informed participants and officers.) Alternative: If the purpose is general education to broaden participants' information base, invite only those on one committee, or on similar committees, or from the same housing unit, or those who eat lunch together.

QUESTIONS FOR DISCUSSION

1. What is the time line planning method? How does it work?
2. What are the most expensive items in arranging meetings?
3. What role does the environment play in the success of a meeting? Give examples.
4. Who is more crucial to the success of a meeting, an effective chairman or a group of active participants? Why?
5. What is the purpose of an agenda? Is it always needed?
6. What seating arrangements are suitable for a board of directors meeting, a general assembly meeting, a pep-talk meeting?

COMPREHENSION EXERCISE

YOUR ISLAMIC ORGANIZATION HAS TAKEN A WELL-CONSIDERED POSITION ON A NEW POLITICAL SITUATION IN THE MUSLIM WORLD. AS PUBLIC RELATIONS OFFICER, YOU ARE ASKED TO SEEK PUBLIC ACCEPTANCE OF THAT POSITION. YOU HAVE DECIDED TO ARRANGE A MEETING FOR LEADERS OF 300 COMMUNITY CENTERS FROM AROUND THE COUNTRY. YOU WANT THE MEETING TO BE HELD IN TWO WEEKS AT A CENTRAL LOCATION. YOU ARE SEEKING THE MEETING'S ENDORSEMENT OF YOUR ORGANIZATION'S POSITION.

1. Write a sample letter or announcement for this meeting. Include an agenda.

2. Draw up a time line plan for the meeting.

3. Draw a diagram to show an effective seating arrangement.

4. Review the checklist and comment on the six most important items.

Chapter

21

How to Chair a Meeting

LEARNING OBJECTIVES

On completing this chapter, you should be able to:
- identify elements of the chairman's role
- chair a meeting effectively
- handle the question and answer period successfully
- assure accurate record keeping

I. The Chairman's Role

You have been asked to chair a meeting. You have done your homework. You have sent out the agenda and other related materials. The meeting is about to begin. Here are some tips on the best way to be effective as chairman:

1. First, ascertain that the room is quiet and without distractions, and that it is well-ventilated and well-lit. Then, attend to seating arrangements. When-

---

ever possible, everyone should be able to see everyone else. Here are some other considerations that can help plan seating arrangements for small committee meetings:

- Face-to-face seating aids opposition. The person seated across from the chairman is most likely to confront him. Seat someone in that position who is more likely to help than hinder your role as chairman. However, we should never use seating to manipulate the meeting but only to create a productive environment.
- Side-to-side seating makes disagreement difficult. Seating a friendly participant next to an antagonistic one can minimize unnecessary opposition.
- The seat to the chairman's right is called the dead man's spot because the person sitting there is hidden from eye contact with the chairman. Placing an antagonistic participant there might diminish the chances of a confrontation.

2. Begin the meeting with recitation of the Qur'an and end it with a *du'a'*. Choosing verses that touch upon the meeting's agenda will help create the right psychological environment, enhance mission orientation, and refresh consciousness of Allah among those present.

3. Handle conflicts tactfully and appeal to the higher mission of the adversaries. When a clash of ideas becomes a clash of personalities, turn to a neutral participant to soften the confrontation. Refer to appropriate selections from the Qur'an and hadith to remind the participants of the Islamic code of conduct.

4. Watch out for and control the gabbers. A talkative person can be controlled by suggesting that he write down his ideas for a concerted study or by picking up a phrase that he has just used, repeating it, and then calling on someone else to continue the discussion.

5. Encourage problem-solving methods like brainstorming. To keep ideas flowing in the right direction, remind the group of the "problem" in front of it.

6. Ask the opinion of the most senior participants present last. This will foster discussion. If their ideas are introduced too early, they may stifle the participation of the newer participants in your meeting.

7. Choose the strongest advocates of a solution when making assignments related to it. They will work hardest to prove that the decision taken was the right one.

8. Set a time frame for each agenda item in proportion to its significance and try to stick to it firmly while allowing enough interaction among participants. Emphasize the agenda as the criteria against which the group should measure its effectiveness. Whenever there is a call for more discussion than time will allow, seek a proper amendment to the agenda. Point out the items that may suffer because of rescheduling and help analyze the costs and benefits of the amendment.

9. Make use of parliamentary procedures whenever needed to keep the meeting orderly; periodically, sum up what has been decided up to that point.

10. Get a verbal commitment from everyone assigned a task. This commitment, made in front of the group, will lead to a greater degree of follow-through than a commitment made in private.

11. Sometimes it may help to introduce controversial subjects just before a scheduled break for prayer, meals, or refreshment. This may allow for intense private exchanges outside the meeting, provide participants an opportunity for understanding varied points of view in a more relaxed setting, and help speed decision making when the meeting resumes.

12. Choose appropriate diction, using positive words and avoiding negative ones. This will enable the participants to feel an "ownership" in the decisions arrived at through the democratic process.

Action point

IF YOU FAIL TO PLAN, YOU PLAN TO FAIL!

Imagine a salesman trying to prove that his customer is wrong! If he succeeds, the client will hate his guts and will not buy. Either way he is a loser. American business has adopted the slogan: The customer is always right! We do not have to accept that concept except within our system of ethics and values. However, we must focus on each activity and clearly define our specific objective in engaging in it. For example, if we are going to meet the leader of the opposition party in the government, we must spell out the particular aim of the meeting and plan among ourselves who is to say what and in what sequence! We have to discuss the issues beforehand and get a consensus on what positions we should jointly adopt. Do not end up in situations where someone dominates the meeting unexpectedly or you quarrel among yourselves in the meeting, or else you will finish the meeting without discussing your own agenda because you are dragged into the opponent's agenda. If you do not plan well, you will be amazed at how many things can go wrong!

II. Question and Answer Period

A. Why?

A Question and Answer (Q & A) period adds to the value of any meeting. It helps the organizers identify the attitudes and concerns of the participants. If extreme criticism or hostile attitudes are expressed, are these directed towards the speaker, the subject, or the organization? In short, the Q & A period provides a powerful feedback tool to the organizers.

At the same time, a Q & A period gives the participants a chance to participate in the meeting, to clarify some ambiguities, to have some important questions answered, to examine the speakers' response and attitude, and to express some of their own opinions. For the speaker, the Q & A period is an excellent feedback instrument.

The Q & A period must not be treated as a casual, unplanned, ten-minute event of the meeting; it has to be thought of and prepared for as one of the main parts of the program.

B. Planning the Q & A Period

Due to lack of planning, most Q & A periods achieve only a fraction of what could be accomplished. The following steps help in good planning:

Step 1: Getting the Participants Set

The participants can be given sample questions that will stimulate other questions. They may be briefed on the particular purpose of the meeting and, if time permits, an outline of the most important issues that will be discussed may be printed and circulated. It should be made clear to the participants that this outline is only suggestive and not restrictive. Another practice is to divide the participants prior to the presentation into three teams: clarification, criticism, and plans-of-action teams. The chairman can introduce these teams to the meeting by seating them into right, center, and left parts of the room.

Step 2: Getting Questions Down

The questions that occur to people in the early part of the program are often forgotten when it is time to ask questions. Papers or cards can be passed out so people can write down questions as they occur to them. Then questions can either be asked after the presentation or collected and quickly sorted systematically so that they can be answered in a logical sequence. Sometimes a break during the meeting may be planned to give participants a chance to write down their questions without missing any part of the presentation.

Step 3: Getting the Most Important Questions

To get questions that are really representative of all the participants is important. Two techniques can be used here: buzz groups and small group discussions. Buzz groups are small discussion groups of six or eight persons, for example. People sometimes have difficulty formulating and expressing questions that bother them. Hearing others' questions usually helps them crystalize their own. Breaking a large meeting into small buzz groups for five or ten minutes can help people frame their questions and ensures that every person takes part in the discussion. Such groups can be quickly organized in a large meeting by asking some people in each row to turn around and team up with someone behind them. Then, one person in each group can report its questions. Small group discussions are another way to get at representative questions. This is done by selecting a small group of representatives from the participants to come up and discuss briefly what questions seem most important to them. If anyone disagrees, he can say so.

Step 4: Sorting Questions

All questions may not be answered in one meeting. Unanswered questions can be collected for future meetings. Questions can be recorded on paper so that the participants are assured that they are not merely being put off and that the questions they raise will be taken up at a future session.

Step 5: Getting Results

This step is very important for the chairman, since most of his activities are focused on motivating people to take action and getting involved with what has been decided. One way to reinforce what has been decided upon or learned is for two or three participants to conduct a panel discussion at the end of the meeting. This discussion should highlight possible courses of action or potential applications of the new knowledge.

III. Taking Minutes

Minutes are not only a legal record of the work accomplished by the group, but they also serve as an informational tool for various committees and the general participants. Even though a chairman normally delegates the writing of minutes to someone designated as secretary, he is responsible for their authenticity. The following are some pointers on how to take good minutes:

1. Since the participant who takes minutes does not have an opportunity to participate fully, it is good practice to have participants take turns at recording minutes. The participant in charge should write out the complete draft from the notes while his memory is still fresh after the meeting.

2. Each item should have its own heading or title in order to separate the items and to make it easier for the reader to locate particular subjects. Each motion should be written down in its exact wording. To make this possible, the chairman could ask each person making a motion to write it down in full.

3. When reporting any item, do not give a word-for-word report of who said what. A summary of the major points for and against is sufficient. Unless the meeting requires it, the names of the participants who make or second a motion need not be written down.

4. The voice votes on motions may be reported as carried or rejected. If a hand count or ballot vote is made, the minutes should show the actual number of supporters and opponents. Include in the minutes all main motions—whether carried or rejected. Do not include motions that were withdrawn.

5. A draft of the minutes should be reviewed by the chairman and, when warranted, by an attorney before it is distributed for approval at the next meeting.

6. Minutes should be as concise as is consistent with full reporting. Committee reports should be presented in writing and may be attached to the minutes, with other material presented at the meeting, or as an appendix.

In summary, to be most beneficial for meeting participants, minutes should be written according to a set format that corresponds to the agenda. In reality, only two things take place in meetings—communication (passing on helpful information) and decisions (deciding to do something). If the item is communication, some form of report should be attached to the minutes, instead of being included in the minutes. If the item is decision, the three W's should be reported:

- 1. The decision made (WHAT)
- 2. Responsibility assigned for action/follow-up (WHO)
- 3. Deadlines for action (WHEN)

Reporting the full discussion is not useful since it is difficult to write, time-consuming to read, and may not add much to the decision made. However, what is written must be at an appropriate level of language and consistent with the level of those receiving the report.

An Acronym for Introducing Speakers

A - Area: What is his area of expertise?
C - Credentials: Why is he qualified to speak?
T - Topic: What will he speak on?
I - Importance: Why is it important to the audience?
O - Organization: What is his affiliation?
N - Name: Who is he?

A
C
T
I
O
N!

FOR CHAIRMEN: HALF A DOZEN WAYS TO WRECK A MEETING

1. Take all telephone calls that come in during the meeting. (Breaks up the best-planned session, interrupting not only the person called but everyone else as well.)

2. Encourage any speakers to employ the lecture method — so successful with some professors — so as not to waste time drawing out ideas from participants. (Very helpful in making everyone — but the speaker — feel useless.)

3. Do not use graphs or charts or any other visual aids. (Such presentations interfere with those who do things "by ear" and have trouble with employing more than one sense at a time. Furthermore, they add interest to meetings, which sometimes prolongs them, ruining schedules.)

4. Do not let participants indicate what is of interest to them. Hold to your guns...and a cast-iron agenda.

5 Encourage private cross-talk between individuals. (Very interesting to those who indulge, although seldom enlightening to anyone else.)

6. Discuss solutions first, and facts later, in solving any problems which may arise. (Increases chances of adopting the first solution that comes along without considering all possibilities. May even let you skip over a few unpopular facts that do not fit in with your favorite solution.)

Action point

ARE YOU THE CHAIRMAN OR THE SPEAKER?

Once at an MSA convention, a session chairman introduced a speaker. His introduction was longer than the speech. Moreover, in the question and answer period he volunteered responses against the wishes of the speaker. In addition, he ventured to summarize the speech after the speaker had spoken, to which the speaker objected. This chairman quarreled with the speaker, ridiculing him, and lecturing him on *adab* and *akhlaq*. The whole session was a flop and the speaker was extremely upset.

From time to time we encounter people like this who mishandle the responsibility of chairing a meeting due to inexperience or lack of knowledge. They need to be educated on the role of the chairman. The main points to remember are:

1. Introduce the speakers, highlighting their achievements relative to the subject matter.
2. Do not say that the speaker is well-known and he will introduce himself. This is an insult. Respectable people do not speak about themselves.
3. Prior to the meeting, prepare a short questionnaire for the speaker to answer.
4. Keep the introductory remarks brief and relevant.
5. Do not become a hindrance or an obstacle between the audience and speaker. Help them to communicate freely.
6. Inform the speaker about the time available and about time signals before the meeting starts.
7. Announce your plan of conducting the meeting, especially time allocation.
8. Do not let the speaker chair his own session. Chairmanship and speaking are two distinct functions and should not be confused.
9. Provide a glass of water for the speaker.
10. Check the audiovisual system before the meeting.
11. Be on the podium ten minutes before time.
12. Keep eye contact with the whole audience during the meeting.
13. Do not leave the stage. Assign someone to be ready to respond to your requests when you point to him.
14. Arrange the table so it is neat, tidy, and without any unnecessary materials. A cloth or paper skirt should be used.
15. Have a pen and paper ready to note things you need to attend to.
16. Appear attentive and interested throughout the talk —no yawning or daydreaming on stage.

IV. The Nuts and Bolts of Creativity

Creativity is the power or the ability to invent, i.e., to use ingenuity in making, developing, or achieving an objective. Creativity calls for originality and imaginativeness in dealing with a situation. When chairing or managing meetings, we can enhance the ability to be creative or depress it by what we say and do or what we allow others to say and do. We will look at how we can be creative in thinking, interpersonal interaction, and innovative performance.

A. Effectiveness in Interaction

The key concepts for effective interaction are:
1. Be positive: Maintain an optimistic rather than a pessimistic attitude and see the good rather than the bad in actions and circumstances.
2. When a speaker is in charge: Let people share themselves and their ideas instead of taking over conversation; do not push people and let them be in charge of action.
3. Speak for "I": Speak for yourself and what you believe; take ownership of what you say.
4. Allow passing: Do not push people who have said or communicated as much as they want to; respect their right to "pass" or quit.
5. Killer statements: Avoid killer statements like put-downs, insults, sarcasm, and anything negative; use empathy and understanding instead.
6. Validation: Use positive comments as much as possible, make people feel comfortable, support them, praise and appreciate honestly, do not delay giving appreciation, give your attention, and practice acceptance.

B. Creativity in Thinking

Creativity in thinking calls for unleashing the process of reaching out with one's imagination and drawing upon the entire spectrum of one's knowledge and experiences. Nothing dampens that process more than the use of everyday phrases that we have become used to when faced with something we have not heard or with which we are not comfortable. Some of these phrases are:

We've never done it that way before!
It's not in the budget!
We're not ready for it yet!
Too academic!
Somebody would have suggested it if it were any good!
Let's discuss it another time!
We're too small/big for that!
We have too many projects now!
It has been the same for twenty years, so it must be good!
I just know it won't work!
No adolescent is going to tell me how to run this organization!

It will increase overhead!
But they won't accept it!
Don't move too fast!
Let's wait and see!
It'll mean more work!
Let's put it in writing!
Won't work in our industry!
It's nuts!
We've never used that approach before!
No regulations covering it!
It won't work!
We lack the manpower!
We've tried that before!
All right in theory, but can you put it into practice?
Too modern!
Too old-fashioned!
You don't understand our problem!

It's their responsibility, not ours!
What airhead thought that up?
Let's form a committee!
That's not our problem!
It's too early!
It's too late!
You'll never sell that to..!
Why something new now?
Our sales are still going up!
Here we go again!
I don't see the connection!
We can't do it under the regulations!
Political dynamite!
It's not in the plan!
It's not in the manual!

C. Stifling Innovation

Innovation is the work of creative minds that look at a situation from a new angle and are willing to offer new interpretation and risk new approaches that may sometimes fail. In many cases, innovation offers the only hope of solving difficult problems or getting out of complicated situations. However, those in charge of a meeting or a project may often act in ways that stifle innovation. Writing in *The Change Masters: Innovation for Productivity in the American Corporation*, R. Kanters lists the following things we do that result in stifling innovation instead of encouraging it.

Suspicion	Regard any new idea from below with suspicion — because it is new and because it is from below.
Approval	Insist that people who need your approval to act first go through several other levels of management to get the necessary signatures.
Challenge	Ask departments or individuals to challenge and criticize each other's proposals. (That saves you the job of deciding — you just pick the survivor.)
Criticism	Express your criticism freely and withhold your praise. (That keeps people on their toes.) Let them know they can be fired at any time.

Problems	Treat identification of problems as signs of failure to discourage people from letting you know when something in their area is not working.
Control	Control everything carefully. Make sure people count anything that can be counted — frequently.
Change	Make decisions to reorganize or change policies in secret and spring them on people unexpectedly. (That also keeps people on their toes.)
Justification	Make sure requests for information are fully justified, and make sure that it is not given out to managers freely. (You don't want data to fall into the wrong hands.)
Delegation	Assign to lower-level managers, in the name of delegation and participation, responsibility for figuring out how to cut back, lay off, move people around, or otherwise implement the threatening decisions you have made.
Know-it-all	Never forget that you, the higher-ups, already know everything important about this business.

Art of *Da'wah*: A Practical Lesson in Unity!

Imam Hasan al Banna was about to pray *tarawih* (nonobligatory prayers during Ramadan) in the mosque when a fierce quarrel erupted among the people. Some wanted to pray eight *raka'at* (sections of prayers) while others insisted on twenty. They asked him: "Who is right and who is wrong?" He did not reply, because an answer either way would only aggravate the situation further. Instead he asked them: "Is *tarawih fard* (obligatory) or *Sunnah*?" They responded unanimously: "It is *Sunnah*, of course!" He added: "But unity of Muslims is a *fard*. Should we violate a *fard* for the establishment of a *Sunnah*? We would be much better off to pray at home and preserve our unity and brotherhood."

V. General Purpose Evaluation Form for Committee Meetings

Please put a check mark in the box on the left of questions you wish to answer by "Yes." Do nothing if your answer is "No."

Part A

[ ] 1. Does the committee understand its assignments?

[ ] 2. Did the members make an agenda or outline of what to discuss?

[ ] 3. Was the agenda carefully planned and thoughtfully worked out by the entire committee?

[ ] 4. Was sufficient advance notice given for members to prepare?

[ ] 5. Did they have a diversity of viewpoints?

[ ] 6. Did they make constructive use of conflict, opposition, or criticism?

[ ] 7. Were there enough good ideas for debate?

[ ] 8. Were they flexible?

[ ] 9 (a). Did they have their facts straight, prepare their homework, study, analyze, and then make decisions as a result of full discussion?

[ ] 9 (b). Did they depend too much on the leader?

Part B

[ ] 1. Was the discussion lively?

[ ] 2. Did the meeting start and stop on time?

[ ] 3. Was there too much expression of opinion instead of trying to integrate ideas?

[ ] 4. Were some members too shy to participate?

[ ] 5. Did any of the members have a tendency to dominate?

[ ] 6. Was there enough progress on the problem, or was the discussion side-tracked?

[ ] 7. Did more than two members wander from the subject? Seem disinterested? Fall asleep? Play with objects?

[ ] 8. Could you spot any of the "problem people" named below?

    [ ] Super-agreeables

    [ ] Negativists

    [ ] Indecisive stallers

    [ ] Hostile aggressors

    [ ] Complete complainers

    [ ] "Know-it-alls"

[ ] 9. Could you spot any "hidden agendas"? In other words, were there members trying to push for their own ideas to get approved as soon as they received enough support without allowing the rest of the group ample time to participate in the discussion?

Part C
[ ] 1. Was there any member that did not participate?
[ ] 2. Was the group enthusiastic and eager to draw up the plan?
[ ] 3. Were there any problems discussed that were not completely solved? State what they are:

1. _____

2. _____

3. _____

[ ] 4. Were there any hostile feelings?
[ ] 5. On the whole, how do you rate this meeting? Please check one of the following:
   [ ] No Good   [ ] Mediocre   [ ] Alright   [ ] Good   [ ] Excellent
[ ] 6. What improvements would you suggest in the conduct of similar meetings?

_____

_____

EVALUATION OF CHAIRPERSONS — A SHORT FORM

Please put a check mark in the box on the left of questions you wish to answer by "Yes." Do nothing if your answer is "No." (Replace "he" by "she" when appropriate in the questions below.)

[ ] 1. Did the session start and end on time?
[ ] 2. Did the group participate well?
[ ] 3. Were the rules for running a meeting followed?
[ ] 4. Was the chairman audible?
[ ] 5. Did he display the intellectual ability to assess situations and make quick, relevant decisions?
[ ] 6. Did he display sensitivity to feelings prevailing in the group without disturbing the meeting?
[ ] 7. Was the chairmanship a function or a person?
[ ] 8. Were the participants present continuously, physically and intellectually?
[ ] 9. Was the speaker introduced properly?
[ ] 10. Was the discussion controlled to focus on the relevant topic?
[ ] 11. Was the chairperson properly dressed?
[ ] 12. Did the stage look tidy?

QUESTIONS FOR DISCUSSION

1. What is the role of an agenda in a meeting's success?
2. Why should controversial subjects be introduced before a break?
3. Why are questions important to the success of a meeting?
4. What is the best way of identifying the most important questions in a large group?
5. What are the three most important purposes of minutes?
6. What are the three W's of decisions that must be recorded in the minutes?

COMPREHENSION EXERCISE

YOUR ISLAMIC ORGANIZATION MUST ISSUE A POSITION PAPER ON A SENSITIVE POLITICAL SITUATION. THE PRESIDENT HAS ASKED YOU TO CHAIR A MEETING OF THIRTY-FIVE SENIOR MEMBERS TO DEVELOP A POSITION. YOU HAVE DECIDED TO ASK THREE MEMBERS TO MAKE PRESENTATIONS ON THE PAST, PRESENT, AND FUTURE OF THE ISSUE. YOU INTEND TO RUN AN EFFICIENT AND PRODUCTIVE MEETING. AT THE SAME TIME, THE MEMBERS ARE ANXIOUS TO HAVE A DEFINITE DECISION-MAKING INPUT IN THIS CASE.

1. Write a memo to the members inviting them to the meeting. Include a complete agenda and schedule.

2. Outline your plan for conducting the meeting. Include how you will ensure full participation, satisfactory response to questions, and agreement on a unified position.

3. Design a form for taking minutes in this meeting.

How to Use Audiovisuals

I. Why Audiovisuals?
II. How to Make an Audiovisual Presentation
   A. Planning
   B. Designing
   C. Presenting
III. Advantages and Disadvantages
IV. Checklist for Using Audiovisuals

LEARNING OBJECTIVES

On completing this chapter, you should be able to:
- identify the elements of good audiovisuals
- prepare supporting and effective audiovisual material
- make a successful audiovisual presentation

I. Why Audiovisuals?

Adult learning researchers tell us that people learn in different ways. Some of us learn more by what we see, others by what we hear. Thus, learning is optimized by conveying information in both visual and audio forms.

The message contained in audiovisuals reaches us through these two channels: the visual and the auditory. We learn more and retain more of what we learn when verbal communication is aided by visual communication. Visual aids also help to add variety and emphasis to a presentation.

We are living in an age accustomed to receiving all kinds of messages through the stimulation of our senses. Giving the audience different kinds of sensory stimulations may help get and keep people's attention in this environment.

Overhead transparencies, 35mm slides, and flip charts are examples of instructional aids, as are props and handouts, where the instructor is in control and active in imparting the training. Films (videotapes or filmstrips), computer-based activities, and slide/tape presentations are examples of instructional media which are self-contained and can deliver training without an instructor being present.

The key to good planning is to choose the aid or medium in which we can produce the most professional visual with the given resources.

II. How to Make an Audiovisual Presentation

A. Planning

Planning what types of audiovisuals to use, and when, is the first step in creating a successful presentation. Our primary considerations are: reliability, ease of use, effectiveness, and cost. We can begin the planning process by gathering data about the learning profile of our audience, the presentation environment including equipment, and the resources available for production.

Once we have made the choice of the medium, we select specific visuals to use by reviewing our presentation for its highlights. Look for key ideas, complex processes, vital information, or inspirational messages. Examine each visual aid that is being considered. It should add depth to the message, not confuse it. It should be simple, clear, and consistent in appearance. Quality, the assurance of getting a good effect, is more important than quantity. One good visual can do more than many dull ones.

Whether it is slides, overhead transparencies, or flip charts, review your plans by asking the following questions:
- ⇒ Is this visual really necessary? If not, drop it.
- ⇒ Is there an idea or process that can be better explained visually than verbally? If you do not have a visual for it, get one.
- ⇒ What single point should the audience take back with it? If you do not have a visual for it, get one.
- ⇒ Are there words or sentences that you plan to emphasize? If you can, use diagrams to give visual life to such words.

B. Designing

Our visuals could be either text or graphics or a combination of the two. Graphics always look more attractive on a visual. Use pictures and designs instead of words when possible. Color brightens visuals. Yellow or orange on dark blue is especially effective.

Text on visual aids should be legible thirty-two feet from the screen. Limit lines to six or seven; limit words per line to six. Use a simple type face and start each visual at the same place. Do not crowd too much, whether it is on a slide, overhead transparency or flip chart. Less text is more effective than more text.

Use of graphics on visuals is often in the form of line, bar, or pie charts. Use bold and thick data lines and do not use grid or axis lines unless they carry information. Show clearly defined and properly spaced bars. Use only essential information on slices of a pie chart. Use diagrams to illustrate components and their relationships, and maps to show spatial arrangements or layouts,

Too many words, words that are too small, words at all angles, or bad use of color can make any visual difficult to view and read. Design your slides for comprehensibility when dealing with charts, engineering drawings, interconnection, or tables of figures. Keep them simple, with only relevant information shown or highlighted.

C. Presenting

Minimize the time you spend with your back or side facing the audience as you attend to your visuals. Do not leave visuals up too long. It's distracting. Do not read your visuals to the audience. It's dull. Do not become dependent on the aids; your presentation aids are there to supplement your presentation. The main attraction of your session should always be you.

Make sure the technology works: check and recheck. Make trial runs. Have backup systems. Know what to do if the technology fails, even if it is merely a felt-tip pen (which many consider to be the leading cause of failure by drying up).

III. Advantages and Disadvantages

Definitions:
- **Slides**: Transparent photographic film that is projected on a distant large screen.
- **Overheads**: Transparent film that can be written on, projected at a nearby large screen.
- **Flip Charts**: Large paper sheets that are placed on an easel and turned over after use.

	Comparative Advantages of Slides, Overheads, and Flip Charts
Slides	⇒ You can rearrange a set of slides for different groups ⇒ Slides are compact and easy to mail or carry ⇒ Slides can be reproduced inexpensively ⇒ They can be used in rear or front projection systems
Overheads (Transparencies)	⇒ The room can remain fully lighted ⇒ You can face the audience and maintain eye contact ⇒ You can make your own overheads quickly and inexpensively ⇒ Overhead projectors are easy to use ⇒ Revising, updating is easy; you can write on the transparency ⇒ You can control sequencing and completeness of visuals ⇒ You can use transparency masters to make handouts ⇒ Your notes on transparencies can stay in front of you
Flip Charts	⇒ They are light and roll up easily for transportation ⇒ They are spontaneous and flexible for live presentations ⇒ The are inexpensive and easy to obtain ⇒ You can maintain normal room lighting ⇒ You can maintain at least partial eye contact ⇒ You can save the record of a group's entire work

Comparative Disadvantages of Slides, Overheads and Flip Charts
Slides   ⇒ You must make a new slide when information changes   ⇒ Room lighting must be dimmed, thus diminishing eye contact   ⇒ You need more lead time to prepare and develop slides   ⇒ Slides tend to discourage discussion until show is over
Overheads   **(Transparencies)**   ⇒ They require screens that can be tilted   ⇒ Widespread distribution is less convenient than for slides   ⇒ Photographs do not reproduce well on transparencies
Flip Chart   ⇒ They do not accommodate a large amount of material   ⇒ Complex preprinted or predrawn charts require much time   ⇒ Prepared flip charts present a rigid sequence of material   ⇒ You must turn your back to the audience when you write   ⇒ Visibility can be a problem

Audio Visual Worksheet

USE AND COST MATRIX

For each training event, review the use and cost of the media that you wish to use.

CONSIDERATIONS	VIDEO TAPE	AUDIO TAPE	SLIDES	PRINT	TRANSPA-RENCY
Useful in:					
⇒ Self-instruction	YES	YES	YES	YES	NO
⇒ Computer based instr.	NO	YES	NO	YES	YES
⇒ Laboratories	YES	YES	NO	YES	NO
⇒ Workshop courses	YES	YES	NO	YES	YES
⇒ Lecture courses	YES	YES	YES	YES	YES
Concerns:					
⇒ Visual	YES	NO	YES	YES	YES
⇒ Audio	YES	YES	YES	NO	NO
⇒ Overall presentation	NO	NO	YES	NO	NO
Costs:					
⇒ Up front/development.	YES	YES	YES	YES	YES
⇒ Installation	YES	NO	YES	NO	NO
⇒ Presentation	NO	NO	NO	NO	NO
⇒ Maintenance	NO	NO	NO	YES	NO
Expense, Overall:					
⇒ High	YES	NO	NO	NO	NO
⇒ Moderate	NO	NO	YES	YES	NO
⇒ Low	NO	YES	NO	NO	YES

IV. Checklist for Using Audiovisuals

(Slides, Overhead Transparencies, and Flip Charts)

ITEM	YES	NO
1. **Accessories:** Do you have		
-a three-prong adapters?	___	___
-an extension cords?	___	___
-a spare pieces of chalk?	___	___
-a grease pencils or marking pen?	___	___
-extra bulbs for projectors?	___	___
2. **Supplies:** Have you		
-met A-V supplier(s)?	___	___
-received instructions on use of equipment?	___	___
-found out how quickly equipment can be replaced?	___	___
-arranged to have backup equipment in the room?	___	___
-tested all equipment in advance?	___	___
3. **Room Check:** Do you know		
-where the light switches are?	___	___
-if curtains will adequately block natural light?	___	___
-where the electrical outlets are?	___	___
-if the power cords are long enough?	___	___
-if they can be taped down to prevent tripping?	___	___
-where the nearest phone is?	___	___
-who you should call for help?	___	___
4. **Physical Set-up:**		
-Did you work on the physical set-up in advance?	___	___
-Is the screen high enough for all to see?	___	___
-Can they be seen from the BACK and the front?	___	___
-Will the viewers' heads NOT be in the beam path?	___	___
-Are volume and balance levels marked with tape?	___	___
5. **Presentation Rehearsal:**		
-Are the visuals in the right order?	___	___
-Are they right side up?	___	___
-Have you run through the program at least once?	___	___

QUESTIONS FOR DISCUSSION

1. What kinds of visual aids may be used without an instructor being present? How?
2. What is the rule of thumb for the number of lines and number of words per line on a slide? What is the purpose of this rule?

COMPREHENSION EXERCISE

AS CHAIRMAN OF THE FUND-RAISING COMMITTEE, YOU ARE ABOUT TO MAKE A PRESENTATION ON A PROPOSED CAMP PROJECT TO AN ASSEMBLY OF VISITORS. YOU MUST TALK NOT ONLY ABOUT THE PROJECT BUT ALSO ABOUT ITS BACKGROUND, INCLUDING THE HISTORY OF THIS TYPE OF WORK IN YOUR ISLAMIC ORGANIZATION. YOU HAVE LIMITED TIME TO PREPARE AND MAKE THE PRESENTATION.

1. *Considering the time available, list the audiovisual items you plan to show and state their format (slides, etc.).*

2. *Outline an emergency plan to substitute any one form of audiovisuals for another form. Explain how the choice may degrade presentation quality.*

Chapter

23

Talking to the Media

I. Introduction
II. Basics of an Interview
III. Writing for the Newspaper

LEARNING OBJECTIVES

On completing this chapter, you should be able to:
- write a more effective press release
- give a more successful interview

I. Introduction

In today's information-oriented world, it may often be impossible to reach the public with our message without the media. Rather than wait for a crisis to generate critical coverage of our issues, we would be smarter to take the initiative to provoke the media's interest. A clear message and correct information, conveyed with integrity, honesty, and willingness to cooperate will help us communicate through the media.

For communication on a regular basis, we must maintain basic information on who is who in the media. This can be done by contacting newsrooms of the local media outlets that interest us. We should follow this up with press kits sent to selected reporters and a call to introduce ourselves as a source for future newsworthy information. This initiative should be backed up with occasional news releases, file information, letters to the editor, and news conferences when necessary. It is important to keep track of any and all interviews and coverage.

There are many different ways of "talking to the media," including letters to the editors for example. However, we shall confine ourselves to a brief presentation of two ways — writing for the newspaper and interviews.

II. Basics of an Interview

The interview is the most common form of communication with the media. Since we are dealing with reporters trained in interviewing, some training on our part is in order.

The underlying approach of our interview should be to state our message, support it, and illustrate it; in that order. The initial answer to the opening question should be brief, not detailed. This will encourage the reporter to ask a followup question. We respond with explanation and supporting evidence of our actions or programs. Again, we use words to encourage further questions. At this time, we expand on our explanation and offer illustrations or analogies. Since the interview will be edited for a news item, short sentences and clever quotes are more likely to convey your message than long statements.

For newsworthy announcements, a well-prepared news conference is an acceptable vehicle. A media kit that includes background material and is handed out to reporters on arrival is always helpful. Designate a chairperson to make introductions, direct questions, and conclude the conference. Open with a short statement containing quotable sentences. These may be repeated during the conference. When possible, we should use audiovisual aids to illustrate the message or important information. Answer questions directly in everyday language and in a calm voice.

Good preparation is the key to effective communication with the media. We can plan our interview on paper by listing all the elements discussed above and rehearsing their delivery. When possible, we should record the interview for later review. This is useful for self-evaluation as well as for countering inaccuracy in coverage.

III. Writing for the Newspaper

Writing for the newspaper is one of the most powerful ways we have to influence, and possibly shape, public opinion. Writing can be done individually as well as in groups, affording an opportunity to contribute from the privacy of one's home as effectively as from a public forum. We can write a letter to the editor, an article on a timely issue, a brief for a breaking story or a press release, etc. The basic rules of writing for the newspaper are the same in each case.

Newspaper writing follows the journalistic style. It is meant to be read quickly. Thus, to get the maximum impact, we must place the most important information at the beginning of the written piece. We begin with the lead sentence or phrase stating what is most newsworthy, relevant and timely to the potential readers. Then we follow with the 5 W's, explaining who did, or was affected by the action the writing is about, what the nature and effects of the action were, when it happened, where it occurred, and why it took place. We state the three or more major points which we want the reader to remember first. We follow this with three or more additional points to elaborate on the major points. Remember, each paragraph should preferably contain only one point. Further paragraphs should follow one another in order of decreasing importance to the writer's objective. Finally, we can place minor details at the end.

The purpose of this type of writing, from most important point to least, is twofold. If the editor has to cut it short, due to space limitations, he will begin to cut at the bottom and thus save the main thrust of the writing. If the reader is in a hurry, he or she will most likely read the opening paragraphs and thus be exposed to the major points you want to get across. This style of writing will apply equally to letters to the editor and articles or background stories. Remember it as a writing pyramid.

THE PYRAMID OF WRITING

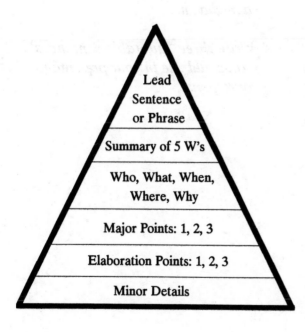

| Lead Sentence or Phrase |
| Summary of 5 W's |
| Who, What, When, Where, Why |
| Major Points: 1, 2, 3 |
| Elaboration Points: 1, 2, 3 |
| Minor Details |

ANATOMY OF A PRESS RELEASE

Title:
⇒ Relate it to what is most newsworthy

Style:
⇒ Most important information first
⇒ Date and location
⇒ One piece of information in one paragraph
⇒ Short sentences
⇒ Direct quotes, with approval

Tense:
⇒ Past tense

Body:
⇒ Answer "Who, What, When, Where, Why, and How"
⇒ End with the sign "-30-" (meaning "end"), or with "more" if needed
⇒ State contact name and number for further information

Size:
⇒ One or two pages

QUESTIONS FOR DISCUSSION

1. What are the differences between an interview and a news conference?
2. What is the function of a media kit?
3. What is the function of a press release?
4. What are the 5 W's that form the body of the press release?

COMPREHENSION EXERCISE

YOUR ISLAMIC ORGANIZATION HAS JUST BEGUN A SOCIAL SERVICE PROJECT IN THE LOCAL COMMUNITY. YOU WANT THIS INITIATIVE TO BE PUBLICIZED SO THAT YOUR SERVICE CAN REACH ITS INTENDED BENEFICIARIES AND, AT THE SAME TIME, YOUR ORGANIZATION CAN GAIN RESPECT AND ACCEPTANCE IN THE COMMUNITY. YOU WANT TO USE THE MEDIA TO ACHIEVE YOUR GOAL. THIS IS THE FIRST TIME YOU ARE DOING THIS, EVEN THOUGH THE MEDIA KNOWS ABOUT YOUR ORGANIZATION.

1. *Select the more appropriate form of media contact in this case — an interview or a press conference. Explain why you chose one or the other.*

2. *Write a sample invitation to the media.*

3. *List all the items you will include in a media kit.*

4. *Write three "quotable sentences" you could use in your presentation or response.*

How to Establish a Local Organization

  I. The Beginning Phase
 II. The Organizational Phase
III. The Stable Phase
 IV. Structure and Administration of an Islamic Organization
     A. The Executive Committee
     B. Sample Job Descriptions

LEARNING OBJECTIVES

On completing this chapter, you should be able to:
- identify specific steps in establishing an organization
- organize a group of people into an organization
- create suitable organizational structures
- write job descriptions of various officers

The establishment of a chapter of a central organization, or the establishment of a local organization, usually begins when a Muslim or a group of Muslims becomes conscious of the need for involvement in an Islamic movement. Let us examine how a local Muslim organization may be established. Let's call it the City Muslim Association (CMA).

I. The Beginning Phase

First, discuss the idea with some active Muslims in your area and obtain their consent to form an organized group. Note who from among your listeners at the mosque is most affected by lectures. Then assemble these people in smaller groups in order to learn, discuss, and preach the cause of Islam. Before you launch any formal organization, try to sit down with the group and map out the goals of your organization. Planning your future course of action is essential; it determines what has to be done. You can worry about when and how these goals can be accomplished later. You need not be too specific in defining your future plans at this stage. Some fairly concrete guidelines should be established first. For example, you need to draw up a list of priorities in terms of what must be done in order of importance.

II. The Organizational Phase

In order to provide stability to the organization, and to delegate responsibilities as smoothly as possible, you need to implement a constitution proceeding as follows:

a) Study an available model constitution.
b) Let someone with related experience write a constitution based on the model but modified to include provisions for local organizational needs.
c) Obtain the potential members' approval to adopt the constitution and
d) Elect officers of the now formal organization at a well-publicized meeting.
e) If there is a genuine Islamic federation or central organization in the country, inquire about the procedure for affiliating yourself with it.
f) If you are an organization operating on a university campus, apply for membership with the campus student union. If you are not on campus, register your organization with the appropriate government department in your state or country.
g) Announce the formation of your organization in the local newspaper or put up a few attractive posters at the nearest places where Muslims gather.
h) If you are on campus, investigate how to obtain funds and other resources from the student union on campus. Otherwise, do the same for grants from social work, research, and similar agencies operated by the city, state, or federal government.

Remember that in the organizational phase:
1. As the organization becomes more complex, the members will by necessity become more specialized in their activities. Do not let bureaucratization divide you.
2. As membership expands, try to improve the channels of communication. Feedback is vital if the organization is to function properly.

3. While Islamic ideology is and should remain the motivating factor of the organization, do not be dogmatic. Original short-term goals can be reassessed, old ones discarded, and some new ones added. If constitutional amendments are necessary, make them in a systematic way.

4. Trial and error will help the organization decide which strategies of membership recruitment are more effective. Do not be discouraged by your mistakes; learn from them.

5. Do not be discouraged by the vulnerability of the Muslim organization to both external and internal threats. As the organization battles for survival, never compromise on Islamic principles, but be flexible in the manner of their application. By altering immediate objectives or even postponing some, the organization will overcome external and internal difficulties, *in sha'a Allah*.

6. If you are faced with internal difficulties, rapid growth may prove dangerous. New members may not understand the plight of the organization and may unknowingly split the group. Guard against disenchantment. Go for quality rather than quantity when you are recruiting new members.

III. The Stable Phase

Fortunately, the problems of the organizational phase will not last forever. If they do, beware:

- Any venture remaining in an extreme state of ferment dissipates its energies, so to speak, to the point of exhaustion. Hence, some degree of stabilization is eventually required.

This stable phase requires more of routinization than "fermentation." We should not go for a bureaucratic structure, but each office should at this point be clearly defined, procedures on how to perform specific tasks established, and qualified Muslims selected. Taking such steps in a timely manner will prevent duplication of efforts and allow for organizational effectiveness.

IV. Structure and Administration of an Islamic Organization

An organization's executive committee usually consists of a president, vice-president, secretary, treasurer, and several members-at-large who are usually the chairmen of various subcommittees. Since the executive committee administers the organization's operations, all chapter officials must be members in good standing and of impeccable Islamic character.

Official continuity being an important consideration, the executive committee must meet regularly, according to a predesignated yearly schedule, to plan and review progress. In fact, the operations of the organization may preserve more continuity if the vice-president is elected to become president automatically in the succeeding year. Similarly, the experience of the outgoing president should be taken advantage of. He may be included in the executive committee as an ex-officio member so that the newly elected officials can benefit from his expertise.

The specific responsibilities of elected officials will be described below. We shall not describe the functions of a "permanent secretariat," since only very few of the major organizations have established such a facility. Here is a tentative organizational chart of your organization:

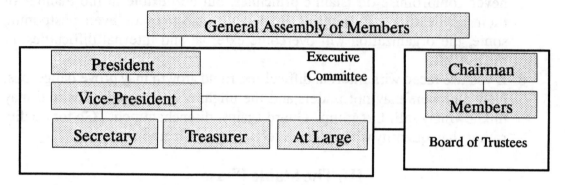

Action Point

THE POLICY OF DISCRETE ORGANIZATIONS

The fact that Islam encompasses every sphere of life does not imply that one organization can perform all sorts of activities. When an organization is successful, we tend to overload it and make it a "do all" type. This is like putting all our eggs in one basket. We have to train ourselves to create distinct structures for various fields of activities. For example, if the major aspect of our organization is *da'wah*, we should isolate it from business ventures. The latter should be carried out by a separate organization. Similarly, a political party should not be burdened with educational, economic, or health concerns. Every aspect should be served by a separate entity. Of course, there has to be coordination and cooperation in setting the objectives and organizational structures.

All this must be done in accordance with the constitutions of these organizations and not haphazardly. Bylaws and constitutions must be followed, and not violated, every inch of the way. If a constitution becomes a hindrance to effective work, it must be modified thoughtfully and through a democratic procedure. Doing so will safeguard the major objectives and principles of the group.

A. The Executive Committee

May Allah help you! You have been chosen by your fellow members to the most important positions that the organization can bestow upon its members. You are now part of the executive committee of an Islamic organization. Your title may be president, vice-president, etc. The title in itself is of no intrinsic importance. You are now accountable to Allah for the protection and promotion of the interests of your fellow members as long as such interests are consistent with the Qur'an and the Sunnah. Here are two questions which you should ask yourself before you begin:

⇒ What am I responsible for in my new position?
⇒ How much authority do I actually have as an executive committee member of this organization?

Of course, you need to be knowledgeable about the organization, its background, history, bylaws, and policies. But you also need a "road map" to guide you in your term of office.

You will need a job description, or at least a series of guidelines to help you navigate through the unfamiliar territory of your position. Your organization may already have such descriptions, or you may have enough ideas to draw up one. The accompanying sample job descriptions may serve as a starting point for you. In either case, think seriously about your role and responsibilities.

B. Sample Job Descriptions

1. President

Basic Functions: The president represents the Muslim community and the best interests of the organization. During his term of office, he:

1. Exercises personal and consultative leadership in motivating other executive committee members, trust members, committee members, staff, and membership;

Action Point

CONFUSING ORGANIZATION WITH FAITH

Some people defend their own ideas on organizational structure with overzealousness. They question the faith of others who do not agree with them. Actually, the type of organization we choose to work with is a matter of opinion and group judgment. It has nothing to do with *'aqidah* (creed) or faith. We can choose confidential organization or public, pyramid structure or not, centralized authority or decentralized, local committees or professional ones, etc. These are all areas of research and ijtihad. There is no one binding system in Islam. The choice of one over the other depends on the *shura*'s determination where the interest of the ummah lies. This is not an area of fiqh where a fatwa is needed. If we discover that one system is wrong, we can modify it or change it with another.

---

2. Influences the establishment of goals and objectives for the organization;
3. Acts as the spokesman of the organization, and monitors and assesses its performance and effectiveness, and
4. Works in partnership with the executive committee.

Within the limits of the constitution, bylaws, and policies, the duties, responsibilities, and authority of the president include the following:

1. Preside at all meetings of the executive committee and general assembly; coordinate agenda material with the secretary;
2. Ensure that the executive committee and the members are kept informed of the conditions and operations of the association;
3. Appoint the chairmen of committees and task forces, outline the purpose and duties of these committees, and monitor their progress;
4. Support and defend policies and programs adopted by the executive committee;
5. Promote interest and active participation in the organization on the part of membership and report activities of the executive committee to the membership by means of letters, publications, and speeches;
6. Present an annual report of activities at the annual meeting and at the end of his term of office;
7. In cooperation with the treasurer, help develop an annual budget and, upon approval, see that the organization operates within it; see to it that the finances are audited annually, and
8. Appoint a nominations committee which selects a suitable slate of candidates for the new term prior to the announced election date, arrange for the election of officials several months before installation, and keep adequate records in order to ensure continuity from one administration to the next.

In terms of relationships with other officers, the president:

a. Is responsible to the executive committee and, through the executive committee, to the membership, for seeing that the programs and the policies of the organization reflect the needs and the aspirations of the membership, and
b. Consults and advises the executive committee on all matters pertaining to organization policies, finances, and programs.

2. Vice-President

It is advisable that the vice-president's (VP's) office be filled by a potential president. A person in this position is able to learn organization management "on-the-job," and is much better prepared to put this learning experience into practice as president later on. As the second-in-command, the VP has the following duties and responsibilities:

1. Act as president in the president's absence;
2. Oversee committee responsibilities as needed and share the workload of the president, and
3. Be chairman of the program and/or membership committees.

3. Secretary

The secretary has an important and exacting task. He may enlist the aid of committee chairmen and other officials in assembling information and drafting reports, but he has the ultimate responsibility of preparing and filing the proper reports on time. A large organization may divide the overload between a correspondence secretary and a records secretary.

The duties, responsibilities, and authority of the secretary are to:

1. Keep detailed records of each meeting of the organization in order to complete the annual report each year; a minimum of six meetings a year are recommended in addition to regular programs.
2. Inform all executive committee members of the time and place of the meetings at least a week prior to their taking place;
3. Maintain the stationery and other supplies according to the needs of the organization;
4. Carry out all necessary communication for the successful operation of the organization and serve as custodian of all records of the organization, including copies of all correspondence;
5. Ascertain whether or not the organization's activities are conducted under the provisions of the current constitution and bylaws, and
6. Arrange for an orderly transfer of all records and information to the incoming secretary.

4. Treasurer

In small Islamic organizations, the elected treasurer may be the one member solely responsible for the financial operations of the organization. Let us, therefore, suggest that in such a case the organization take extreme care to follow established accounting procedures. Then should the treasurer change, any other individual who takes over will already know what procedures his predecessor was using. An audit of the accounts will also be easier if standard accounting procedures are followed. Whoever he is, the treasurer should be a practicing Muslim and should be selected from among the most trustworthy brothers.

Whatever the size of his organization, the treasurer must abide by the policies that the executive committee establishes. Such policies cover the following:

1. The frequency and type of financial statements to be received by the executive committee and the accounting method (cash or accrual) to be used by the organization,
2. The authority for making and implementing procedures relating to Islamic investments, and
3. The collection and disbursements of *sadaqah*, zakah, and special funds.

How can you as treasurer ensure that your organization is financially sound and following appropriate financial procedures? Using the following checklist, you may verify whether the actions listed below are being taken:

1. Dues, fees, and membership rates are periodically reviewed and adjusted to the needs of the membership and economic fluctuations;
2. The accounting system is adequate for the size and complexity of the organization;
3. There is a reserve fund for unanticipated contingencies;
4. An audit is conducted by an outside auditor reporting directly to the executive committee;
5. The executive committee reviews and approves annual programs and budget plans;
6. Periodic income and expense statements, including comparisons with the current budget and with the previous year's expenses, if appropriate, are analyzed by the executive committee.

Action Point	THE FIVE-YEAR PRINCIPLE
	In this fast-moving world, individuals are growing up faster than ever before. They are developing, maturing, and becoming highly mobile. It is found that a man can contribute best to his position of responsibility during the first five years of his service. If he is retained there longer, his rate of return, or productivity, diminishes. If he stays for too long, he may become more of a liability than an asset. The longer he stays, the more negatives he will accumulate and the fewer positives he will contribute. The position becomes too personalized for him. His aspirations and dreams become stifled by the walls of his office and position. A rule of thumb is to transfer to other positions every five years and get a chance to use acquired experiences in other positions and projects. Similarly, others will not stagnate in their positions as they move to fill in these vacancies and get the opportunity for new training. Such moves are quite healthy for the organization and the individuals. Five is not a magic number for the length of time in one position; it may be four or six years.

Following in their footsteps ...

Okay, you have established the local organization. As a leader or a part of the leadership, you have a variety of models to follow.

Imam al Ghazzali indicates in *Kimya' al Sa'adah* that a learned man once told the great *khalifah* Harun al Rashid to be aware on which chair he was sitting!

This was the chair on which:

Abu Bakr (RA) once sat	— so be **truthful**
'Umar (RA) once sat	— so differentiate between **right and wrong**
'Uthman (RA) once sat	— so be **modest and benevolent**
'Ali (RA) once sat	— so be **learned and just**

Think About.....

⇒ How does this composite model formed by these special characteristics of the *khulafa'* apply to your particular situation?

QUESTIONS FOR DISCUSSION

1. What is the very first step you should take if you want to establish an organization?
2. What specific role will communication and feedback play in the initial stages?
3. How do the roles of the executive committee and the board of trustees differ in our example?
4. In what areas must the secretary and the treasurer work closely together?

COMPREHENSION EXERCISE

DUE TO THE RELOCATION OF A LARGE MANUFACTURING PLANT, THE MUSLIM POPULATION HAS INCREASED IN YOUR SMALL TOWN. ESTABLISHING AN ORGANIZATION SEEMS TO BE FEASIBLE. HOWEVER, MOST MUSLIMS ARE NOT YET INTERESTED AND ONLY SOME HAVE BEEN IN AN ISLAMIC ORGANIZATION BEFORE. EDUCATIONAL AND ECONOMIC LEVELS VARY AMONG THEM, AND THEY COME FROM MANY BACKGROUNDS. YOU HAVE ONLY TWO MONTHS TO ORGANIZE BEFORE YOU ARE TRANSFERRED TO ANOTHER AREA BY YOUR EMPLOYER.

1. *Draw up a step-by-step plan that will address the special problems of this group.*

2. *Set up an organizational structure that will suit them.*

3. *List the difficulties that the group may encounter after you leave the area. Also list possible solutions.*

Chapter

25

Attitudes for Personal Growth and Development

Skill enhancement and self-development are twin aspects of training for exercising leadership. In this part of the *Guide*, we have so far discussed selected individual and group skills. This chapter deals in a nontraditional way with selected aspects of self-development. Through a combination of anecdotes, cases, and reminders we will highlight areas of personal growth that are critical to self-development even though they are not always obvious to us. This is a three-step do-it-yourself model which directs you to

- Know Yourself
- Discipline Yourself
- Express Yourself

We are making no attempt to be all-inclusive. What is pointed out should lead a potential leader to reflect on what is not. On this basis, we can develop an individualized action plan for personal growth and self-development.

I. Know Yourself

A. Do Not Be Like Mr. Averageman!

Born 1901, grades between C and D, married Miss Mediocre in 1924, had one boy named Averageman Jr. and one girl named Baby Mediocre. He had forty years of undistinguished service and held several unimportant positions. He never took a risk or chance, managed not to develop his talents, never became involved in anything with anyone. His favorite book was "Noninvolvement: The Story of Playing It Safe." He lived sixty years without goals, plans, desires, confidence, or determination. On his tombstone, you read

Here Lies
Mr. J. Averageman
Born 1901, Died 1921, Buried 1964
He never tried to do anything
He asked little of life
Life paid his price

B. Disparity of Expectations

We often come to a situation where, between two brothers, each thinks he has done great favors to the other and received none in return. It is worse when we think that others owe us a lot and we owe them nothing. These propositions are unfounded. It is in human nature to magnify what we give to others and minimize what we receive. Our behavior reflects the saying "When I am right nobody remembers, when I am wrong nobody forgets." If we truly want to find our balance of accounts with others, we should jot down on a piece of paper all our debits and credits objectively. Our only criterion must be Islam; and in identifying the debits and credits, we should consult with people of knowledge. If Islam has a specific ruling we should submit to it. For example, in deciding about inheritance, we should go according to the Shari'ah and not our own biases or emotions. There is great wisdom in the Arabic lines "When you are pleased with someone, you don't see his mistakes, and when you are displeased, you pronounce his mistakes."

C. Do Not Compare Yourself to Others!

There is a saying that "He who watches people dies of grief." This is a cancer that can eat away your life. You concentrate on others and start wondering why you do not get their positions, salaries, riches, personalities, respect, health, family, etc. You do not ask yourself: What have they done to deserve what they have? How much hard work have they put in? How many years of struggle they have gone through? You forget that *rizq*, sustenance, comes from Allah alone, and that He does as He wills. No one can question Allah!

One day a brother came to me and asked why he didn't get the same salary as others. I said: "Have you asked yourself why you do not produce the same as others? Look at their efficiency and productivity!"

Islam has taught us:
1. In worldly affairs, compare yourself with the poor, destitute, or handicapped and say *al hamdu li Allah*, Allah has given me much more than I deserve.
2. In knowledge and piety, compare yourself with the great scholars and saints and strive hard to achieve more. Ask Allah for forgiveness.

Remember that what you know about your shortcomings is a certainty. What you think you know about others' shortcomings is only a doubt. It is ridiculous to indulge in comparisons, because what you do not know about others is much more than the little you do know! Do not be shocked if, after an objective analysis, you discover that you are actually a liability to the organization while others are assets! Before you ask what the organization is doing for you, examine what you are offering to it.

D. Mixing the Personal with the Institutional

We tend to mix personal feelings with institutional feelings. This mixing is very taxing on our performance and human relations. The result of this has become a standard pattern. We start as brothers and end up as enemies.

Unfortunately, nowadays committed brothers may avoid dealing with one another. They fear they will end up in hostilities. When we confuse what is institutional with what is personal, we lose both. One such application is that if a brother needs financial help, we employ him in the organization even if he does not fit there. The organization becomes inefficient and a refuge for retirees. Eventually we lose the employees and

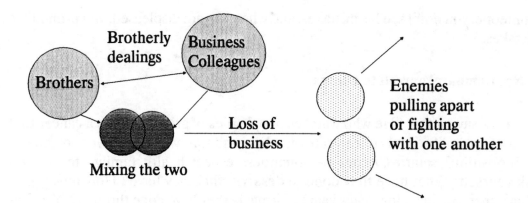

the organization, because we are confusing charity with professionalism. We should help the brother from charity and not kill the functioning institution. A brother asked me to lend him money from the institution to buy a house. I told him this was not my money. It belongs to the ummah and I am a trustee for it. How can I give it away for personal reasons? Instead of being very appreciative, he became very angry. The rule here is simple: If you qualify to receive *sadaqah* according to the criteria of fiqh, you may be entitled to be helped from public *waqf* funds.

We are not an employment agency; we have objectives to fulfill. We have to learn not to confuse the heart with the mind. We may disagree on many things, but our hearts should always be united. We can disagree but agreeably. If someone commits a mistake in the work place, he must expect punishment and be pleased about justice. I know of a highly successful businessman who punishes his sons with double the punishment of others. Allah tells the wives of the Prophet(SAW) of such double punishment:

O women of the Prophet, if any of you were guilty of evident unseemly conduct, the punishment would be doubled to her, and that is easy for Allah (33:30).

يَٰنِسَآءَ ٱلنَّبِيِّ مَن يَأْتِ مِنكُنَّ بِفَٰحِشَةٍ مُّبَيِّنَةٍ يُضَٰعَفْ لَهَا ٱلْعَذَابُ ضِعْفَيْنِ وَكَانَ ذَٰلِكَ عَلَى ٱللَّهِ يَسِيرًا (سورة الأحزاب)

Such was the prophetic practice: No favoritism!

II. Discipline Yourself

A. Be Careful about Becoming a Full-Time *Da'iyah!*

Some people become very enthusiastic about *da'wah* and decide to leave their studies or positions to work full time in *da'wah*. Beware of this! Great as it may appear, it is a very daring step. Never leave your studies or job before considering the following carefully:

1. Know the exact details of your new job description in *da'wah*. Do not accept generalities like working for the sake of Allah. You are also working full-time for Allah when you earn wages to support your family.

2. How are you going to be paid, how much, and for how long? Can they provide your income indefinitely or for a certain period only?

3. The decision must come in writing from the highest *shura* or appropriate authority of the organization. The president's signature may be enough, but he may be changed or change his opinion later! Make sure that other decision makers in the organization have been consulted and have given their support.

4. Compare your service to the group now with the new promised position. It may not justify giving up your current job; you may be able to do both without resigning.

5. Study the long-range effects on your professionalism, your family's future, and personal plans. Do not claim later that you did not know or did not consider these vital issues.

6. Know to whom you will be reporting and who will be reporting to you in order to avoid possible future conflict.

7. Study the new job environment regarding travel, location, nature, etc., and see if it suits your interests, abilities, and training.

8. Realize that you cannot reverse the decision later and expect things to be the same.

9. Think of what will happen in case of disagreements. There must be an amicable plan to "divorce" with kindness and understanding.

After you have considered all of the above and have decided to go ahead, do it on a trial basis for a few months or part-time, if possible. This will open your eyes to the hidden aspects and give you a taste of the real work.

The ideal situation is to personally support yourself fully and work as a volunteer. Obviously this cannot always be done. However, young Muslims should plan for it early in life so that Allah may bless them with the right opportunity later.

Remember, whenever possible, try a project on a small scale, a minibudget, and on a part-time basis. If successful, commit your full-fledged resources according to a well-thought-out plan.

B. Honesty to Superiors

One day a division head came to me complaining that he needed more staff. I responded that he had extra employees and must lay off some! Then I asked him how about Mr. X? He said: "He is useless!" I asked him why he did not recommend his termination to the vice-president? He replied: "Well! You know I cannot tell the vice-president that because he likes him, but you can do so from your top position." I answered with conviction that the reason I was in my position was because I always said what was right and what was wrong regardless of personal relations! Do not be afraid of differing with superiors; just be honest and objective. Allah will help you sail through life from one *falah* to another.

C. *Masjid* Rome

In the summer of 1977, Dr. Jamal Barzinji, then chairman of the North American Islamic Trust, and I were going overseas to raise funds. We were delayed in Rome for a day due to an outbreak of fighting between Libya and Egypt. We headed for the mosque where we met the imam for the first time. As soon as we sat down he started saying: "In this mosque I do everything and the director does nothing. I deliver Friday *khutab*, arrange marriages, take care of funerals, meet visitors and explain Islam to them, but the director gets all the credit. His salary keeps increasing while mine stays the same." After this strange reception we exclaimed: "Why don't you tell that to the board of directors and ask them to rectify the situation?" He replied: "I always tell them, but they do not listen to me, and are biased."

What kind of image does one get from such a reception? A very negative one, about the organization as well as the imam himself. Such a person has no loyalty to the organization; he only thinks about what he gets. He is dynamiting the whole organization with himself in the center. Do you have such self-centered members in your organization? They are willing to demolish the entire setup for a small personal benefit! Remember, if you sacrifice for the objectives of the organization, you and the organization will grow. If you degrade the organization, hoping that you will rise, both you and the organization will fall. The organization's strengths and weaknesses reflect directly on the members, officers, and directors. They are all in one boat.

D. Leaving Our Own Inventory and Borrowing from Outside!

Imagine that you contest an election and discover that your own family did not go to vote. Or you call for a public meeting and your close relatives and committed members do not attend. In fund-raising, you may address others and neglect your close contacts. It is amazing how we work very hard to gain outsiders and forget our own supporters. This can be attributed to disorganization, lack of planning, and no follow-up. It certainly disheartens us. A lot of improvements result if this function — enlisting support of those close to you — is assigned to a specific person or a committee.

E. We Only See You in Times of Distress

In a Muslim country, the head of state once asked why Islamists visited him only on sad occasions! This gives the movement an image of being formal without being concerned, and it becomes associated with calamities and stressful moments only. The movement should be active and visit at 'Id festivals and other celebrations as well! We have to continue our contacts with people on a regular basis and not only when we need something from them. Imagine if you only see your son or employee when he asks you for money? You will become unconsciously wary whenever such people appear in your sight!

F. The Sandwich Strategy

People commit themselves to Islam through various doors. A lot of them come to it through indirect means. For example, if you call for a sports game (or any other Islamically permissible activity) and you couple it with salah and a short reminder, a number of those participants who did not pray before will start praying. Similarly, in social gatherings and dinner parties when you sandwich the Islamic content with other activities, the Islamic impact will be stronger. On the other hand, if you present Islam through dull preaching alone, it tends to be unattractive. Sandwiching is a powerful tool of *da'wah*. It can be used in collective functions as well as on an individual friendly basis.

III. Express Yourself

A. Verbalize Appreciation, Loudly!

Once the Messenger of Allah (SAW) was sitting with some companions when a man passed by. One of the companions said: "This is a very good man. I love him." The Messenger inquired: "Have you ever told him that?" The companion responded: "No!" The Prophet said: "Go and tell him that you love him."

Nowadays, we criticize others loudly. When it comes to good deeds deserving praise, we keep quiet. The Prophet (SAW) teaches us to verbalize our appreciation. Others must hear it from us loud and clear. The pivotal principle of a Muslim is to praise Allah, the Most Praiseworthy. But this should spread to our fellow men. Listen to the Prophet's saying:

«مَنْ لَمْ يَشْكُرِ النَّاس لَمْ يَشْكُرِ الله»

He who does not thank people, does not thank Allah.[1]

The Qur'an explains this in a very special way:

And remember! Your Lord caused to be declared [publicly]: "If you are grateful, I will add more [favors] to you; But if you show ingratitude, truly My punishment is terrible indeed." (14:7)

وَإِذْ تَأَذَّنَ رَبُّكُمْ لَئِن شَكَرْتُمْ لَأَزِيدَنَّكُمْ وَلَئِن كَفَرْتُمْ إِنَّ عَذَابِي لَشَدِيدٌ ۝

(سورة إبراهيم)

---

1   Sunan Abu Dawud, Sunan al Tirmidhi, and Musnad Ahmad ibn Hanbal.

The key to more favors from Allah is to thank Him! Let us practice giving thanks to our people for any good thing they do. We will be rewarded with more good things coming from them. Appreciation is the watering needed for the tree of goodness to bear more fruit.

For parents, remember that the healthy blood needed for your children is appreciation with encouragement. Do not deprive them of it; they may become anemic!

If we practice more vocalized appreciation and less loud criticism, our society will be flooded with love and encouragement.

B. Vocalize Your Dislikes, Softly!

In my office I was addressing a brother by his last name for two years. He hated it and told people about it, but I never knew until one day another brother told me in confidence. I immediately changed the way I addressed him. Several mistakes were committed in this case:
1. He did not tell me about it;
2. He told others about it;
3. Those who knew did not inform me.

Why should a minor issue continue to hurt us if we can settle it in ten seconds! Allah will hold us accountable if we do not express our feelings and opinions frankly and objectively!

C. Thinking Alike

When you meet an Islamically committed person, do not take it for granted that he thinks as you do. You may perform *ibadah* (worship) alike, but thinking alike is a very slow and lengthy process. There are no two identical things in life. Allah made us all different; even for electrons, each one has a unique state. To come closer in thinking, we must discuss our viewpoints to reach a better understanding. We are deceived sometimes when we see a whole nation united to fight a common enemy. It is easy to unite people against an invader, but it is extremely difficult to unite them on a plan of action. There will be many factions. This happens within the same movement too. If you are calling for reforms, you may form a group to support you against the incumbents. But as soon as your group takes control, you will discover how divided you are on many things. The seemingly united reformist group may turn out to be more divided than the one it replaced. Beware of this time bomb! Make sure you have agreed upon a plan of action before you start the battle for reform. This is applicable on national political issues as well as within an organization or a family. If you do not follow this principle, your actions will be unproductive, regardless of how good your intentions are.

D. Moderation in Friendship and Hostility

People go to extremes in loving and hating a person or an issue. When they love someone, they become overwhelmed and forget objectivity and rationality in their dealings. Similarly, if they dislike somebody, they think that he is good for nothing. The Prophet (SAW) taught us a lesson of objective moderation in both cases:

«أَحْبِبْ حَبِيبَكَ هَوْناً مَا، عَسَى أَنْ يَكُونَ بَغِيضَكَ يَوْماً مَا، وَأَبْغِضْ بَغِيضَكَ هَوْناً مَا، عَسَى أَنْ يَكُونَ حَبِيبَكَ يَوْماً مَا»

Temper your love for your friend, for one day he may be your enemy. And temper your hate for your enemy, for one day he may be your friend. [1]

What a far-sighted principle! We need it so often.

E. *Shura* with Children

When *shura* is mentioned, our minds jump to political and organizational aspects only. There is a great need for *shura* with children and families. How many husbands consult with their wives? How many wives consult with their husbands? This is not to mention if children are ever consulted on anything. Possibly, *shura* is the most blessed gift given to the limited human mind. Through *shura* the individual draws from the pool of many minds. You may blame yourself for not consulting others, but you will hardly regret any decision if you exercise *shura*. Try to practice *shura* with your spouse and children. You will be amazed at the generous rewards you get. The advantages of such a family practice are innumerable. Do not belittle the contribution of children. They add a new dimension to information and decision making. One great scholar told me: "I cannot remember a single incident where I consulted a child and did not benefit from it."

F. Think!

It is impossible not to think. However, there are too many things in life to think about. It is a Qur'anic duty to think. What do we want you to think about? Consider, at least, the repetitive words and phrases we utter every day. Any time you say them, think of their great meaning. You will become a better person. We suggest you think deeper when you say the following:

---

1   Sunan al Tirmidhi.

⇒ *Al salamu 'alaykum* (Peace be upon you)   السَّلامُ عَلَيْكُم

⇒ *Allahu Akbar* (Allah is the Greatest)   الله أَكْبَر

⇒ *Subhana Rabbiya al Adhim* (I glorify my Lord, the Greatest)   سُبْحانَ رَبِّيَ العَظيم

⇒ *Subhana Rabbiya al A'la* (I glorify my Lord, the Highest)   سُبْحانَ رَبِّيَ الأَعْلى

⇒ *Astaghfiru Allah* (Oh Allah, Forgive me)   اسْتَغْفِرُ الله

⇒ *Al hamdu li Allah* (All praise be to Allah)   الحَمْدُ لله

⇒ *Ihdina al Sirat al Mustaqim* (Guide us to the Straight Path) اهْدِنا الصِّراطَ المُسْتَقيم

Did You Know?

- How do you talk to Allah?

- How does Allah talk to you?

- You talk to Allah when you perform prayers.

- Allah talks to you when you read the Qur'an.

There are four types of men:

- A man that knows, but does not know that he knows; that one is negligent, so remind him.
- A man that does not know, and does not know that he does not know; that one is foolish, so abandon him.
- A man that does not know, and knows that he does not know; that one is ignorant, so teach him.
- A man that knows, and knows that he knows; that one is a knower, so follow him.

Al Khalil ibn Ahmad al Farahidi

Things to Remember!

FOR BETTER PERFORMANCE

1. DO ONE THING AT A TIME

2. KNOW THE PROBLEM

3. LEARN TO LISTEN

4. LEARN TO ASK QUESTIONS

5. DISTINGUISH SENSE FROM NONSENSE

6. ACCEPT MISTAKES

7. ADMIT MISTAKES

8. SAY IT SIMPLY

9. BE CALM

10. SMILE

EXERCISE Hypocrisy or Psychology?

FIRST READ THIS LETTER!

Don't Be Fooled by My Mask. Hear What I Am Not Saying!

Don't be fooled by me. Don't be fooled by the mask I wear. I wear a thousand masks, masks that I'm afraid to take off, and none of them is me. Pretending is an art that is second nature with me, but don't be fooled.

I give the impression that I'm secure, that all is sunny and unruffled with me, within as well as without; that confidence is my name and coolness is my game; that the waters are calm and that I'm in command and I need no one. But don't believe it; please don't.

My surface may seem smooth, but my surface is my mask, my ever-varying and ever-concealing mask. Beneath lies no smugness, no coolness, no complacence. Beneath dwells the real me, in confusion, in fear, in loneliness. But I hide this; I don't want anybody to know it. I panic at the thought of my weakness being exposed. That's why I frantically create a mask to hide behind, a nonchalant sophisticated facade to help me pretend, to shield me from the glance that knows. But such a glance is precisely my salvation. It's the only thing that can liberate me from myself, from my own self-built prison walls, from the barriers that I so painstakingly erect. But I don't tell you this. I don't dare. I'm afraid to.

I'm afraid your glance will not be followed by love and acceptance. I'm afraid that you will think less of me, that you'll laugh, and your laugh will kill me. I'm afraid that deep down inside I'm nothing, that I'm just no good, and that you'll see and reject me. So I play my games, my desperate, pretending games, with a facade of assurance on the outside and a trembling child within.

I'd really like to be genuine, spontaneous, and me; but you have to help me. You have to help me by holding out your hand, even when that's the last thing I seem to want or need. Each time you are kind and gentle and encouraging, each time you try to understand because you really care, my heart begins to grow wings. Very small wings. Very feeble wings. But wings. With your sensitivity and sympathy and your power of understanding, I can make it. You can breathe life into me. It will not be easy for you. A long conviction of worthlessness builds strong walls. But love is stronger than strong walls, and therein lies my hope. Please try to beat down those walls with firm hands, but with gentle hands, for a child is very sensitive, and I AM a child.

Who am I, you may wonder? I am someone you know very well. For I am every man, every woman, every child... every human you meet. Signed . . . Anonymous.

Now, answer these questions.
1. Do you consider this letter a form of hypocrisy?
2. Do you relate any traits of human psychology in this letter with the contents of Surat Yusuf?

Wherever you are, death will find you out

...when their term is reached, not an hour can they cause delay, nor [an hour] can they advance [it in anticipation] (7:34).

... فَإِذَا جَاءَ أَجَلُهُمْ لَا يَسْتَأْخِرُونَ سَاعَةً وَلَا يَسْتَقْدِمُونَ (سورة الأعراف)

This is the tale of an Average Man,
Who acts contrary to Allah's plan,
If you are reflected herein,
Then repent and commit no sin.

It was early in the morning at four,
When death knocked upon a bedroom door,
"Who is there?" the sleeping one cried.
"I am Isra'il, let me inside."

At once the man began to shiver,
As one sweating in deadly fever,
He shouted to his sleeping wife:
"Don't let him take away my life."

"Please go away, O Angel of death!
Leave me alone, I'm not ready yet,
My family on me depend,
Give me a chance, O please perpend!"

The Angel knocked again and again.
"Friend, I'll take your life without a pain,
It is your soul that Allah requires,
I come not with my own desire."

Bewildered the man began to cry.
"O Angel, I am so afraid to die,
I'll give you gold, and be your slave,
Don't send me to the unfit grave."

"Let me in, O Friend!" the Angel said.
"Open the door, get up from your bed.
If you do not allow me in,
I will walk through it like a Jinn."

The man held a gun in his right hand,
Ready to defy the Angel's stand.
"I'll point my gun towards your head,
You dare come in, I'll shoot you dead."

By now the Angel was in the room,
Saying: "O Friend! Prepare for your doom.
Foolish man, Angels never die,
Put down your gun and do not sigh."

"Why are you afraid! Tell me, O man,
To die according to Allah's plan?
Come smile at me, do not be grim.
Be happy to return to Him."

"O Angel! I bow my head in shame.
I had no time to take Allah's name.
From morning till dusk, I made my wealth,
Never even caring for my health."

"Allah's commands I never obeyed.
Nor five times a day I ever prayed,
A Ramadan came and a Ramadan went,
But no time had I to repent."

"The Haj was already fard on me,
But I would not part with my money.
All charities, I did ignore,
Taking usury, more and more."

"Sometimes I sipped my favorite wine.
With flirting women I sat to dine.
O Angel! I appeal to you,
Spare my life for a year or two."

"The laws of Qur'an, I'll obey,
I'll begin to Salat this very day,
My fast and Haj I will complete,
And keep away from self-conceit."

"I will refrain from usury,
And give all my wealth to charity.
Wine and wenches I will detest.
Allah's Oneness I will attest."

"We Angels do what Allah demands.
We cannot go against His commands.
DEATH is ordained for everyone,
Father, mother, daughter, son."

"I'm afraid this moment is your last.
Now be reminded more of your past.
I do understand your fears,
But it's now too late for tears."

"You lived in this world two score or more.
Never did you your people adore.
Your parents, you did not obey.
Hungry beggars you turned away."

"Your two ill-gotten female offsprings,
In nightclubs for livelihood they sing.
Instead of making more Muslims,
You made your children non-Muslims."

"You ignored the muezzin's adhan,
Nor did you read the Holy Qur'an.
Breaking promises all you life,
Backbiting friends, and causing strife."

"From hoarded goods, great profits you made,
And your poor workers you underpaid.
Horses and cards were your leisure,
Money-making was your pleasure."

"You ate vitamins, and grew more fat.
With the very sick you never sat.
A pint of blood, you never gave,
Which could a little baby save."

"O Human, you have done enough wrong.
You bought good properties for a song.
When the farmers appealed to you,
You did not have mercy, it's true."

"Paradise for you? I cannot tell.
Undoubtedly you will dwell in hell.
There's no time for you to repent.
I'll take your soul, for which I'm sent."

The ending, however, is very sad.
Eventually, the man became mad.
With a cry he jumped out of bed,
And suddenly, he fell down dead.

Wherever you are death will find you out, even if you are in towers built up strong and high!... (4:78)

أَيْنَمَا تَكُونُوا يُدْرِككُّمُ الْمَوْتُ وَلَوْ كُنتُمْ فِي بُرُوجٍ مُشَيَّدَةٍ ... (سورة النساء)

Part Four

Training for Trainers

The function of training calls for a disciplined and systematic approach to impart selected skills, attitudes, and values to the prospective trainees. Part Four of the *Guide* addresses itself to providing information, instruments, and know-how to the established and would-be trainers so that they may successfully train others. Training, and human development in general, must optimize the limited resources available for this purpose, must show a clear benefit from the expenditure of these resources, and must follow through with its results. This is most likely to happen when training and development are part of the general strategy and plans of the organizations involved, and when a commitment to training is clearly expressed at the highest levels of decision making.

This part of the *Guide* discusses how we may assess and analyze needs for training, what characterizes effective training programs, what are the different types of training, what are training programs composed of, what techniques might be used to train, and how we can plan and implement a training program.

Chapter

26

Needs Assessment and Analysis

LEARNING OBJECTIVES

On completing this chapter, you should be able to:
- identify the role of an analyst in program design
- research and define training objectives in a given situation
- use various instruments to gather and analyze data

An effective training program must have a purpose that springs from a determined need for training. A proper assessment of needs ensures that training will be relevant and the cost of the program will be justified by the benefit it produces. Needs assessment also reduces the risk of funding unproductive programs.

A need is the difference between the actual knowledge, skills, and performance of the prospective trainee and what is expected of him or her. We can measure this difference through the use of interviews, observation, questionnaires, and tests. Such measurement requires accurately gathering, analyzing, verifying, and reporting relevant data.

I. The Analyst's Role

As analysts who are engaged in assessing and analyzing needs, our first task is to identify the knowledge and skills necessary to perform certain tasks and then evaluate the ability of individuals to actually function satisfactorily. We must observe and describe their behavior objectively. We must develop effective methods for collection and analysis of data, followed by processing, synthesizing, and forming appropriate conclusions about the data.

II. Basic Steps for Needs Analysis

A. Define Objectives

The purposes and objectives for conducting a needs analysis can be to distinguish workers who need training, identify performance problems, deficiencies and their root causes, determine whether training is the best solution to the problems, and generate data that will be useful in measuring the impact of the training program. Another purpose can be to provide specific recommendations for training program methods, frequency, cost, and location.

B. Identify the Necessary Data

Data collection must focus on facts and figures that will be relevant to the performance expectations from trainees. We must identify the specific types of data needed to establish conclusions.

C. Choose or Design a Method for Gathering Data

Methods of gathering data must be adequate for the type of data being collected and must also be acceptable within the norms of the organization. We must be objective and thorough without being redundant.

D. Collect the Data

Collecting data is the heart of the needs analysis effort. Adequate preparation and time for collection will add to the accuracy, and thus validity, of the data.

E. Analyze and Confirm the Data

How the data is analyzed depends on the nature of the data and the method of its collection. We must test the validity of the data by cross-examining it with equivalent data obtained from other sources or by other methods.

F. Prepare Final Report

Our final report should specify what form of training program will most effectively address the needs that the analysis has identified. The report could be a graphic presentation of data and conclusions drawn from it, a written summary of considerations and solutions, or it could be just an oral review of what is needed. In all cases, however, it should be conclusive so as to help program designers design a training program that will fulfill the training needs.

III. Instruments for Needs Analysis

Instruments used for analyzing needs are tools such as questionnaires, tests, checklists, surveys, and scales that systematically gather data about individuals, groups, or entire organizations. When applied objectively, they indicate both weak and strong areas.

Effective instruments are those that can be quickly and easily administered, administered in groups without disturbing the work place, scored quickly and accurately on the computer, and whose results are objective and do not require interpretation.

A. Questionnaires

Questionnaires are generally used to reach a large or a geographically dispersed population in a limited period of time. Their main purpose is to determine areas of inquiry that require further investigation through other assessment methods and to then verify information gathered from other sources.

B. Interviews

Interviews are generally used to gather background data at the beginning of analysis or to supplement and expand data from instruments and observation. They are also used to obtain input from those people who better express their views in person than on written surveys or questionnaires. Interviews help identify causes of problems and possible solutions by encouraging interviewees to reveal their feelings and opinions on these matters. Interviews often give participants pride of ownership in the analysis process by inviting them to provide the data for diagnosing training needs.

C. Observation

Observation is used to obtain background information on topics such as group dynamics, the organization's culture or the work climate, to supplement interviews and questionnaires, and to validate information derived from them. Observation is also used to investigate possible communication problems; inefficient use of time, resouces, and personnel; declining operational standards; ineffective procedures; and conflicts between management and staff. In addition, observation helps identify positive or strong characteristics.

D. Work Samples

Work samples are generally used to identify problem areas that may require further analysis, to supplement other assessment methods, to validate other data, and to gather preliminary information for the study.

E. Records and Reports

Records and reports are generally used to gather background information and acquire a general sense of the organization's culture and traditions, to verify information generated by other methods, and to understand how particular problems have influenced individual and organizational competency in the past.

ACTION POINT

SEX EDUCATION AND PRACTICES

Halal sex is a very important aspect of a Muslim's life. Teaching about it must be dealt with properly and correctly. For married Muslims, total sexual satisfaction is crucial to normal behavior. If they cannot satisfy their sexual needs through marriage, they might be tempted to look for it outside. It is astonishing how a considerable number of spouses have major problems in their sexual life. As a result of this, they often feel miserable and may end up in divorce. The rules of our fiqh teach us that there is no shyness (or bashfulness) in asking about matters of religion.

Yet we find that the majority of us hesitate to ask about sexual manners and etiquette in Islam. With some basic education on sex life, we can save a lot of families from agony. Due to the lack of education, there exists a lot of misconceptions about the Islamic practice of sex. For example, some think the less the sexual activity in one's life, the greater the piety. This is contrary to the teaching of Islam. Others believe that sex is a necessary evil. Again for a Muslim, man or woman, all *halal* things are for one's enjoyment and bring a reward from Allah if he or she uses them for His sake.

Certainly, we have to be careful about how, when, and who should give and receive sexual education. But we should also realize that if we do not teach it ourselves the right way, our youth will get it the un-Islamic (wrong) way from society. Then it will be too late to be sorry. It is a crime on our part to let our youths get married without the proper Islamic sexual education. Our training programs must contain this aspect in a well-measured and controlled manner. It is not sufficient to read books, although they are very useful. Some senior, knowledgeable spouses must explain various aspects of sex, followed by a question and answer session.

IV. Sample of Needs Analysis Worksheet

Focusing on Training Goals: What Should Be vs. What Is

EXAMPLE:

WHY? The Reason: Decisions of the executive committee are not being implemented the way they are intended to be implemented.

WHAT? The Goal: Implement executive committee decisions as required.

What Is?	What Should Be?	Is Training Needed? Area?	Any Other Solutions	Notes
Assignees are not informed fully and in time	Assignees should be informed sufficiently to carry out decisions	Yes; Communi–cation	Oversight by a designated official	Talk to President
Poor turn out	Good turn out	Yes; Publicity	Better program	Talk to editor

Exercise on Needs Assessment

Complete the Needs Assessment Forms for the Directors/Imams of Islamic Centers and derive conclusions about their most pressing needs.

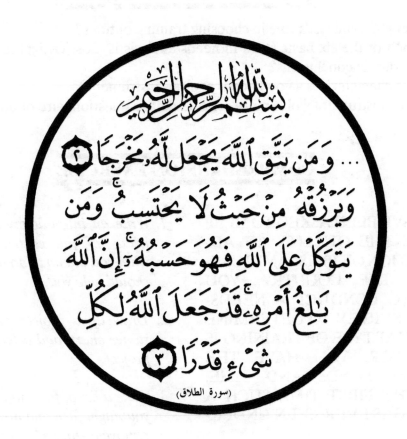

(سورة الطلاق)

... And for those who fear Allah, He [ever] prepares a way out, And He provides for him from [sources] he never could imagine. And if anyone puts his trust in Allah, sufficient is [Allah] for him. For Allah will surely accomplish His purpose: Verily, for all things has Allah appointed a due proportion (65:2-3).

QUESTIONS FOR DISCUSSION

1. What is the analyst's role in choosing training options?
2. Which of the six basic steps in needs analysis is most critical to attain accuracy in conclusions?
3. What characterizes a good needs analysis instrument?
4. Which instrument yields more reliable data: a questionnaire or an interview?

COMPREHENSION EXERCISE

YOU HAVE BEEN ASKED TO HELP UPGRADE THE QUALITY OF ADMINISTRATION OF 100 ISLAMIC CENTERS IN THE COUNTRY. YOU DECIDE TO CONDUCT A NEEDS-ANALYSIS SURVEY TO DETERMINE IF AND WHAT TYPE OF TRAINING IS CALLED FOR. YOU HAVE THE NECESSARY FUNDS AND TIME. THIS IS THE FIRST TIME SUCH A PROJECT HAS EVER BEEN UNDERTAKEN.

1. *Write an introductory letter to the heads of the centers explaining what you intend to do and why they should help you.*

2. *Draw up a project plan, a milestones chart, and a budget for this project.*

3. *Make a list of five major difficulties you might face and how you would remove them.*

Characteristics of Effective Training Programs

I. Continuity
   A. Planned Continuity
   B. Data Base
II. Audience Specificity
   A. Targeting the Audience
   B. Special Needs
III. Follow-Through Material
IV. Experiential Learning
V. Adult Learning
VI. Limits to Training

LEARNING OBJECTIVES

On completing this chapter, you should be able to:
- identify the factors that make training effective
- recognize the concerns that require training to be audience specific
- focus on the learning features of adult training

I. Continuity

Good training is a process of progressively enhancing ideological and organizational commitment. It is also a system of acquiring relevant skills and continually practicing the same to further develop and update them. For that reason, good training embodies progressively increasing sophistication of the training material.

A review of the present situation in training shows that even when training programs are well thought out and geared to an audience, there may be no continuity from one program, or one part of it, to the other. No one program may qualify as a planned sequel to another, and participants may not be generally advancing from one level to another.

A. Planned Continuity

An effective training program must be characterized by planned continuity. Such continuity will ensure that trainees do not stagnate but grow in their capabilities. It will also eliminate repetition and redundancies, thus conserving scarce training resources. When subjected to formal classification, a training program with built-in continuity can provide a measure of evaluation of trainees and their posttraining placement in fieldwork.

B. Data Base

One consequence that follows from planned continuity is the need to maintain a data base of trainees and another of training resources. The data base of trainees should include at least their name, contact information, bio-data, and training credentials. Selected information from this data base can be made available to community and field leaders in Islamic work.

The data base of training resources should include similar information about experienced and potential trainers. In addition, it should include content and access information about training material like books, articles, audiovisuals, and the like. Selected information from this data base will be very helpful for individual trainers organizing training programs. Its use will optimize their search for suitable standardized material.

II. Audience Specificity

Good training must be audience specific, taking into account the present level of education and understanding of the participants.

Islamic training programs have generally tended to be broad-based in an attempt to address the needs of the wide variety of experience and exposure among the participants. Trainers have not succeeded in organizing programs for specific audiences and using material that will be neither too easy nor too difficult or irrelevant for them.

A. Targeting the Audience

Targeting its contents to specific audiences is an important characteristic of good training programs. There is a wide variety of potential training audiences to whom trainers must direct their efforts. Different audiences have different backgrounds, roles, expectations, and above all varying receptivity to selected learning experiences. If these differences are studied and utilized in program design and implementation, the outcome will be a more focused program. The result will be better training.

B. Special Needs

Surveys and questionnaires from potential trainees and experienced trainers can help determine special needs. These could vary from special vocabulary, to span of attention, to suitable subject matter, etc. Examples of specific audiences will be youth, women, minorities, field-workers, educationists, community leaders, imams, parents, and so on.

III. Follow-Through Material

Good training must be supported by take-home follow-through material that participants can use at their own pace. The type and nature of this material should be such as to reinforce the learning material used in the program itself. Such joint use of on-site and take-home materials will optimize the effectiveness of the training effort as a whole.

Experience shows that even when training programs tend to include good material in the on-site presentation and handouts, not all of it can be read, properly covered, or absorbed at the time. This makes it necessary to make material available to trainees packaged in effective learning forms so that they can take it home for follow-up and refresher learning. Examples of this type of material will be audio-cassettes, videotapes, summaries of texts, case studies, etc.

IV. Experiential Learning

Good training must include learning by doing and getting involved. The importance of learning through experiencing or doing things oneself cannot be overstated.

At times, training programs may tend to deliver training to an audience as opposed to involving them in a training process. To be effective, each training program must have participant involvement in the form of role-playing, leadership assignment in program operation, or challenging tasks that require the exercise of the skills being taught.

A number of suggestions can be made about designing special experiential activities for individual or group involvement. These could be indoor or outdoor. Outdoor activities could be organized around physically demanding goals that may be reached only through the exercise of teamwork, cooperation, and similar leadership skills.

V. Adult Learning

Good training must recognize the special character of adult learning. It must provide an appropriate learning environment and incorporate the basic principles of adult learning into the preparation and presentation of each element of the training program. Effective training material must:

1. Attract
   a. To learn, adults must be attracted to and then respond to information.
   b. To get adult learners' attention, tell them what they have to gain from learning.
2. Relate
   a. To remember what they pay attention to, learners need to relate new information to what they already know.
   b. To make new information meaningful, use at least one concrete example to illustrate each concept or skill you introduce.
3. Simplify
   a. To present new information clearly, start with basic principles, rules, warnings, and advice.
   b. To help learners remember lengthy or complex information, present it in blocks.
4. Reinforce
   a. To keep learners on track, provide feedback.
   b. To reinforce new learning, allow plenty of practice and some personalized pacing.
   c. To prepare learners for moving on to new information, wind up with a summary of key points and a few questions.

VI. Limits to Training

We often speak of training everyone to excel in performance. However, there is a limit to training; the individual has to be trainable. We quote below a fable of the "Administration of the School" curriculum in Cincinnati, Ohio. Allah has endowed every one with special gifts of excellence. We must enhance the qualities we have and train for other traits in moderation and within limits.

The Animal School

Once upon a time, the animals decided they must do something heroic to meet the problems of a "New World," and so they organized a school. They adopted an activity curriculum consisting of running, climbing, swimming, and flying. To make it easier to administer, all animals took all the subjects.

The duck was excellent in swimming, better in fact than his instructor, and made excellent grades in flying, but he was very poor in running. Since he was low in running he had to stay after school and also drop swimming to practice running. This was kept up until his web feet were badly worn and he was only average in swimming. But average was acceptable in school, so nobody worried about that except the duck.

The rabbit started at the top of the class in running, but had a nervous breakdown because of so much makeup in swimming.

The squirrel was excellent in climbing until he developed frustrations in the flying class where his teacher made him start from the ground up instead of from the treetop down. He also developed a charley horse from overexertion and he got C in climbing and D in running.

The eagle was a problem child and had to be disciplined severely. In climbing class he beat all the others to the top of the tree, but insisted on using his own way of getting there.

At the end of the year, an abnormal eel that could swim exceedingly well and also could run, climb, and fly a little had the highest average and was valedictorian.

QUESTIONS FOR DISCUSSION

1. Why is continuity important to training effectiveness?
2. When must training be targeted to a specific audience? How?
3. How does take-home material reinforce classroom work?
4. In what way does understanding how adults learn help design more effective training programs?

COMPREHENSION EXERCISE

YOU ARE PLANNING A TRAINING PROGRAM FOR A GROUP OF THIRTY FIVE EXPERIENCED VOLUNTEER LEADERS, BOTH YOUNG AND OLD, WHO HAVE GONE THROUGH TWO OTHER TRAINING PROGRAMS IN RELATED AREAS. THEY HAVE LIMITED TIME TO ATTEND A SEMINAR BUT ARE COMMITTED TO SELF-TRAINING. SOME OF THEM ARE COMMITTED TO LONG-TERM SERVICE WITH THE ORGANIZATION.

1. *State your underlying assumptions for designing an effective training program for this group.*

2. *Design a simulated computer screen for a data base that will help in making a five-year training plan for them.*

3. *Determine which of the factors in adult learning is critically important for this group.*

Chapter

28

Types of Training

LEARNING OBJECTIVES

On completing this chapter, you should be able to:
- distinguish between various types of training events
- select appropriate types in a particular case
- adapt a training program to a selected need

I. By Duration

The duration of the training program or of any training activity is one of the important parameters of planning. How long a training event should last depends on the training objectives as well as the availability of trainees. Several possibilities exist:

A. Weekend

A weekend training activity is practically the shortest viable training event. It usually begins on a Friday afternoon and ends on a Sunday afternoon. However, depending on the availability of the trainees, sessions on Friday may or may not be well-attended. Similarly, some participants may have to leave before the program ends on Sunday. Thus, Saturday tends to be the most productive day with the largest uninterrupted and focused attendance. Program planners and trainers should schedule sessions and activities so that they peak on Saturday. Friday activities should build towards Saturday activities and a brief summarizing session Saturday morning should update late-comers. Sunday activities should be of the reinforcing and winding-down type, and a brief what's-to-come session the night before should explain to those who will leave early what they must later pick up on their own.

B. Week

A week-long program is possible only when the prospective trainees are free from their regular assignments, whether at college or at work. Alternatively, they have to obtain leave from college or work for a week. The program would normally begin on a Friday and end on the following Friday, but other possibilities exist, especially Monday through Sunday.

A week-long training event offers the opportunity to establish a more deliberative pace. A more varied and detailed program can be offered with some opportunity to engage in exercises and to test the learning accomplished. A week is also sufficient time to build relationships among participants and cultivate a team spirit.

C. Quarter-Year

A quarter-year program is called for when the objective is to train selected trainees who are committed to Islamic work on a long-term and occasionally full-time basis. A program of such duration is also needed to effectively train those who will be commissioned to prepare others for Islamic work. Such programs can be designed for imams and directors of Islamic centers.

From a programming design point of view, a quarter-year-long program consists of a number of theoretical and practical courses on selected topics in leadership training. Each course consists of lectures, practice, exams, and special projects. A significant element of the program is the on-going interaction among students and faculty in both planned and spontaneous settings. The restrictions of work or college are bound to limit the number of participants in a quarter-year training event. However, such a program may be conveniently scheduled during the summer.

II. By Purpose

Training events can be organized around several purposes, from development of skills to that of the spirit. The underlying purposes influence the selection of contents and techniques. Some situations are discussed below.

A. Skill Development

New challenges or simply new developments in the environment of our work may call for new skills. Acquiring skills in which a deficiency has been indicated and enhancing already-acquired skills are important parts of being a leader.

Skill development training programs focus on imparting proficiency in specific skills that the trainees lack. The duration of such programs depends on the complexity of the skills to be developed and the capacity of the trainees to learn. A hands-on type approach shapes much of the program. Examples of such skills are writing, public speaking, political campaigning, imam duties, audiovisual use, journalistic writing, and so on.

B. Spiritual Growth

Developing spiritual qualities and enhancing one's personal relationship with Allah (SWT) are the underlying foundations of Islamic leadership.

Specialized training events may be focused on promoting spiritual growth among participants through intensive study of the Qur'an and hadith literature. Success is directly related to the quality of programming and the environment in which it takes place. Besides learning activities like lectures and study circles, such programs may involve the participants in collective worship such as night prayers and fasting.

C. Knowledge Enhancement

Increasing one's knowledge about Islamic and contemporary sciences, including history, ideology, culture, and the like, prepares the potential leader to see contemporary challenges in the right perspective.

Training events may be focused on the acquisition of knowledge and education relevant to the functions of leadership. Such programs may consist of lectures, seminars and discussions by experts in the topics covered as well as guided self-study by trainees.

D. Field Training

The exercise of leadership in the field, among members and organizations at the local level, is at the heart of a national organization's mission. Decisions and plans must filter down to the field and members must be mobilized, motivated, and instructed to act upon them.

Programs that specialize in field training generally involve hands-on type of interactive activities like workshops, case studies, role-play, and the like. These focus on developing one's ability for effective leadership on the interpersonal and group dynamics levels.

III. By Geography

Training events may also be classified by the locality and jurisdiction of the participants. They could range from being local in a city to being worldwide.

A. Local

Local training events attract participants from the vicinity of the site. Such programs draw largely upon local talent for presentation, though often one or more resource persons may be invited from outside the area to enrich the program.

B. Sub-national (Regional)

When a country is divided into regions, each region may hold its own training activities. Participants are drawn from the entire region and overnight accommodations become necessary. Attendees would normally be driving to the site, thus reducing transportation expenses. Regional trainees could be picked from a slate of graduates of local training events.

C. National

Participants in the national training activities come from all over the nation and are generally leading Islamic workers of the sponsoring national organizations. The program draws upon national human resources for presentations and organization. Since considerable travelling may be involved, the program usually lasts two or more days with overnight sleeping planned.

D. International (Regional)

Several countries of the world may be grouped to form regions like North America, South America, Europe, South Asia, the Arab world, North Africa, etc., for the purpose of training leaders of national organizations. As it happens at the national level, international regional training events permit wider participation from several nations with less travelling than for worldwide events.

E. Worldwide

These are at the top of the hierarchy of training events. The presenters and participants come from all over the world. Due to high travelling expenses, trainees must be carefully selected to have the maximum impact on Islamic work at the world level. It is best to organize worldwide events as the culmination of a series of programs that may begin at the local level. The duration of such activities must not be less than a week.

IV. By Age and Specialization

For best results, we must tailor training to the needs and orientation of different ages or specializations among the trainees. Youth and women must receive special attention in this respect.

A. Youth
The younger trainees, preparing for the responsibilities of adulthood, and young adults are a special group from the training perspective. Programs for them should include structured physical exercises and out-of-door activities. Presentations should be at the appropriate intellectual level and of a duration that will allow them to maintain their active interest.

B. Women
Women are another group that must be given special attention when we design training programs. Physical arrangements should allow for separate sleeping quarters for women when both genders are participating in an event. The selection of subjects should reflect their special interests. The current situation of the Muslim community calls for extra efforts to train Muslim women for appropriate leadership roles in the community.

C. Specialization

While most training activities are directed at the general trainee, some training events may be organized for those with special vocations or aptitudes. These could include programs for workers engaged in *da'wah* in prisons, or those running small businesses, like publishing, for example.

Action Point

TARBIYAH BETWEEN PRIVATE AND PUBLIC

The debate continues on whether *tarbiyah* should be in private *halaqat* or on public platforms. It is a byzantine, fruitless argument. What is the purpose of *tarbiyah* in seclusion? Is it not to be utilized in public? On the other hand, how can a member perform well in the public arena if he misses the internal self-*tarbiyah*? Both aspects complement each other. We should plan to switch the roles of members and expose them to both positions so that they can appreciate the benefits on both sides. In this way, the conflict between the two will eventually disappear.

COMPREHENSION EXERCISE

YOU HAVE BEEN ASKED BY A COORDINATING COUNCIL OF ISLAMIC ORGANIZATIONS TO PROPOSE A STRATEGY FOR TRAINING LEADERS OF LOCAL GROUPS. THEY ARE SPREAD OVER A LARGE GEOGRAPHICAL AREA, DIFFER AMONG THEMSELVES IN PROFESSIONAL AFFILIATION, FAMILY LIFE, AND GENERAL FIELD EXPERIENCE. YOUR TASK IS TO COME UP WITH A PLAN OUTLINING HOW TO GROUP POTENTIAL TRAINEES AND SCHEDULE THEIR RESPECTIVE TRAINING PROGRAMS.

1. *Set up criteria for making groups among the leaders for training purposes.*

2. *List the pros and cons of running training programs at the national level versus the local level.*

3. *Write a brief note to a critic of your decision in defence of what you have planned.*

Components of the Training Program

I. Training Resource Material (Training Aids)
    A. Printed Material
    B. Audiovisual Material
    C. What Kind of Material Should We Use — and How?
II. The Training Environment: Activities and Programs
    A. Set-up Procedure
    B. Training Potential
    C. Useful Time Span
    D. Courseware Support

LEARNING OBJECTIVES

On completing this chapter, you should be able to:
- identify the type of material you can use to help in training
- recognize the major considerations in selecting training alternatives
- use training aids more effectively

I. Training Resource Material (Training Aids)

Resource materials are the key components of a successful training program. These may range from the printed text to videotapes and a number of other formats in between. In general, resource materials may be defined as learning aids that help explain, test, or remind the participants about what they learn. Such materials must directly assist learning to be classified as resource material. Material that will only help add information, or otherwise supplement what is learned, may be classified as reference material.

A. Printed Material

The printed word is the most common medium for resource material. It can be produced less expensively and in shorter time than other forms of material. It is also easily reproducible and can be transported and distributed rather conveniently. Compared to other forms, printed material does not need special equipment like video-players or computers to read it. It is cost-effective, reliable, familiar, accessible, and versatile.

The limitations of printed material include the difficulty of making it attractive, the inability to visually illustrate real-life situations, larger physical size than computer diskettes and electronic media, difficulty in changing the original, and the lack of interactiveness with the learner.

1. Handouts

Handouts are the the most popular form of printed material. They include notes or outlines, tables or illustrations that supplement lectures or workshops. Notes supplied to learners enable them to write during presentations; added fill-in or comments sections help them participate in the instructional process. Handouts are often used to briefly explain one aspect of a topic.

2. Worksheets

Worksheets include reading lists, assignments and problems, briefing sheets, etc. They allow the learner to think more creatively. Structured worksheets strengthen memory and retention.

3. Study Guides

These include learning aids and instructor's manuals in the form of structured notes, off-line courseware, workbooks, and other short supplemental texts that provide information, learning activities, and directions. Such guides and manuals clearly specify what must be learned and how it should be studied. They are much more detailed than handouts.

4. Group Activity Resources

These include all materials used to support group learning such as role-play scripts, instructions, background reading, data sheets, and briefing material.

5. Manuals and Seminar and Workshop Packages

The individual chapters of this *Guide* are an important source of resource material for leadership training. In addition, the Islamic Leadership Training Library at the IIIT has a collection of booklets on a variety of subjects in the areas of Islamics, contemporary sciences, organization, personal development, and field work. This material can be used as how-to manuals and packages for distribution at seminars and workshops.

B. Audiovisual Material

Examples of audiovisual material are flip charts, overhead transparencies, slides, props, audiotapes, videotapes, film strips, computer screen projections, and the like. Any Islamic leadership training library should have a good collection of audiotapes and videotapes. In addition, some recordings made at training sessions held by Islamic organizations should be edited for reproduction.

C. What Kind of Material Should We Use — and How?

The training program in itself is a system for change. Its overall objective is to effect a transformation in the attitude and behavior of the participants, using a variety of appropriate techniques and events assembled as a training program. To select the most effective resource material for this purpose, we must examine the levels of experience, education, and the cultural and socioeconomic backgrounds of the trainees. We can then map the most suitable strategies for achieving our training objectives for this particular audience.

When and how to use various forms of training resource material is influenced by several factors, including size of audience, nature of physical facilities, age and experience of participants, and the complexity and availability of the material itself for the subject at hand. A combination of printed material with audiovisual aids is the best choice in most circumstances. However, audiovisual aids must be of good quality to be effective.

> **TIPS ON EFFECTIVE USE OF TRAINING AIDS**
>
> * Keep training aids—materials and media—organized.
> * Encourage trainees to interact with the training aid.
> * Use aids only to support and extend core instruction.
> * Practice the use of media and material before class time.
> * Be ready to rearrange and skip aids during presentation.
> * Avoid the fatal mistake of distributing anything before examining it carefully yourself.

II. The Training Environment: Activities and Programs

There are a variety of activities and program elements that can be used to construct a training program. What is selected is dictated by who the participants are and the environment in which the training is taking place. Some of the most important considerations are:

A. Set-up Procedure

The training environment — classroom, outdoor setting, workplace, or other locations — may influence our choice of activity. We must make sure that the environment is adequately equipped with, for example, audiovisual equipment for indoor presentations or open spaces for outdoor activities. The setup procedure should be under the control of the trainer and backup facilities and equipment should be available when needed.

B. Training Potential

The training potential of an activity is related to the level of the trainees as much as to the activity itself. It is important to establish a profile of the participants. The kind of information needed will include age, gender, education and Islamic knowledge levels, Islamic leadership responsibility, organizational affiliation, etc. In addition, it will be important to know what the participants view as their principal concerns and what they want to learn. Certain kinds of activities may be more useful than others in answering the training needs of the group.

C. Useful Time Span

One can prolong or overdo a training activity to the point that it loses its effectiveness. This can happen when the activity becomes repetitive or the audience gets tired of it. Each activity can hold the audience's attention for a certain length of time during which participants are likely to benefit the most from it. Beyond its useful time span, the activity can create repressed hostility toward the entire training effort.

D. Courseware Support

The selected activity must be properly supported by available courseware for use by the trainer as well as the trainees. This could be in the form of books, manuals, audio or visual tapes, computer diskettes, or any other form that can be used in the training environment. Some support should also be available for participants to follow up on their learning experience after the program has ended. In the absence of any cour-

their learning experience after the program has ended. In the absence of any courseware support, the selection of an activity would be limited by the ability of the trainer to prepare material for such support.

CHECKLIST FOR ASSESSING THE TRAINING ENVIRONMENT

(Two hypothetical activities or options are considered here briefly. Not all factors have been taken into account. The purpose is to illustrate a manner of assessing different ways of creating the right training environment.)

	Activity or Option #1	Activity or Option #2
A. Set-up Procedure	Classroom, projector and screen, blackboard	Work area, computers, microphone
B. Training Potential	Younger, less experienced workers	Older, more experienced workers
C. Useful Time Span	One and a half hours	Three hours
D. Courseware Support	Manual, handouts, textbooks	Handouts, manuals

QUESTIONS FOR DISCUSSION

1. What are the limitations of printed material in training?
2. In what ways are audiovisual materials and aids more effective than printed material?
3. Why is a profile of the trainees important in training?
4. How does the concept of time span apply to training?

COMPREHENSION EXERCISE

AS VICE-PRESIDENT FOR TRAINING IN A LARGE ISLAMIC ORGANIZATION, YOU ARE PLANNING AN ADVANCED LEVEL SEMINAR FOR FIFTEEN VERY BUSY VOLUNTEER LEADERS. YOU HAVE THE NECESSARY FUNDS BUT YOU ARE SHORT ON TIME. THE TRAINEES NEED TO IMPROVE THEIR PERFORMANCE RIGHT AWAY, EVEN THOUGH THEY ARE OLDER AND EXPERIENCED PEOPLE.

1. *List the type of resource material you would use.*

2. *Design a chart showing the advantages of the selected material over others in this situation.*

3. *Describe how you would determine the length of your program.*

Training Techniques

LEARNING OBJECTIVES

On completing this chapter, you should be able to:
- identify the characteristics of training techniques
- understand their setup requirements and courseware needs
- enhance effectiveness and retention value for various audiences
- develop case studies for use in training

I. Selection Factors

The selection of training techniques to use in a particular case depends on several factors related to the learning style of the participants. Some learn better through the print, visual, or oral media; others do so through discussion, hands-on activity, or drills involving physical action. In addition, the availability of resources, the nature of the learning material, and the needs of the individual learner and the group also influence the choice of training techniques.

Other factors that determine the suitability of one technique over another include the size and profile of the group, training goals and objectives, resources, equipment and materials, and time limits. In addition, one must consider presentation and facilitation skills, a group's barriers to learning, the best approach to the subject, and facilities for the physically disabled.

Adult trainees learn from activity and variety in teaching methods. They learn best when they can relate new knowledge to previous knowledge. They must see learning as based on their life experience. They must practice and apply what they learn. Their learning is reinforced when they know how training will help them and when the training imparted actually does help them solve work-related problems. Above all, adults do not learn unless they have the desire to learn.

The trainer also must have certain qualities in a combination that delivers training effectively. These include knowledge of the subject, technical skill, awareness of others, willingness to lead when necessary, and a sense of humor.

In the final analysis, success in training is measured not by how well we train but by how well the participants learn. Learning by the participants depends on our being well-prepared, well-versed in the subject matter, and conscientious about using the appropriate training technique.

II. Basics of Common Training Techniques

A. Lectures

A lecture is a talk delivered by a designated person who has the information and knowledge about his subject and presents its various points in a sequence leading to a final conclusion. The lecture is prepared in advance and delivered by reading from a script or by expanding on notes. Audiovisual aids may help make the message of the lecture clearer. By use of telephone and video conferences, a lecture may be beamed simultaneously to one or more remote audiences, thus saving time, travel, and cost.

To set up a lecture, we first identify the topic and then select a speaker who is willing and able to speak about it. We inform the speaker about our expectations from the lecture, the time allotted for it, and nature of the audience. We make sure that all arrangements, including the public address system, are made and operating as expected.

The lecture is effective as a training technique when our purpose is either to motivate the audience to take specific action or to inform it. When followed by questions and answers, the lecture serves to educate the audience on the basis of the speaker's expertise and experience.

> *A good format to follow in the outline comes in three stages:*
>
> *1. Tell them what you are going to tell them.*
> *2. Tell them.*
> *3. Tell them that you have told them.*

A total of ninety minutes is generally the maximum time that the audience can remain attentive to a lecture. The lecture should generally last no longer than forty-five minutes. The balance of the time should be taken up by general discussions or questions and answers.

An outline, an abstract, or the full text of the lecture can help the audience follow the presentation, especially if complex or unfamiliar ideas are being presented.

B. Workshops

A workshop is like a working meeting in which the participants are actively involved. They acquire new knowledge, relate it to their work, identify needed changes in behavior, learn new skills, and practice behaviors and skills in simulated work environments. An effective workshop is built around what is practical and relevant from the learners' perspective. It is specific and focused in its subject matter.

The physical setting of a workshop must be conducive to interaction and involvement among the participants. This character of the workshop must be reinforced by its program design from planning to execution. The program designer and trainer must seek input from prospective participants to determine their training needs, their learning styles, and their motivation for attending the workshop. Worksheets, case studies, role-play scripts, checklists, and other training instruments should all be ready before the workshop begins.

An effective workshop has a high potential for focused training of the participants and subsequent retention of what is learned. The willing individual actively engages all his faculties — mental, visual, auditory, and the like — in the learning process as opposed to his passive involvement in, for example, lectures.

Workshops can last from a several-hour session to several sessions over a period of days. The length is generally determined by the complexity of the subject and the availability of the prospective participants. The useful time span in which participants continue to learn is greatly increased due to their active engagement with the learning material and exercises.

Courseware support needed for workshops depends on the type of learners, their jobs, their educational level, their learning styles, and the time frame of the workshop. Films on specific skills, case studies in relevant situations, and worksheets to supplement instruction can be useful support material. It helps to relate the summary and conclusions of all workshops to all participants in a special session. This way members of the audience benefit from the findings of the workshops they did not attend.

C. Seminars

A seminar is a topic-oriented event designed to educate and inform an audience about a broad subject of interest. The program of a seminar usually consists of a series of lectures or panel discussions on topics within the seminar's main theme. Sometimes parallel workshops or discussions in small groups may be included.

Seminars are set up by first picking a subject and its major component topics. Next we select speakers and panelists who are qualified and available to speak on those topics. The main characteristic of the seminar program is the progressive development of the subject from the basics to the specifics and the interconnection between all topics.

The training potential of well-designed seminars is significant. This is especially true when they aim at improving the participants' attitudes through motivation or enhancing their knowledge base so that they may make informed decisions. Though audience participation is limited, the variety of presentation methods used can keep interest high enough to encourage learning.

Seminars generally last a day or two. Since they are designed to give out information, their useful time span is constrained by the learners' capacity to digest that information. Complex subjects, if not well-presented, can reduce the learning effectiveness of a seminar.

Handouts that contain outlines of talks, purposes of panel discussions, and workshop objectives are helpful in creating a context for the information received by the audience. References to reading material for followup also help the learning process.

D. Camps

A camp is a live-in activity that requires the participants to stay on the camp site day and night from the beginning to the end of the program. The site is selected with special consideration for facilities needed for lodging, food, meeting, prayers, and recreation. The program is usually fully structured and designed to utilize all available time from wake up to sleep. The purpose is to create an environment that promotes pertinent values and reinforces practical skills through participation in camp management. The physical setting and on-site living offer a chance to include variety and interaction into learning methods and presentations. One purpose of this is to enhance team spirit and promote collective work.

The selection of a proper site is critical to the success of the camp. This depends significantly on the nature and purpose of the camp program. For example, camps for younger participants and those aimed at developing broader values rather than narrow skills require a number of facilities for physical activities. Other important factors include accessibility to the camp by normal means of travel, climate control in extreme weather, security for isolated location, help in medical or other emergencies, etc. Even though rural, out-of-town sites are generally preferred for camps, urban location on college campuses, in hotels, or in conference centers can also be used for this purpose, though with less opportunity for physical activities. They must be safe and well-protected against crime.

As a vehicle for training, the camp is highly effective. The participants learn and practice values and skills by exercising them among peers. Friendships are built and strengthened. A spirit of camaraderie helps inspire commitment to higher goals and superior behavior, both objectives of the camp program.

Camps generally last from a weekend to two weeks. Longer periods call for a creative program that holds the participants' attention and keeps their spirits high. A week is often the optimum duration and allows enough time for an absorbing program that involves everyone without wearing them out.

The live-in nature of the camp permits the use of more extensive reading and reference material than would be practical for other training techniques. For maximum benefit, a temporary reading and reference library can be set up and its use incorporated into the program itself.

To enhance control, communication, cooperation, and competition, camp participants may be divided into groups of ten, each with a group leader. Each group should be identified by a meaningful name like that of a prophet, a *sahabi*, an Islamic event, a Muslim city, etc.

E. Role-Playing

Role-playing, a short presentation dramatizing a problem or situation, is a combination of discussion and demonstration. The demonstrators are group members who, with or without the benefit of scripts or rehearsals, act out specific situations that require particular skills. An instructor or group leader explains the situations and outcomes to be dramatized, giving each actor directives on his or her character, behavior, and actions.

Role-playing is easy to set up unless special props are needed to create a meaningful scene. Props are usually not needed, and the trainees can imagine the scene being played out. The room must allow for rearrangement of seating so that everyone in the audience can view the actors as they perform. Microphones, if needed, must be movable to suit the requirements of the roles being played.

Role-playing is informative and entertaining at the same time and is a good attention-getter. Collective analysis and critique allow the group to pool their experience and talents and to benefit from sharing these strengths with one another.

Effective role-playing is usually short and fast-moving. Five minutes is an optimum length of time for a single role-play situation, though a longer duration may be acceptable if the play entertains as it teaches. Each play should illustrate one major point. Long plays covering several issues should be avoided.

Occasionally, prepared scripts may be available for role-play situations. Sometimes, however, they may be more distracting than useful. It is helpful for the trainer to distribute a handout briefly describing the nature of the roles being played when a detailed script is not advisable.

F. Conferences

Conferences are generally used to tackle single problems or sets of problems. The sponsors usually set up the agenda in advance. The structure of the program includes sessions of various types, including lectures, panel discussions, workshops, and the like.

Planning for a conference may be conveniently divided into two sections. One group can draw plans for the program and another can plan the administrative arrangements and services. The latter include registration, meeting rooms, housing, recreation, physical facilities, and other such arrangements.

Besides solving problems, conferences may also motivate and inspire and thus supplement the training efforts of the sponsoring organization. Other than that, the larger size, structured program, and limited interaction keep the training potential of a conference rather low.

Conferences generally last from two to five days. The attention and interest of the audience can be kept up with creative programming that includes appropriately timed breaks and recreational activities.

A printed program distributed in advance with adequate information about topics to be discussed is essential for the success of the conference. It is also advisable to distribute reports and documents that may be presented during the program.

G. One-on-One

The one-on-one mode of training is a direct transfer of skills and attitudes from a more experienced person to a less experienced one. It works in cases from the very simple to the fairly complex. The trainer may be a supervisor on the job, a senior volunteer, or even a more seasoned peer. The trainee must not be shy or hesitant to benefit from personal interaction. Individualized training techniques like this one offer a much greater opportunity to practice what is being taught than do group training methods.

One-on-one training can be imparted in special sessions or on the job itself. A bond of trust and confidence must exist between the trainer and the trainee for this method to be effective.

On the one hand, this method is very costly since only one trainee benefits from the trainer's time. On the other hand, personal attention and close supervision result in quality training. Since training is individualized, it is more likely to be retained over a period of time.

How long one-on-one training may be conducted and what courseware is needed depends on the style of the trainer and the trainee.

H. Panel Discussions

A panel discussion is a presentation from the podium by a number of speakers or panelists. At the outset, each panelist speaks briefly, for ten minutes or so, and addresses a part of the subject or expresses a point of view on the subject as a whole. A moderator then directs the discussion on the presentations made as well as on questions and comments from the floor. At times, and at the end, the moderator briefly summarizes and reflects on the highlights of the discussion without overshadowing the panelists. It is of paramount importance that the moderator should coordinate among the panelists to cover all aspects of the discussion without the panelists overlapping or duplicating one another. This must be done well in advance.

A topic that generates audience interest, panelists who can present their ideas concisely, and a moderator who can take charge are the essential ingredients of a successful panel discussion. A panel discussion is not simply a number of lectures scheduled in one session. Its essence is an effective coverage of the subject by the panelists and an exchange of ideas among them. This exchange benefits and is stimulated by the audience. Three to five panelists is generally the standard; too few may not cover the subject fully and too many may result in repetition.

A good panel discussion that involves the audience with the panelists has a high training potential. Information is extracted from a greater pool of expertise than is possible at a lecture. Ideas and applications are explained with a greater degree of clarity. Audience involvement promotes a longer retention of what is learned at a panel discussion.

The length of a panel discussion can be greater than that of a lecture because it has more variety. However, two hours is about the maximum that a discussion can hold the audience's attention. As a rule of thumb, we recommend sessions of ninety minutes or less for any training technique.

Just as for lectures, handouts containing information about the panelists, the topic for discussion, conflicting points of views, and abstracts of the presentations can be helpful to the audience of a panel discussion.

I. Parallel Sessions

Parallel sessions are simply two or more sessions of the same or different types taking place at the same time. Such sessions can have separate topics for several parts of the group or the same topic for participants of different age, gender, or prior training. Sometimes a group may be split into smaller subgroups attending parallel sessions on the same topic if it is too large to meet all at once.

Parallel sessions are set up just like full sessions. They must be located close to one another if the nature of the program permits participants to move between sessions.

Holding sessions in parallel increases their training potential by targeting the training effort to the audience or by reducing the audience size. This leads to more effective interaction within the group and thus improves learning.

The useful time span and courseware support for the sessions depend on the nature of the program.

III. Other Useful Techniques

A. Debates and Discussions

Debate and discussion are participative methods as opposed to lectures or the like. The methods are interactive and involve learners in exploring a specific topic through analysis, review, and evaluation of the subject. Debates are formal and governed by strict time rules, whereas discussions are informal in that they allow for an unstructured exchange of views without constraints placed by leaders or rules. However, for effective discussions, the group must focus on a subject and must not be too large for general participation. A leader must moderate the discussion, but the leader or the more vocal members of the group should not dominate the discussion.

The physical arrangements for a debate are of formal theatre style. Each debater speaks from one of the two opposite sides of the center seat the moderator occupies. Seating style for a discussion can be less formal, like sitting in one or two circles. The presentation of opposing points of view stimulates critical thinking among the presenters as well as the audience. This enhances their ability to learn.

If presentations are interesting and relevant, the length of a debate or discussion session can be longer than usual. However, we should still break up sessions longer than two hours into subsessions. No particular material is needed except what we have recommended for the panel discussions. The debate becomes more interesting when the issue being debated is voted upon both before the debate starts and after it is concluded. Doing so enhances the spirit of the competition.

B. Dialogue

Like a debate, a dialogue is an exchange of views, but one limited to two presenters. Each presenter represents a position on the issue. However, unlike a debate, a dialogue seeks to explain and understand the opposing ideas and does not determine which is better. In matters of setup procedures, training potential, useful time span, and courseware support, dialogue and debate are alike.

C. Brainstorming

Brainstorming is a technique for gathering ideas from a group of people assembled in a meeting. The technique is discussed in detail elsewhere in this *Guide*.

D. Demonstration

Unlike lectures, demonstrations teach by showing as well as by telling. Trainees learn by observing and sometimes practicing the skills, processes, functions, or relationships demonstrated in action.

E. Entertainment

Entertainment can also be a powerful learning tool when it is done tastefully and with a purpose. By helping to relax the mind and providing a relief from tensions, an entertainment session can positively contribute to better learning during the entire experience. In addition, certain topics and concerns themselves can be taught through the creative use of purposeful and wholesome entertainment. However, we must make extraordinary efforts to ensure that entertainment sessions are not corrupted by non-Islamic influences. Indeed, there is a dire need to produce Islamically acceptable entertainment material.

IV. A Comparative Review

Among the more popular techniques of training mentioned above are lectures, workshops, seminars, camps, role-playing, conferences, one-on-one, panel discussions, and parallel sessions.

The following chart shows how these techniques differ in terms of:
- Organization   difficulty or ease in setting it up
- Presenters   number of trainers needed to present it
- Audience role   active or passive nature of the audience
- Retention value   how well will the audience remember afterwards

Technique	Organization	Presenters	Audience Role	Retention
Lectures	Easy	One each	Passive	Low
Workshops	Difficult	One to three	Active	High
Seminars	Medium	Several	Passive	Low
Camps	Difficult	Several	Active	High
Role-playing	Difficult	One	Semiactive	Medium
Conference	Difficult	Several	Passive	Low
One-on-One	Easy	One	Active	High
Panel Discussion	Easy	One to five	Passive	Medium
Parallel Session	Easy	Several	Passive	Low

V. Case Study

A case is a record of an actual situation complete with issues that have actually been faced. However, it offers no conclusion. The record includes facts, opinions, and prejudices upon which viewpoints are developed and decisions must depend.

A. How to Develop a Case

To develop a case, write out a concise and accurate description of each of the following items: the central issue, situation, background, and documentation.

Note that the central issue relates to the main problem to be solved. The situation is the events, circumstances, characters, actions, and dialogue from which the central issue evolves. The background refers to basic information related to the work environment and relevant to the case situation. The documentation consists of exhibits that support the case situation.

B. When to Use the Case Method

The case study technique is used when the training objective is to develop analytical thinking, problem-solving, and decision-making skills. The participants should be capable of using logical skills to analyze information. In addition, the group should be small enough for an effective discussion of the case.

The case method offers an opportunity to make decisions without damaging an actual situation. One can practice resolving problems of a certain nature by use of similar cases.

The method requires a case that is clearly written, a facilitator who has the experience to direct discussion to the central issue, and participants who can verbalize their ideas.

C. How to Prepare a Case

To develop a case, we first identify the objectives of the session. After this, we choose one or more relevant cases in the field of interest. We then plan our research for the case situation, background, and documentation. Finally, we conduct the research and write out the case. Before we use the case, we must evaluate it for suitability.

D. How to Conduct a Successful Case Method Session

First we introduce the session objectives and the case study technique. Then we read the case, preferably aloud, to the group. Next we discuss the case in order to arrive at one or more solutions to the problem. At the end, we summarize the session and highlight the conclusions.

Sample Worksheet: How To Develop A Case

Write out descriptions of each item below, concisely and accurately. For extra space, use an additional sheet and number the items. An example is shown below.

ITEM / DESCRIPTION: _____

1. Central issue

The MSA needs a permanent site for its proposed general secretariat.

2. Situation

The space and facilities at the present headquarters are no longer sufficient. Expansion required to deliver services is not possible. The location is not attractive for volunteers or visitors.

3. Background

The headquarters is housed in the mosque in Gary, Indiana, purchased by the MSA in the late 1960s. The main floor has an office for the director, a masjid, and a fixed seating auditorium. The basement has a work area for the secretary, toilets and showers, kitchen and dining area, and storage. The neighborhood is somewhat stagnant. The available land does not allow significant expansion.

4. Documentation

Report of the planning committee on plans for the general secretariat, report of the headquarters site selection committee, report of the director on the present use of space, and unpublished surveys of active members about their expectations from the MSA.

5. Comments

Review criteria for the selection of suitable site and examine conclusions.

VI. Defining Instructional Groups

Training groups can be formed and seated in at least three distinct ways depending on the interaction between the instructor and the trainees. These groups are shown below. The circles represent the instructor and the squares represent the students.

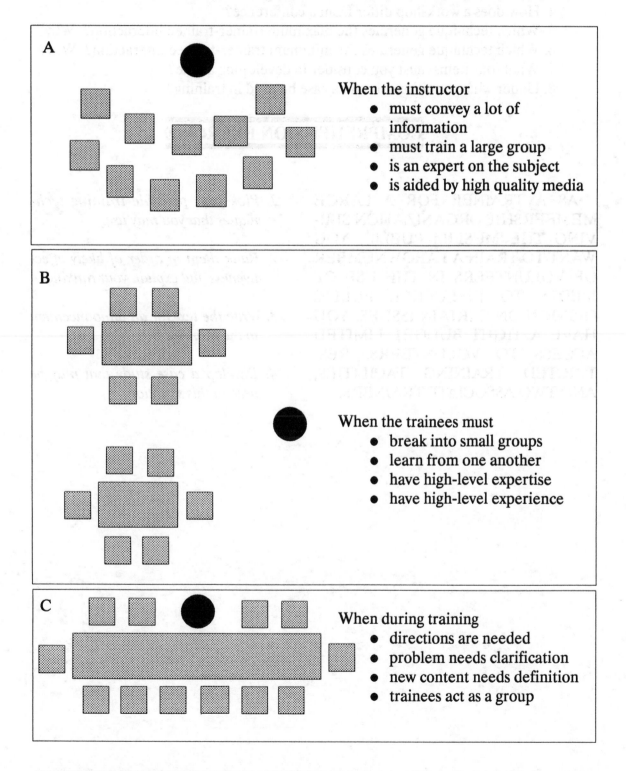

A

When the instructor
- must convey a lot of information
- must train a large group
- is an expert on the subject
- is aided by high quality media

B

When the trainees must
- break into small groups
- learn from one another
- have high-level expertise
- have high-level experience

C

When during training
- directions are needed
- problem needs clarification
- new content needs definition
- trainees act as a group

QUESTIONS FOR DISCUSSION

1. What are the three major factors in good training?
2. What are the three major factors in adult learning?
3. What are the three most common training techniques?
4. How does a workshop differ from a conference?
5. Which technique generates the maximum trainer-trainee interaction? Why?
6. Which technique generates the minimum trainer-trainee interaction? Why?
7. What four items must you consider in developing a case?
8. Under what conditions should a case be used in training?

COMPREHENSION EXERCISE

AS A TRAINER FOR A LARGE MEMBERSHIP ORGANIZATION SERVING THE MUSLIM PUBLIC, YOU WANT TO TRAIN A LARGE NUMBER OF VOLUNTEERS IN THE USE OF MEDIA TO INFLUENCE PUBLIC OPINION ON CERTAIN ISSUES. YOU HAVE A TIGHT BUDGET, LIMITED ACCESS TO VOLUNTEERS, RESTRICTED TRAINING FACILITIES, AND TWO ASSOCIATE TRAINERS.

1. *Pick four possible training techniques that you may use.*

2. *Rank them in order of likely effectiveness and explain your ranking.*

3. *Write the text for an announcement to the trainees.*

4. *Develop a case study that may be used in this situation.*

How to Plan and Implement a Training Program

I. Effective Program Planning
    A. Basic Principles
    B. Step-by-Step Procedure
II. Implementation
    A. Resource Constraints
    B. Action Tracking

LEARNING OBJECTIVES

On completing this chapter, you should be able to:
- identify various parts of the program you must plan for
- develop a practical schedule of activities
- establish a method of following up on implementation

I. Effective Program Planning

A. Basic Principles

Effective planning of programs always develops directly out of the interests and needs of the prospective audience. Programs are best planned in terms of topics satisfying stated needs, not in terms of available resource persons.

Those who will carry out the program and participate in it must be able to contribute to the making of the plan. We work most enthusiastically for programs we have made or helped make. We should fully record the planning process in order for it to serve in evaluating the program and guiding future programs.

B. Step-by-Step Procedure

We should outline plans for the year or a longer period in order to tie individual programs into an integrated plan with a long-range goal.

Most failures in program planning occur when the details of how the program will be organized have not been thought through. Most of the time, this calls for detailed answers to "Who? What? When? Where? Why? How? and How Much?"

Issues of central concern in planning a program are:
   a. **Time**: Set up a time line covering deadlines for completion of tasks and activities necessary for the execution of the program.
   b. **Funds**: Estimate cost for the program, identify possible sources of funds, set up a budget, and plan for contingencies and obligations in case of a cancellation.
   c. **Space and Equipment**: Reserve facilities for all elements of the program and arrange equipment and necessary electrical requirements.
   d. **Leadership**: Assign tasks and responsibilities to those capable of leading others to work. Distribute assignments among several people without splitting them to the extent that coordination may become difficult.
   e. **Materials**: Obtain in advance literature and other training materials for reference and distribution at the program.
   f. **Evaluation**: Identify criteria to be used for assessing the success or failure of the program.

II. Implementation

A. Resource Constraints

The availability of resources for program planning is often the principal constraint on what can be done. These include, other than financial means, speakers, resource people, ideas and guidance, films, printed matter, and the like. The planning committee for the program should know where to get the following:
   a. **Up-to-date files and records** of all available sources and resources.
   b. **Membership list** with information about special qualifications, interests, and experience of members.
   c. **Library and clipping systems** of books, periodicals, and pamphlets on subjects of interest and other programs.
   d. **Filing system** that maintains statements of policy and objectives, legislation affecting the organization, and records of its past efforts and achievements.

e. **Directory of resource people** with leadership roles or needed expertise from outside the organization.

f. **Catalog of supplementary sources** like films, books, tapes, and the like. Some of these may be available from the national headquarters of the local organization, the local library, related government agencies, colleges, and businesses.

The financial means available for planning and implementing a training program is often the most serious constraint. To overcome this limitation, we must work out a budget of income and expenses in the early stages of planning. If a deficit is indicated, we must review cost-cutting possibilities in expenses and launch an effort to raise additional funds either in cash or in kind, like airline tickets, printed materials, telephone bills, secretarial help, etc.

B. Action Tracking

A plan is only as good as the way it is implemented. Implementation calls for action. A checklist or a chart with stated responsibilities and deadlines helps monitor progress. When possible, we should assign one individual the task of checking progress of all actions and reporting any deviations from planned activity.

SAMPLE OF ACTION TRACKING CHART
(Add more details as needed to keep track of action)

	Person(s) Responsible	Resources Needed	Cost	Funding Source(s)	Deadline(s)
Facilities					
Speakers					
Setup					
Publicity					
Food					
Invitations					
Thank You's					
(Add your own)					

A SAMPLE DAILY PROGRAM
SUGGESTED FORMAT

	Wake up
	Iqamah for *Salat al Fajr*
	Brief reminder (10 min.)
	Qur'anic study Circle (30 min.)
	Wash up (30 to 45 min.)
8:30 - 9:00 am	Breakfast
9:15 - 10:30	Session I
10:30 - 11:00	Break
11:00 - 12:30 pm	Session II
1:00	*Iqamah* for *Salat al Zuhr*
	Lunch
	Free Time — sports
	Iqamah for *Salat al 'Asr*
4:15 - 6:00	Session III — Workshops (3 to 4 groups)
	Iqamah for *Salat al Maghrib*
	Dinner
7:30 - 8:30	Session IV — Reports from each group
9:30 - 9:45	Evaluation and reflection
10:00	*Iqamah* for *Salat al 'Isha'*
10:15	Required rest

THE BOTTOM LINE!

When all is said and done, it does not matter how hard we worked, or how well we planned. What matters is what we achieved. And we cannot achieve unless we implement.

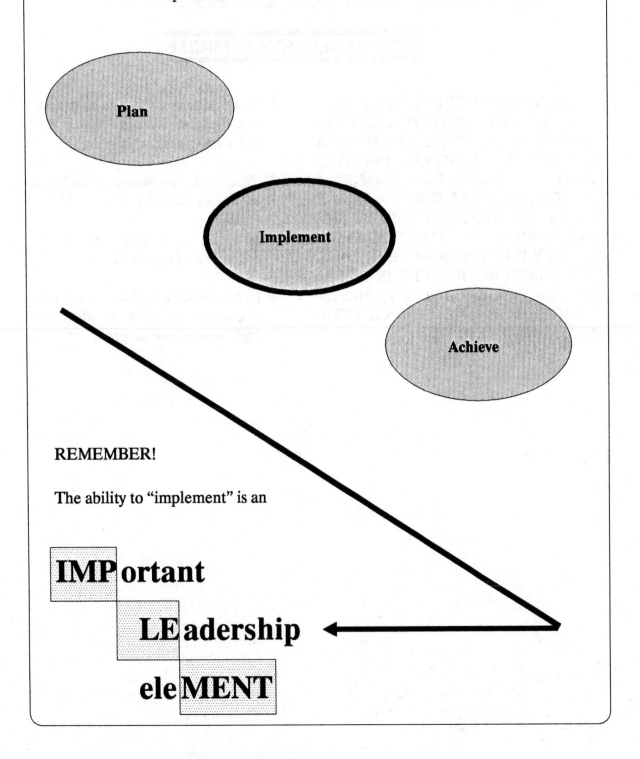

REMEMBER!

The ability to "implement" is an

IMPortant

LEadership

ele**MENT**

QUESTIONS FOR DISCUSSION

1. Who should be involved in designing the program?
2. How can you use a time line in program development?
3. What are the principal resource constraints in planning?
4. How can you use a checklist to help implement the plan?

COMPREHENSION EXERCISE

THE VICE-PRESIDENT FOR TRAINING AT THE UNITED CENTRAL SOCIETY HAS DECIDED TO HOLD A THREE-DAY PERSONAL PRODUCTIVITY TRAINING PROGRAM IN A CONFERENCE CENTER IN A SMALL TOWN. THE TRAINEES WILL BE THE PRESIDENTS OF THIRTY LOCAL UNITS WITHIN A 300-MILE RADIUS. THE PARTICIPATION FEE IS SET AT $45 PER PERSON AND THE HONORARIUM FOR THE TWO OUTSIDE TRAINERS IS $750 EACH.

1. *Name five checklists and charts you could use to plan and implement the above program.*

2. *Design the program, including a schedule of activities.*

3. *Draw up a budget showing all incomes and expenses.*

4. *Write a motivating letter to the participants explaining to them the highlights of your program.*

Part Five

The Youth Camp in Theory and Practice

The Youth Camp has become a venerable institution in Islamic work. Even though not restricted to training *per se*, most types of youth camps are oriented to developing leadership qualities and skills. For some, the youth camp is an opportunity to reinforce existing proficiencies and practice them in a model setting.

This part of the *Guide* deals with the purpose of the youth camp, preparation, program design, participation, curriculum and projects, and its evaluation. A chapter on Islamic manners is also included. The discussion lays down the foundation for understanding youth camps and using them to train for leadership.

Chapter

32

Purpose of the Youth Camp

I. Purpose
II. Recommended Subjects
    A. Islamic and General Knowledge
    B. Physical Education and Arts
    C. Management and Organizational Skills
    D. Community Projects
    E. Special Assistance
III. List of References

LEARNING OBJECTIVES

On completing this chapter, you should be able to:
- define the purpose of a youth camp
- determine what kind of training can be given in the camp
- specify areas of training and their place in the program

I. Purpose

The youth camp is one of the most effective methods for the Islamic training of young potential leaders. The camp is a combination of a special type of environment and a package of planned activities for the youth. We generally organize youth camps with the following objectives in mind:

⇒ To increase the participants' faith, knowledge, and commitment to Islam through guided living;
⇒ To develop an Islamic personality;
⇒ To develop skills required for Islamic work;
⇒ To provide opportunities to gain general experience in cooperative living; and

---

⇒ To develop an understanding and provide an opportunity for the natural development of true Islamic brotherhood and sisterhood.

The principal purpose of the youth camp is to achieve these objectives through one or more of the following means:

a. Education in Islamics and training in general skills and physical arts;

b. Training in management and organizational skills;

c. Experience through involvement in community affairs; and

d. Special programs to assist the youth.

We should select appropriate topics for various presentations during the camp program according to the need, environment, age group, and level of understanding of the participants. In addition, assigning camp participants to individual or collective projects for social work in the community immediately surrounding the camp site is a valuable training concept. Any community can offer a number of such projects. It is advisable to make initial contacts with local agencies ahead of time to facilitate arrangements for social work during the camp. Most agencies will welcome the help. We give below a list of possible subjects and projects. After reviewing the list, try this exercise: Make your own list of particular items to respond to the needs of a youth camp that you might have to plan.

II. Recommended Subjects

A. Islamic and General Knowledge

Review of Islamic Literature

Rising above Cultural Barriers

World Affairs and Issues

Unity of Muslims

Contemporary Situation of the Muslim Ummah

Concept of *Tawhid*

Islamic Brotherhood: How to Achieve It

Basic Beliefs

Sources of Islamic Shari'ah

Love of Allah *Subhanahu wa Ta'ala*

Fiqh of Salah

Concept and Purpose of Life in Islam

Love of the Prophet (SAW)

Fiqh of *Siyam*

Qur'an and Hadith

How Islam Was Spread

Lessons from the *Sirah*

Siyam

Islamic *Da'wah* — Our Responsibility

Islamic Resurgence
Sabr
Fiqh of *Niyah* (Intention) and *Taharah* (Purity)
How to Build an Islamic Personality
What is a Muslim Family
Dedication of *Sahabah* (Companions of the Prophet [PBUH])
Fiqh of Zakah and Hajj
Prohibitions in Islam
Nasihah
Islam and Other Religions
Islamic Movements
Role of a Muslim — Especially the Youth
Dhikr
Hijrah: A Turning Point
Status of Women in Islam
Pursuit of Knowledge
Life of Muhammad (SAW)
Punishment in Islam
Economic System of Islam
Islamic *Da'wah*
Social and Political Systems of Islam
Shura and Leadership in Islam
Muslim State
Organization in Islam
Difference of Opinion vs. Tolerance

B. Physical Education and Arts

Arts
Calligraphy
Scouting
Self-Defense
First Aid
Recreation in Islam
Islamic Approach to Martial Arts
Sports in Islam

C. Management and Organizational Skills

A number of subjects in this area can be selected from this *Guide*. Only additional ideas are suggested below.

Preparing Budgets
Organizing Groups
Preparing a Calendar of Activities

Writing Proposals
How to Serve through Islamic Organizations
Group Dynamics

D. Community Projects

Routine Work at Islamic Centers
Help with *'Id* Functions
Assistance in Transportation
Message Delivery
News Reporting
Disseminating Information
Visiting to Strengthen Islamic Bonds
Baby-sitting
First Aid
Children's Schools
General Behavior (Workshop)
Being a Parent — Your Responsibilities
Combining Motherhood and Career
Careers — How to Choose Them
Participating in Lobbying Efforts
Teaching Self-Development Courses
Volunteering with Scouts
Raising Funds for Local Causes
Feeding the Hungry
Visiting and Assisting Senior Citizens
Helping Refugees
Conducting Literacy Classes
Responding to Defamation of Islam

E. Special Assistance

Opportunities for Self-Development
Public School Problems
Interaction Analysis (Parents, Teachers, Peers, etc.)
Marriage
Family Counseling
Career Counseling
Job Placement
Educational Opportunities and Scholarships
How to Apply to Universities
Loans for Small Business
International/National Youth Activities

The purpose of a youth camp is to provide a well-rounded program in the areas outlined above. The underlying emphasis of the program and all its activities should be that all our work is for the pleasure of Allah (SWT). We have a responsibility to prepare ourselves to play a role in this world so as to establish righteousness. With our efforts will come the help of Allah, as the Qur'an promises:

That they would certainly be assisted and that Our forces—they surely must conquer (37:172-73).

إِنَّهُمْ لَهُمُ ٱلْمَنصُورُونَ ﴿١٧٢﴾ وَإِنَّ جُندَنَا لَهُمُ ٱلْغَٰلِبُونَ ﴿١٧٣﴾
(سورة الصافات)

III. List of References

Besides the Qur'an, its well-known commentaries, and the well-known hadith works, a number of reference books may be available in the local community or college libraries. The current catalog of an established book distributor — such as the Islamic Book Service in Indianapolis, Indiana, in the U.S.A. — can serve as a valuable source for making a list of references on various subjects from an Islamic perspective.

QUESTIONS FOR DISCUSSION

1. How can youth camp trainees train for community work?
2. In what ways does the camp serve as a forum for advice?
3. What are the three most vital purposes of a youth camp?
4. Can vocational training play a role in such a camp? How?

COMPREHENSION EXERCISE

AS COORDINATOR OF YOUTH AC-TIVITIES, YOU HAVE BEEN ASKED TO ARRANGE A PROGRAM FOR THE YOUTH. YOU DECIDE TO ORGANIZE A YOUTH CAMP FOR A FULL WEEK WITH SEVERAL COLLEGE TEACH-ERS AS PRESENTERS OF VARIOUS PARTS OF THE PROGRAM. YOU HAVE BEEN ADVISED THAT THE PARTICIPATING YOUTH ARE NEW TO YOUTH WORK, STUDY AT VARIOUS ACADEMIC INSTITUTIONS, ARE GENERALLY BRIGHT, AND QUITE PROMISING FOR ISLAMIC WORK.

1. *Explain why you chose the youth camp as the training vehicle in this case.*

2. *State what kind of education and training you plan to incorporate in the camp program and in what mix.*

3. *Considering their backgrounds and potentials, list the ways in which you can train them for community work.*

4. *Design a checklist to illustrate your answers to the three questions above.*

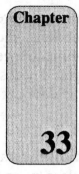

Chapter

33

Camp Preparation – Physical Arrangements

LEARNING OBJECTIVES

On completing this chapter, you should be able to:
- identify factors essential in the selection of sites
- identify major components of a budget for the camp
- identify main methods for selection of participants

I. Site Selection

For the camp to be effective, we must make an effort to select a place which provides an Islamic environment without any distractions; a place which offers an atmosphere of freedom and simplicity where brotherly and sisterly relationships are enhanced. In addition, the location should offer rooms for meetings, teaching, and other functions of the camp program. Classrooms, dining hall, gymnasium, lounge areas, first aid room, library, kitchen, storage room, and offices are the typical needs. An open area, a water reservoir, and a pleasing landscape are also desirable for outdoor activities and sports.

We could select a site that is located in either a rural area or an urban one. The rural setting needs a wooded area with some clearing, potable water on site or close by, and permanent buildings or tent sites suitable for sleeping and all other planned activities. Mountains, rivers, lakes and the seashore add to potential recreational opportunities like swimming and hiking. Nearby historical or archaeological sites can offer invaluable learning experiences.

On the other hand, urban settings bring together a wide variety of facilities within a close distance or even within one building. Museums, monuments, parks, factories, and colleges allow sophisticated programming for the camp. Athletic fields and swimming pools owned by nearby schools or the city can add to what is available on the main urban site.

Usually, programs conducted in a rural camp environment are found to be more effective than those in the urban setting, because the former provides a place which is open, isolated, and free from everyday disturbances.

We should begin the planning and processing of site selection early, from six months to a year before the opening day of the camp. The sponsoring organization should form a committee for this purpose. This committee may delegate specific tasks such as search for the site, evaluation of available sites, and negotiations with the favored one to subcommittees. We should consider factors such as cost, centrality of location, accessibility and nearness to a large Muslim population, and availability of local manpower during the site selection phase. The organizers should ensure that participants are not exposed to scenes such as unclothed swimmers on beaches or swimming pools in the proximity of the camp. Similarly, areas where crime rates are high must be avoided.

II. Physical Facilities

Here are some tips for preparing the physical facilities:

A. Space Planning

Each type of activity needs a certain size and kind of space. For meetings, as an example, we determine the room size by calculating the square feet of space required for sitting, locating equipment, and walking around. The room should not be too big, just as it should not be too small. We should partition a room that is too big by placing removable dividers so as to create a cozy feeling of togetherness. Some "rules of thumb" for space planning are given below:

Type of Activity	Space Needed (sq. ft.)
Receptions	About 9 - 10
Meals	About 12 - 13
Theater Seating	About 9 - 10
Classroom Seating	About 15 - 17
Conference Seating	About 23 - 25
Prayers	About 7 - 8

B. Screen Placements

Whether it is for slides or transparency presentations or for films, we should place the screen such that the audience can view it with comfort. Discomfort and strain often result from screen height, screen distance, or obstructions. The rule of thumb is that the distance between the screen and front row of seats should be at least twice the width of the screen; from the front to the back, all rows should be no deeper than four screen widths. Each row should be no wider than three screen widths. The screen should be placed just high enough for people in the last row to see the bottom of the screen above the heads of those sitting in front of them.

C. Messaging

"No interruption" should be the general rule during a program. However, communication with and by the participants may be necessary in certain situations. We can allow for that by placing an alphabetized message board in a central location and by assigning an operator to receive and post messages on the board. It is not advisable to place a telephone in an instructional area or to read individual messages to the participants in such a setting.

D. Rest Rooms

The need for and time of making *wudu'* should be a major concern in determining the size and location of rest rooms. The men's and women's rest rooms should be large enough to accommodate the participants in each group and allow for children if present. They should be close enough to the meeting rooms with convenient routes to the prayer areas.

III. Budgeting

Preparing a budget and then sticking to it are critical to the successful operation of a camp program. We should begin by listing all possible sources of expense and income. The difference between the two must be made up by fund-raising efforts early in the preparation.

We should use budgeting as a decision-making tool. This is done by examining alternatives in buying goods or services and deciding in favor of those that are consistent with program objectives both in quality and cost.

Generally, travel expenses are a major portion of the camp budget. Efforts made to minimize them could be very rewarding. Whenever possible, carpooling should be encouraged. In case of air travel, we must purchase tickets in advance (seven to thirty days depending on the market) to save significantly. Because of competition, many airlines offer bargain fares between selected cities. It pays a lot to shop around.

IV. Selection of Participants

It is expected that candidates for a leadership training camp are already practicing Muslims. The camp program seeks to make them potential leaders. We must therefore select youth not only on the basis of their commitment to Islam but also for their desire to work for the cause of Islam. We should follow the age limits chosen for the camp. If the participants' ages are too far apart, the camp will be difficult to manage and unlikely to succeed.

One possible selection method would be a competition in the form of an essay or a quiz. We could hold it on local levels, have local winners compete at a regional level, and then judge among regional winners nationally. Those scoring above a certain level could be chosen for camp participation. Regardless of the method, the event must be widely publicized so that we may select the best from a wide field of candidates.

A. Outside the City

The regional representatives or publicity chairman should contact various organizations in each city or county through letters, faxes, telegrams, telexes, and phone calls. Presidents of these organizations should select young Muslims in the chosen age group. Selection of the participating youth must conform to the established criteria.

B. Inside the City

The local committee should be asked to contact various Islamic organizations in the city to assist in selection.

C. Reception

A local reception committee consisting of persons from various local organizations may be appointed to receive the arriving participants and bring them to the camp. The camp program may start with a brief opening ceremony. It may be beneficial to invite local officials to participate in the camp and become familiar with its objectives. After the opening ceremony, we should thoroughly discuss the purpose, management, and rules of camp conduct in an orientation session.

QUESTIONS FOR DISCUSSION

1. What are the major differences between rural and urban sites?
2. Why is a meeting room that is too large as bad as one that is too small?
3. What is the major expense item in most camp budgets? How can you reduce it?
4. What is one good way to select potentially qualified participants for the camp?

COMPREHENSION EXERCISE

YOU ARE CHAIRMAN OF A COMMITTEE TO MAKE PHYSICAL ARRANGEMENTS FOR THE YOUTH CAMP. YOU MUST CHOOSE BETWEEN A FEW RECOMMENDED SITES, PREPARE A BUDGET WITH A VIEW TO MAKING THE CAMP SELF-SUFFICIENT, AND SELECT PARTICIPANTS. THIS IS GOING TO BE A NATIONAL TRAINING CAMP FOR THE FUTURE LEADERSHIP. YOU HAVE SIX MONTHS TO MAKE ALL ARRANGEMENTS.

1. *Explain why you chose the site you did over others.*

2. *Prepare a circular to announce the camp to potential participants. Tell them what they need to do to qualify.*

3. *Develop a budget for the camp. Include an optimum level of spending and a bare minimum level. Explain and justify your budget cuts.*

Chapter

34

Program Design – General Considerations

LEARNING OBJECTIVES

On completing this chapter, you should be able to:
- identify the most important considerations in scheduling
- select the right speakers and plan visual aids use
- make a suitable daily program for the youth camp

I. Elements of Program Design

As stated before, the youth camp is one of the most effective ways of imparting Islamic leadership training to youth. The phrase "youth camp" generally refers to a program of activities spread over a period of one to a few weeks in a somewhat secluded

---

setting. The objective is to train potential leaders between twenty and thirty years of age. The many facets of training have been discussed in the other chapters of this *Guide*. This chapter and the other material in this part will focus on the practical aspects of organizing and managing such youth camps.

A good program is at the heart of a successful youth camp. In this section, we will deal with some general and specific considerations in making a program and offer an outline schedule to use. However, we must carefully tailor each program to its audience and, whenever possible, seek input from that audience. A profile of the prospective participants helps to determine the level and extent of the program that will benefit them most.

A program committee of three to five persons, plus a youth representative, should prepare a program for the camp. The program should be carefully designed to generate an Islamic attitude, enhance team spirit, contribute to developing an Islamic personality, and encourage commitment to Islam among the youth. It should be structured around a well-thought-out curriculum using a variety of training techniques as discussed in appropriate chapters of this *Guide*, including lectures, workshops, practical exercises, demonstrations, and the like. It should also allocate time for sports and recreational activities.

In the light of the objectives of the camp, appropriate topics may be selected for presentation. Some suggested topics are listed in another chapter of Part Five.

A. Basics of Scheduling

How to schedule a program has been discussed in details elsewhere in this *Guide*. Here we will restate only the basic principles of scheduling a program for a youth camp.

The dual objective in program scheduling is to simplify the task of managing and coordinating the various activities and to provide comfort for the participants. Both concerns aim at improving the learning environment at the camp.

Except for the opening day, daily programming should begin with waking up for *salat al fajr*. The early morning beginning takes advantage of the full night's rest. Similarly, daily programming should end with *salat al 'isha'*, after which participants should prepare for bed. Personal private study or reading may be allowed only in special cases for persons who can function well the next day with reduced sleep. In between *fajr* and *'isha'*, periods of rest should be strategically placed before and after activities that may drain the participant's energies. A tired audience does not learn well and a packed program does not fulfil the objectives of the camp.

The length and nature of the camp will determine how various activities should be spread out over the entire duration. Generally speaking, the intellectually demanding activities should be scheduled earlier in the day and on earlier days of the camp. These include academically-oriented sessions of an hour and a half each which should be placed in the morning and during times of greatest absorptive capacity of the mind. Sports, outdoor activities, and recreational events, which may include audiovisual presentations, should be scheduled during the afternoon and early evening. This takes advantage of daylight and provides a physically stimulating break between the major intellectual parts of the day's program. Whenever possible, the skeleton of the schedule, including meal and prayer times, should stay the same from day to day for convenience and to facilitate greater punctuality.

For camps of longer than a week's duration, a whole day or two may be set aside for learning excursions to places outside the camp site. This can help break monotony, offer opportunity to study the environment, and challenge participants to practice some of the things they have learnt. Another day may be set aside for an open forum for discussion and exchange of ideas among the trainers and the trainees. Subjects could range from what has been studied so far to new topics of practical importance to the Islamic movement and the youth.

The last day of any camp should be an opportunity for the participants to evaluate the camp experience and to discuss their plans and resolutions with others. This helps them translate what they have learnt into blueprints for action. In this exercise, they identify and consider problems peculiar to the social milieu from which they come and how these affect the Islamic movement locally. Written statements help a discussion of the salient features among the trainers and the trainees.

B. Speaker Selection

After we have specified a curriculum and set up a schedule, the most important task is to select speakers, discussants, and other presenters who will be engaged in the task of training. In this *Guide* we have discussed the characteristics of trainers and resource persons.

To identify resource persons, we can enlist the aid of national and international organizations that maintain lists of qualified speakers. However, it is important to select speakers who will best communicate with the audience at the proper intellectual and emotional levels. It is as ineffective to speak to an audience at too high a level as it is to speak at too low a level. Further, we should select speakers not only for their expertise in specific subject areas but also their ability to relate to the social, cultural, or political context of the camp and the participants. It is a good practice to avoid having the same speaker in several camps. Avoid choosing a speaker just for his famous name.

C. Audiovisual Use

The types and techniques of audiovisual media have been discussed earlier. Since camp sites are often less equipped than conference sites, we must pay special attention to the availability of power, the right kinds of outlets and cords, and backup equipment. Advance arrangement may be necessary to ensure that the viewing room can be darkened when required. If advanced technology like computerized projection is to be used, we should ensure the availability of adequate technical support. All audiovisuals must be tested in advance on site.

D. Sports and Recreation

Sports and recreational activities form an important part of the camp and should be properly organized. We should allow reasonable time for them in the program and make sure appropriate and safe equipment is available on time. We can group the camp participants into teams for sports like soccer, football, volleyball, basketball, swimming, and so forth. Even in the case of camps with families present, care should be taken to guard and control mixing of the sexes Islamically in these and other activities or during the camp. Intracamp and, when practical, intercamp competitions can be a good way to create enthusiasm and the spirit to excel among the players as well as the nonplaying participants of the camp. We should recognize special efforts and award prizes to those who perform outstandingly.

E. Opening and Closing Sessions

The opening and closing sessions of the camp are among the most important parts of the program. We often do not give them the attention they need to be effective.

The opening sessions may begin with the recitation of the Qur'an and translation of its meaning in the local language. We must select passages as close to the theme of the camp as possible and plan for the best reciter available to recite them. Then, representatives of the host and sponsoring organization should speak to establish their identity and role in the program. Next, the participants should be adequately oriented to what is to come by the chairman of the program committee and the chairman of the physical arrangement committee. We could then introduce selected guests. A model of such an opening session is shown below. Note that the chairman of the camp should preside.

Opening Session: Friday, 2:30-4:00 pm (for example)

2:30	Recitation of the Qur'an followed by translation
2:40	Remarks by an official of the national organization
2:45	Remarks by an official of the local host organization
2:50	Remarks by officials of other sponsoring organizations
3:00	Orientation talk by program committee chairman, assignment of groups, and allocation of individual responsibilities
3:15	Orientation talk by camp committee chairman
3:40	Introduction of selected guests by camp chairman
3:45	Questions from the participants
4:00	End of session

The opening session must set the tone of the program to follow. It should prepare the participants for the theme.

The closing session is equally important. It must bring the program to a graceful and enjoyable end. We must take the opportunity to recognize everyone's contribution to the success of the program. When possible, we should briefly highlight the presentations made and offer suggestions on how to benefit from what the participants learned. A sample of a concluding session is shown below:

Closing Session: Sunday, 2:30-4:00 pm (for example)

2:30	Remarks by selected guests
2:50	Summary of presentations in the program
3:10	Presentation of conclusions and/or assignments
3:15	Remarks by participants
3:30	Remarks by an official of the local host organization
3:35	Remarks by an official of the national organization
3:40	*Du'a'* from the Qur'an and hadith and their translation, followed by an appropriate collective departure song
4:00	End of session

Note: If the camp is for three days or less, it is better to do the evaluation in the closing session. If the program is for more than three days, a separate evaluation session is warranted.

Action point	This question must be asked by the organizers for every activity, whether it is a lecture, a camp, a social event, a political gathering, or a *qiyam al layl*. Plan for the participants to take something home with them. Otherwise, the function is done and forgotten, and will have no lasting effect. It becomes next to a waste of time and money. If this question is dealt with from the beginning, the organizers will make sure that the participants get some benefits in the form of material to take home.
WHAT DO I TAKE HOME WITH ME **?**	

II. How to Make a Daily Program

A. Elements of Program Scheduling

1. Divide the day into its natural divisions around prayers and meals.
2. Estimate time for specific activities on the basis of factors that affect the attention span and the movement of participants, like number and age of participants, the type of activity, capacity of physical facilities, number and size of entrances and exits, weather conditions, distance between different facilities, and so on.
3. Include preparation time for things like *wudu'* before salah, and wash up before breakfast and other meals.
4. Seek input from participants and counsellors/instructors.
5. Schedule activities for each division and then integrate them to complete the day's program. For longer than a day, repeat the day's schedule with appropriate modifications, like registration on the opening day and evaluation on the closing day.

B. How to Put Together the Daily Schedule

From a scheduling point of view, days are of two types: long in summer and short in winter. On a long day the sun rises early and sets late. Thus the time of *salat al fajr* is early and that of *salat al 'isha'* is late. The time for sleeping at night between *'isha'* and *fajr* becomes insufficient in the middle of summer. To compensate for lost sleep, rest periods must be scheduled after Qur'anic study following *salat al fajr* and after lunch. Participants may sleep, nap, or just relax in these rest periods to perhaps make up for insufficient sleep at night.

Similarly, the time between *'asr* and *maghrib* is long in summer and short in winter. Thus dinner may be scheduled before *maghrib* in summer and after *maghrib* in winter.

Time between *maghrib* and *'isha'* is also somewhat longer in summer and shorter in winter. Thus, a social period could be scheduled before *'isha'* in summer with participants going to sleep immediately following *'isha'*, and after *'isha'* in winter when there is still sufficient sleeping time left.

The time required for various **types of activities** is discussed below. Care should be exercised to take into account local conditions, constraints, and habits.

a) Wake Up and Wash Up

A fixed time must be announced for wake-up. How long it should be before *salat al fajr* depends on the number of participants in relation to the number of toilet and washing facilities and their distance from sleeping areas. As a rule of thumb, divide the number of participants by the number of facilities and multiply by three to get number of minutes before *iqamah* for wake-up time.

b) Wudu'

The time allowed for *wudu'* for prayers other than *fajr* need not be more than half that allowed for *fajr*. Participants should be encouraged to make *wudu'* as time permits during the day. Indeed, they should be encouraged to be in the state of *wudu'* all day.

c) Tea

Sometimes it may be possible to have tea before *fajr*. This may help in making the participants more alert for the prayers and the following Qur'anic study. The time allowed should be related to the number of participants and the size of the serving facility. At least half the time will overlap with the time for making *wudu'*.

d) Prayers

As a rule of thumb, the total time allotted for prayers should be three times the time it takes to perform the particular prayer.

e) Rest

On long summer days, periods of rest in the morning and afternoon are essential to compensate for the short nights. To calculate the maximum time available for rest in the morning, subtract time for wash up from the time between end of Qur'anic study and beginning of breakfast. In the afternoon, adequate time for rest should be about ninety minutes.

f) Meals

Scheduling adequate time for meals is important. Even if the meal is not accompanied by a lecture or presentation, it is a valuable part of the program because eating together brings people closer. The time needed will depend on whether the facility allows for everyone to eat at the same time or in groups and how fast the service is going to be. If properly planned, an hour and a half is a good time to allow for meals, wash-up, and some relaxation.

g) Sessions

Generally, sessions should not last longer than one hour and a half in order to retain the full attention of the participants. This time should be shortened if the meeting room or the seating is uncomfortable. It may be extended if the reverse is true and the session involves the audience interactively, thus holding their attention for a longer time.

As a rule, sessions containing nonparticipatory activities like lectures should be scheduled in the mornings or evenings when the audience is fresh or has had a chance to freshen up. Afternoons are best for participatory activities, like workshops, where a higher degree of involvement keeps the participants engaged in the learning process.

h) Breaks

Breaks of fifteen to thirty minutes duration are necessary to break the monotony of some programs. In addition, breaks help participants digest the information presented, collect their thoughts, interact with speakers, socialize with others, stretch their legs, and become better prepared for the following session than they would be if there was no break between sessions. A break should not be longer than thirty minutes to discourage participants from engaging in other activities, like private meetings.

i) Recreation

In programs lasting longer than two days, a set time for recreational activities enhances the quality of learning. Recreation releases tensions and restores energy after program segments that call for concentration and participation from participants. Generally, two hours are adequate for this purpose, other than the time required to commute to off-site facilities if necessary.

j) Sports

Scheduling time for sports is essential for youth camps and other programs for younger audiences lasting more than three days. Two hours are generally sufficient in addition to time needed for preparation and commuting. We must organize the sports activity well, otherwise it will be a waste of time and will become a negative element of the program. The organizer will benefit much by playing with the trainees and watching them. They will be able to recognize personality traits from the trainees' behavior in sports, very useful information that cannot be obtained from lectures and the like.

k) Socials

Getting to know one another in order to nourish brotherhood and sisterhood and to establish networks is an important purpose of Islamic gatherings like camps, conferences, and conventions. The most appropriate time for social activities is near the end of the day. One hour is usually sufficient.

l) Sleep

How much sleep is enough will depend on the personal habits of the participants as well as their age and health. A minimum of seven hours in summer and six hours in winter should be allowed for. The amount of time available for sleep will also vary with the season. The general principle should be to encourage participants to be well-rested through sleep and naps. A tired audience is not ready to learn well.

C. Suggested Format of Daily Program

	Wake up
	Salat al fajr
	Brief talk (10 min.)
	Qur'anic study circle (half hour)
	Wash up (half hour to 45 min).
8:30 - 9:00 am	Breakfast
9:15 - 10:30	Session I
10:30 - 11:00	Break
11:00 - 12:30 pm	Session II
1:00	*Iqamah* for *salat al zuhr*
	Lunch
	Free-time for sports
	Iqamah for *salat al 'asr*
4:00 - 6:00	Session III: Workshops (3 to 4 groups)
	Iqamah for *salat al maghrib*
	Dinner
7:30 - 9:00	Session IV: Reports from each group
9:30 - 9:45	Evaluation
10:00	*Iqamah* for *salat al 'isha'*
10:15	Required rest/sleep

EXERCISE	
Statistics of the Daily Program	Devise a daily program of the camp. Calculate the time for activities like salah, food, breaks and recreation, sports, sessions, sleep, etc. Then calculate the total. It should be twenty-four hours. Calculate the percentage of time for each activity. Analyze this data and discuss whether the cost of the program is justified by the planned schedule. For example, is there too much time for sleep, recreation, breaks, and so on, and not enough for the learning sessions? Modify the daily schedule accordingly.

A panoramic view of *Ka'bah* — "the House of Allah."

QUESTIONS FOR DISCUSSION

1. In what way is a profile of participants helpful in designing a youth camp program?
2. What is the best time of day for academic-type programs? Why?
3. What are the major concerns in the selection of speakers?
4. Why are the opening and closing sessions important?
5. What are the major activity types in a daily program?
6. What are the major effects of winter and summer on program scheduling?

COMPREHENSION EXERCISE

YOU HAVE ALREADY CHOSEN THE MAJOR PROGRAM ELEMENTS OF THE YOUTH CAMP. NOW YOUR TASK IS TO DESIGN AN EFFECTIVE PROGRAM. YOU BEGIN BY IDENTIFYING THE SPEAKERS, PLANNING USE OF VISUAL AIDS, AND MAKING A PRELIMINARY SCHEDULE. WHILE YOU HAVE SUFFICIENT TIME BEFORE THE CAMP, YOU MUST BE THOROUGH SINCE THIS IS AN ANNUAL CAMP AND ANY MISSED OPPORTUNITIES CANNOT BE MADE UP UNTIL NEXT YEAR.

1. *Design a detailed chart to keep track of arrangements about speakers from the initial contact to the final presentation.*

2. *Write a concise letter to the prospective trainees to get their personal profiles and their input on program design. Explain clearly what information you want and why.*

The Art of Participation

LEARNING OBJECTIVES

On completing this chapter, you should be able to:
- identify differences between individual and group actions
- select tasks for group participation
- plan activities for intellectual involvement

I. Training by Delegation

How many times have you heard the complaint "Too many lectures, no participation from the audience!" Slogans like "Too much theorizing, not enough 'peoplizing'" are becoming quite popular. This is a general feature among us, where very few people run the entire show. They become overloaded, exhausted, and their efficiency drops drastically. The audience feels neglected, underutilized, and unconsulted. It becomes increasingly critical and negative. Morale plummets and dissatisfaction spreads. Some organizers feel that the camp program is a method whereby information is poured from the mouth of the speakers into the brain containers of the participants. Far from it. Such leaders miss the great opportunity of training by participation and example during the few precious contact hours of the camp. They do not realize that the trainees are watching their actions and attitudes much more than the lips of their trainers and leaders. They give lip service to *nasihah* and do not practice it. They advocate discipline, order, sacrifice, punctuality, kindness, cost-cutting, efficiency, piety and tolerance but fail to exemplify them in their own behavior. Many shortcomings in the movement exist because we say what we do not do and do what we do not say.

The valuable few contact hours provide a golden opportunity to demonstrate training by example.

The organizer's golden rule should be to delegate all tasks in the camp to the participants and leave nothing for themselves, whenever possible. This enables trainers to watch everything and fill in the gaps as soon as they appear. It also makes them available to provide trainees with "on-the-job" training. Learning through doing is much more effective and lasts longer. The camp environment must provide a model to be emulated in its format and essence. In short, the camp should be conducted as a model Islamic society in every respect.

One may argue that it is easier, faster, and more efficient to do the thing yourself rather than teach someone else to do it for you. This is true in the short run, but in the long run it is much better to teach others to do it. Otherwise, you will end up doing everything yourself because you can do it better. We should be patient to accept less than perfection from others until they learn. We have to train ourselves to tolerate others' mistakes.

II. How to Accomplish Group Participation

After presenting the opening remarks in the first session, the camp leader should explain the various tasks and assign them to individuals. These tasks are in addition to the other preestablished committees of the camp, like the program, transportation, food, budget, guests, sports, security, baby-sitting, entertainment, camp evaluations, and the like. Each participant must be in charge of a specific item.

A. Physical Facilities
1. Announcements
2. Heating and air-conditioning
3. Sleeping rooms
4. Bathrooms
5. Lighting
6. Parking arrangements
7. Refreshments

B. Discipline and Order
1. Cleanliness and tidiness
2. Shoe arrangements
3. Odors and smells
4. Timings and punctuality
5. Personal appearance
6. Garbage removal

C. Sessions
1. Seating arrangements
2. The podium
3. Audiovisuals
4. Ushers to help people to be in the session and not outside in the corridors
5. Language correction (Arabic and English)
6. Jokes and entertainment
7. Evaluation of speakers
8. Evaluation of chairpersons
9. Evaluation of participants

D. Salah
1. *Adhan*
2. Assigning the imams
3. Appointing the "after salah" speakers
4. Waking up
5. Assigning Qur'anic reciters
6. *Du'a's*

E. Office Work
1. Copying/duplicating
2. Typing
3. Stationery supplies
4. Lost and found
5. Telephone
6. Camp newsletter

F. Miscellaneous
1. Photography
2. Complaints
3. Donations
4. Safety
5. Health (first aid)
6. *Nasihah* in general
7. Communication with the outside (parents, media, etc.)
8. Books (library)
9. Bazaar stands/tables
10. Fiqh (must necessarily be broad-minded; must be aware of various opinions and schools of thoughts)

Each task may be assigned to one or more individuals, or several of them may be performed by one depending on the nature of the task and the number of participants. They could be changed during the camp. This assignment of tasks to individuals does not excuse others from doing their duty without being reminded. It will also teach the trainees how not to interfere in other people's authority except through the right channels.

III. Intellectual Participation

Participation on the academic level can be achieved through the following:

A. Three-Minute Presentations

This activity is organized by dividing the camp into group workshops of about fifteen each. Each person is given three minutes to speak about the most important thing he wants to convey to the group. The chairman of the session assigns a time controller.

B. Three-Minute Self-Introduction Workshop

Each trainee presents his life background to the group in a self-introduction workshop. It is amazing how enriching this can be. This is a powerful application of the verse:

O mankind! We created you from a single [pair] of a male and female, and made you into nations and tribes, that you may know each other [not that you may despise each other] ... (49:13).

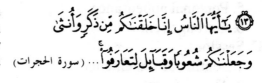

C. Presenting Somebody Else's Article

This activity is to train someone to read an article at short notice and present it to an audience. The presenter must be honest in conveying the author's views regardless of what he thinks of them. If he wants to relate his own personal opinions, he must clearly indicate so. If the author happens to be among the audience, it will be a great training for him as well. It is appropriate to give the author the privilege to respond in three minutes only.

D. A Short Memorization

A great feeling of participation is experienced by memorizing collectively some short *ayat* or hadith, preferably in the *du'a'* format. What is memorized will stay with the trainees for the rest of their lives. This experience gives them the nice feeling of taking something home with them. It may be the thing from the camp that they remember most in their lives.

E. Purposeful Jokes

The camp may adopt the format of starting each session with a purposeful joke. Each time a different trainee may narrate it. If the number is large, two jokes per session may be narrated, one at the beginning and one at the end. Such a practice will uplift the camp morale enormously. The Prophet (SAW) teaches us:

«رَوِّحوا القُلوبَ ساعةً وَساعةً، فَإِنَّ القُلوبَ إِذا كَلَّتْ عَمِيَتْ»

Entertain the hearts in between hours, for if the hearts get tired, they become blind.[1]

Participation Drill

Set up a competition. "Who remembers the names of the largest number of participants?" The key to remembering names is to register them consciously in your memory by associating them with someone you know very well!

---

1   Sunan al Daylami.

QUESTIONS FOR DISCUSSION

1. What are the advantages of assigning camp administration responsibilities to participants? What are the disadvantages?
2. What considerations you should keep in mind when assigning a responsibility to more than one person?

COMPREHENSION EXERCISE

YOU HAVE BEEN ASKED TO BE PROGRAM DIRECTOR OF A YOUTH CAMP. THE PARTICIPANTS WILL SPEND A WEEK OF ACTIVITIES IN A RURAL SETTING. AT LEAST HALF OF THEM WILL BE FROM FARAWAY PLACES AND ALSO NOT FAMILIAR WITH THE PEOPLE AND PRACTICES IN THE CAMP. THE GROUP SIZE WILL BE FIFTY AND THE NUMBER OF COUNSELLORS AND PRESENTERS FIFTEEN. YOUR GOAL IS TO TRAIN THE PARTICIPANTS FOR LEADERSHIP IN THEIR LOCAL ORGANIZATIONS AS WELL AS FOR TEAM WORK AT THE REGIONAL LEVEL.

1. *Draft a letter to the potential participants explaining to them how they will have a group experience at the camp.*

2. *List ten tasks that you may assign to individuals in the group. Rank the tasks by degree of effectiveness of each for training.*

3. *Design a model for self-introduction by participants. Underline the information that will be most useful in this group.*

Chapter

36

Islamic Manners

LEARNING OBJECTIVES

On completing this chapter, you should be able to:
- understand the concept of *adab* (manners) in Islam
- identify Islamic manners in daily life situations
- appreciate the unity of style in Islamic manners

I. *Adab* **for Daily Living**

Islam concerns itself extensively with manners. It places a very high premium on manners, a premium so high that it includes them in the scripture as Allah's commandments. As the profusion of hadith on the subject indicates, the Prophet (SAW) devoted a great portion of his efforts to teaching his companions new manners. Distinctive manners are always noticeable; but in the case of the Muslim, they are his lifestyle, his culture, his refinement, and his humanity. In all their details, Islamic manners are consistent with and reflect the Muslim's identity. The Prophet (SAW) was the best exemplar of them. Rightly, he said:

$$\langle\langle\text{أَدَّبَني رَبِّي فَأَحْسَنَ تَأْدِيبي}\rangle\rangle$$

My Lord has taught me good manners; and He mannered me well.[1]

The Islamic camp is bound to teach the manners of Islam to its members and to uphold their observance everywhere and at all times. Islamic manners can be classified according to the topics or the situations with which they deal.

A. *Adab* of Communication

1. Always smile and avoid frowning.
2. Always speak softly; do not raise your voice.
3. Laugh softly; do not thunder.
4. Stand up and stay standing if the person with whom you are communicating is standing. Otherwise, invite him to sit down. You sit down after he does.
5. Be first to greet the other person with *al salamu 'alaykum* unless (a) you are stationary and he is moving toward you on foot or by vehicle or (b) you are in company and he is alone.
6. Answer *al salamu 'alaykum* with a complete *wa 'alaykum al salam wa rahmatu Allah wa barakatuhu.* Do so with a cheerful, inviting and engaging voice.
7. Do not yawn in public. If a yawn comes, suppress it politely or cover your mouth with your hand. If it must come, follow it with *la hawla wa la quwata illa billah.*
8. Keep your posture straight at all times. Do not slump or lean unless you are alone.
9. Give full attention to what is being said to you.
10. When you talk to a person of the same gender or are being talked to similarly, look at your communicant in the face.
11. If anyone in your company sneezes and follows it with *al hamdu li Allah*, answer promptly with *yarhamukum Allah*, may Allah bless you!
12. Say as little about yourself to others as possible. Avoid saying anything ill of anyone even if it is absolutely true.
13. Learn to compliment your communicant on all occasions and to invoke Allah's blessings upon him in the conversation.

B. *Adab* of Appearance

1. Always and everywhere be clean. Cleanliness is integral to *iman.* To this end, take showers regularly.
2. Keep your hair well trimmed and short.

---

1   Al Sam'ani in *Adab al Imla'.*

3. Do not allow your fingernails to grow; every Friday before prayer, clip them before they begin to gather dirt under them. Wash hands and face, rinse mouth, and comb hair several times a day.

4. Do not wear your clothes tight, especially your trousers.

6. When you sit, keep your legs together and your arms close to your sides. Avoid motioning with your arms.

7. Avoid grimacing with your face and maintain a natural appearance. A smiling appearance is better.

8. If you perspire a lot, use a deodorant or a suitable perfume.

C. *Adab* of Attending Class

1. Be in your seat one or two minutes before the appointed hour. Always bring with you your notebook and pens.

2. Sit properly and fix your eyes on the speaker. Do not allow yourself to look elsewhere while he is talking.

3. While the teacher talks, listen well and take notes. Do not speak to your neighbor.

4. Never interrupt your teacher. Signal that you need to speak by raising your hand. If you are not recognized, then know that it is not desired that you speak. Lower your hand and speak to the teacher after class.

5. Do not agitate when the time is up for a session. Avoid leaving the room before the teacher or before he has signalled termination of the session.

6. Never eat, drink, or smoke at any meeting.

7. If you disagree with the teacher, express your opinion softly and with decorum.

D. *Adab* of Eating

1. Before sitting at the table, wash your hands and face and rinse your mouth.

2. Do not be the first to start eating. Wait until others have started. If there is insufficient room for another diner to sit with you, squeeze yourself to your neighbor and make room for the new comer.

3. Start with an audible recitation of *bismillahi al rahmani al rahim.*

4. Never take more than you can eat. It is far better to go for a second helping, or to remain somewhat hungry, than to leave food on your plate.

5. Do not "swallow." Take time to chew.

6. Eat with your right hand. This means that when you use a fork to eat you hold the fork with the right hand. Dish and cut with your right hand.

7. Do not speak while your mouth is full of food.

8. Be of help and service to your fellow diners. If you rise to get something, ask if you may get something for them.

9. If there is doubt about to whom a certain thing is served, never touch it. If someone takes what is served to you, try to get it replaced and do not ask the taker to return it.

10. If you finish eating before others, wait until the others have finished too.
11. Keep the table around your plate and the ground around your place impeccably clean and appetizing. If you drop any food anywhere, stop eating at once, remove it, and wipe the spot clean.
12. Always complete your eating with an audible *al hamdu li Allah*.
13. Wash hands and rinse mouth after eating.

E. *Adab* of Sleeping

1. Retire as soon after *salat al 'Isha'* as possible. If you must read and work, go to the reading room to do so.
2. Rise at the first call for waking up and do not tarry in bed. Between the first call and the first duty there is plenty of time to do all that you want to do; but not if you wait till the last call. Recite your morning *du'a'*.
3. Brush your teeth, take a shower, and put on your clothes quickly.
4. Always arrive for *salat al fajr* before the *iqamah*.
5. If for any reason you are going to be late for *salat al fajr*, go to the mosque notwithstanding and there perform your salah as a *qada'* (overdue).

F. *Adab* of Salah

1. Always arrive at the mosque ahead of the *iqamah*. One late arrival in one week is too much.
2. Do not carry your shoes inside the mosque, but keep them outside in orderly rows on the floor. If there are shoe racks, put them in one.
3. Upon arrival, find a place as close to the *mihrab* as possible, sit down, and recite the Qur'an softly.
4. Never talk to anyone before or during the salah, even to silence somebody else who is talking. Talk to such a person about his improper conduct after the salah and outside the mosque.
5. If the Qu'ran is being recited aloud anywhere, stand or sit still and listen. Do not talk or move about.
6. Stand to salah with feet apart, feet and shoulders close to those of your neighbors, in absolutely straight lines.
7. Never anticipate the movements of the imam, but follow his movements when signalled by his recitation of *Allahu Akbar*, etc. Perform the final *salam* only after the imam has completed his fully, not half of it.
8. Avoid stretching your legs in the direction of the *qiblah*. If you cannot sit cross-legged for a certain time, stretch them sideways, or sit on your knees and heels for a change of posture.
9. In the salah, your voice should be such that even your immediate neighbor cannot hear it.
10. During a sermon or a Friday *khutbah*, never talk, yawn, move around, or laugh loudly even when the imam has told a joke; smile instead.

G. General Rules of *Adab*

1. **Punctuality** in Islamic life and work is as important as the fulfillment of religious and moral duties. This cannot be over emphasized to Muslims the world over, who are notorious in their neglect of this prime Islamic virtue. If you are in the habit of arriving late, advance your watch enough to counter your habit.

There is no escape from your having to break this un-Islamic and unworthy habit. In the Islamic camp, as well as in the Islamic movement, every member or worker must be aware of time and absolutely serious in his utilization of it. Whatever the activity, Muslims must be bound to its precise time. Life is purposeful and man is responsible for every moment of time. So, whether the time calls for food or salah, for sports or study, you should be there not only on time, but before time. Failure to start your duty on time is failure in your Islamicity, in your very *iman*.

2. **Readiness to give aid** is an Islamic virtue par excellence. The Muslim is always ready to come to the assistance of other Muslims in need. He does not wait to be asked to extend assistance. He is always on the lookout for the situation where he can actualize his benevolence. As far as doing the good (*al ma'ruf*) is concerned, or stopping or prohibiting an evil (*al munkar*), the Muslim must even be aggressive at times. This readiness to jump into any situation in order to be of service to fellow humans is the highest, the noblest expression of *iman*.

In the Islamic camp, a member's *iman* is rightly measured by his active *ihsan*, his doing good on all occasions. If he enters a meeting room and finds the table dirty, he wipes it clean. If the chairs are not properly arranged, he arranges them in proper order. If the blackboard is full of writing, he wipes and makes it ready for use. In the bathroom, the gym, the dining room, the athletic field, the mosque, walkways—everywhere, the Muslim is the first one to set right that which is not right. If a service calls for volunteers, he is the first to offer his service. The Muslim thus makes himself worthy of his Prophet (SAW) who said: "...And the beginning of *ihsan* is removing refuse from the public highway." (Bayhaqi)

3. **Amiability** is a prerequisite of *falah*. The Muslim struggles as hard as he can to make himself amiable, loveable, befriendable, and trustworthy. The ever-present smile on his face is the index of a tenderness of heart toward other Muslims. When they talk, he listens; when they cry, he cries with them; when they are in a good mood, he joins in their joyfulness. He is generous, good, and permanently concerned with their welfare. He is so determined by their good and so inclined toward realizing it by his personal effort that he can never be said to be neutral where questions of good and welfare arise. If he is not neutral, how can he ever be antagonistic, alienated, hateful, contemptuous, unconcerned? The Muslim is responsive to the Creator (SWT), the good-

ness of the Almighty, with a similar beneficence toward all creatures and especially toward humans.

4. **Optimism** is the highest principle of Islamic ethics. Islam implies the conviction that Allah, (SWT) is beneficent and merciful, just and willing our welfare. He committed Himself to have mercy on us (6:12, 54) to give the *mu'minun* (believers) victory over their enemies (22:40), and generally to harm none (4:39, 10:44). This world is His theater. It cannot be evil, nor can its outcome be evil. Certainly it is an arena for action, for testing our piety and morality. But it is a world in which the good will always preponderate. That is because Allah (SWT) is indeed Allah, and there is none else beside Him.

The implication of this view for the Muslim is self-reassurance, self-confidence, and trust that his efforts are worth exerting; that Allah will pay him back with tremendous dividends in this world and the next. The Muslim will, therefore, inspire and induce this self-reassurance to everyone around him. His counsel will never be one of pessimism and despair. His consistent attitude towards all things is that they are good and becoming better. When fortune smiles at him, he exclaims with all his heart and mind and being:

Praise and thanks to Allah. Allah is greater than all.

الحَمْدُ لله ، وَالله أَكْبَر

When tragedy strikes, he says and thinks and believes:

To Allah we belong and to Him we shall all return.

إنَّا لله وَإنَّا إلَيْهِ رَاجِعُون

and:

There is neither strength nor power except through Allah.

لا حَوْلَ وَلا قُوَّةَ إلاَّ بالله

Then he moves on to do his next duty. The advice of the Prophet (SAW) is on his mind:

«إنْ قامَتِ السَّاعةُ وَبِيَدِ أَحَدِكُمْ فَسِيلَةً فَاسْتَطَاعَ أنْ يغرِسَهَا فَلْيَغرِسْها»

If the last hour strikes and finds you carrying a nursling tree to the grove for planting, go ahead and plant it.[1]

---

1   Musnad Ahmad ibn Hanbal.

II. Unity of the Islamic Style

All the foregoing rules of conduct, when complemented by observance of the five salahs, fasting of Ramadan, disbursement of zakah and *sadaqah,* the laws of the Shari'ah, and guided by the underlying faith in *tawhid* and its implications, constitute a unique style of life. The style is comprehensive, like Islam, and affects every aspect of life. The Islamically-committed individual is a person observing the Islamic style, for the style is the outward expression of his commitment.

To begin with, the Muslim does not hanker after the fashions of the West, changing his wardrobe whenever the fashion in vogue changes. Whatever he wears, he does so with class and dignity. His clothes are never tight, showing the outline of his body, but ample, giving him freedom of movement and drawing attention from his body to his face and to what he says. Above all, his clothes are absolutely spotless and always tidy and well-pressed. So is his hair or hat, his fingernails always clipped, his shoes always shiny , and laces always tied. If he wears a beard and/or moustache, they are always well- groomed and tidy. He is especially careful not to soil them with food when he eats or drinks, and to clean them forthwith in case of an accident.

The committed Muslim will observe every one of the directives outlined in the foregoing section. Instantly, one recognizes his commitment because he shows his constant awareness of Allah (SWT), of his mission, of his smiling satisfaction with whatever Allah (SWT) has disposed for him, of his optimistic trust in the holy cause, and his resolution to press ever forward towards its fulfillment. Whether one finds him listening or speaking, eating, drinking or fasting, working or resting, coming or going, there is an Islamic way of doing any of these and he is observing that way to perfection. There is order and mission in his life as well as beauty and discipline. One could sense he belongs to a higher level of humanity: he is an Islamic Muslim.

III. Principles of Ethical Conduct

Ethical conduct is the anchor of the Islamic personality of the *da'iyah*. It is the standard by which a leader is judged by the people and which, in the long run, is the only way to assure people's confidence in his or her ability to lead. There are many aspects of ethical conduct, but the major principles may be boiled down to the five illustrated below.

E = Ethical Conduct

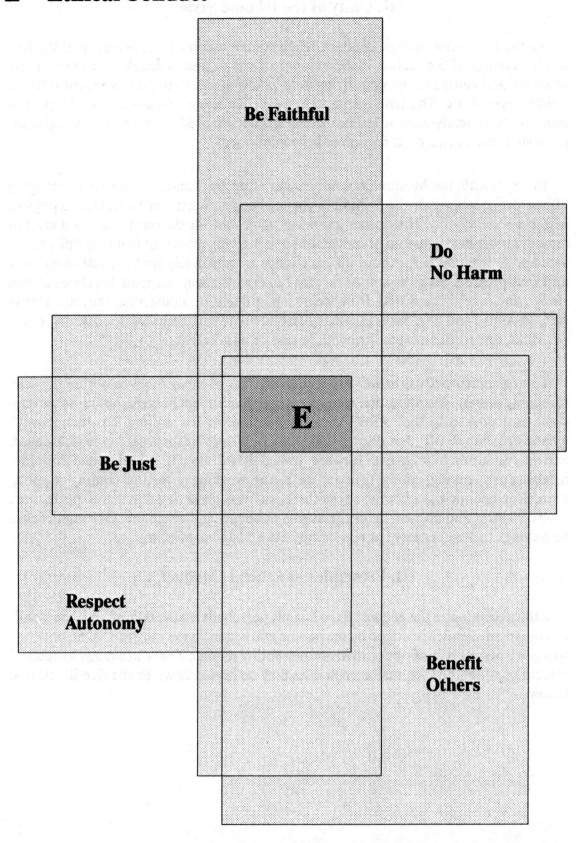

The Principle	Its Description	Its Roots in Hadith
RESPECT AUTONOMY	It is assumed that individuals have the right to decide how they live their lives, as long as their actions do not interfere with the welfare of others. One, therefore, has the right to act as a free agent and has the freedom of thought and choice.	«مِنْ حُسْنِ إِسْلامِ المَرْءِ تَرْكُهُ مَا لا يَعْنِيهِ» Part of someone being a good Muslim is his leaving alone that which does not concern him (Sunan Al Tirmidhi).
DO NO HARM	The obligation to avoid inflicting either physical or psychological harm on others and to avoid actions that risk harming others may be a primary ethical principal.	«لا ضَرَرَ وَلاَ ضِرار» There should be neither harming nor reciprocating harm (Sunan Ibn Majah).
BENEFIT OTHERS	There is an obligation to improve and enhance the welfare of others, even where such enhancements may inconvenience or limit the freedom of the persons offering assistance.	«مَنْ فَرَّجَ عَنْ مُسْلِمٍ كُرْبَةً مِنْ كُرَبِ الدُّنْيَا، فَرَّجَ اللهُ عَنْهُ كُرْبَةً مِنْ كُرَبِ يَوْمِ القِيَامَةِ» Whosoever removes a worldly grief from a believer, Allah will remove from him one of the griefs of the day of judgment (Sahih Muslim).
BE JUST	To be just in dealing with others assumes equal treatment of all, to afford each individual his due position, and, in general, to observe the Golden Rule ("Honesty is the best policy.")	«لا يُؤْمِنُ أَحَدُكُمْ حَتَّى يُحِبَّ لأخِيهِ ما يُحِبُّ لِنَفْسِهِ» None of you [truly] believes until he wishes for his brother what he wishes for himself (Sahih al Bukhari and Sahih Muslim).
BE FAITHFUL	One should keep promises, tell the truth, be loyal, and maintain respect and civility in human discourse. Only insofar as we sustain faithfulness can we expect to be seen as being trustworthy.	«المُسْلِمُ أَخُو المُسْلِمِ لاَ يَظْلِمُهُ وَلاَ يَخْذُلُهُ» A Muslim is a brother of a Muslim; he neither treats him unjustly nor does he fail him (Sahih Muslim).

QUESTIONS FOR DISCUSSION

1. Under what circumstances do you need not be the first one to say *al salamu 'alaykum?*
2. Why is optimism part of Islamic manners?

COMPREHENSION EXERCISE

YOU ARE IN CHARGE OF A GROUP OF PARTICIPANTS AT A MUSLIM YOUTH CAMP FOR NEW MEMBERS WHO HAVE NEVER BEEN IN A CAMP ENVIRONMENT BEFORE. THE OBJECTIVE OF THE CAMP IS TO MOTIVATE MEMBERS TO RETURN FOR FUTURE CAMPS AND TO INSPIRE THEM TO RECRUIT OTHERS FOR CAMPS TO COME. SEVERAL PARENTS AND COMMUNITY LEADERS ARE UNCONVINCED ABOUT THE UTILITY OF THIS PARTICULAR CAMP AND THE EFFECTIVENESS OF ITS PROGRAM FOR FIRST-TIME PARTICIPANTS. YOUR ONLY CHANCE TO SOLICIT THEIR SUPPORT LIES WITH HOW THIS CAMP AFFECTS THE PARTICIPANTS.

1. Outline a talk you will give to those under your charge about how observing Islamic manners can make the camp enjoyable for everyone. Be specific.

2. List five Islamic manners you intend to enforce and how. List five manners that you feel unable to enforce and why.

3. Write a letter to parents and community leaders stating specifically how the camp has improved the manners of the participants and how they can help reinforce this improvement.

Chapter

37

Camp Evaluation

LEARNING OBJECTIVES

On completing this chapter, you should be able to:
- identify how evaluation helps managing the camp
- choose appropriate methods for evaluation of the camp
- use evaluation forms to get information

I. Evaluation during the Camp

Once the camp program is underway, we should make its ongoing evaluation a part of our managing routine. A good approach is for the organizers to meet every night for an hour or so to discuss ways of correcting any shortcomings and preventing their repetition. Any changes agreed upon should be properly communicated to all concerned and implemented the following day. We may form different groups to evaluate the program, the physical arrangements, participants' performance, and other matters. We should encourage group leaders to invite suggestions from members and to bring problems to their attention for consultation and solution. Besides, we should also make an overall evaluation of the camp to help in planning future events.

II. Post-camp Follow Up

Muslim youth camps generate a great deal of interest among Muslim youth and involved adults. The camp environment inspires them, and the experience of living and practicing Islam together during a camp gives them plenty of motivation and ideas for arranging Islamic activities in their own areas.

Post-camp evaluation is critically important to assess effectiveness. The true measure of success of a program is how much the participants retain and practice from what they have learned during the camp after they return. As such, we should evaluate the changes in the participants' attitudes, behavior, and performance three months after the camp. This can be done through questionnaires, surveys, and other techniques addressed to the participants and their supervisors.

We also need to follow up with them on a regular basis and provide them with the necessary programming resources and educational materials to help them remain Islamically active. A data base of participants, articles, speakers and so on can be invaluable in making proper decisions about new camp planning. For example, the data base could identify, for priority attention, topics not dealt with in previous camps or individuals needing additional learning in specific areas.

III. Sample Evaluation Forms

Evaluation should be both quantitative and qualitative. A general meeting with opportunity for open discussion is a very useful forum for qualitative evaluation. Quantitative evaluation is best done through questionnaires or surveys that require specific answers to pointed questions. Some samples follow.

A. Evaluation of Participants

Answer each question by grading the indicated behavior on a scale from 1 to 5 (5 being the most desirable standard in the indicated behavior). Circle the grade.

Answers pertain to the individual being evaluated or to the average condition of a group if a number of participants are being evaluated as a group.

Was the participant or the group of participants:

Attentive?	1 2 3 4 5
Quiet?	1 2 3 4 5
Punctual?	1 2 3 4 5
Tidy in appearance?	1 2 3 4 5
Obedient to the chairperson?	1 2 3 4 5

Did the participant or the group of participants:

Use proper sitting posture?	1 2 3 4 5
Refrain from cross-talking?	1 2 3 4 5
Refrain from distractions?	1 2 3 4 5
Maintain good housekeeping?	1 2 3 4 5

Did the participant or the group of participants display the following characteristics in response to the presentations:

Comprehension?	1 2 3 4 5
Quality of questions and comments?	1 2 3 4 5
Organization of questions/comments?	1 2 3 4 5
Relevance of questions/comments?	1 2 3 4 5
Discussion dominated by individuals?	1 2 3 4 5
Cooperation?	1 2 3 4 5

B. Evaluation of Camp — Overall

1. Was the program effective in in- [ ] Yes   [ ] No
   creasing your knowledge about
   Islam?

2. If your answer to question no. 1 is No, please check your reasons:
   - The camp was overcrowded   [ ] Yes   [ ] No
   - The speakers were ineffective [ ] Yes   [ ] No
   - The environment was   [ ] Yes   [ ] No
     unsuitable
   - The program was too long   [ ] Yes   [ ] No

3. To increase the effectiveness of this type of program, would you like
   to have more:
   - Lectures   [ ] Yes   [ ] No
   - Workshops   [ ] Yes   [ ] No
   - Quizzes   [ ] Yes   [ ] No
   - Question & Answer Sessions [ ] Yes   [ ] No
   - Recreation   [ ] Yes   [ ] No
   - Rest Periods   [ ] Yes   [ ] No

4. Do you think this program will
   make you a better person?   [ ] Yes   [ ] No

5. Did you offer all prayers in con- [ ] Yes   [ ] No
   gregation?

6. If No, what prevented you from
   doing so?
   - Laziness   [ ] Yes   [ ] No
   - Not important   [ ] Yes   [ ] No
   - Doing something else   [ ] Yes   [ ] No
   - Lack of ample time for *wudu'* [ ] Yes   [ ] No

7. Did you assist others in offering [ ] Yes   [ ] No
   prayers on time?

8. The sleeping facilities were: [ ] adequate [ ] clean
                                      [ ] inadequate

9. The quality of food was: [ ] excellent [ ] adequate [ ] poor

10. The quantity of food was: [ ] too much [ ] adequate
                                       [ ] too little

11. I prefer by way of style: [ ] family   [ ] cafeteria

12. Were the program coordinators [ ] Yes   [ ] No
    helpful?

13. If you were the organizer, what would you do differently?

_____

14. Name the five best sessions/lec-
    tures/workshops you attended: _____
    _____
15 Who do you think were the three _____
    best (that is, more informative _____
    and interesting) guest lec- _____
    turers/speakers?
16. Other suggestions/comments?

_____
_____

C. General Evaluation for a Leadership Training Program (LTP)

1. Name, Address, and Tel. No(s):

_____
_____

2. Why did you come to the LTP?

_____

3. Did the LTP fulfill the objective for which you came?
   If not, where did it fall short?

_____

4. What do you think was the highlight of the program?

_____

5. From which aspect did you benefit the most?

_____

6. What disappointed you most at the LTP?

_____

7. How efficient were the physical arrangements overall?
   (e.g., eating, seating, sleeping, grouping, etc.)
   [ ] better than expected [ ] as expected [ ] worse than expected
   best aspect: _____
   worst aspect: _____
8. How would you rate the level of the presentation?
   [ ] too high [ ] too low [ ] just right
9. Have you learnt anything from the LTP? [ ] Yes [ ] No
   If yes, list three important aspects:
   a) _____
   b) _____
   c) _____
10. Have you clearly understood the objectives of the LTP?
                [ ] Yes [ ] No
11. Do you have any suggestions to strengthen the LTP?

_____

QUESTIONS FOR DISCUSSION

1. How does ongoing evaluation help you run a better camp?
2. What is the most critical information you should seek from a post-camp evaluation.

COMPREHENSION EXERCISE

AS THE CHAIRMAN OF THE YOUTH CAMP COMMITTEE, YOU WANT TO RUN AN EFFECTIVE CAMP PROGRAM NOW AND IN THE FUTURE. SINCE MOST OF THE PARTICIPANTS ARE NEW, THEY ARE HESITANT TO GIVE FEEDBACK FACE TO FACE. ALSO, THEY DO NOT KNOW WHAT THEY SHOULD EXPECT. THE EXECUTIVE COMMITTEE HAS ASKED FOR A REPORT. THEY HAVE NOT BEEN TO THE CAMP, BUT DO HAVE A STANDARD IN MIND.

1. *Make a checklist of what you must do, when and involving whom, to gather material for your report.*

2. *Write a note to yourself to use as an aid when you explain to camp participants how and why to complete the forms that you will pass out.*

3. *Decide which evaluation forms you would use if you had time to use only two.*

Conclusion

Have you ever wondered why such a great religion can have such backward followers? How can we explain the tremendous gap between Islam and Muslims today? Something is wrong.

Certainly, the problem is in the messengers — us — and not in the message. It is our static reading and literal understanding of our religion. All the energy and power are there.

... But power [honor] belongs to Allah, and His Messenger and the believers, but the hypocrites know not (63:8).	... وَلِلَّهِ ٱلْعِزَّةُ وَلِرَسُولِهِ وَلِلْمُؤْمِنِينَ وَلَٰكِنَّ ٱلْمُنَٰفِقِينَ لَا يَعْلَمُونَ (سورة المنافقون)

But this is only potential power. We need to transfer it to dynamic and kinetic energy that can change conditions and environments. This *Guide* attempts to bring about the inner potential energy and direct it to establish the needed renaissance. Five spoons of sugar in a cup of tea will not make it sweet, but when you stir it you get the sweetness. This *Guide* is the stirrer, *in sha'a Allah*. Having comprehended this *Guide*, if you can visualize yourself as a trustee placed on the globe to think and plan how to Islamize your environment and improve the society around you, the *Guide* has achieved its objective. It compresses the time needed to acquire such lessons from a few decades to a few months, maybe a year at most.

The *Guide* attempts to lead you through a simple Do's and Don't's format to optimize your understanding of the art and science of *da'wah* in this century. While some may argue that leadership is an inborn quality that has to do with genes, we believe that much of it can be acquired. This *Guide* tries to fill in the gap by pointing out how we learn what it takes to be a leader on the individual and the collective levels. We are confident that, with the permission of Allah (SWT), if the *Guide* is fully comprehended and practiced, at least a 50% jump in achievement and effectiveness of Islamic activities will result. Such achievement will be manifest in the areas of concepts, management, administration, communication, camps, conferences, and meetings.

This *Guide* is supplemented by workbooks to facilitate teaching of various chapters. The workbooks are not included in this volume.

We do not consider this *Guide* to be the ultimate, but rather the gate opener for the improvement (*ihsan*) process, which extends from the cradle to the grave.

We pray that Allah (SWT) will guide you to the Straight Path — *al Sirat al Mustaqim*.

Selected Bibliography

Qur'an

1. Ali, Abdullah Yusuf, *Meaning of the Holy Qur'an*: Text and Translation, Amana Corporation, Brentwood, Md: 1411/1991.
2. Asad, Muhammad, *The Message of the Qur'an* (with Arabic Text). Dar al Andalus, Gibraltar, Spain 1980.

Sunnah

1. Abu Dawud, *al Sunan*, 4 vols. ed. by M.M.'Abd al Hamid, 2nd imp. Cairo, 1369/1950.
2. Bayhaqi, Abu Bakr al, *al Sunan al Kubra*. 10 vols., Hyderabad, India. 1344 A.H.
3. Bukhari, Muhammad b. Isma'il al, *al Jami' al Sahih*, 9 vols., ed. by M. al Nawawi, M. Abu al Fadl and M. Khifaji, Cairo, 1376 A.H.
4. Ibn Hanbal, Ahmad b Muhammad, *Kitab al Ashribah*, ed. by Subhi Jasim, Baghdad, 1369 A.H.
5. Ibn Majah, Muhammad Ibn Yazid, *al Sunan*, 2 vol. ed. by M.F.A. Baqi, Cairo, 1374 A.H.
6. Muslim Ibn Hajjaj al Qushayri, *al Sahih*, ed. by M.F.A. Baqi, Cairo, 1374 A.H.
7. Nasa'i, Ahmad ibn Shu'ayb al, *Kitab al Du'afa*, Hyderabad, India.
8. Shafi'i, Muhammad ibn Idris al, *Al Risalah*, Bulaq, Cairo, 1321 A.H.
9. Tirmidhi, Muhammad ibn 'Isa al, *al Sunan*, ed. by M. A. Shakir and others, 5 vols., Cairo.
10. Daraqutni, Abu al Hasan al, *al Sunan*, 4 vols., ed by Hashim Yamani, Dar al Mahasin, Cairo, 1386 A.H.
11. Darimi, 'Abd Allah ibn 'Abd al Rahman, *al Sunan*, 2 vols., ed. by M. A. Rahman, Damascus, 1349 A.H.
12. Daylami, Abu Mansur al, *Firdaws al Akhbar bi Ma'thur al Khitab*, ed. Fawwaz Ahmad Zumurli and Muhammad al Mu'tasim billah al Baghdadi, Beirut, Dar al Kitab al Arabi, 1987.

Others

1. Ahmad, Mumtaz (ed), *State, Politics and Islam*, American Trust Publications, Indianapolis, Indiana 1986.

2. Altalib, Hisham, *Report of the MSA Training Course* (Unpublished), The MSA of the US and Canada, Indianapolis, Indiana, 1976.

3. Al 'Alwani, Taha J., *Adab al Ikhtilaf Fi al Islam* (Arabic), International Institute of Islamic Thought, Herndon, Virginia, 1987.

4. *Association Management*, American Society of Association Executives, Washington, D.C.

5. Duncan, J., *Essentials of Management*, Dryden, Hinsdale, Illinois, 1975.

6. Drucker, P.F., *Management: Tasks, Responsibilities, Practices*, Harper & Row, New York, 1974.

7. Fisher, R., and Ury, W., *Guide to Yes - Negotiation*, Houghton Miflin Company.

8. Hamid, A. W., *Companions of the Prophet*, (adapted from Arabic), Umran Publications, London, 1982.

9. Mirza, M. Yaqub, *Youth Activities and Camps*, The MSA of the US and Canada, Plainfield, Indiana, 1979.

10. Nu'mani, Shibli, *Life of Umar the Great* (Translated from Urdu by Muhammad Saleem, Sh. Muhammad Ashraf), 1981.

11. Omer, Abdel Hadi M., *Let Us Learn: Issues of Your Concern*, Beloit, Wisconsin, 1987.

12. Safi, Louay, *Islamic Leadership* (Unpublished), Detroit, 1990.

13. Ibn Taymiya, Imam Taqi al Din Ahmad, *Public Duties in Islam* (Translated from Arabic by Muhtar Holland), Islamic Foundation, Leicester, England, 1982.

14. Terry, G.R. and Stephen G. F., *Principles of Management*, 8th ed., Richard D. Irwin, Inc., Homewood, Illinois, 1982.

15. Unus, Iqbal J. and Beekun, Rafik, *A Management Guide for Islamic Organizations* (Unpublished), Plainfield, Indiana, 1982.

A limited number of selections from other references could not be properly identified for inclusion in the selected bibliography. As soon as we are able to identify those sources, we will include them in the bibliography in future editions of the Guide.

Indexes

Ayat Index

Ahadith Index

Subject Index

Names Index

Places Index

Organizations Index

Index and Glossary
of Islamic Terms

Ayat Index

O you who believe! Remain conscious of Allah, and [always] say words that are true to the mark [truthful, relevant and to the point] (33:70). [F]

﴿٧٠﴾ يَٰٓأَيُّهَا ٱلَّذِينَ ءَامَنُوا ٱتَّقُوا ٱللَّهَ وَقُولُوا قَوْلًا سَدِيدًا (سورة الأحزاب)

We have indeed created man in the best of molds, then do We abase him [to be] the lowest of the low — except those who believe and do righteous deeds: for they shall have a reward unfailing (95:4-6).

Part One, Page 13

﴿٤﴾ لَقَدْ خَلَقْنَا ٱلْإِنسَٰنَ فِىٓ أَحْسَنِ تَقْوِيمٍ ﴿٥﴾ ثُمَّ رَدَدْنَٰهُ أَسْفَلَ سَٰفِلِينَ ﴿٦﴾ إِلَّا ٱلَّذِينَ ءَامَنُوا وَعَمِلُوا ٱلصَّٰلِحَٰتِ فَلَهُمْ أَجْرٌ غَيْرُ مَمْنُونٍ (سورة التين)

That man can have nothing but what he strives for; that [the fruit of] his striving will soon come in sight; then will he be rewarded with a reward complete (53:39-41).

Chapter 1, Page 15

﴿٣٩﴾ وَأَن لَّيْسَ لِلْإِنسَٰنِ إِلَّا مَا سَعَىٰ ﴿٤٠﴾ وَأَنَّ سَعْيَهُ سَوْفَ يُرَىٰ ﴿٤١﴾ ثُمَّ يُجْزَىٰهُ ٱلْجَزَآءَ ٱلْأَوْفَىٰ (سورة النجم)

Nor did We send before you [as messengers] any but men, whom we did inspire — [men] living in human habitations. Do they not travel through the earth, and see what was the end of those before them? But the home of the hereafter is best, for those who do right. Will you not then understand? (12:109).

Chapter 1, Page 16

﴿١٠٩﴾ وَمَآ أَرْسَلْنَا مِن قَبْلِكَ إِلَّا رِجَالًا نُّوحِىٓ إِلَيْهِم مِّنْ أَهْلِ ٱلْقُرَىٰٓ أَفَلَمْ يَسِيرُوا فِى ٱلْأَرْضِ فَيَنظُرُوا كَيْفَ كَانَ عَٰقِبَةُ ٱلَّذِينَ مِن قَبْلِهِمْ وَلَدَارُ ٱلْءَاخِرَةِ خَيْرٌ لِّلَّذِينَ ٱتَّقَوْا أَفَلَا تَعْقِلُونَ (سورة يوسف)

Do you not see that Allah has subjected to your [use] all things in the heavens and on earth, and has made His bounties flow to you in exceeding measure, [both] seen and unseen? Yet there are among men those who dispute about Allah, without knowledge and without guidance, and without a book, to enlighten them (31:20).

Chapter 1, Page 17

﴿٢٠﴾ أَلَمْ تَرَوْا أَنَّ ٱللَّهَ سَخَّرَ لَكُم مَّا فِى ٱلسَّمَٰوَٰتِ وَمَا فِى ٱلْأَرْضِ وَأَسْبَغَ عَلَيْكُمْ نِعَمَهُ ظَٰهِرَةً وَبَاطِنَةً وَمِنَ ٱلنَّاسِ مَن يُجَٰدِلُ فِى ٱللَّهِ بِغَيْرِ عِلْمٍ وَلَا هُدًى وَلَا كِتَٰبٍ مُّنِيرٍ (سورة لقمان)

Read! In the name of your Lord and Cherisher, who created — created man, out of a mere clot of congealed blood: Read! And your Lord is Most Bountiful, — He Who taught [the use of] the pen, — taught man that which he knew not (96:1-5).

Chapter 1, Page 22

﴿١﴾ ٱقْرَأْ بِٱسْمِ رَبِّكَ ٱلَّذِى خَلَقَ ﴿٢﴾ خَلَقَ ٱلْإِنسَٰنَ مِنْ عَلَقٍ ﴿٣﴾ ٱقْرَأْ وَرَبُّكَ ٱلْأَكْرَمُ ﴿٤﴾ ٱلَّذِى عَلَّمَ بِٱلْقَلَمِ ﴿٥﴾ عَلَّمَ ٱلْإِنسَٰنَ مَا لَمْ يَعْلَمْ (سورة العلق)

[F] There is an entry for this verse in the front of the book before the table of contents.

Against them make ready your strength to the utmost of your power, including steeds of war, to strike terror into [the hearts of] the enemies, of Allah and your enemies, and others besides, whom you may not know, but whom Allah does know ... (8:60).

Chapter 1, Page 22

۞ وَأَعِدُّواْ لَهُم مَّا ٱسْتَطَعْتُم مِّن قُوَّةٍ وَمِن رِّبَاطِ ٱلْخَيْلِ تُرْهِبُونَ بِهِۦ عَدُوَّ ٱللَّهِ وَعَدُوَّكُمْ وَءَاخَرِينَ مِن دُونِهِمْ لَا تَعْلَمُونَهُمُ ٱللَّهُ يَعْلَمُهُمْ ... (سورة الأنفال)

... If you turn back [from the path], He will substitute in your stead another people; then they would not be like you (47:38).

Chapter 2, Page 36

... وَإِن تَتَوَلَّوْاْ يَسْتَبْدِلْ قَوْمًا غَيْرَكُمْ ثُمَّ لَا يَكُونُوٓاْ أَمْثَٰلَكُم (سورة محمد)

... Give just measure and weight, and do not withhold from the people the things that are their due ... (7:85).

Chapter 2, Page 36

... فَأَوْفُواْ ٱلْكَيْلَ وَٱلْمِيزَانَ وَلَا تَبْخَسُواْ ٱلنَّاسَ أَشْيَآءَهُمْ ... (سورة الأعراف)

Go, both of you, to Pharaoh, for he has indeed transgressed all bounds; but speak to him mildly; perchance he may take warning or fear [Allah] (20:43-44).

Chapter 2, Page 38

۞ ٱذْهَبَآ إِلَىٰ فِرْعَوْنَ إِنَّهُۥ طَغَىٰ ۝ فَقُولَا لَهُۥ قَوْلًا لَّيِّنًا لَّعَلَّهُۥ يَتَذَكَّرُ أَوْ يَخْشَىٰ (سورة طه)

If not Him, you worship nothing but names which you have named — you and your fathers — for which Allah has sent down no authority: the command is for none but Allah: He has commanded that you worship none but Him: that is the right religion, but most men understand not (12:40).

Chapter 2, Page 38

۞ مَا تَعْبُدُونَ مِن دُونِهِۦٓ إِلَّآ أَسْمَآءً سَمَّيْتُمُوهَآ أَنتُمْ وَءَابَآؤُكُم مَّآ أَنزَلَ ٱللَّهُ بِهَا مِن سُلْطَٰنٍ إِنِ ٱلْحُكْمُ إِلَّا لِلَّهِ أَمَرَ أَلَّا تَعْبُدُوٓاْ إِلَّآ إِيَّاهُ ذَٰلِكَ ٱلدِّينُ ٱلْقَيِّمُ وَلَٰكِنَّ أَكْثَرَ ٱلنَّاسِ لَا يَعْلَمُونَ (سورة يوسف)

Behold, your Lord said to the angels: "I will create a vicegerent on earth." They said: "Will You place therein one who will make mischief therein and shed blood? — While we do celebrate Your praises and glorify Your holy [name]?" He said: "I know what you know not" (2:30).

Chapter 3, Page 41

۞ وَإِذْ قَالَ رَبُّكَ لِلْمَلَٰٓئِكَةِ إِنِّي جَاعِلٌ فِي ٱلْأَرْضِ خَلِيفَةً قَالُوٓاْ أَتَجْعَلُ فِيهَا مَن يُفْسِدُ فِيهَا وَيَسْفِكُ ٱلدِّمَآءَ وَنَحْنُ نُسَبِّحُ بِحَمْدِكَ وَنُقَدِّسُ لَكَ قَالَ إِنِّيٓ أَعْلَمُ مَا لَا تَعْلَمُونَ (سورة البقرة)

And He taught Adam the names of all things;
then He placed them before the angels, and
said: "Tell Me the names of these if you are
right." They said: "Glory to You: of knowledge
we have none save what you have taught us: in
truth it is You who are perfect in knowledge and
wisdom" (2:31-2).

Chapter 3, Page 42

٣١ وَعَلَّمَ ءَادَمَ ٱلْأَسْمَآءَ كُلَّهَا ثُمَّ عَرَضَهُمْ عَلَى ٱلْمَلَٰٓئِكَةِ
فَقَالَ أَنۢبِـُٔونِى بِأَسْمَآءِ هَٰٓؤُلَآءِ إِن كُنتُمْ صَٰدِقِينَ
٣٢ قَالُوا۟ سُبْحَٰنَكَ لَا عِلْمَ لَنَآ إِلَّا مَا عَلَّمْتَنَآ
إِنَّكَ أَنتَ ٱلْعَلِيمُ ٱلْحَكِيمُ (سورة البقرة)

We said: "Get you down all from here: And if,
as is sure, there comes to you guidance from Me,
whosoever follows my guidance, on them shall
be no fear, nor shall they grieve" (2:38).

Chapter 3, Page 42

٣٨ قُلْنَا ٱهْبِطُوا۟ مِنْهَا جَمِيعًا فَإِمَّا يَأْتِيَنَّكُم مِّنِّى هُدًى
فَمَن تَبِعَ هُدَاىَ فَلَا خَوْفٌ عَلَيْهِمْ وَلَا هُمْ يَحْزَنُونَ (سورة البقرة)

He who created death and life that He may
try which of you is best in deed; and He is
the Exalted in Might, Oft-Forgiving (67:2).

Chapter 3, Page 42

٢ ٱلَّذِى خَلَقَ ٱلْمَوْتَ وَٱلْحَيَوٰةَ لِيَبْلُوَكُمْ أَيُّكُمْ
أَحْسَنُ عَمَلًا وَهُوَ ٱلْعَزِيزُ ٱلْغَفُورُ (سورة الملك)

Do men think that they will be left alone on
saying: "We believe," and that they will not be
tested? (29:2).

Chapter 3, Page 42

٢ أَحَسِبَ ٱلنَّاسُ أَن يُتْرَكُوٓا۟ أَن يَقُولُوٓا۟
ءَامَنَّا وَهُمْ لَا يُفْتَنُونَ (سورة العنكبوت)

And we shall try you until We test those among
you who strive their utmost and persevere in
patience; and We shall try your reported
[character] (47:31).

Chapter 3, Page 42

٣١ وَلَنَبْلُوَنَّكُمْ حَتَّىٰ نَعْلَمَ ٱلْمُجَٰهِدِينَ مِنكُمْ
وَٱلصَّٰبِرِينَ وَنَبْلُوَا۟ أَخْبَارَكُمْ (سورة محمد)

When Yusuf attained his full manhood, We gave
him power and knowledge: thus do We reward
those who do right (12:22).

Chapter 3, Page 43

٢٢ وَلَمَّا بَلَغَ أَشُدَّهُۥٓ ءَاتَيْنَٰهُ حُكْمًا وَعِلْمًا
وَكَذَٰلِكَ نَجْزِى ٱلْمُحْسِنِينَ (سورة يوسف)

And our duty is only to proclaim the clear message
(36:17).

Chapter 3, Page 43

١٧ وَمَا عَلَيْنَآ إِلَّا ٱلْبَلَٰغُ ٱلْمُبِينُ (سورة يس)

Therefore, do you give admonition, for you are
one to admonish. You are not one to control
[men's] affairs (88:21-22).

Chapter 3, Page 43

٢١ فَذَكِّرْ إِنَّمَآ أَنتَ مُذَكِّرٌ
٢٢ لَّسْتَ عَلَيْهِم بِمُصَيْطِرٍ (سورة الغاشية)

Therefore, give admonition in case the admonition
profits [the hearer] (87:9).

Chapter 3, Page 43

٩ فَذَكِّرْ إِن نَّفَعَتِ ٱلذِّكْرَىٰ (سورة الأعلى)

Invite [all] to the way of your Lord with wisdom and beautiful preaching; and argue with them in ways that are best and most gracious; For your Lord knows best, Who have strayed from His path, and who receive guidance (16:125).

Chapter 3, Page 43

﴿١٢٥﴾ ٱدْعُ إِلَىٰ سَبِيلِ رَبِّكَ بِٱلْحِكْمَةِ وَٱلْمَوْعِظَةِ ٱلْحَسَنَةِ وَجَٰدِلْهُم بِٱلَّتِي هِيَ أَحْسَنُ إِنَّ رَبَّكَ هُوَ أَعْلَمُ بِمَن ضَلَّ عَن سَبِيلِهِۦ وَهُوَ أَعْلَمُ بِٱلْمُهْتَدِينَ (سورة النحل)

Let there be no compulsion in religion; Truth stands out clear from error: Whoever rejects evil and believes in Allah has grasped the most trustworthy handhold, that never breaks. And Allah hears and knows all things (2:256).

Chapter 3, Page 43

﴿٢٥٦﴾ لَآ إِكْرَاهَ فِي ٱلدِّينِ قَد تَّبَيَّنَ ٱلرُّشْدُ مِنَ ٱلْغَيِّ فَمَن يَكْفُرْ بِٱلطَّٰغُوتِ وَيُؤْمِنۢ بِٱللَّهِ فَقَدِ ٱسْتَمْسَكَ بِٱلْعُرْوَةِ ٱلْوُثْقَىٰ لَا ٱنفِصَامَ لَهَا وَٱللَّهُ سَمِيعٌ عَلِيمٌ (سورة البقرة)

It is true that you will not be able to guide those whom you love; but Allah guides those whom He will and He knows best those who receive guidance (28:56).

Chapter 3, Page 44

﴿٥٦﴾ إِنَّكَ لَا تَهْدِى مَنْ أَحْبَبْتَ وَلَٰكِنَّ ٱللَّهَ يَهْدِى مَن يَشَآءُ وَهُوَ أَعْلَمُ بِٱلْمُهْتَدِينَ (سورة القصص)

Say you: "This is my way: I do invite unto Allah — on evidence clear as the seeing with one's eyes — I and whoever follows me. Glory to Allah! And never will I join gods with Allah!" (12:108).

Chapter 3, Page 44

﴿١٠٨﴾ قُلْ هَٰذِهِۦ سَبِيلِىٓ أَدْعُوٓا۟ إِلَى ٱللَّهِ عَلَىٰ بَصِيرَةٍ أَنَا۠ وَمَنِ ٱتَّبَعَنِى وَسُبْحَٰنَ ٱللَّهِ وَمَآ أَنَا۠ مِنَ ٱلْمُشْرِكِينَ (سورة يوسف)

Who is better in speech than one who calls [men] to Allah, works righteousness, and says: "I am of the Muslims?" (41:33).

Chapter 3, Page 44

﴿٣٣﴾ وَمَنْ أَحْسَنُ قَوْلًا مِّمَّن دَعَآ إِلَى ٱللَّهِ وَعَمِلَ صَٰلِحًا وَقَالَ إِنَّنِى مِنَ ٱلْمُسْلِمِينَ (سورة فصلت)

For each [such persons] there are angels in succession, before and behind him: they guard him by command of Allah. Verily never will Allah change the condition of a people until they change within their own souls... (13:11).

Chapter 3, Page 44

﴿١١﴾ لَهُۥ مُعَقِّبَٰتٌ مِّنۢ بَيْنِ يَدَيْهِ وَمِنْ خَلْفِهِۦ يَحْفَظُونَهُۥ مِنْ أَمْرِ ٱللَّهِ إِنَّ ٱللَّهَ لَا يُغَيِّرُ مَا بِقَوْمٍ حَتَّىٰ يُغَيِّرُوا۟ مَا بِأَنفُسِهِمْ... (سورة الرعد)

He said: "O my people! See you whether I have a clear [sign] from your Lord. And He has given me sustenance [pure and] good as from Himself? I wish not, in opposition to you, to do that which I forbid you to do. I only desire [your] betterment to the best of my ability; and my success [in my task] can only come from Allah. In Him I trust, and unto Him I look" (11:88).

Chapter 3, Page 45

﴿٨٨﴾ قَالَ يَٰقَوْمِ أَرَءَيْتُمْ إِن كُنتُ عَلَىٰ بَيِّنَةٍ مِّن رَّبِّى وَرَزَقَنِى مِنْهُ رِزْقًا حَسَنًا وَمَآ أُرِيدُ أَنْ أُخَالِفَكُمْ إِلَىٰ مَآ أَنْهَىٰكُمْ عَنْهُ إِنْ أُرِيدُ إِلَّا ٱلْإِصْلَٰحَ مَا ٱسْتَطَعْتُ وَمَا تَوْفِيقِى إِلَّا بِٱللَّهِ عَلَيْهِ تَوَكَّلْتُ وَإِلَيْهِ أُنِيبُ (سورة هود)

Nor can goodness or evil be equal. Repel [evil] with what is better: Then will he between whom and you was hatred become as it were your friend and intimate (41:34).

Chapter 3, Page 46

سُورَةُ فصلت) وَلَا تَسْتَوِى الْحَسَنَةُ وَلَا السَّيِّئَةُ ادْفَعْ بِالَّتِى هِىَ أَحْسَنُ فَإِذَا الَّذِى بَيْنَكَ وَبَيْنَهُ عَدَاوَةٌ كَأَنَّهُ وَلِىٌّ حَمِيمٌ

Those, who, if we give them power in the land, establish worship and pay zakah and enjoin kindness and forbid inequity... (22:41).

Chapter 4, Page 52

(سُورَةُ الحج) الَّذِينَ إِنْ مَكَّنَّهُمْ فِى الْأَرْضِ أَقَامُوا الصَّلَوٰةَ وَءَاتَوُا الزَّكَوٰةَ وَأَمَرُوا بِالْمَعْرُوفِ وَنَهَوْا عَنِ الْمُنْكَرِ...

And those who answer the call of their Lord and establish prayer, and who conduct their affairs by consultation and spend out of what We bestow on them for sustenance (42:38).

Chapter 4, Page 52

(سُورَةُ الشورى) وَالَّذِينَ اسْتَجَابُوا لِرَبِّهِمْ وَأَقَامُوا الصَّلَوٰةَ وَأَمْرُهُمْ شُورَىٰ بَيْنَهُمْ وَمِمَّا رَزَقْنَهُمْ يُنْفِقُونَ

It is part of the mercy of Allah that you do deal gently with them. Were you severe or harsh hearted, they would have broken away from about you: so pass over [their faults], and ask for [Allah's] forgiveness for them; and consult them in their affairs [of moment]. Then, when you have taken a decision, put your trust in Allah. For Allah loves those who put their trust [in Him] (3:159).

Chapter 4, Page 52

فَبِمَا رَحْمَةٍ مِنَ اللهِ لِنْتَ لَهُمْ وَلَوْ كُنْتَ فَظًّا غَلِيظَ الْقَلْبِ لَانْفَضُّوا مِنْ حَوْلِكَ فَاعْفُ عَنْهُمْ وَاسْتَغْفِرْ لَهُمْ وَشَاوِرْهُمْ فِى الْأَمْرِ فَإِذَا عَزَمْتَ فَتَوَكَّلْ عَلَى اللهِ إِنَّ اللهَ يُحِبُّ الْمُتَوَكِّلِينَ (سُورَةُ آل عمران)

Allah does command you to render back your trusts to those to whom they are due, and when you judge between man and man, that you judge with justice... (4:58).

Chapter 4, Page 53

(سُورَةُ النساء) إِنَّ اللهَ يَأْمُرُكُمْ أَنْ تُؤَدُّوا الْأَمَانَتِ إِلَىٰ أَهْلِهَا وَإِذَا حَكَمْتُمْ بَيْنَ النَّاسِ أَنْ تَحْكُمُوا بِالْعَدْلِ...

...And let not the hatred of others to you make you swerve to wrong and depart from justice. Be just, that is next to piety... (5:8).

Chapter 4, Page 53

(سُورَةُ المائدة) وَلَا يَجْرِمَنَّكُمْ شَنَئَانُ قَوْمٍ عَلَىٰ أَلَّا تَعْدِلُوا اعْدِلُوا هُوَ أَقْرَبُ لِلتَّقْوَىٰ...

O you who believe! Stand out firmly for justice, as witnesses to Allah, even as against yourselves, or your parents or your kin, and whether it be against rich or poor, for Allah can protect both... (4:135).

Chapter 4, Page 53

يَأَيُّهَا الَّذِينَ ءَامَنُوا كُونُوا قَوَّمِينَ بِالْقِسْطِ شُهَدَاءَ لِلَّهِ وَلَوْ عَلَىٰ أَنْفُسِكُمْ أَوِ الْوَالِدَيْنِ وَالْأَقْرَبِينَ إِنْ يَكُنْ غَنِيًّا أَوْ فَقِيرًا فَاللهُ أَوْلَىٰ بِهِمَا... (سُورَةُ النساء)

...And We raise some of them above others in ranks so that some may command work from others. But the mercy of your Lord is better than the [wealth] which they amass (43:32).

Chapter 4, Page 60

وَرَفَعْنَا بَعْضَهُمْ فَوْقَ بَعْضٍ دَرَجَٰتٍ لِيَتَّخِذَ بَعْضُهُمْ بَعْضًا سُخْرِيًّا وَرَحْمَتُ رَبِّكَ خَيْرٌ مِمَّا يَجْمَعُونَ (سُورَةُ الزخرف)

...Verily, the most honored among you is the most Allah conscious ... (49:13).

Chapter 5, Page 61

...إِنَّ أَكْرَمَكُمْ عِندَ اللَّهِ أَتْقَنكُمْ ... (سورة الحجرات)

It is part of the mercy of Allah that you do deal gently with them. Were you severe or harsh-hearted, they would have broken away from about you: so pass over [their faults], and ask for [Allah's] forgiveness for them; and consult them in their affairs [of moment]. Then, when you have taken a decision, put your trust in Allah. For Allah loves those who put their trust [in Him] (3:159).

Chapter 7, Page 88

﴿١٥٩﴾ فَبِمَا رَحْمَةٍ مِّنَ اللَّهِ لِنتَ لَهُمْ وَلَوْ كُنتَ فَظًّا غَلِيظَ الْقَلْبِ لَانفَضُّوا مِنْ حَوْلِكَ فَاعْفُ عَنْهُمْ وَاسْتَغْفِرْ لَهُمْ وَشَاوِرْهُمْ فِي الْأَمْرِ فَإِذَا عَزَمْتَ فَتَوَكَّلْ عَلَى اللَّهِ إِنَّ اللَّهَ يُحِبُّ الْمُتَوَكِّلِينَ (سورة آل عمران)

O You who believe! Why say you that which you do not? (61:2).

Chapter 8, Page 94

﴿٢﴾ يَا أَيُّهَا الَّذِينَ آمَنُوا لِمَ تَقُولُونَ مَا لَا تَفْعَلُونَ (سورة الصف)

... Then, when you have taken a decision, put your trust in Allah. For Allah loves those who put their trust [in Him] (3:159).

Chapter 8, Page 94

... فَإِذَا عَزَمْتَ فَتَوَكَّلْ عَلَى اللَّهِ إِنَّ اللَّهَ يُحِبُّ الْمُتَوَكِّلِينَ (سورة آل عمران)

O you who believe! Stand out firmly for Allah, as witnesses to fair dealing, and let not the hatred of others make you swerve to wrong and depart from justice. Be just: that is next to piety: and fear Allah. For Allah is well acquainted with all that you do (5:8).

Chapter 11, Page 142

﴿٨﴾ يَا أَيُّهَا الَّذِينَ آمَنُوا كُونُوا قَوَّامِينَ لِلَّهِ شُهَدَاءَ بِالْقِسْطِ وَلَا يَجْرِمَنَّكُمْ شَنَآنُ قَوْمٍ عَلَى أَلَّا تَعْدِلُوا اعْدِلُوا هُوَ أَقْرَبُ لِلتَّقْوَى وَاتَّقُوا اللَّهَ إِنَّ اللَّهَ خَبِيرٌ بِمَا تَعْمَلُونَ (سورة المائدة)

O My Lord! Expand my breast, and ease my task for me; and remove the knot from my tongue that they may understand my saying (20:25-28).

Chapter 12, Page 153

﴿٢٥﴾ قَالَ رَبِّ اشْرَحْ لِي صَدْرِي ﴿٢٦﴾ وَيَسِّرْ لِي أَمْرِي ﴿٢٧﴾ وَاحْلُلْ عُقْدَةً مِّن لِّسَانِي ﴿٢٨﴾ يَفْقَهُوا قَوْلِي (سورة طه)

I [Hud] deliver to you the messages of my Lord and I am to you a sincere advisor (7:68).

Chapter 14, Page 172

﴿٦٨﴾ أُبَلِّغُكُمْ رِسَالَاتِ رَبِّي وَأَنَا لَكُمْ نَاصِحٌ أَمِينٌ (سورة الأعراف)

... I [Shu'ayb] delivered to you [his people] the messages of my Lord and I gave you good advice ... (7:93).

Chapter 14, Page 172

... لَقَدْ أَبْلَغْتُكُمْ رِسَالَاتِ رَبِّي وَنَصَحْتُ لَكُمْ ... (سورة الأعراف)

He [Iblis] swore to them [Adam and his wife] both that he was their sincere advisor (7:21).

Chapter 14, Page 173

﴿٢١﴾ وَقَاسَمَهُمَا إِنِّي لَكُمَا لَمِنَ النَّاصِحِينَ (سورة الأعراف)

... We [Yusuf's brothers] are his sincere well-wishers (12:11).

Chapter 14, Page 173

... وَإِنَّا لَهُ لَنَاصِحُونَ (سورة يوسف)

... I [Salih] certainly delivered to you [his people] the message of my Lord and I gave you good advice; but you do not love those who give good advice (7:79).

Chapter 14, Page 174

... لَقَدْ أَبْلَغْتُكُمْ رِسَالَةَ رَبِّي وَنَصَحْتُ لَكُمْ وَلَكِنْ لَا تُحِبُّونَ النَّاصِحِينَ (سورة الأعراف)

And remind, surely reminding benefits the believers (51:55).

Chapter 14, Page 174

وَذَكِّرْ فَإِنَّ الذِّكْرَى تَنْفَعُ الْمُؤْمِنِينَ (سورة الذاريات) ٥٥

Men who celebrate the praises of Allah, standing, sitting and lying down on their sides, and contemplate [the wonders of] creation in the heavens and the earth, [with the thought]: "Our Lord! not for naught have You created [all] this! Glory to You! Give us salvation from the penalty of the fire" (3:191).

Chapter 14, Page 174

الَّذِينَ يَذْكُرُونَ اللَّهَ قِيَامًا وَقُعُودًا وَعَلَى جُنُوبِهِمْ وَيَتَفَكَّرُونَ فِي خَلْقِ السَّمَوَاتِ وَالْأَرْضِ رَبَّنَا مَا خَلَقْتَ هَذَا بَاطِلًا سُبْحَانَكَ فَقِنَا عَذَابَ النَّارِ (سورة آل عمران) ١٩١

[Allah] Most Gracious! It is He Who has taught the Qur'an. He has created man: He has taught him speech [and the art of communication] (55:1-4).

Chapter 15, Page 179

الرَّحْمَنُ ١ عَلَّمَ الْقُرْآنَ ٢ خَلَقَ الْإِنْسَانَ ٣ عَلَّمَهُ الْبَيَانَ ٤ (سورة الرحمن)

Now has come unto you a messenger from among yourselves; it grieves him that you should perish: ardently anxious is he over you: to the believers is he most kind and merciful (9:128).

Chapter 15, Page 181

لَقَدْ جَاءَكُمْ رَسُولٌ مِنْ أَنْفُسِكُمْ عَزِيزٌ عَلَيْهِ مَا عَنِتُّمْ حَرِيصٌ عَلَيْكُمْ بِالْمُؤْمِنِينَ رَءُوفٌ رَحِيمٌ (سورة التوبة) ١٢٨

It is part of the mercy of Allah, that you deal gently with them. Were you severe or harsh-hearted, they would have broken away from you ... (3:159).

Chapter 15, Page 181

فَبِمَا رَحْمَةٍ مِنَ اللَّهِ لِنْتَ لَهُمْ وَلَوْ كُنْتَ فَظًّا غَلِيظَ الْقَلْبِ لَانْفَضُّوا مِنْ حَوْلِكَ ... (سورة آل عمران) ١٥٩

Not a word does he utter but there is a sentinel by him, ready [to note it] (50:18).

Chapter 15, Page 183

مَا يَلْفِظُ مِنْ قَوْلٍ إِلَّا لَدَيْهِ رَقِيبٌ عَتِيدٌ (سورة ق) ١٨

O women of the Prophet, if any of you were guilty of evident unseemly conduct, the punishment would be doubled to her, and that is easy for Allah (33:30).

Chapter 25, Page 268

يَا نِسَاءَ النَّبِيِّ مَنْ يَأْتِ مِنْكُنَّ بِفَاحِشَةٍ مُبَيِّنَةٍ يُضَاعَفْ لَهَا الْعَذَابُ ضِعْفَيْنِ وَكَانَ ذَلِكَ عَلَى اللَّهِ يَسِيرًا (سورة الأحزاب) ٣٠

And remember! Your Lord caused to be declared [publicly]: "If you are grateful, I will add more [favors] to you; But if you show ingratitude, truly My punishment is terrible indeed" (14:7).

Chapter 25, Page 271

۞ وَإِذْ تَأَذَّنَ رَبُّكُمْ لَئِن شَكَرْتُمْ لَأَزِيدَنَّكُمْ وَلَئِن كَفَرْتُمْ إِنَّ عَذَابِى لَشَدِيدٌ (سورة إبراهيم)

... when their term is reached, not an hour can they cause delay, nor [an hour] can they advance [it in anticipation] (7:34).

Chapter 25, Page 276

... فَإِذَا جَآءَ أَجَلُهُمْ لَا يَسْتَأْخِرُونَ سَاعَةً وَلَا يَسْتَقْدِمُونَ (سورة الأعراف)

Wherever you are death will find you out, even if you are in towers built up strong and high ! ... (4:78).

Chapter 25, Page 276

۷۸ أَيْنَمَا تَكُونُوا يُدْرِككُّمُ الْمَوْتُ وَلَوْ كُنتُمْ فِى بُرُوجٍ مُّشَيَّدَةٍ ... (سورة النساء)

... And for those who fear Allah, He [ever] prepares a way out, and He provides for him from [sources] he never could imagine. And if anyone puts his trust in Allah, sufficient is [Allah] for him. For Allah will surely accomplish His purpose: verily, for all things has Allah appointed a due proportion (65:2-3).

Chapter 26, Page 285

... وَمَن يَتَّقِ اللَّهَ يَجْعَل لَّهُ مَخْرَجًا ۝ وَيَرْزُقْهُ مِنْ حَيْثُ لَا يَحْتَسِبُ وَمَن يَتَوَكَّلْ عَلَى اللَّهِ فَهُوَ حَسْبُهُ إِنَّ اللَّهَ بَلِغُ أَمْرِهِ قَدْ جَعَلَ اللَّهُ لِكُلِّ شَىْءٍ قَدْرًا (سورة الطلاق)

That they would certainly be assisted and that Our forces — they surely must conquer (37:172-3).

Chapter 32, Page 331

۱۷۲ إِنَّهُمْ لَهُمُ الْمَنصُورُونَ ۝ ۱۷۳ وَإِنَّ جُندَنَا لَهُمُ الْغَلِبُونَ (سورة الصافات)

O mankind! We created you from a single [pair] of a male and female, and made you into nations and tribes, that you may know each other [not that you may despise each other] ... (49:13).

Chapter 35, Page 354

۱۳ يَأَيُّهَا النَّاسُ إِنَّا خَلَقْنَكُم مِّن ذَكَرٍ وَأُنثَى وَجَعَلْنَكُمْ شُعُوبًا وَقَبَآئِلَ لِتَعَارَفُوا ... (سورة الحجرات)

... But power [honor] belongs to Allah, His Messenger, and the believers, but the hypocrites know not (63:8).

Page 373

... وَلِلَّهِ الْعِزَّةُ وَلِرَسُولِهِ وَلِلْمُؤْمِنِينَ وَلَكِنَّ الْمُنَفِقِينَ لَا يَعْلَمُونَ (سورة المنافقون)

[This will be] their cry therein: "Glory to You, O Allah!" And peace will be their greeting therein! And the close of their cry will be: "Praise be to Allah, the Cherisher and Sustainer of the Worlds!" (10:10).

Page 397

۱۰ دَعْوَلهُمْ فِيهَا سُبْحَنَكَ اللَّهُمَّ وَتَحِيَّتُهُمْ فِيهَا سَلَمٌ وَءَاخِرُ دَعْوَلهُمْ أَنِ الْحَمْدُ لِلَّهِ رَبِّ الْعَلَمِينَ (سورة يونس)

Ahadith Index

«إِنَّ اللهَ كَتَبَ الإِحْسَانَ على كُلِّ شَيْءٍ، فإذا قَتَلْتُمْ فَأَحْسِنوا الْقِتْلَةَ، وإذا ذَبَحْتُمْ فَأَحْسِنوا الذِّبْحَةَ،
وَلْيُحِدَّ أَحَدُكُمْ شَفْرَتَهُ، وَلْيُرِحْ ذَبِيحَتَهُ»

Allah has decreed that for everything there is a better way. Then, when you kill in battle, do it in
the best way; and when you slaughter [an animal] in sacrifice, do it in the best way. So every one of
you should sharpen his knife, and let the slaughtered animal die comfortably.[1]

Page 13

«الخَلْقُ عِيالُ اللهِ، أَحَبُّهُمْ إِلَيْهِ أَنْفَعُهُمْ لِعِيالِهِ»

People are the dependents of Allah; the closest to Him are the most useful to His dependents.[2]

Page 16

«ارْحَمُوا مَنْ في الأرضِ يَرْحَمْكُمْ مَنْ في السَّمَاءِ»

Have mercy on those in the land, so that the One in Heaven will have mercy on you.[3]

Page 16

«جُعِلَتْ لِي الأرضُ مَسْجِدًا وَطَهُورًا»

The Earth has been made for me a *masjid* and a means of purification.[4]

Page 18

«سَيِّدُ القَوْمِ خادِمُهُمْ»

The leader of the nation is their servant.[5]

Page 19

«إنَّ هَذا الدِّينَ مَتِينٌ فَأَوْغِلْ فيهِ بِرِفْقٍ»

This religion is strong, so deal with it delicately and nicely.[6]

Page 35

---

1   Sahih Muslim, Sunan Abu Dawud, Sunan al Tirmidhi, Sunan al Darimi, Sunan ibn Majah, and
    Sunan al Nasa'i.
2   Sahih Muslim.
3   Sunan al Tirmidhi.
4   Sahih Muslim, Sunan Abu Dawud, Sunan al Tirmidhi, Sunan al Nasa'i, Sunan ibn Majah, Sunan al
    Darimi, and Musnad Ahmad ibn Hanbal.
5   Sunan al Daylami and Sunan al Tabarani.
6   Musnad Ahmad ibn Hanbal.

«اللَّهُمَّ أَعِزَّ الإِسْلامَ بِأَحَبِّ هٰذَيْنِ الرَّجُلَيْنِ إِلَيْكَ،

بِأبِي جَهْلٍ (عمرو بن الحكم) أَوْ بِعُمَرَ بْنِ الخَطَّابِ»

Oh Allah! Strengthen Islam by the more lovable one to You of the two men: Abu Jahl (meaning 'Amr Ibn al Hakam) or 'Umar ibn al Khattab.[1]

Page 35

«كُلُّكُمْ رَاعٍ، وَكُلُّ رَاعٍ مَسْئُولٌ عَنْ رَعِيَّتِهِ»

Every one of you is a shepherd and every one is responsible for what he is shepherd of.[2]

Pages 47, 143

«الدِّينُ النَّصِيحَةُ» قُلْنا لِمَنْ؟ قَالَ «لله، وَلِرَسُولِهِ، وَلِكِتَابِهِ، وَلِأئِمَّةِ المُسْلِمِينَ وَعامَّتِهِم»

"Religion is sincere advice." We said: "To whom?" He said: "To Allah, His Book, His Messenger, the leaders of Muslims, and to their common folk."[3]

Page 54

«النَّاسُ مَعَادِنُ خِيَارُهُمْ في الجَاهِلِيَّةِ خِيَارُهُمْ في الإِسْلامِ، إذا فَقُهُوا»

People are like mines [in terms of their nature]. Thus the best of them in Jahiliyah [period of ignorance] will be the best of them in Islam; so long as they attain a proper understanding of Islam.[4]

Page 62

«إنَّما النَّاسُ كَإِبِلٍ مائَةٍ، لاَ يُوجَدُ فيها رَاحِلَةٌ»

People are like camels; you may not find one suitable mount from even a hundred of them.[5]

Page 98

«يَدُ اللهِ مَعَ الجَمَاعَةِ، وَمَنْ شَذَّ شَذَّ إلى النَّارِ»

The Hand of Allah is with the *jama'ah*. Then, whoever singles himself out (from the *jama'ah*), will be singled out for the hell-fire.[6]

Page 134

«الدِّيْنُ النَّصِيْحَة»

Religion is sincere advice.[7]

Page 171

«المُؤمِنُ مِرآةُ المُؤمِنِ»

The believer is the mirror of the believer.[8]

Page 175

1   Musnad Ahmad ibn Hanbal and Sunan al Tirmidhi.
2   Sahih al Bukhari, Sahih Muslim, Sunan al Tirmidhi and Sunan Abu Dawud.
3   Sahih Muslim.
4   Sahih al Bukhari, Sahih Muslim, Sunan al Darimi, and Musnad Ahmad ibn Hanbal.
5   Musnad Ahmad ibn Hanbal, Sahih al Bukhari, Sahih Muslim, Sunan al Tirmidhi, and Sunan ibn Majah.
6   Sunan al Tirmidhi.
7   Sahih Muslim.
8   Sunan Abu Dawud and Sunan al Tirmidhi.

«لا يُؤْمِنُ أَحَدُكُمْ حَتَّى يُحِبَّ لِأَخِيهِ مَا يُحِبُّ لِنَفْسِهِ»

You shall not attain *iman* until you love for others what you love for yourself.[1]

Page 175

«تَبَسُّمُكَ في وَجْهِ أَخِيكَ صَدَقَة»

Your smile in the face of your brother is an act of charity (*sadaqah*).[2]

Page 187

«مَا مِنْ فَجْرِ يَوْمٍ يَنْشَقُّ إِلاَّ وَيُنادي مَلَكان، يا ابْنَ آدَمَ أَنَا يَوْمٌ جَديدٌ، وَعَلى عَمَلِكَ شَهِيدٌ، فَتَزَوَّدْ مِنِّي فَإِنِّي لا أَعُودُ إلى يَوْمِ القِيامَةِ».

Not a single dawn breaks out without two angels calling out: "Oh! Son of Adam, I am a new day and I witness your actions, so make the best out of me because I will never come back till the Day of Judgment."[3]

Page 190

«مَنْ اسْتَوى يَوْمَاهُ فَهُوَ مَغْبُون»

He whose two days are equal [in accomplishments] is a sure loser![4]

Page 194

«مَنْ لَمْ يَشْكُرِ النَّاس لَمْ يَشْكُرِ الله»

He who does not thank people, does not thank Allah.[5]

Page 271

«أَحْبِبْ حَبِيبَكَ هَوْناً مَا، عَسى أَنْ يَكُونَ بَغِيضَكَ يَوْماً مَا، وَأَبْغِضْ بَغِيضَكَ هَوْناً مَا، عَسى أَنْ يَكُونَ حَبِيبَكَ يَوْماً مَا»

Temper your love for your friend, for one day he may be your enemy. And temper your hate for your enemy, for one day he may be your friend.[6]

Page 273

---

1   Sahih al Bukhari and Sahih Muslim.
2   Sunan al Tirmidhi.
3   Al Ma'thur of the Prophet (SAW).
4   Sunan al Daylami.
5   Sunan Abu Dawud, Sunan al Tirmidhi and Musnad Ahmad ibn Hanbal.
6   Sunan al Tirmidhi.

«رَوِّحوا القُلوبَ ساعةً وَساعةً، فَإِنَّ القُلوبَ إذا كَلَّتْ عَمِيَتْ»

Entertain the hearts in between hours, for if the hearts get tired, they become blind.[1]

Page 355

«أدَّبَني رَبِّي فَأَحْسَنَ تَأْديبي»

My Lord has taught me good manners; and He has mannered me well.[2]

Page 358

«إِنْ قامَتِ السَّاعةُ وَبِيَدِ أَحَدِكُمْ فَسيلَةً فَاسْتَطاعَ أَنْ يغرِسَها فَلْيَغرِسْها»

If the last hour strikes and finds you carrying a nursling tree to the grove for planting, go ahead and plant it.[3]

Page 362

«مِنْ حُسْنِ إِسلامِ المَرْءِ تَرْكُهُ ما لاَ يَعْنيهِ»

Part of someone being a good Muslim is his leaving alone that which does not concern him.[4]

Page 365

«لا ضَرَرَ وَلاَ ضِرارَ»

There should be neither harming nor reciprocating harm.[5]

Page 365

«مَنْ فَرَّجَ عَنْ مُسْلِمٍ كُرْبَةً مِنْ كُرَبِ الدُّنْيا، فَرَّجَ اللهُ عَنْهُ كُرْبَةً مِنْ كُرَبِ يَوْمِ القِيَامَةِ»

Whosoever removes a worldly grief from a believer, Allah will remove from him one of the griefs of the Day of Judgment.[6]

Page 365

«لا يُؤْمِنُ أَحَدُكُمْ حَتَّى يُحِبَّ لِأَخيهِ ما يُحِبُّ لِنَفْسِهِ»

None of you [truly] believes until he wishes for his brother what he wishes for himself.[7]

Page 365

«المُسْلِمُ أَخُو المُسْلِمِ لاَ يَظْلِمُهُ وَلاَ يَخْذُلُهُ»

A Muslim is a brother of a Muslim; he neither treats him unjustly nor does he fail him.[8]

Page 365

---

1   Sunan al Daylami.
2   Al Sam'ani in *Adab al Imla'*.
3   Musnad Ahmad ibn Hanbal.
4   Sunan al Tirmidhi.
5   Sunan ibn Majah.
6   Sahih Muslim.
7   Sahih al Bukhari and Sahih Muslim.
8   Sahih Muslim.

Subject Index

Names Index

SAW = Salla Allahu 'Alayhi Wa Sallam
AS = 'Alayhi al Salam
RA = Radiya Allahu 'Anhu

[F] There is an entry for this name in the front of the book before the table of contents.

Places Index

[F] There is an entry for this place in the front of the book before the table of contents.

Organizations Index

Index and Glossary of Islamic Terms

Note: Arabic words found in standard English dictionaries have not been italicised below.

A

Adab, manners, etiquette 357, 359, 360-1, أدب

Adab al ikhtilaf, manner of differing 35 أدب الاختلاف

Ahadith, plural of hadith 377, 386 أحاديث

Allahu Akbar, God is the Greatest 274, 360 الله أكبر

Amir, commander or leader 27 أمير

Amwal, properties 27 أموال

'Aqidah, creed 259 عقيدة

AS, 'Alayhi Al Salam, upon him be peace عليه السلام

'Asr, time; afternoon (prayer) 345 عصر

Astaghfiru Allah, I seek forgiveness from Allah 274 أستغفر الله

Ayah, a verse from the Qur'an, a phenomenon pointing to the Creator 4, 22,353 آية

Ayat, plural of *Ayah* 377, 378 آيات

B

Basirah, vision 44 بصيرة

Bismillah al Rahman al Rahim, In the name of Allah, Most Gracious, Most Merciful 359 بسم الله الرحمن الرحيم

D

Da'iyah, (plural: du'at) one who is engaged in da'wah 4, 17-22, 24, 37, 39, 44, 47, 147, 268 داعية

Da'wah, inviting people to Islam 2-4, 6-9, 11-2, 22, 29, 33, 37, 39, 46, 106, 113, 123, 126, 166, 258, 268, 271, 329 دعوة

Dhikr, the remembrance of Allah 17, 174, 329 ذكر

Du'a', invocation (prayer) addressed to Allah 29, 343, 353, 360 دعاء

F

Fajr, dawn (prayer) 345 فجر

Falah, success in attaining full conviction and realization of the divine will 361 فلاح

Fard, an obligatory action 239 فرض

Fatawa, a juristic opinion given by an *'alim* (scholar) on any matter pertinent to Islamic law 38 فتاوى

Fiqh, knowledge of Islam through its laws, science of the laws of Islam 27, 329 فقه

G

al Ghayb, the transcendental realm the knowledge of which is impossible for man to achieve except through revelation 18-9 الغيب

H

Hadith, the verbalized form of a tradition of the Prophet Muhammad (SAW) constitutive of his Sunnah 4, 15, 17-9, 21-2, 36-7, 47, 295, 343, 357 حديث

Hajj, pilgrimage to Makkah, the fifth pillar of Islam 329 حج

Halal, that which Allah (SWT) has made legitimate 38, 283 حلال

Halaqah, a circle or group 22, 177, 298 حلقة

al Hamdu li Allah, praise be to Allah 267, 274, 360 الحمدلله

Haram, that which Allah has explicitly forbidden humans to do and for which He has specified a penalty 38 حرام

Hijrah, the departure of the Prophet Muhammad (SAW) from Makkah to Madinah ; designation for the Islamic lunar calender which began on the day of that departure from Makkah (July, 622 AD) 329 هجرة

Hikmah, wisdom based on revelation of the will of Allah (SWT) 43, 145 حكمة

I

'Ibadah, act of obedience and worship to Allah (SWT) 272 عبادة

'Id, celebration, festival (to mark end of Ramadan or to commemorate Prophet Ibrahim's willingness to sacrifice his son at the command of Allah SWT) of 271, 330 عيد

Ifsad, destruction, corruption 45 إفساد

Ihdina al Sirat al Mustaqim, Guide us to the Right Path 274 إهدنا الصراط المستقيم

Ihsan, the perfect fulfillment of the commandments of Allah; the state of the person whose deeds achieve such fulfillment; betterment 20, 45, 64, 361 إحسان

Ijtihad, Islamic research 27, 31, 151, 259 اجتهاد

Iman, the conviction that Allah is indeed the one and only God and that Muhammad is His last prophet 38, 45, 194, 358, 361 إيمان

In sha'a Allah, Allah willing 257 إن شاء الله

Iqamah, the inception of salah or any other ritual of worship 322, 345, 348, 360 إقامة

'Isha', late evening (prayer) 345 عشاء

Islah, improvement, rectification 41, 45 إصلاح

Itqan, perfection 45 إتقان

J

Jahannam, hell 37 جهنم

Jahiliyyah, ignorance; pre-Islamic period 62 جاهلية

Jama'ah, group 18, 31, 37, 51, 182 جماعة

Jannah, the Garden, paradise, the eternal abode of the meritorious humans who have been granted the reward of Allah (SWT) on the Day of Judgment 17, 37 جنة

Jihad, self-exertion in the cause of Allah (SWT) including peaceful as well as violent means 59 جهاد

K

Khilafah, vicegerency, caliphate 41, 59 خلافة

Khulafa', vicegerents, caliphs 54 خلفاء

Khutbah, sermon 59, 270, 360 خطبة

L

La hawla wa la quwwata illa billah, there is neither strength nor power except through Allah SWT 358 لا حول ولا قوة إلاّ بالله

M

Madhahib, schools of thought in fiqh 20 مذاهب

Maghrib, time of sunset (prayer) 345 مغرب

al Ma'ruf, the good actions 361 المعروف

Sunnah, the pattern of Allah (SWT) in ordering creation or any part or aspect of it 17, 239, 259   سنّه

Usrah, family; a closely knit group 22   أسرة

T

Taharah, purification 329   طهارة

Tarawih, nonobligatory prayers on the nights of Ramadan 329   تراويح

Tarbiyah, training 298   تربية

Tasbih, praise of Allah (SWT) 17   تسبيح

Tawhid, the Oneness of Allah (SWT) 2, 9, 328, 363   توحيد

U

'Ulama', scholars 31   علماء

Ummah, the community as identified by its ideology or culture 24, 26, 27, 28, 30, 31, 38   أمة

W

Wa 'alaykum al Salam, and on you be peace 358   وعليكم السلام

Wahy, revelation 59   وحي

Waqf, trust; property in trust for service to Islam 268   وقف

Wudu', ablutions 336, 344-5   وضوء

Z

Zakah, the obligatory sharing of wealth with the needy 329, 363   زكاة

Zalim, oppressor 39 5, 240, 260   ظالم

[This will be] their cry therein: "Glory to You, Allah!" And peace will be their greeting therein! And the close of their cry will be: "Praise be to Allah, the Cherisher and Sustainer of the Worlds!" (10:10)

أحدث إصدارات المعهد العالمي للفكر الإسلامي

العنف وإدارة الصراع السياسي بين المبدأ والخيار

يكتسب هذا البحث أهميته من الرؤية والطرح الجديدين اللذين يقدمهما، متسماً بمنهجية شمولية تحليلية منضبطة بالرؤية القرآنية والسياسات النبوية في هذا المجال.

والكتاب يضع في أسلوبٍ علمي إسلامي أحد معالم وشروط التقدم والاستقرار للأمة الإسلامية، وهو بذلك إضافة ثرية لكل مثقف مسلم يُعنى بمستقبل الأمة وحاضر همومها.

يقع الكتاب في 61 صفحة وهو من إصدارات عام 2000

مسألة المعرفة ومنهج البحث عند الغزالي

تتميز هذه الدراسة عن صوفية الغزالي، رحمه الله، بأنها حققت النظرة المعرفية التي يتبناها، ومناهج البحث التي تسندها وتبعاً لهذه فإنها وفقت في ملاحقة واستنباط معالجة العديد من القضايا التي حفل بها فكره، وهي متشعبة، ونجحت في وضعها في مكانها المناسب من البنية المنطقية والمنهجية في فكره، فأثبتت، من غير شك، بأن خطاب الغزالي متماسك الرؤى متلاحم الأجزاء، على عكس ما أشيع عنه، الأمر الذي خفف حدة الإشكالية التي اصطبغ بها وساعد، بالتالي، على تخليصه مما ألحق به من أوهام أو ألصق به من مثالب.

وتقع هذه الدراسة في 374 صفحة وهو من إصدارات المعهد بالاشتراك مع دار الفكر في سورية.

قواعد المقاصد عند الإمام الشاطبي

يعرض الكتاب حول "قواعد المقاصد" موضوعاً جديداً من موضوعات علم مقاصد الشريعة الإسلامية، يستهدف بيان أهمية ضبط هذا العلم المتسع عن طريق قواعد محددة، حتى لا يدخل فيه ما ليس منه، ولا يخرج منه ما هو من صميم مداولاته.

وعَمَدَ المؤلِّف إلى دراسة هذه القواعد عن طريق ما ساقه الإمام الشاطبي في كتابه "الموافقات في أصول الشريعة"، وأظهر أثر المقاصد في ضبط عملية فهم النصوص، حتى يأتي هذا الفهم صحيحاً راشداً، متبصراً بغاية المشرِّع ومقصده.

ويقع الكتاب في 488 صفحة وهو من إصدارات عام 2000 بالاشتراك مع دار الفكر في سورية.

نحو نظام معرفي إسلامي

وهو أعمال الحلقة الدراسية التي عقدها المعهد في الأردن صيف عام 1998 وقام بتحريره د فتحي حسن ملكاوي.

ويتضمن الكتاب ثلاث عشرة ورقة عرضت في الحلقة الدراسية، مع التعقيبات الخاصة بكل ورقة والمناقشات العامة لكل جلسة، وتعريف بالمشاركين في الحلقة، ومستخلصات من مداخلات المشاركين، إضافة إلى مخطط لمشروع كتاب منهجي حول النظام المعرفي الإسلامي.

يقع الكتاب في 510 صفحات وصدر صيف عام 2000.

ومن إصدارات المعهد الجديدة:

1- العطاء الفكري لأبي الوليد بن رشد.

2- جمال الدين الأفغاني: عطاؤه الفكري ومنهجه الإصلاحي.

3- في مصادر التراث الإقتصادي الإسلامي.

4- بطاقات الائتمان: دراسة فقهية إقتصادية.

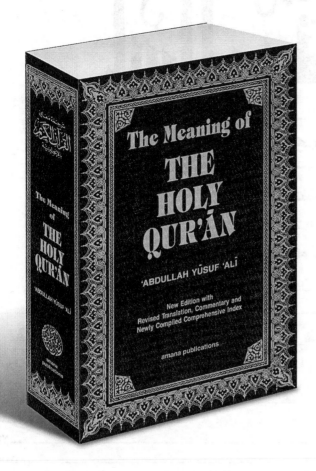
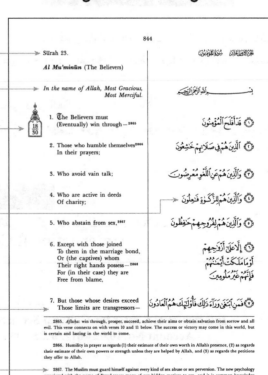

مجلّة فكرية فصلية محكّمة يصدرها المعهد العالمي للفكر الإسلامي

رئيس التحرير

جمال البرزنجي

أعضاء هيئة التحرير

التيجاني عبدالقادر * محيي الدين عطية * لؤي صافي * فتحي ملكاوي

قسيمة اشتراك في إسلامية المعرفة

أرجو قبول / تجديد اشتراكي بـ (   ) نسخة اعتباراً من (   )

ولمدة (   ) عام.

طيه صك / حوالة بريدية. بقيمة ـــــــــــــ

إرسال فاتورة ـــــــــــــ

الإسم ـــــــــــــ

العنوان ـــــــــــــ

ـــــــــــــ

التوقيع ـــــــــــ التاريخ ـــــــــــ

الإشتراك السنوي

في دول الخليج، أمريكا، استراليا، اليابان، أوروبا، نيوزيلندا:

للأفراد ٥٠ دولاراً أمريكياً   للمؤسسات ١٠٠ دولار أمريكي

في باقي دول العالم:

للأفراد ٢٥ دولاراً أمريكياً   للمؤسسات ٧٠ دولاراً أمريكياً

التسديد

شيك مصرفي مسحوب على أحد المصارف الأجنبية لأمر المركز الدولي للخدمات الثقافية

(International Center for Cultural Services)

أو

تحويل المبلغ إلى العنوان التالي:

International Center for Cultural Services - Bank of Kuwait & the Arab World s.a.l. Main branch
Account No. 10.02 4612. 61352.00 - Telex: 23778 P 22383 Bencott Le Beirut - Lebanon

سعر العدد:

لبنان ٥٠٠٠ ل.ل. * سوريا ٧٥ ل.س. * الأردن ٢.٥٠ دينار * العراق دينار واحد * الكويت ١.٥ دينار * الإمارات العربية ٢٠ درهماً * البحرين ١.٥ دينار * قطر ٢٠ ريالاً * السعودية ٢٠ ريالاً * الجمهورية اليمنية ١٥٠ ريالاً * مصر ٤ جنيهات * السودان ٦٠٠ جنيه * الصومال ٢٠ شلناً * ليبيا ٢ دينار * الجزائر ٥٠ ديناراً * تونس ٢ دينار * المغرب ٢٠ درهماً * موريتانيا ٢٥٠ أوقية * قبرص ٣ جنيهات * اليونان ٣٠٠ دراخما * فرنسا ٤٠ فرنكاً * ألمانيا ١٠ ماركات * إيطاليا ٥٠٠٠ ليرة * بريطانيا ٤ جنيهات * سويسرا ١٤ فرنكاً * هولندا ١٠ فلورن * أمريكا وسائر الدول الأخرى ١٠ دولارات.

International Center for Cultural Services
P.O. Box: 153242
Telefax: 961-1654250
Beirut, Lebanon

THE AMERICAN JOURNAL OF ISLAMIC SOCIAL SCIENCES

What are Muslim Intellectuals saying about Islam and Muslims? How are the thinking Muslims negotiating with modernity without losing their traditional intellectual heritage? Does Islam have anything to offer to the contemporary world, or has it lost its relevance due to the unstoppable onslaught of secularism/modernization/westernization/globalization which continues to spread throughout the globe?

For answers which might surprise you, read the American Journal of Islamic Social Sciences (AJISS). We have spent the last 15 years answering these and other questions of concern to contemporary Muslims.

AJISS is a refereed academic journal published quarterly by the Association of Muslim Social Scientists (AMSS) and the International Institute of Islamic Thought (IIIT). It publishes research articles, books reviews, conference reports and abstracts of doctoral dissertations relating to various Islamic sciences, social science disciplines and philosophy with particular attention to their attendant epistemological paradigms.

SUBSCRIPTION INFORMATION:

☐ Bill Me   ☐ Check Enclosed

(Subscriptions are for one calender year)

($30.00 individual-$45.00 institution)

Name:..

Address:..

City: .... State: .... Zip: ....

IIIT Publications

SOCIAL JUSTICE IN ISLAM
Dina Abdulkader

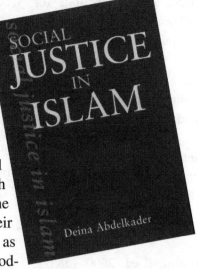

Using the two sources of maqasid and maslaha, and through the examination of the dialectical link between fiqh and reality, the author shows their idispensability as important methodological tools for the study of the social sciences and, indeed, of social phenomena.

216 pp.   **$14.95**

CONTEMPLATION
An Islamic Psychospiritual Study
Malik Badri

Combining the rich traditional Islamic wisdom with contemporary knowledge, the author advances a unique approach to the understanding of the human psyche and the self that gives a central position to meditation and contemplation as forms of worship in Islam.

136 pp.   **$13.95**

THE VICEGERENCY OF MAN
'Abd al Majid al Najjār

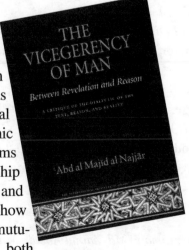

The Vicegerency of Man is a truely contributioin to the debate on Revelation and reason that has always been a central issue in Islamic thought. The book aims to clarify the relationship between reason and Revelation and to show that far from being mutually exclusive, they both contribute to a correct portrayal of reality.

90 pp.   **$9.95**

A THEMATIC COMMENTARY ON THE QUR'AN
Shaykh Muhammad al Ghazali

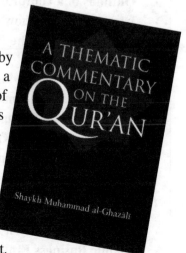

No exegesis is by itself sufficient for a full understanding of the Qur'an. But this work is an indispensable companion in the quest for a better comprehension of, and a closer affinity with, the sacred text.

804pp.   **$24.95**

IIIT Publications

(English Language)

Islamization of Knowledge

- **Toward an Islamic Theory of International Relations: New Directions for Methodology and Thought**, *AbdulHamid A. AbuSulayman*, 2ⁿᵈ ed., 1993, 240 p.
- **Islam and Economic Development**, *M. Umer Chapra*, published jointly with the Islamic Research Institute (Pakistan), 1ˢᵗ ed., 1993, 166 p.
- **Contribution of Islamic Thought to Modern Economics (Vol. 2)**, *Misbah Oreibi (ed.)*, 1998, 274 p.
- **Islam and Other Faiths**, *Ismail Raji al-Faruqi,* published jointly with The Islamic Foundation, 1998, 370 p.
- **Islamization of Knowledge: Historical Background and Recent Developments**, *Danjuma Abubakar Maiwada,* 1999, 42 p.
- **Economic Guidelines in the Qur'an**, *S.M. Hasanuz Zaman*, 1999. 398 p.
- **Islamization of Knowledge: A Research Guide**, *Bashir Shehu Galadanci, (ed.)* 2000, 90 p.
- **Islamization of Knowledge: Background Models and the Way Forward**, *Sa'idu Sulaiman,* 2000, 59 p.

Issues in Contemporary Islamic Thought

- **The Ethics of Disagreement in Islam**, *Taha Jabir al Alwani*, 4ᵗʰ ed., 2000, 158 p.
- **Madinan Society at the Time of the Prophet**, *Akram Diya' al Umari*, (2 Parts in one volume), 2ⁿᵈ ed.,1995, 472 p.
- **Thematic Commentary on the Qur'an (Vol. 1)**, *Shaykh Muhammad al Ghazali*, 1997, 175 p.
- **Thematic Commentary on the Qur'an (Vol. 2)**, *Shaykh Muhammad al Ghazali*, 1998, 204 p.
- **Thematic Commentary on the Qur'an (Vol. 1+2)**, *Shaykh Muhammad al Ghazali*, 1999, 204 p.
- **Thematic Commentary on the Qur'an (3Vols. in one)**, *Shaykh Muhammad al Ghazali*, 2000, 804 p.
- **Proceedings of the IIIT Lunar Calendar Conference**, 2ⁿᵈ ed., *Imad-ad-Dean Ahmad*, 1998, 76 p.
- **Tawhid: Its Implications for Thought and life**, *Ismail Raji al Faruqi*, 5ᵗʰ ed. 2000, 236 p.
- **Contemplation: An Islamic Psycho Spiritual Study**, Malik Badri, 2000, 136 p.

Occasional Papers

- **Outlines of a Cultural Strategy**, *Taha Jabir al Alwani*, 1st ed., 1989, 20 p..
- **Islamization of Knowledge: A Methodology**, *Imad al Din Khalil*, 1st ed., 1989, 32 p.
- **The Qur'an and the Sunnah: The Time-Space Factor**, *Taha Jabir al Alwani/Imad al Din Khalil*, 1st ed., 1991, 68 p.
- **Laxity, Moderation and Extremism in Islam**, *Aisha B. Lemu*, 1st ed., 1993, 48 p.
- **Islamization: Reforming Contemporary Knowledge**, *AbdulHamid AbuSulayman*, 1st ed., 1994, 48 p.
- **Toward Global Cultural Renewal**, *Mona Abul-Fadl*, 1st ed.,1995, 32 p.
- **The Islamization of Knowledge: Yesterday and Today**, *Taha Jabir al Alwani*, 1st ed., 1995, 40 p.
- **Missing Dimensions in Contemporary Islamic Movements**, *Taha Jabir al Alwani*, 1st ed., 1996, 72 p.

Human Development

- **Leadership: Western and Islamic**, *Muhammad Anisuzzaman / Md. Zainul Abedin Majumder*, 1996, 67 p.
- **Islamic Business Ethics**, *Rafik Issa Beekun*, 1997. 80 p.

Perspectives on Islamic Thought

- **Nationalism and Internationalism in Liberalism: Marxism and Islam**, *Tahir Amin*, 1st ed., 1991, 106 p.
- **Theories of Islamic Law: The Methodology of Ijtihad**, *Imran Ahsan Khan Nyazee*, 1994, 344 p.

Islamic Methodology

- **Crisis in the Muslim Mind**, *AbdulHamid AbuSulayman*, 2nd ed., 1997, 160 p.
- **The Vicegerency of Man**, *'Abd al Majid al Najjār*, 1st ed., 2000, 90 p.

Academic Dissertations

- **Business Ethics in Islam**, *Mushtaq Ahmad*, published jointly with International Institute of Islamic Economics (Pakistan), 1995, 211 p.
- **Qur'anic Text: Towards a Retrieval System**, *Hani Attiyah*, 1st ed.,1996, 288 p.
- **Working Principles for an Islamic Model in Mass Media Communication**, *Suhaib Jamal al Barzinji*, 1998, 94 p.
- **The Variant Readings of the Qur'an : A Critical Study of Their Historical and Linguistic Origins**, *Ahmad A. M. 'Abdallah*, 1998, 191 p.
- **Social Justice in Islam**, *Deina Abdelkader*, 2000, 1st edition, 216 p..

Supplementary Social Studies Teaching Units

- **I am a Muslim: A Modern Storybook** (kindergarten), *Susan Douglas*, published jointly with Kendall/Hunt Publishing Company, 1st ed., 1995, 142 p.
- **Eid Mubarak! Islamic Celebration Around the World** (1st grade), *Susan Douglas*, published jointly with Kendall/Hunt Publishing Company, 1st ed., 1995, 108 p.
- **Muslims in Our Community & Around the World** (2nd grade), *Susan Douglas*, published jointly with Kendall/Hunt Publishing Company, 1st ed., 1995, 68 p.
- **Traders & Explorers in Wooden Ships** (5th grade), *Susan Douglas*, published jointly with Kendall/Hunt Publishing Company, 1st ed., 1995, 72 p.
- **Islam & Muslim Civilization** (6th grade), *Susan Douglas*, published jointly with Kendall/Hunt Publishing Company, 1st ed., 1995, 106 p.
- **Muslims Cities Then & Now** (3rd grade), *Susan Douglas*, published jointly with Kendall/Hunt Publishing Company, 1st ed., 1996, 288 p.
- **Introduction to Geography: Where in the World Do Muslims Live?** (4th grade*)*, *Susan Douglas*, published jointly with Kendall/Hunt Publishing Company, 1st ed., 1996, 147 p.

Islamic Law and Jurisprudence

- **Islamic Law of Business Organization Partnerships**, *Imran Ahsan Khan Nyazee*, 1997, 89 p.
- **Islamic Jurisprudence**, *Imran Ahsan Khan Nyazee*, 2000, 405 p.

Comparative Religion

- **Muslim Understanding of Other Religions**: A Study of Ibn Hazm's Kitab al-Fasl fi al-Milal wa al-Ahwa' wa al-Nihal, *Ghulam Haider Aasi*, Published jointly with the Islamic Research Institute, 2000, 231 p.

Distributors of IIIT Publications

Egypt

Center of Epistemological Studies, 26-B Al Jazirah al Wosta Street, Zamalek, Cairo.
Tel: (20-2) 340-9825 Fax: (20-2) 340-9520

France

Libraire du Monde Arabe, 220 Rue Saint Jacques 75005 Paris.
Tel: (33-1) 4329-4022 Fax: (33-1) 4329-6629

India

Genuine Publications & Media (Pvt.) Ltd., P.O. Box 9725, Jamia Nagar, New Delhi 110 025.
Tel: (91-11) 630-989 Fax: (91-11) 684-1104

Jordan

IIIT Office, P.O. Box 9489, Amman.
Tel: (962-6) 639-992 Fax: (962-6) 611-420

Morocco

Dar al Aman for Publishing and Distribution, 4 Zangat al Ma'muniyah, Rabat.
Tel: (212-7) 723-276 Fax: (212-7) 200-055

Saudi Arabia

International Islamic Publishing House, P.O. Box 55195, Riyadh 11534.
Tel: (966-1) 465-0818 Fax: (966-1) 463-3489

United Arab Emirates

Reading for All Bookshop, P.O. Box 11032 Dubai.
Tel: (971-4) 663-903 Fax: (971-4) 690-084

United Kingdom

- Zain International, 84 Whitehorse Lane, London EI 4LR U.K.
  Tel. and Fax: (44-171) 704-1489

- The Islamic Foundation, Markfield Conference Centre,
  Ratby Lane, Markfield, Leicester LE67 9SY
  Tel: (44-530) 244-944/45 Fax: (44-530) 244-946
  www.Islamic-Foundation.org.uk/IslamFound

USA

- **Astrolabe Pictures,** 201 Davis Drive, Suite 1, Sterling, VA 20164
  Tel: (703) 404-6800 Orders: 1-800-39-ASTRO
  Fax: (703) 404-6801
  online order: http://www.astrolabepictures.com

- **amana publications,** 10710 Tucker Street, Beltsville MD, 20705-2223.
  Tel: (301) 595-5777 Fax: (301) 595-8888
  Email: ig@igprinting.com
  http://www.amana-publications.com

- **Islamic Book Service,** 2622 East Main Street, Plainfield, IN 46168
  Tel: (317) 839-8150 Fax: (317) 839-2511

- **Halalco Books,** 108 East Fairfax Street, Falls Church, VA 22046
  Tel: (703) 532-3202 Fax: (703) 241-0035